COURSE 7: KISU DAY

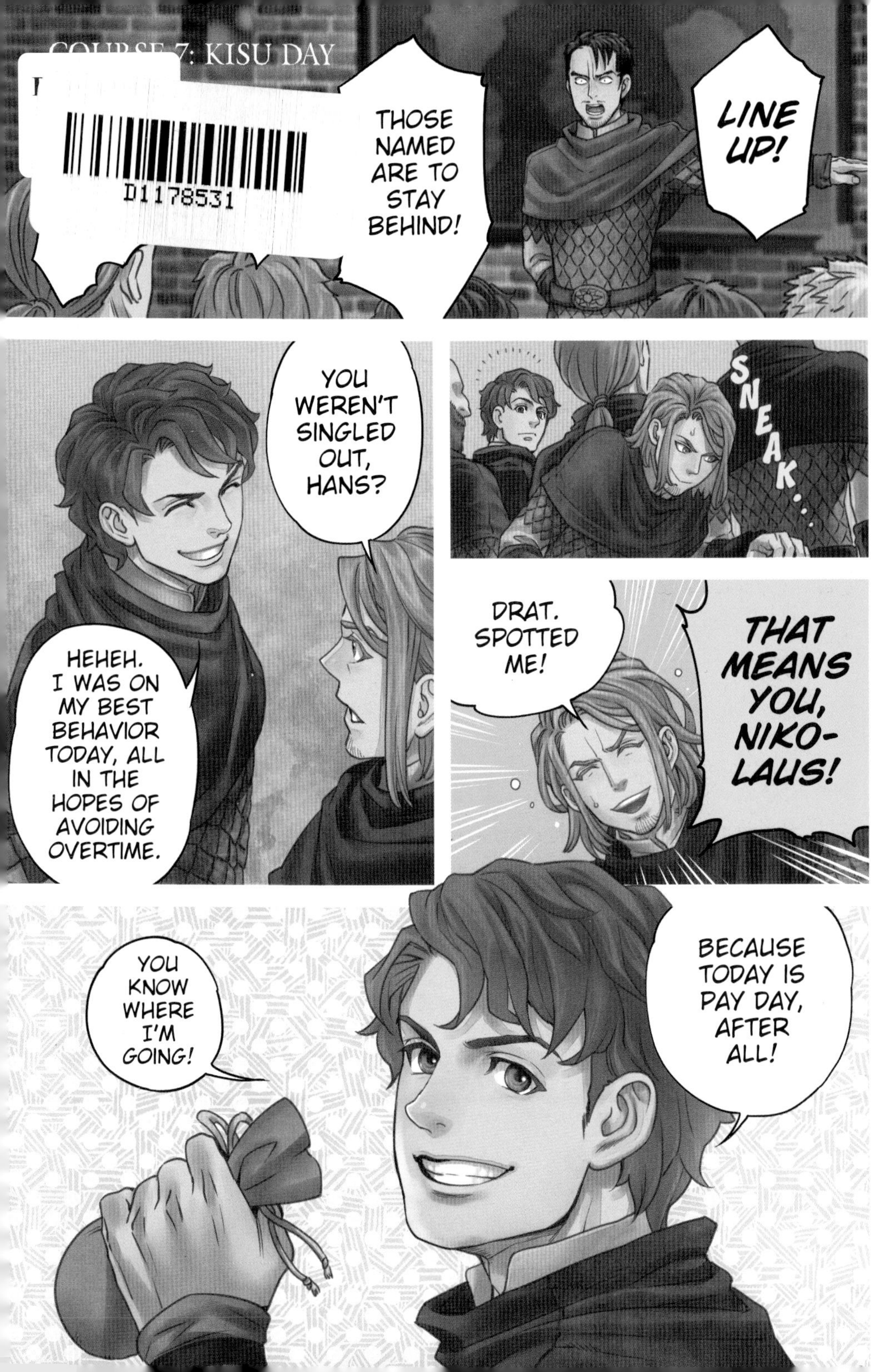
LINE UP!
THOSE NAMED ARE TO STAY BEHIND!
SNEAK...
THAT MEANS YOU, NIKO-LAUS!
DRAT. SPOTTED ME!
YOU WEREN'T SINGLED OUT, HANS?
HEHEH. I WAS ON MY BEST BEHAVIOR TODAY, ALL IN THE HOPES OF AVOIDING OVERTIME.
BECAUSE TODAY IS PAY DAY, AFTER ALL!
YOU KNOW WHERE I'M GOING!

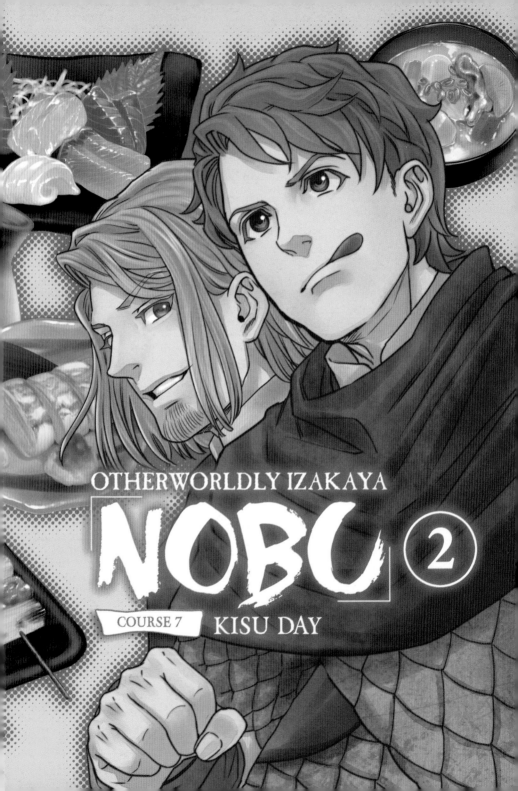

OTHERWORLDLY IZAKAYA

「NOBU」②

COURSE 7   KISU DAY

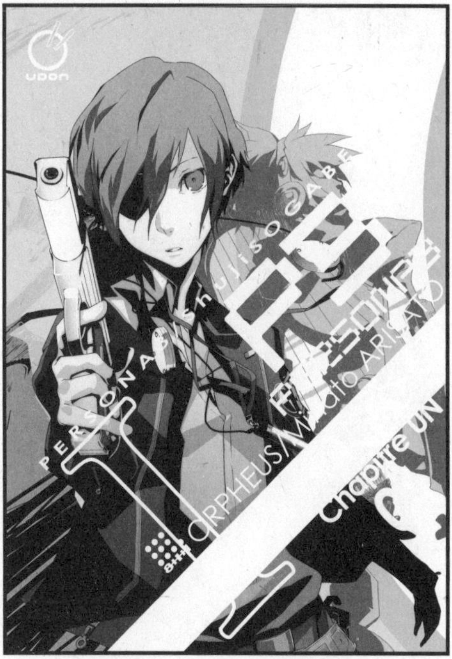
udon
Chapitre UN

PERSONA 3 VOL.1
ISBN-13: 978-1927925850

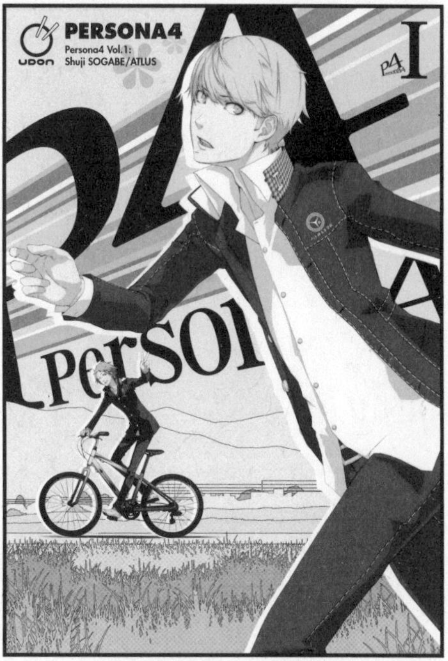
PERSONA4
Persona4 Vol.1:
Shuji SOGABE/ATLUS
udon
I

PERSONA 4 VOL.1
ISBN-13: 978-1927925577

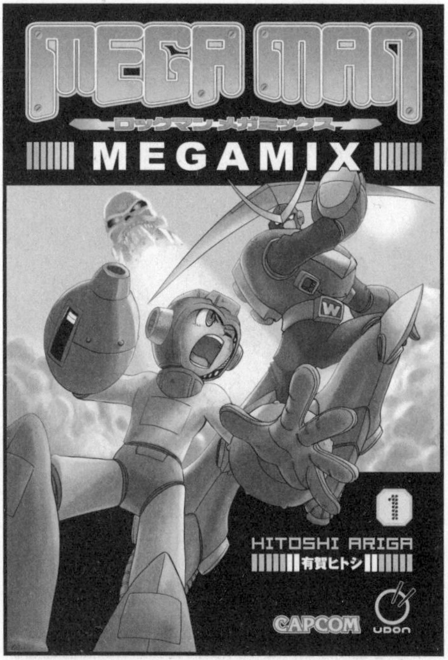
MEGA MAN
MEGAMIX
1
HITOSHI ARIGA
有賀ヒトシ
CAPCOM
udon

MEGA MAN MEGAMIX VOL.1
ISBN-13: 978-1897376164

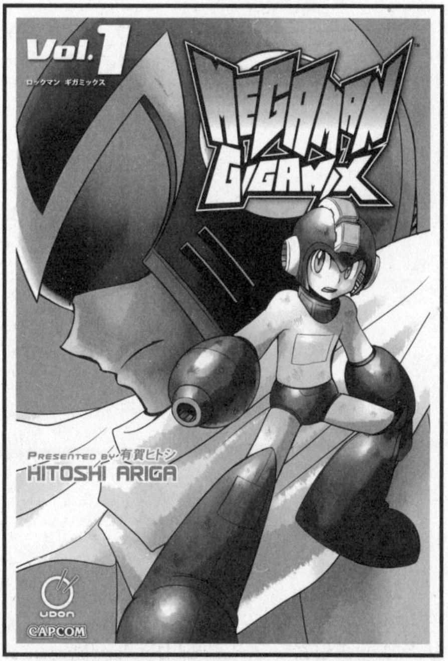
Vol.1
ロックマン ギガミックス
MEGAMAN GIGAMIX
PRESENTED BY 有賀ヒトシ
HITOSHI ARIGA
udon
CAPCOM

MEGA MAN GIGAMIX VOL.1
ISBN-13: 978-1926778235

OTHERWORLDLY IZAKAYA NOBU ROUGH CHARACTER DESIGNS 7

ダミアン

DAMIEN

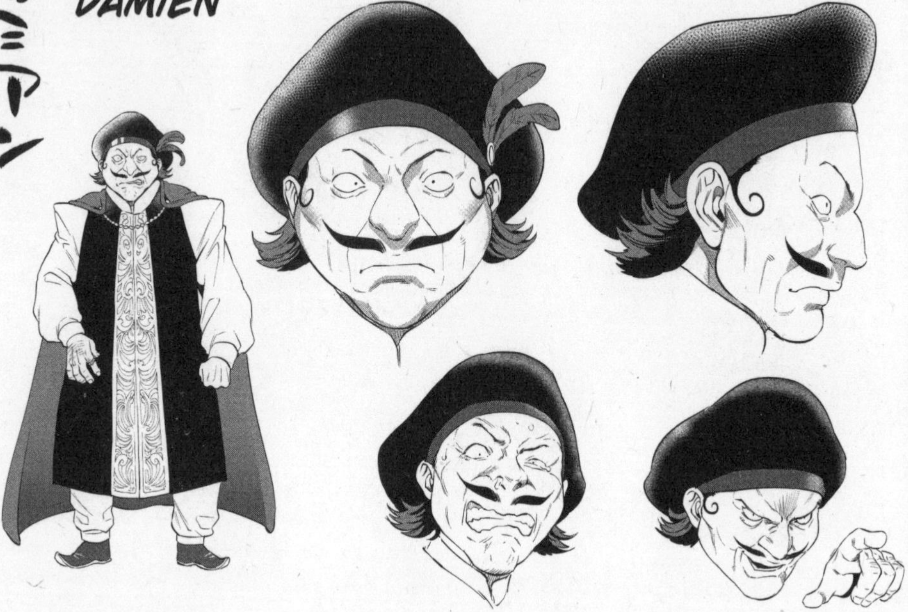

白狐

SHIROGITSUNE

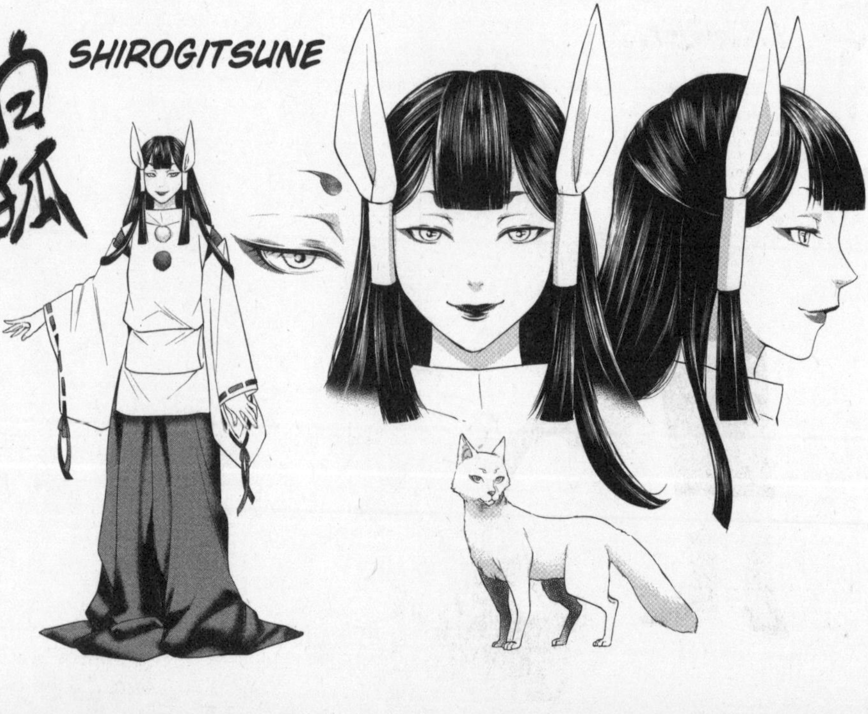

OTHERWORLDLY IZAKAYA NOBU ROUGH CHARACTER DESIGNS 6

ホルガー
HOLGA

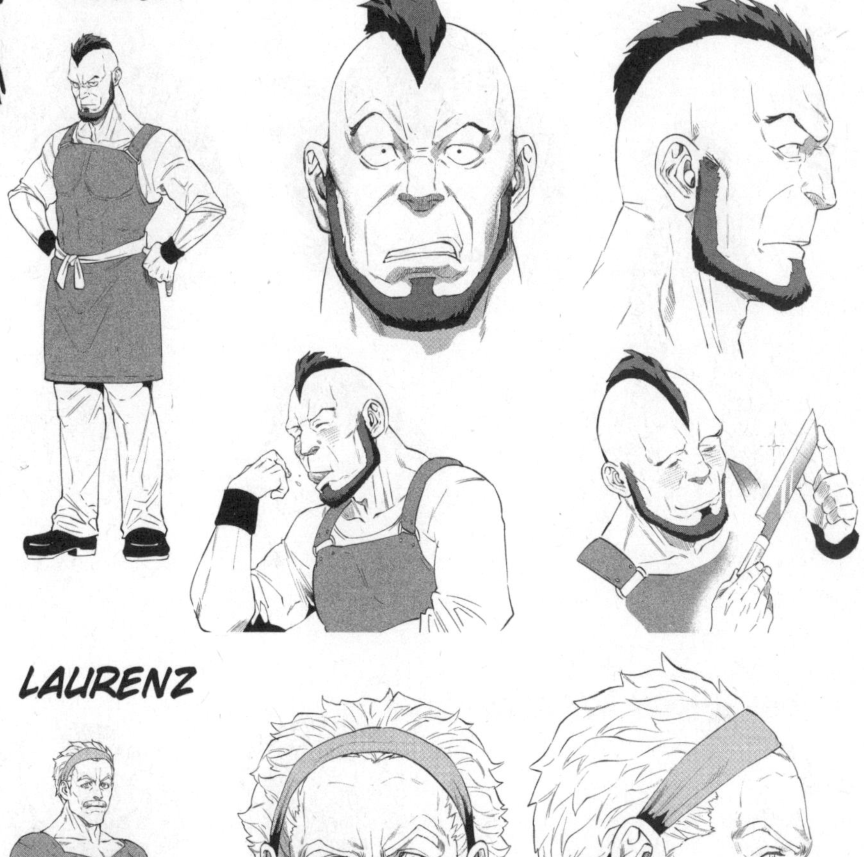

ローレンツ
LAURENZ

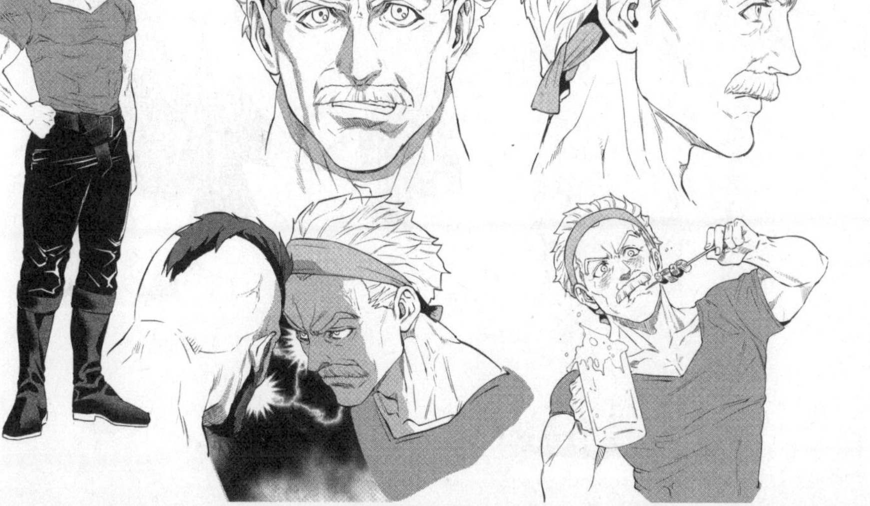

OTHERWORLDLY IZAKAYA NOBU ROUGH CHARACTER DESIGNS 5

ベルトホルト

BERTHOLD

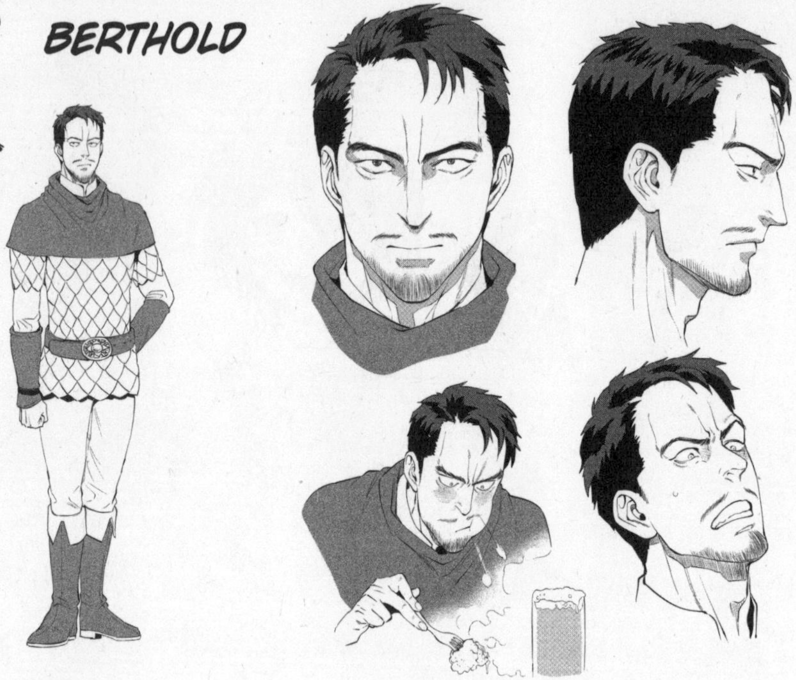

ヘルミーナ

HERMINA

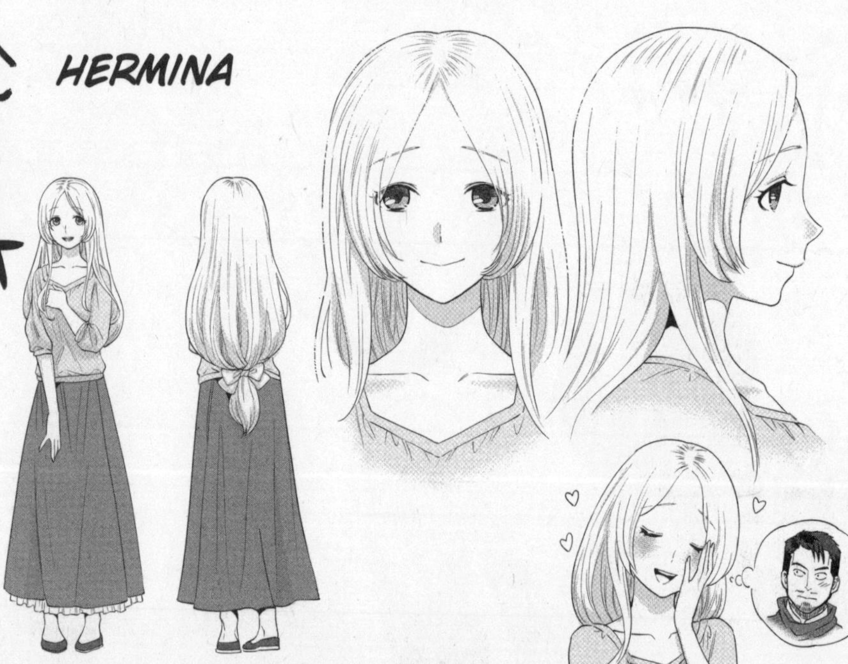

OTHERWORLDLY IZAKAYA NOBU ROUGH CHARACTER DESIGNS 4

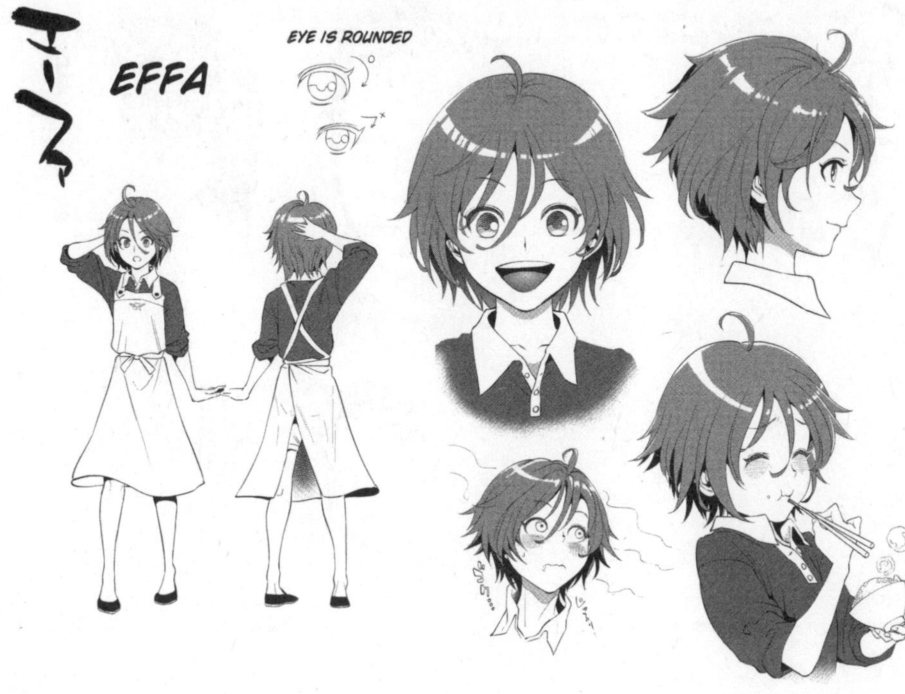
エーファ
EFFA
EYE IS ROUNDED

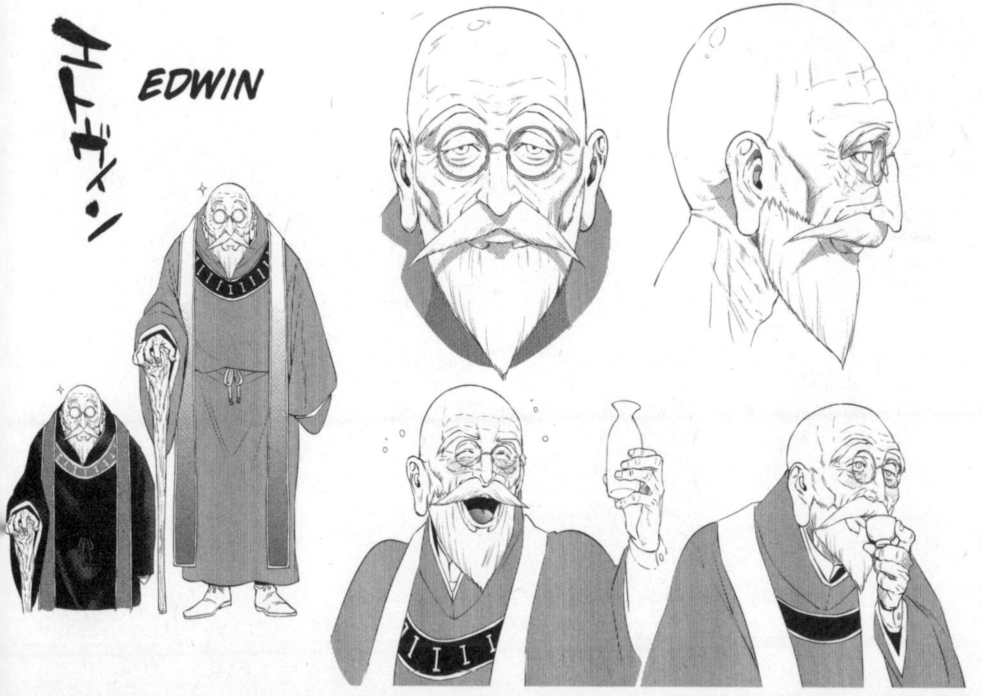
エドヴィン
EDWIN

FOOD VOCABULARY ENCOUNTERED IN THIS BOOK:

The fantasy world of "Nobu" brings together speakers of Japanese and German for a delicious cross-cultural exchange. Hans, Nikolaus, Chief, Shinobu, and the gang use a variety of foreign food vocabulary throughout, so here's a quick review of what came up in this volume!

JAPANESE

Abura-age: deep-fried tofu skin

Ankake yudofu: boiled tofu topped with viscous ankake sauce

Atsukan: hot sake

Ayu shioyaki: sweetfish, salted and grilled

Croquette: In the Japanese style, a breaded and fried food usually filled with a potato and meat mixture

Edamame: soybeans still in the shell, boiled and salted

Hirekatsu: lean pork loin, deep-fried

Hokke: a type of mackerel

Hotaruika okizuke: firefly squid, pickled and eaten whole

Ichimi: cayenne pepper powder

Inarizushi: sushi rice wrapped in abura-age

Katsuo tataki: seared skipjack tuna

Katsuretsu: generic term for tonkatsu, hirekatsu, etc., from the Japanese pronunciation of "cutlet"

Kisu: sillago fish (also known as Japanese whiting)

Ninuki: "hard-boiled egg" in the Kansai dialect

Omuraisu: Japanese omelet draped over a mound of seasoned fried rice

Omusoba: yakisoba with an omelet draped on top

Onigiri: the quintessential riceball, filled with any number of ingredients and wrapped in dried seaweed

Oshibori: hot, rolled towels provided to restaurant customers before the meal

Reishu: chilled sake served in a bottle so the customer can pour for themselves

Sashimi: slices of raw fish served on their own (without rice), distinct from sushi

Shiokara: fermented seafood entrails

Shishamo: a type of smelt fish whose name is Ainu in origin

Shuto: pickled tuna entrails

Squid dango: squid paste formed into balls

Squid shogani: squid meat boiled with ginger and soy sauce

Squid somen: raw squid, sliced into strips

Surume geso: dried squid tentacles

Tarako: cod roe

Tempura: Japanese deep-frying technique that uses flour and egg batter

Tentsuyu: a thin, slightly sweet, slightly salty dipping sauce for tempura dishes

Tonkatsu sauce: a thick, sweet sauce paired with katsuretsu (tomato and soy sauce base)

Yakisoba: soba noodles fried up with a sweet sauce

GERMAN

Brot: bread

Ei(er): egg(s)

Eintopf: stew

Fisch: fish

Fleisch: meat

Huhn: chicken

Kartoffel(n): potato(es)

Nudeln: pasta

Obst: fruit

Reisbrei: rice porridge

Rindfleisch: beef

Schnitzel: meat that's been pounded thin and fried

Speck: bacon

Tintenfisch: squid

Zwiebel: onion

OTHERWORLDLY IZAKAYA

NOBU

Inarizushi

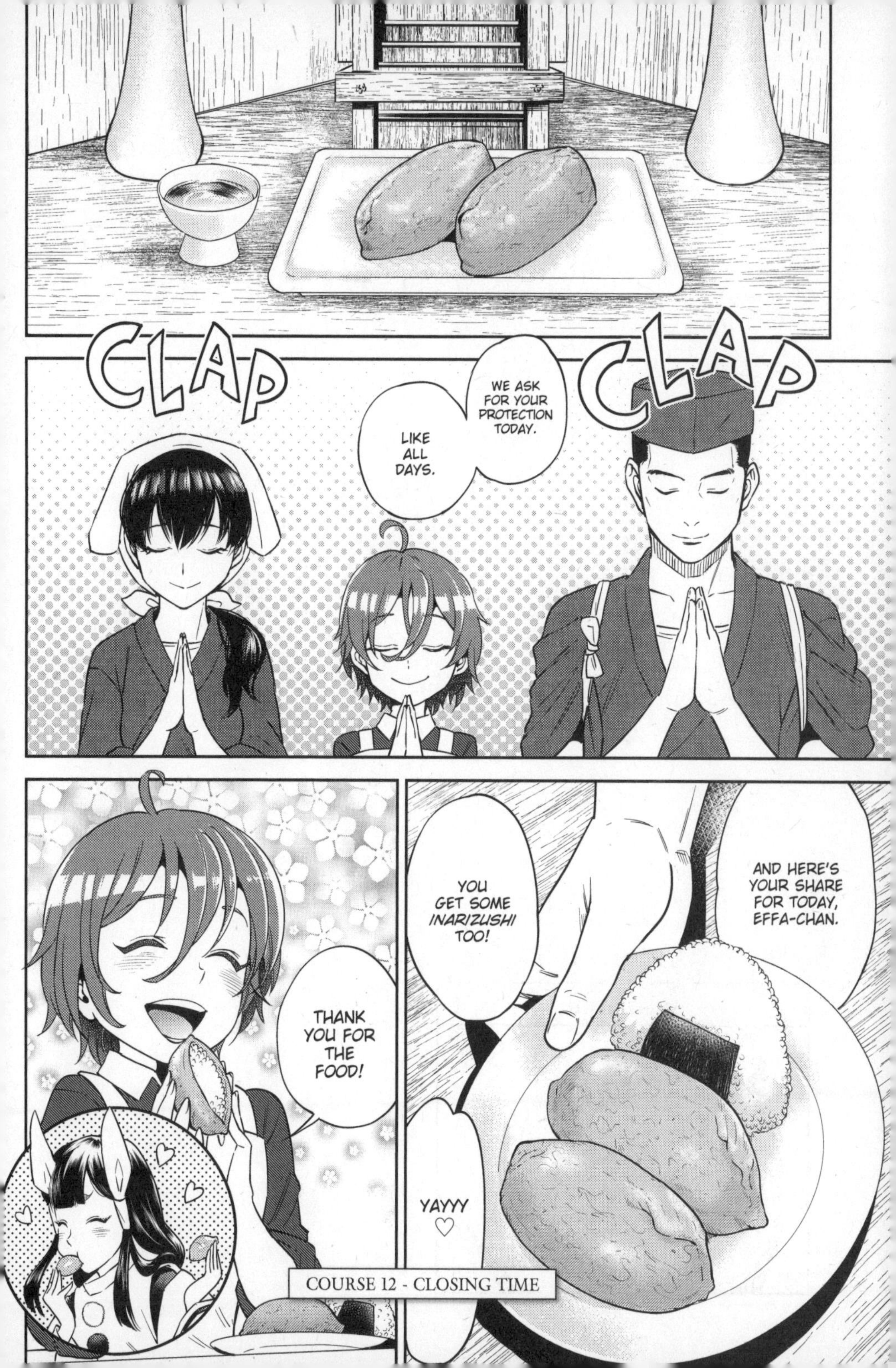
CLAP
WE ASK FOR YOUR PROTECTION TODAY.
LIKE ALL DAYS.
CLAP
AND HERE'S YOUR SHARE FOR TODAY, EFFA-CHAN.
YOU GET SOME *INARIZUSHI* TOO!
YAYYY ♡
THANK YOU FOR THE FOOD!
COURSE 12 - CLOSING TIME

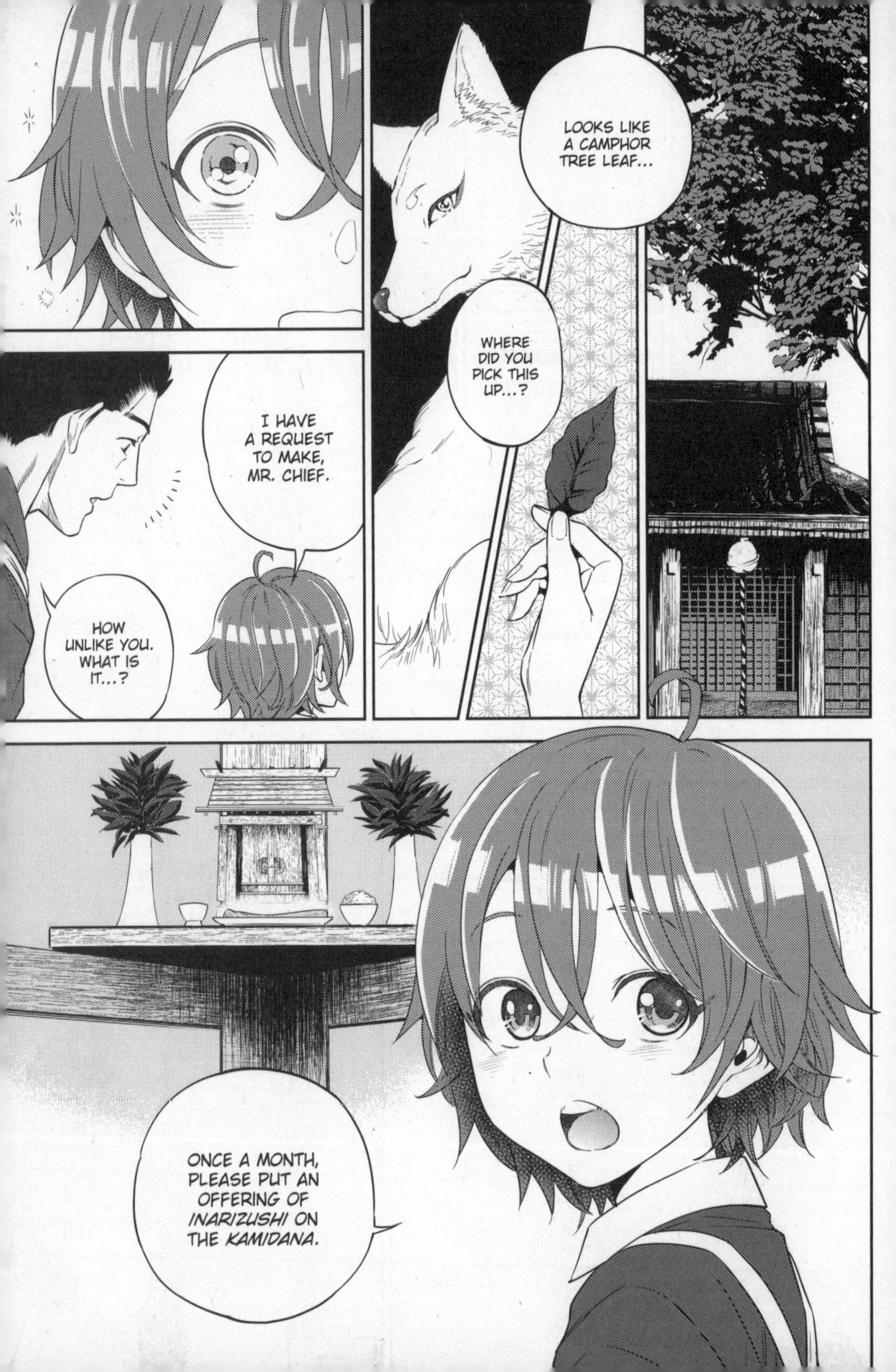
LOOKS LIKE A CAMPHOR TREE LEAF...
WHERE DID YOU PICK THIS UP...?
I HAVE A REQUEST TO MAKE, MR. CHIEF.
HOW UNLIKE YOU. WHAT IS IT...?
ONCE A MONTH, PLEASE PUT AN OFFERING OF *INARIZUSHI* ON THE *KAMIDANA*.

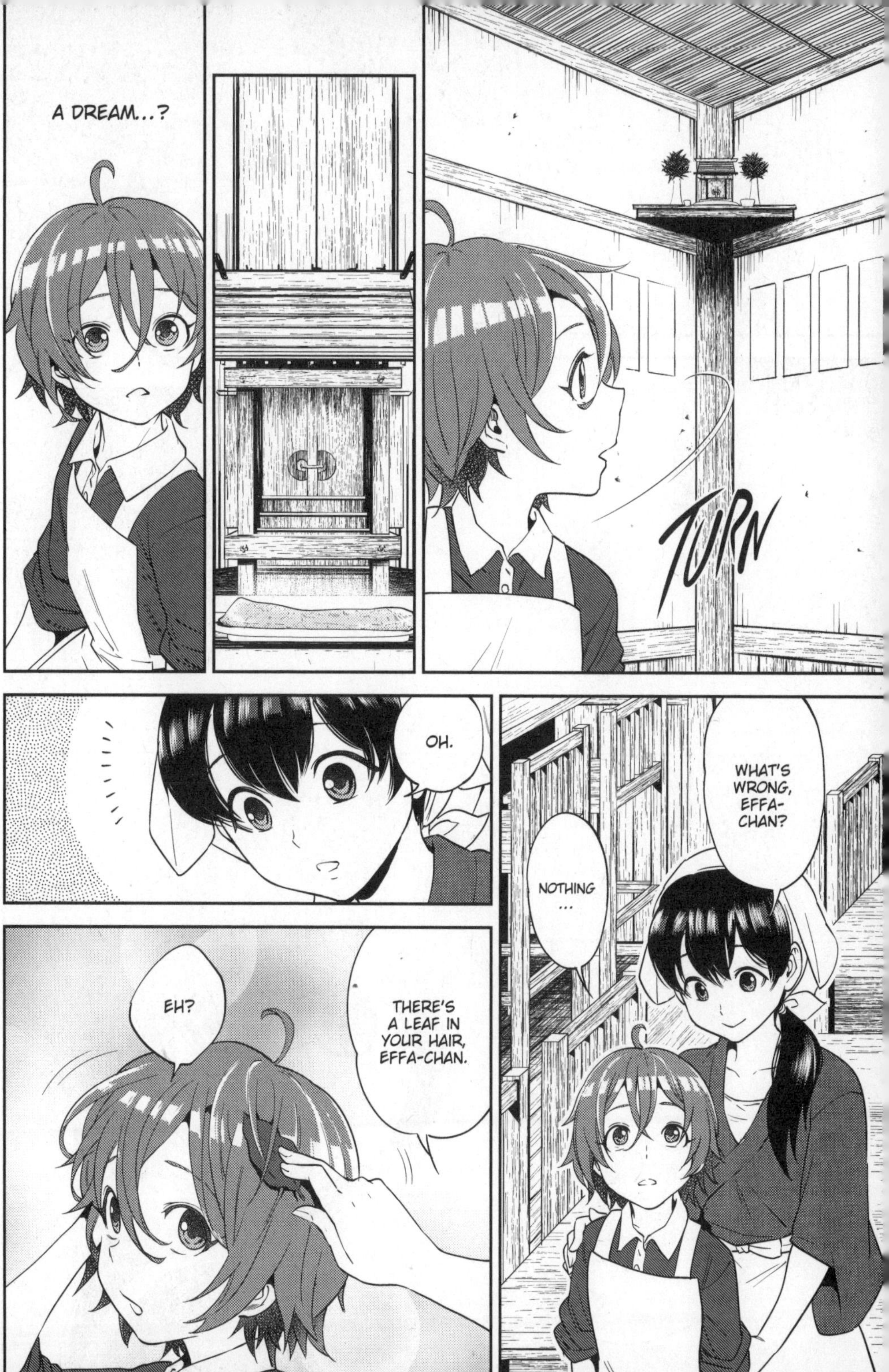
TURN
A DREAM...?
WHAT'S WRONG, EFFA-CHAN?
NOTHING ...
OH.
THERE'S A LEAF IN YOUR HAIR, EFFA-CHAN.
EH?

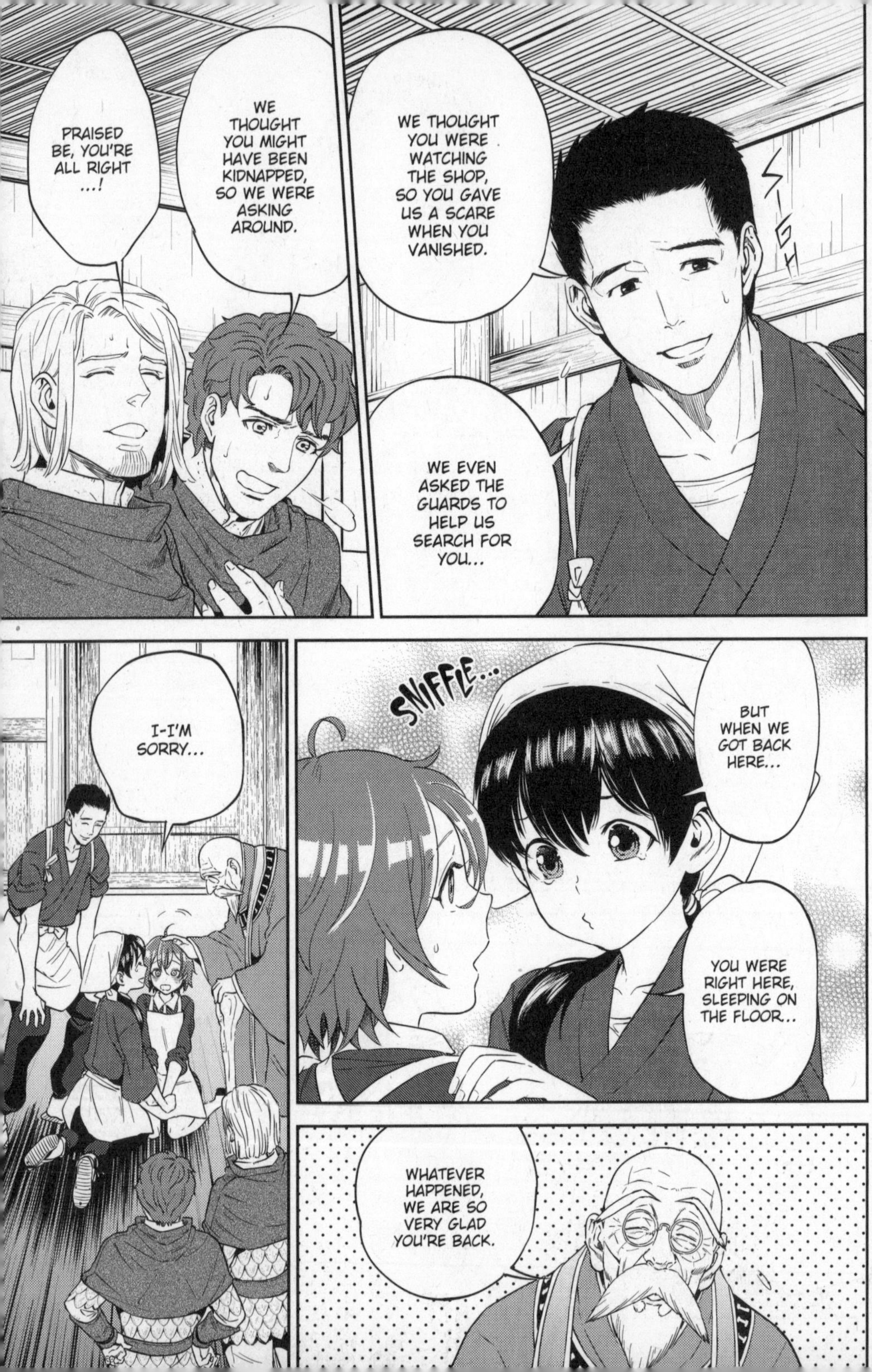
WE THOUGHT YOU WERE WATCHING THE SHOP, SO YOU GAVE US A SCARE WHEN YOU VANISHED.
SIGH
WE EVEN ASKED THE GUARDS TO HELP US SEARCH FOR YOU...
WE THOUGHT YOU MIGHT HAVE BEEN KIDNAPPED, SO WE WERE ASKING AROUND.
PRAISED BE, YOU'RE ALL RIGHT ...!
BUT WHEN WE GOT BACK HERE...
SNIFFLE...
YOU WERE RIGHT HERE, SLEEPING ON THE FLOOR...
WHATEVER HAPPENED, WE ARE SO VERY GLAD YOU'RE BACK.
I-I'M SORRY...

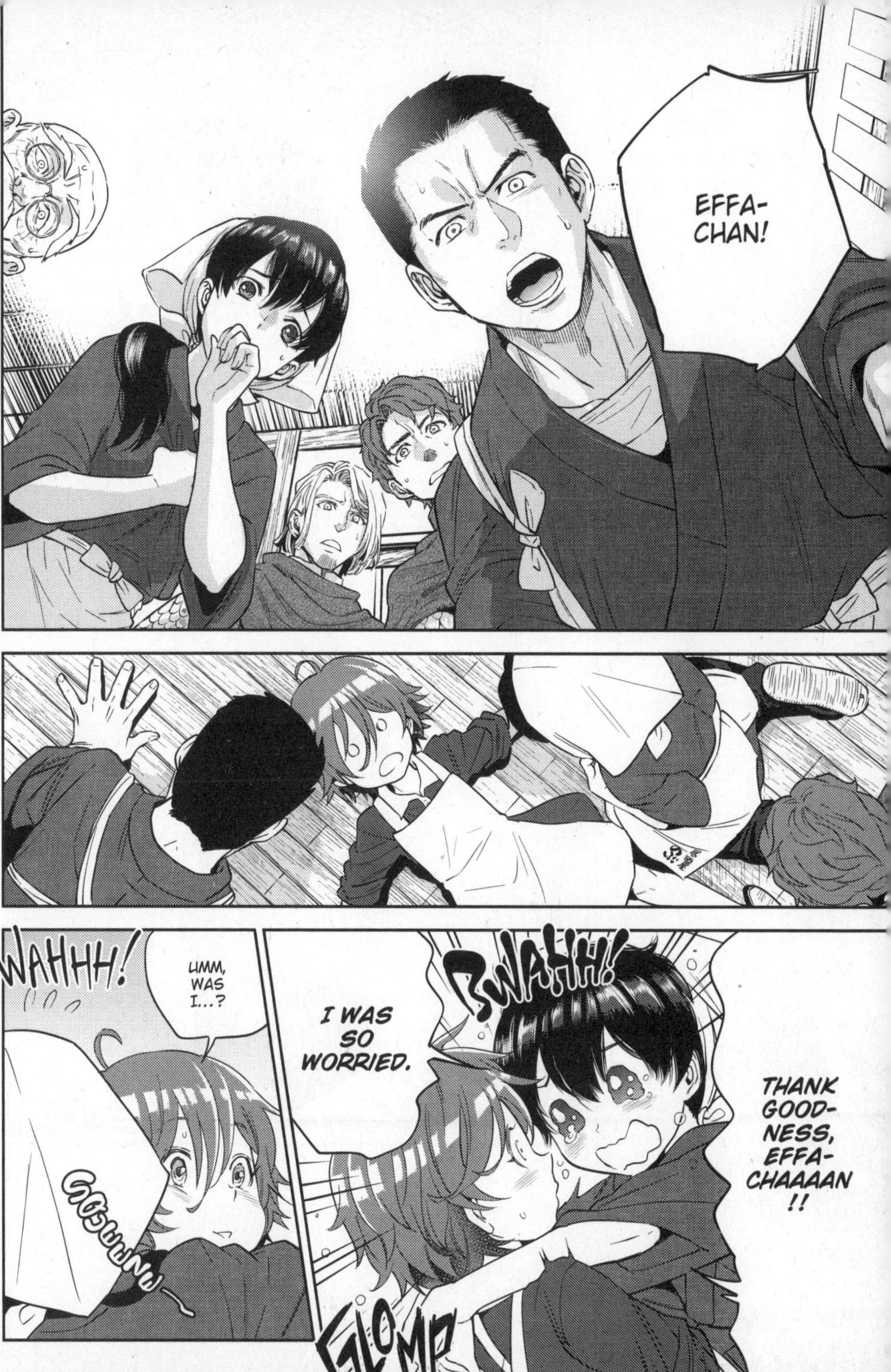
EFFA-CHAN!
BWAHH!
THANK GOODNESS, EFFA-CHAAAAN!!
I WAS SO WORRIED.
GLOMP
WAHHH!
UMM, WAS I...?

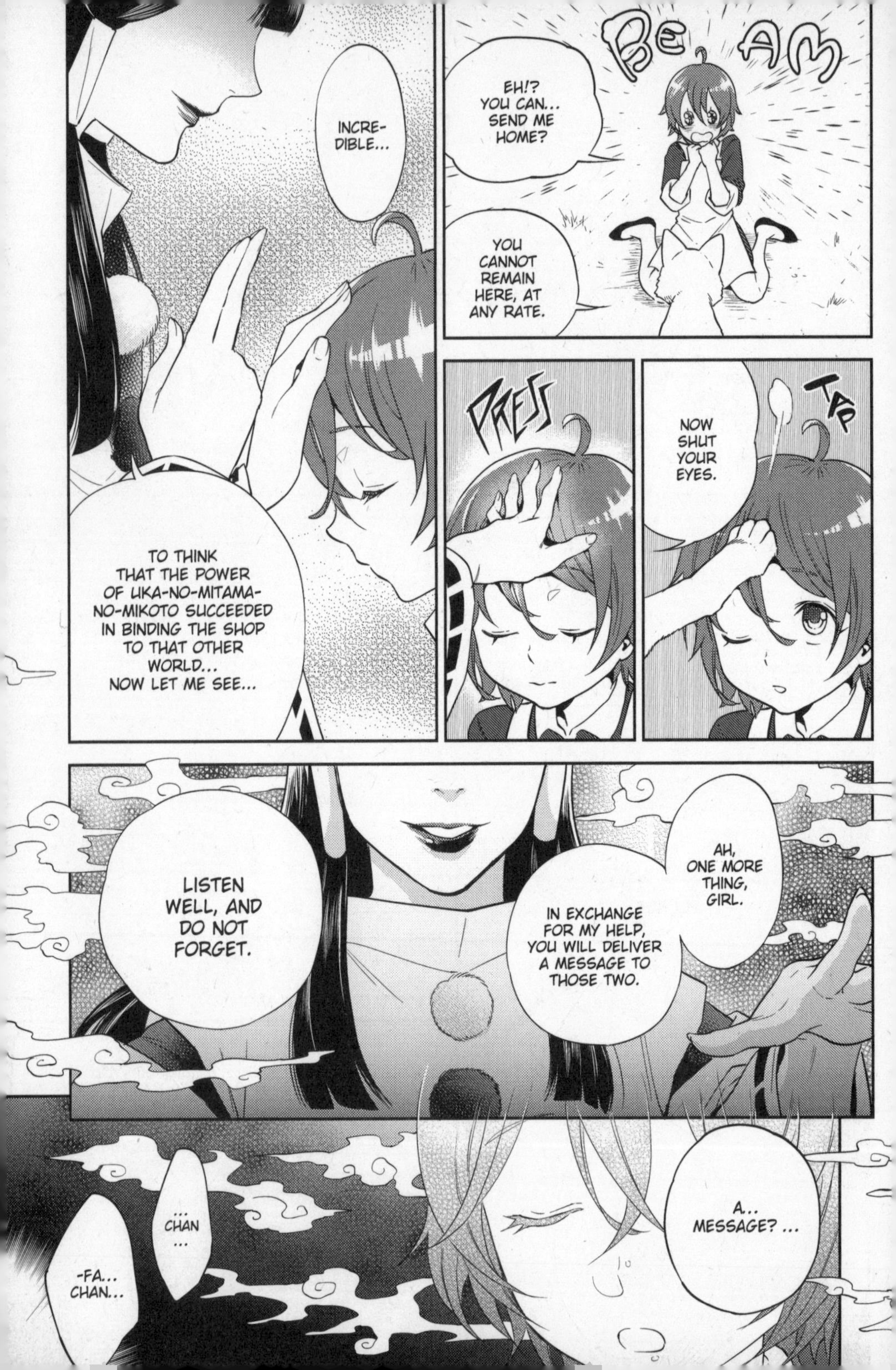
BE AM
EH!? YOU CAN... SEND ME HOME?
YOU CANNOT REMAIN HERE, AT ANY RATE.
TAP
NOW SHUT YOUR EYES.
PRESS
INCREDIBLE...
TO THINK THAT THE POWER OF UKA-NO-MITAMA-NO-MIKOTO SUCCEEDED IN BINDING THE SHOP TO THAT OTHER WORLD... NOW LET ME SEE...
AH, ONE MORE THING, GIRL.
IN EXCHANGE FOR MY HELP, YOU WILL DELIVER A MESSAGE TO THOSE TWO.
LISTEN WELL, AND DO NOT FORGET.
A... MESSAGE? ...
... CHAN ...
-FA... CHAN...

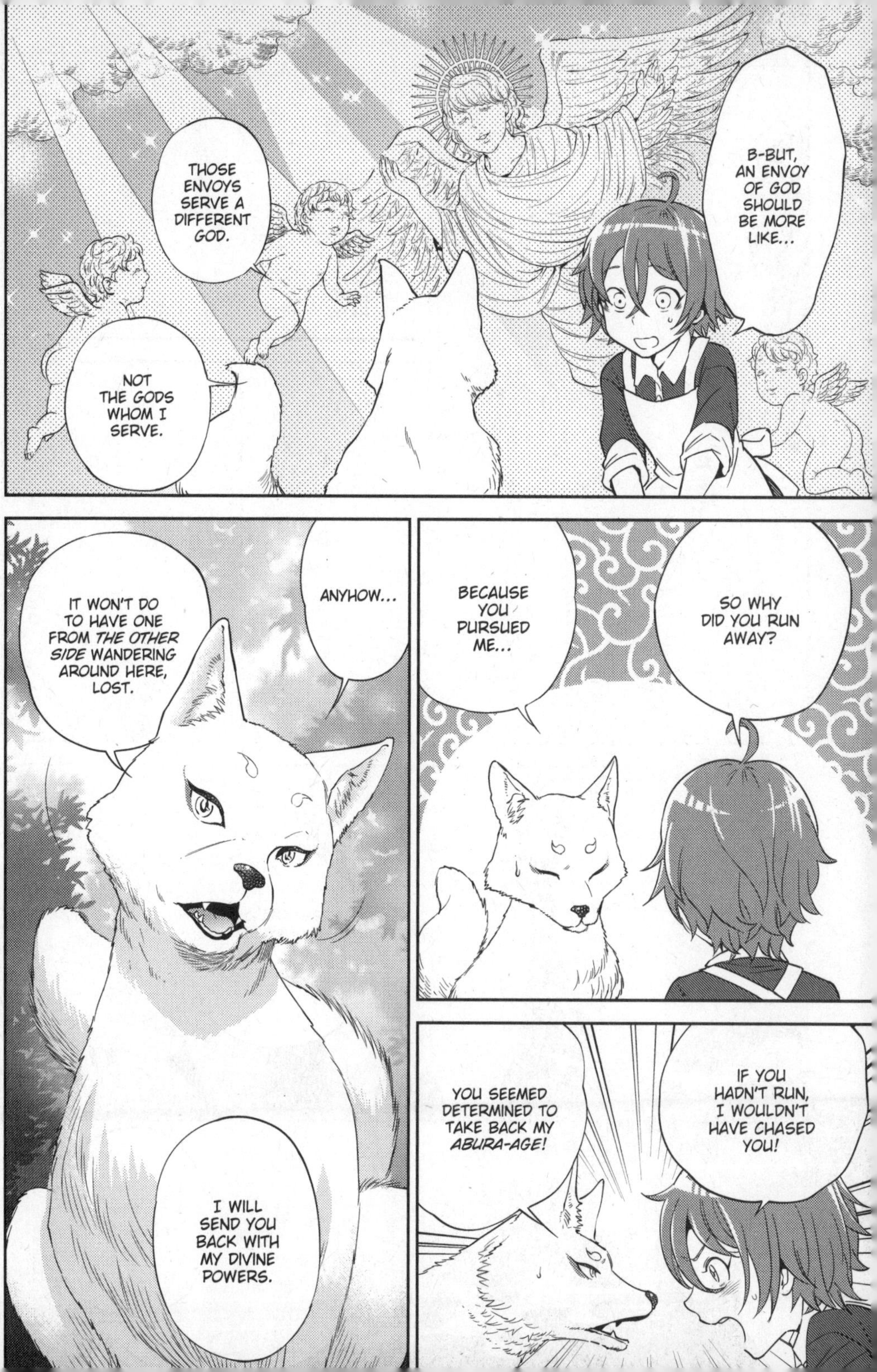
B-BUT, AN ENVOY OF GOD SHOULD BE MORE LIKE...
THOSE ENVOYS SERVE A DIFFERENT GOD.
NOT THE GODS WHOM I SERVE.
SO WHY DID YOU RUN AWAY?
BECAUSE YOU PURSUED ME...
IF YOU HADN'T RUN, I WOULDN'T HAVE CHASED YOU!
YOU SEEMED DETERMINED TO TAKE BACK MY *ABURA-AGE*!
ANYHOW...
IT WON'T DO TO HAVE ONE FROM *THE OTHER SIDE* WANDERING AROUND HERE, LOST.
I WILL SEND YOU BACK WITH MY DIVINE POWERS.

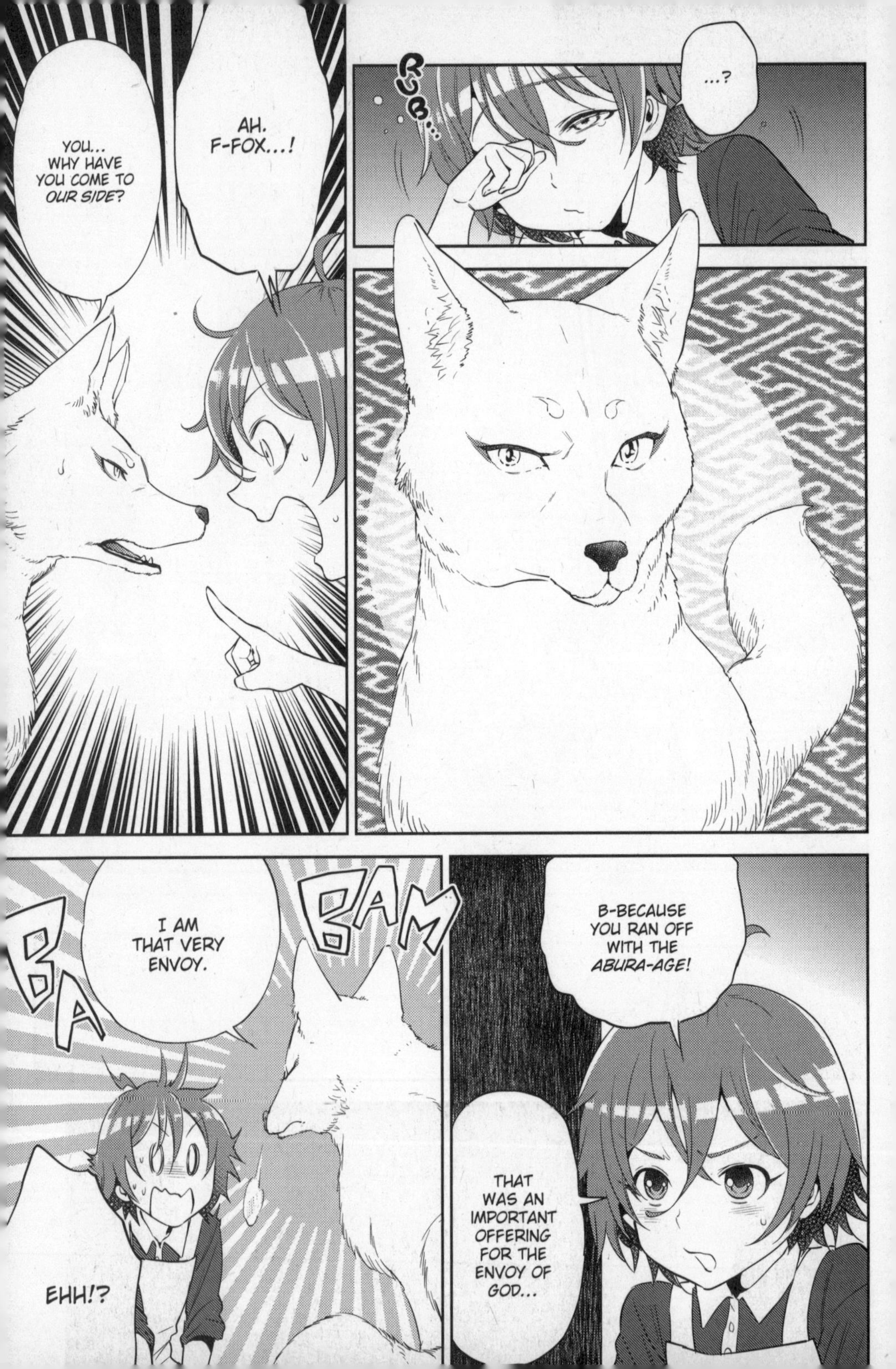
...?
RUB...
AH. F-FOX...!
YOU... WHY HAVE YOU COME TO OUR SIDE?
B-BECAUSE YOU RAN OFF WITH THE ABURA-AGE!
THAT WAS AN IMPORTANT OFFERING FOR THE ENVOY OF GOD...
BAM
I AM THAT VERY ENVOY.
BA
EHH!?

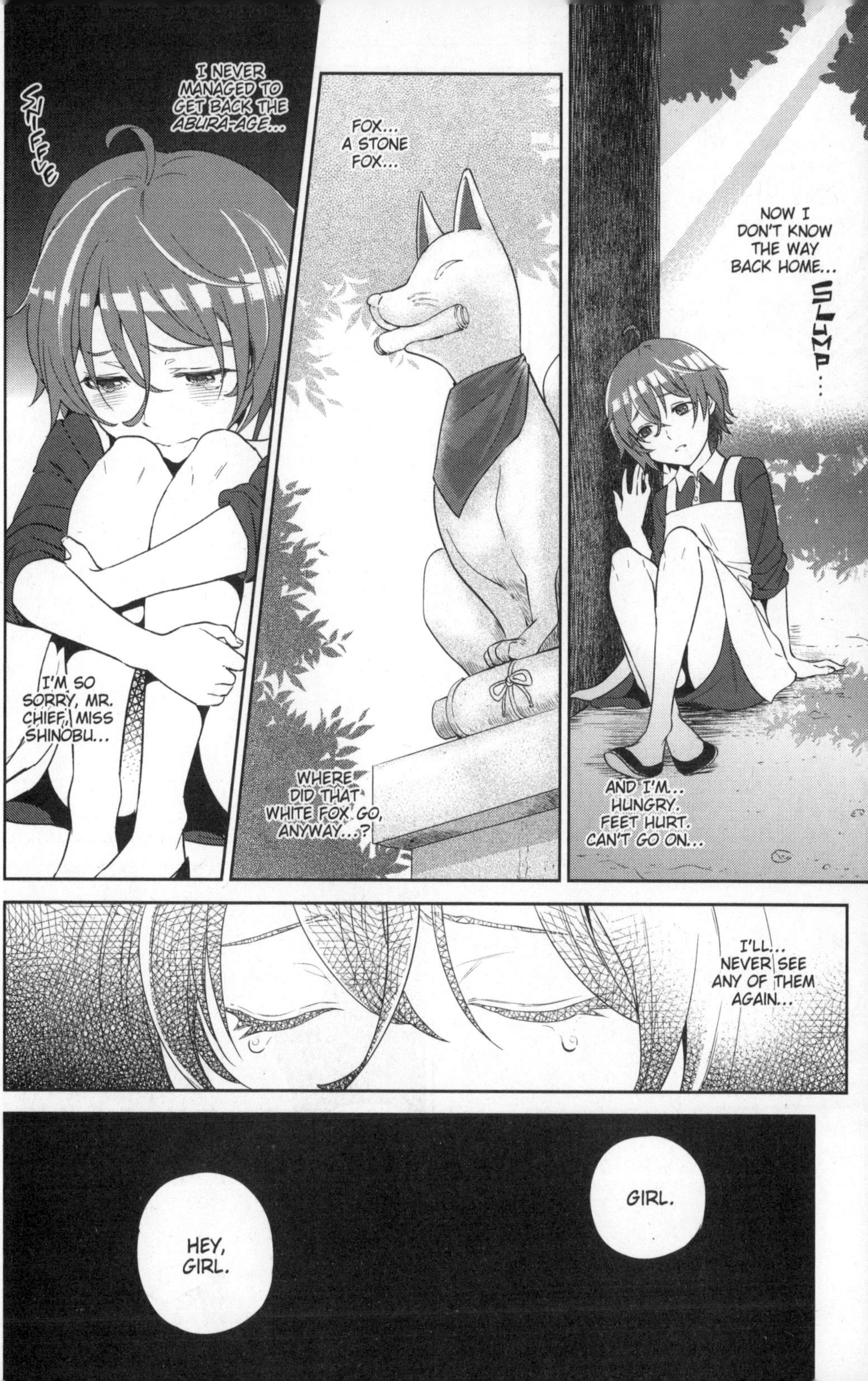
NOW I DON'T KNOW THE WAY BACK HOME...
SLUMP...
AND I'M... HUNGRY. FEET HURT. CAN'T GO ON...
FOX... A STONE FOX...
WHERE DID THAT WHITE FOX GO, ANYWAY...?
I NEVER MANAGED TO GET BACK THE ABURA-AGE...
SNIFFLE
I'M SO SORRY, MR. CHIEF, MISS SHINOBU...
I'LL... NEVER SEE ANY OF THEM AGAIN...
GIRL.
HEY, GIRL.

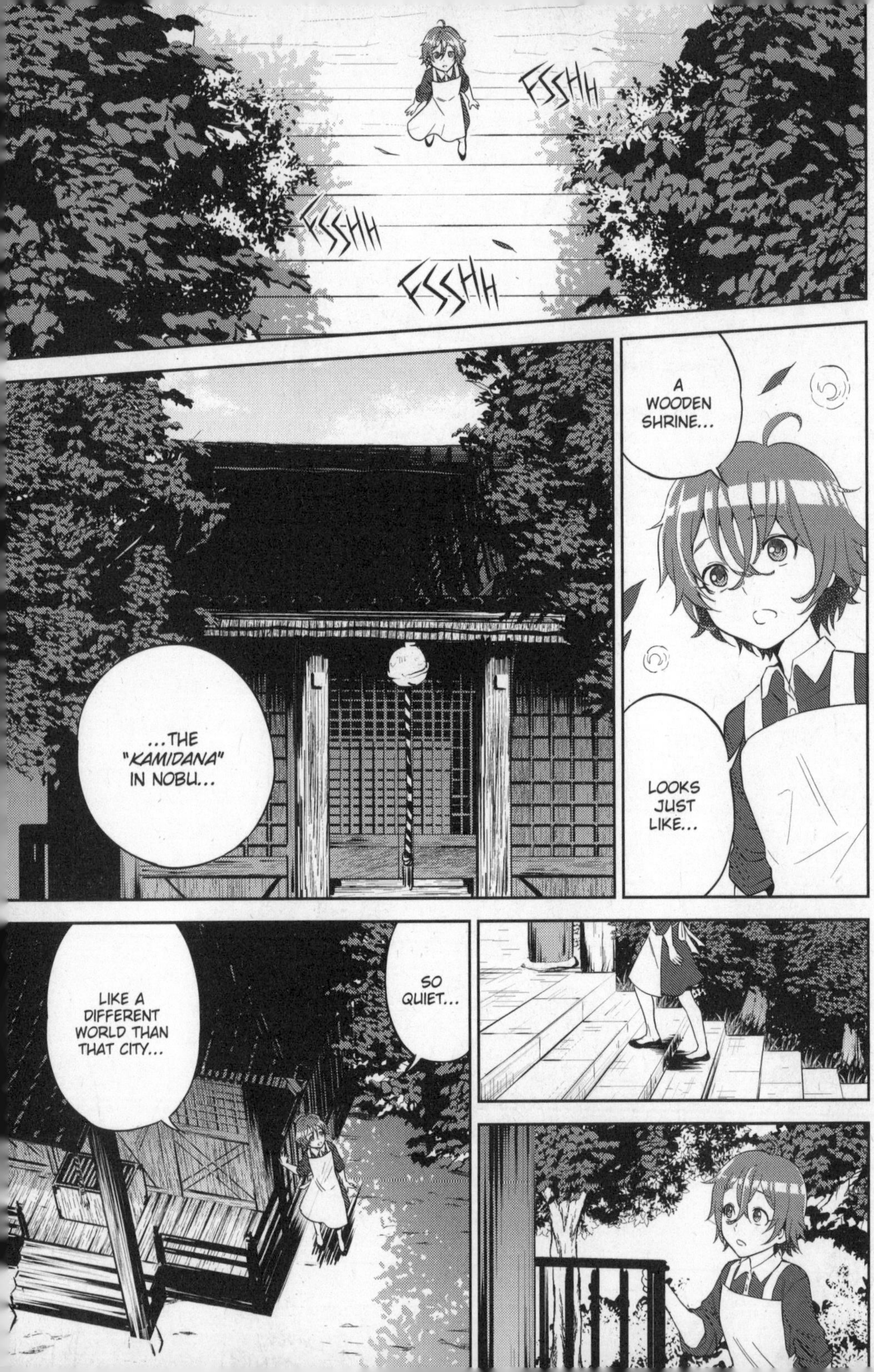
FSSHH
FSSHH
FSSHH
A WOODEN SHRINE...
LOOKS JUST LIKE...
...THE "*KAMIDANA*" IN NOBU...
SO QUIET...
LIKE A DIFFERENT WORLD THAN THAT CITY...

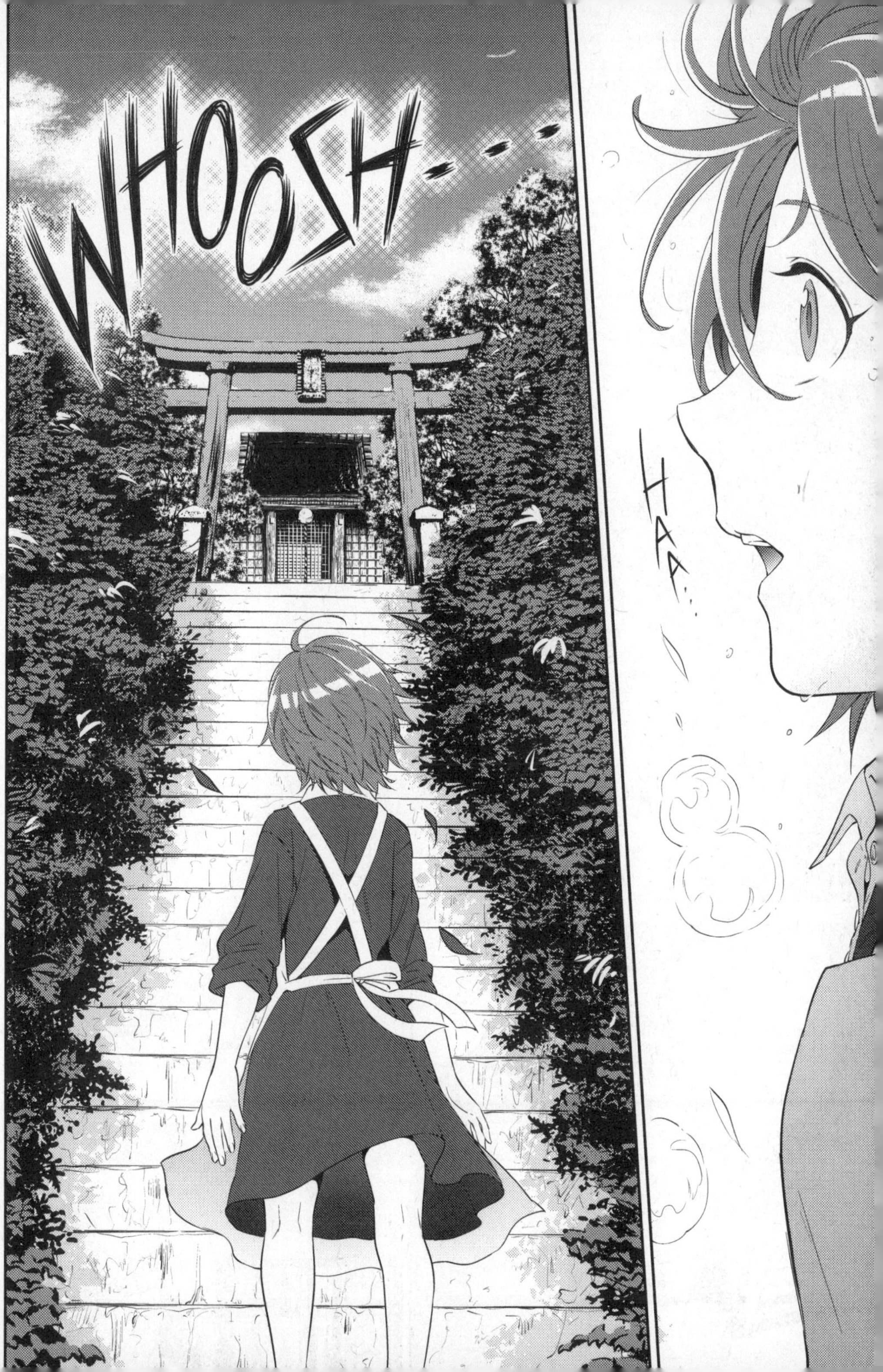
HAA...
WHOOSH...

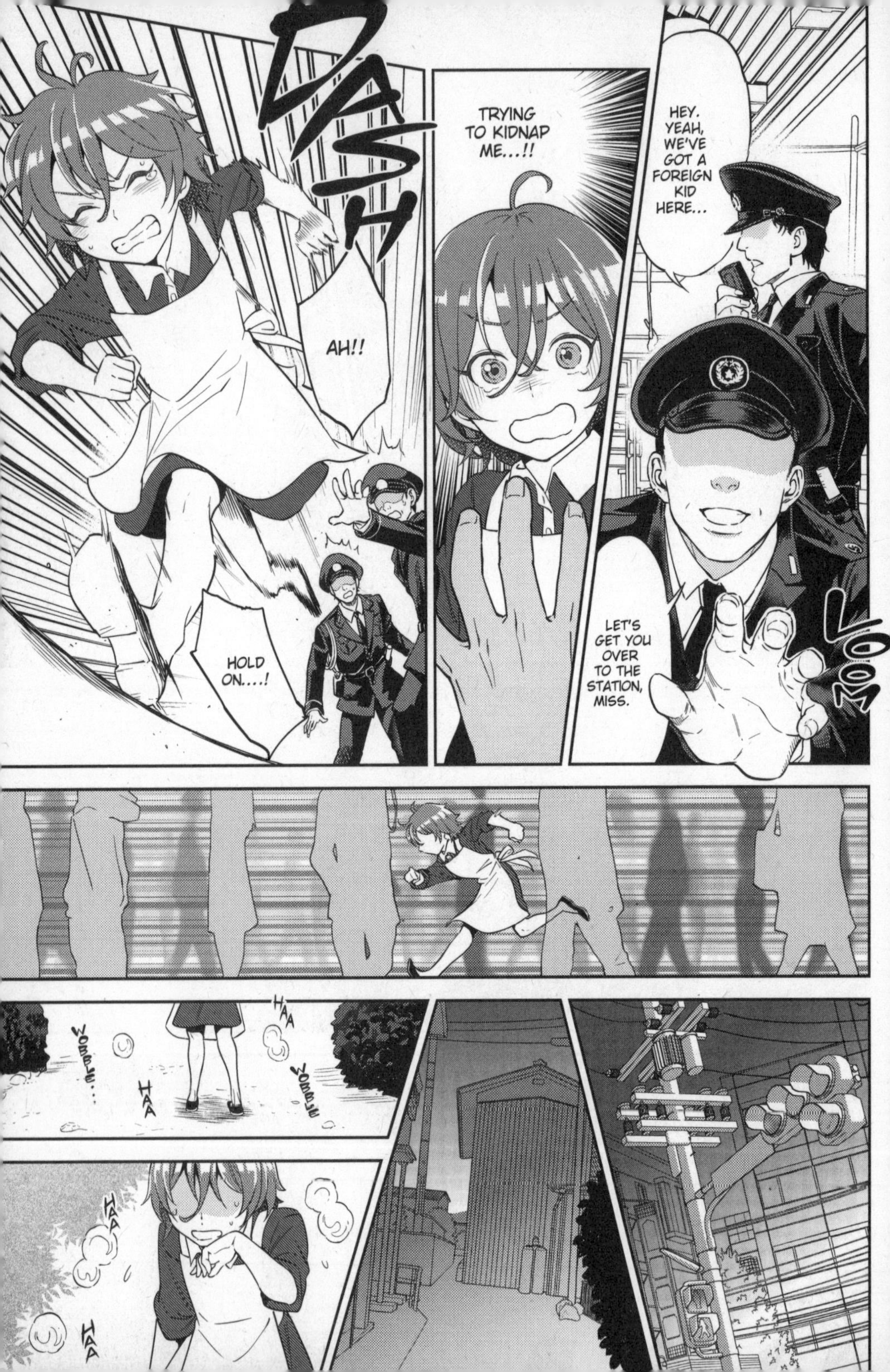
HEY. YEAH, WE'VE GOT A FOREIGN KID HERE...
LET'S GET YOU OVER TO THE STATION, MISS.
VOOM
TRYING TO KIDNAP ME...!!
DASH
AH!!
HOLD ON....!
HAA
WOBBLE...
HAA
WOBBLE
HAA
HAA

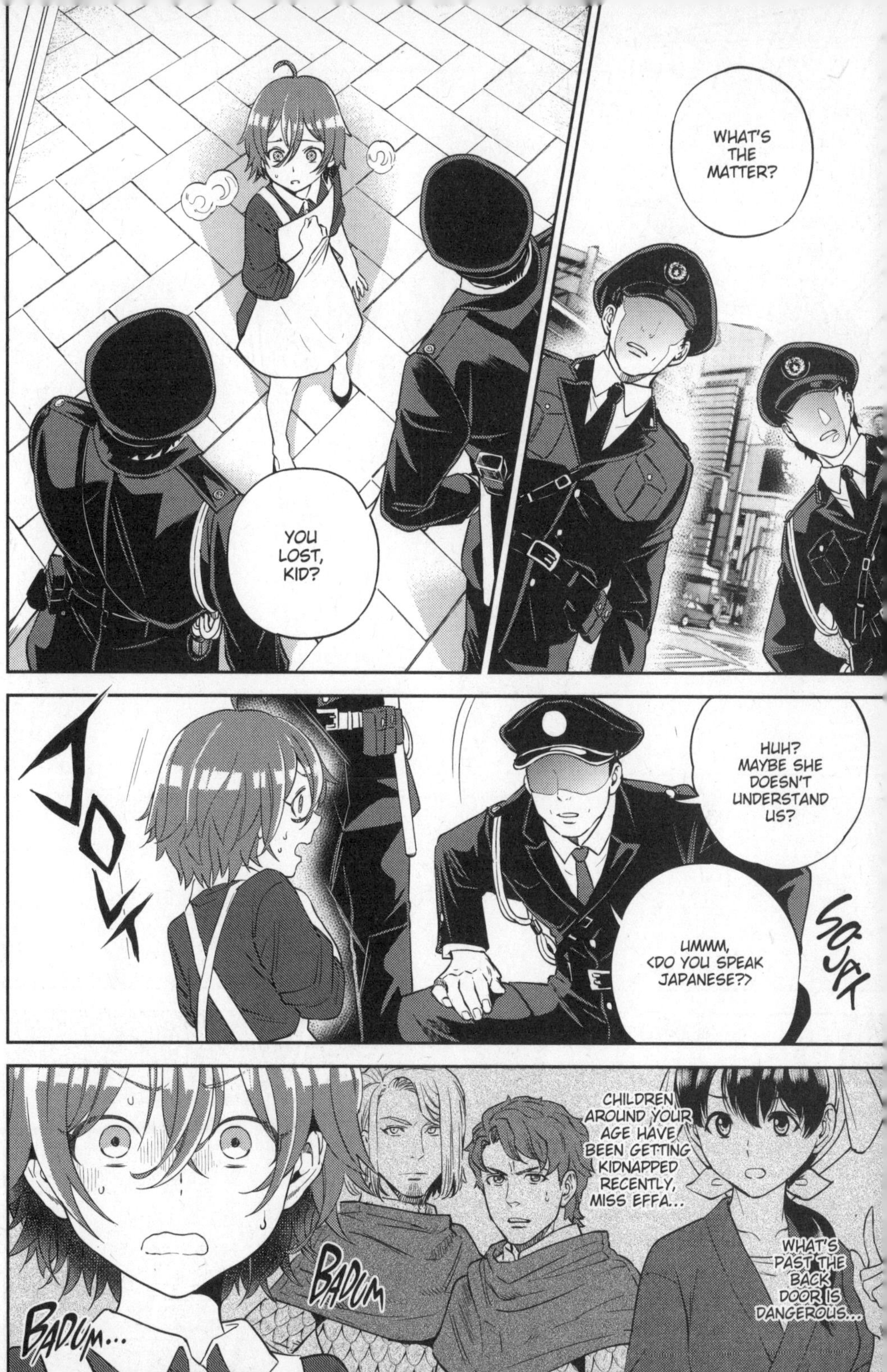
WHAT'S THE MATTER?
YOU LOST, KID?
SQUAT
HUH? MAYBE SHE DOESN'T UNDERSTAND US?
UMMM, <DO YOU SPEAK JAPANESE?>
JOLT
WHAT'S PAST THE BACK DOOR IS DANGEROUS...
CHILDREN AROUND YOUR AGE HAVE BEEN GETTING KIDNAPPED RECENTLY, MISS EFFA...
BADUM
BADUM...

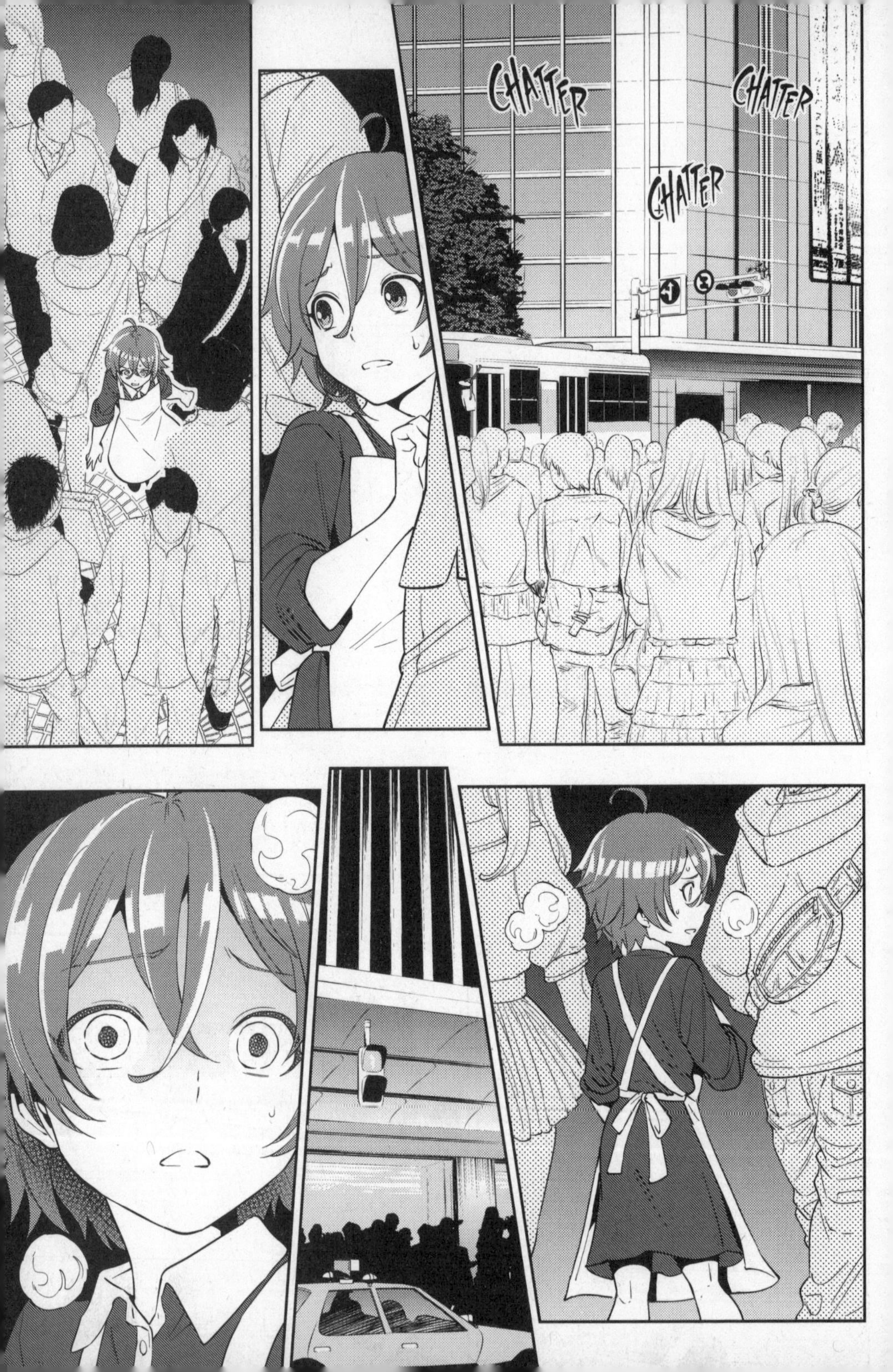
CHATTER
CHATTER
CHATTER

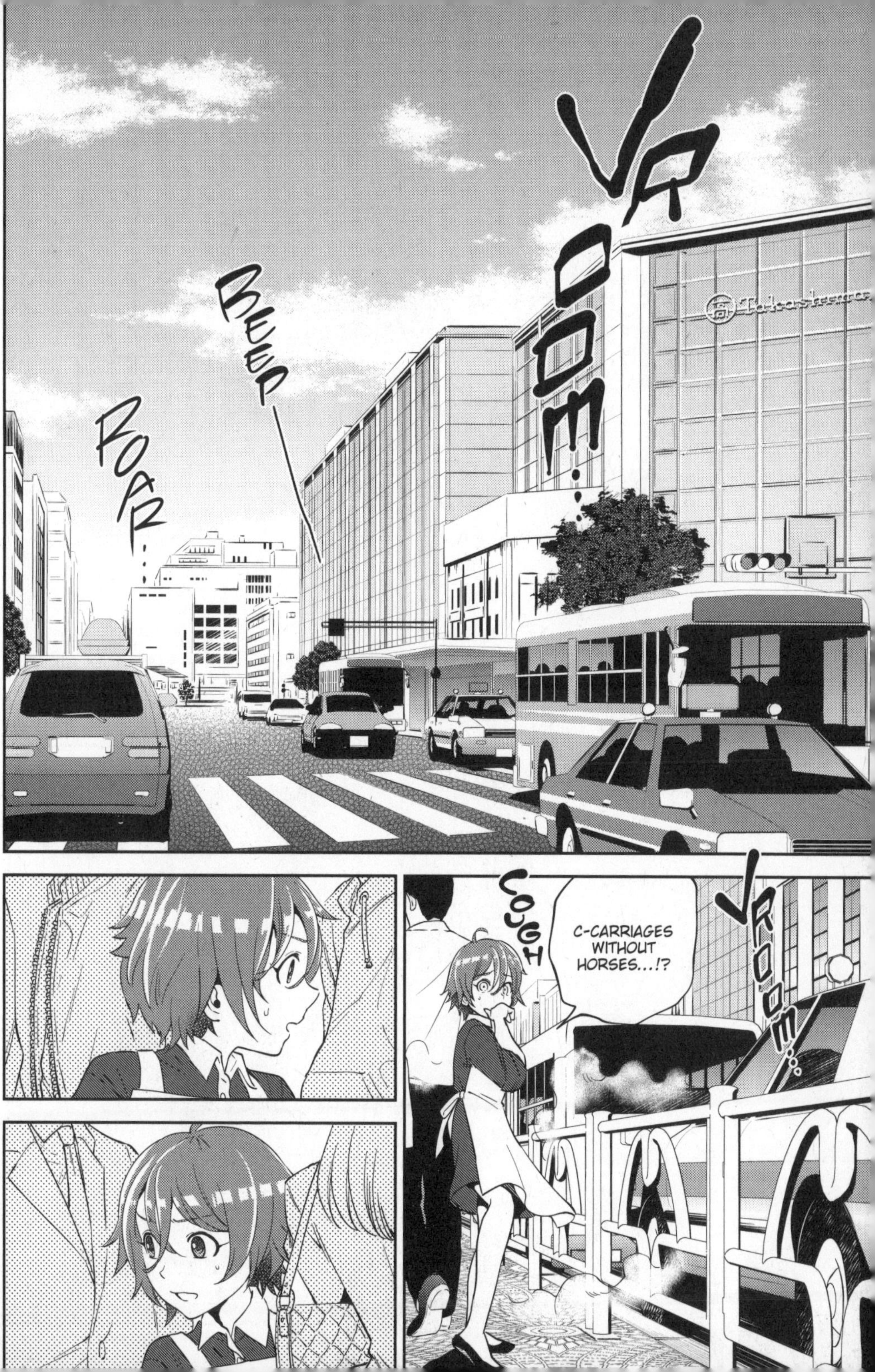
VROOM!!...
BEEP
ROAR...
VROOM...
C-CARRIAGES WITHOUT HORSES...!?
COUGH

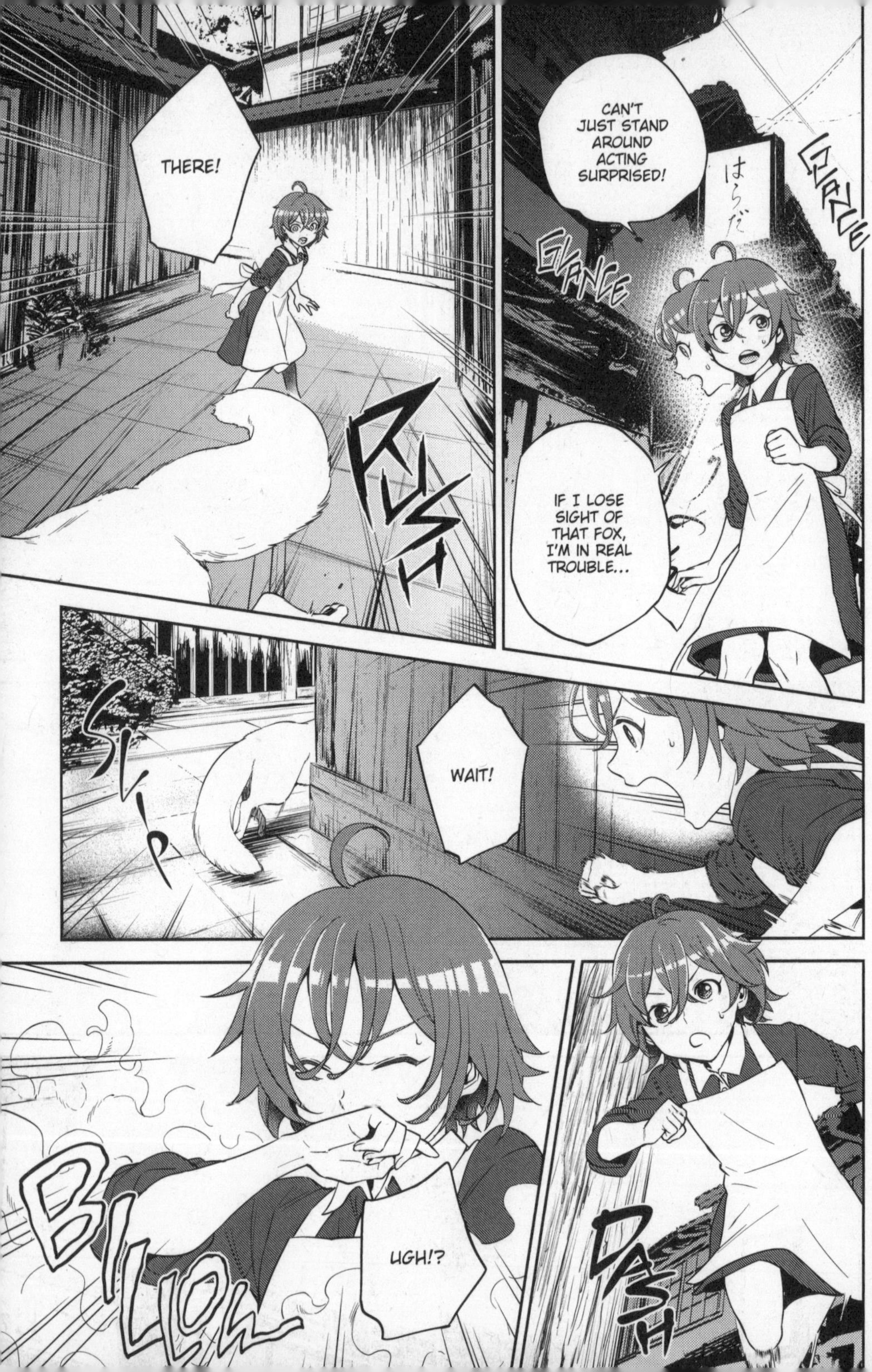
CAN'T JUST STAND AROUND ACTING SURPRISED!
はらだ
GLANCE
GLANCE
IF I LOSE SIGHT OF THAT FOX, I'M IN REAL TROUBLE...
THERE!
PUSH
WAIT!
SLIP
DASH
UGH!?
BILLOW

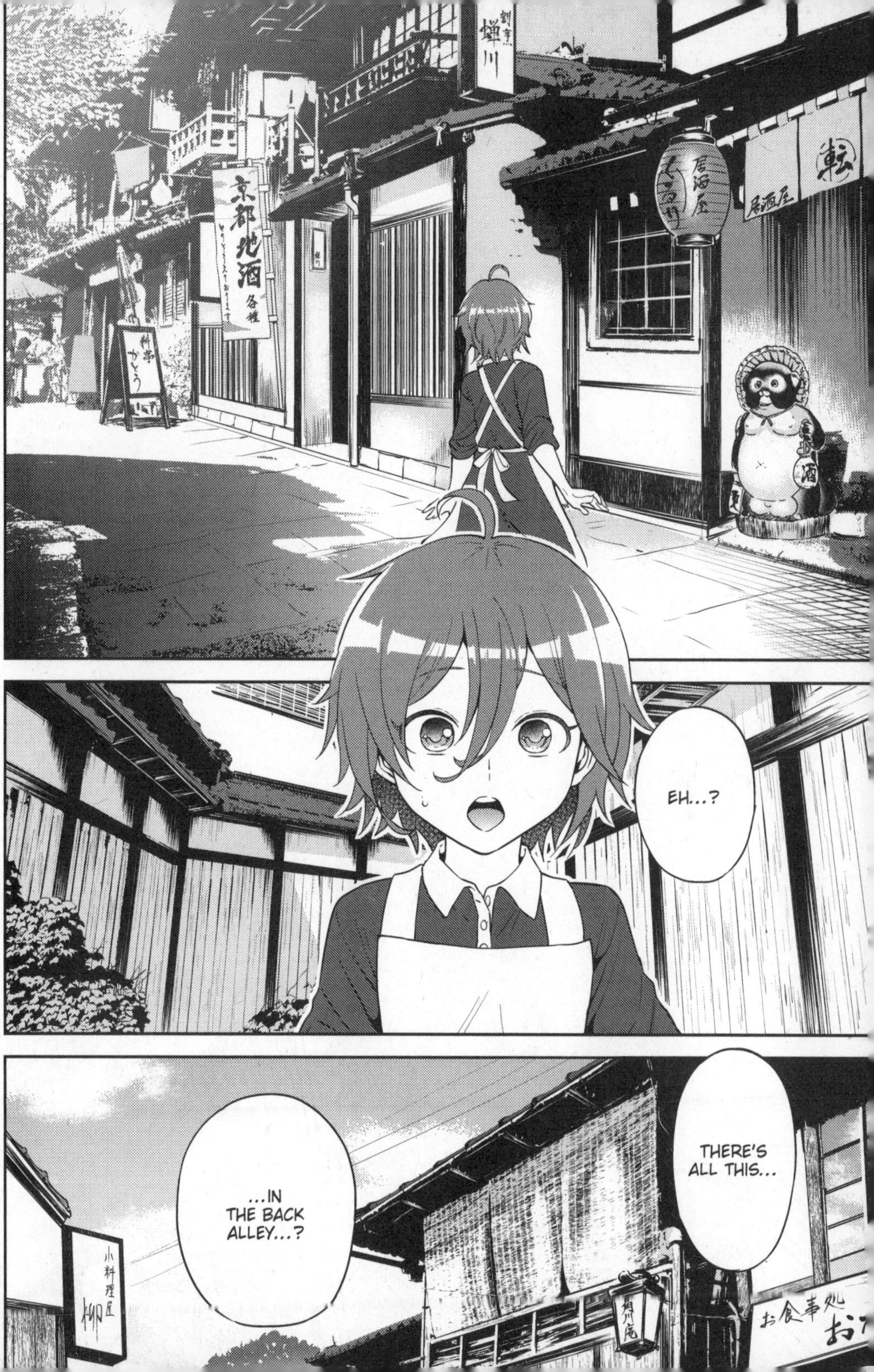
京都地酒
各種
居酒屋
居酒屋
EH...?
THERE'S ALL THIS...
...IN THE BACK ALLEY...?
お食事処
小料理屋
柳

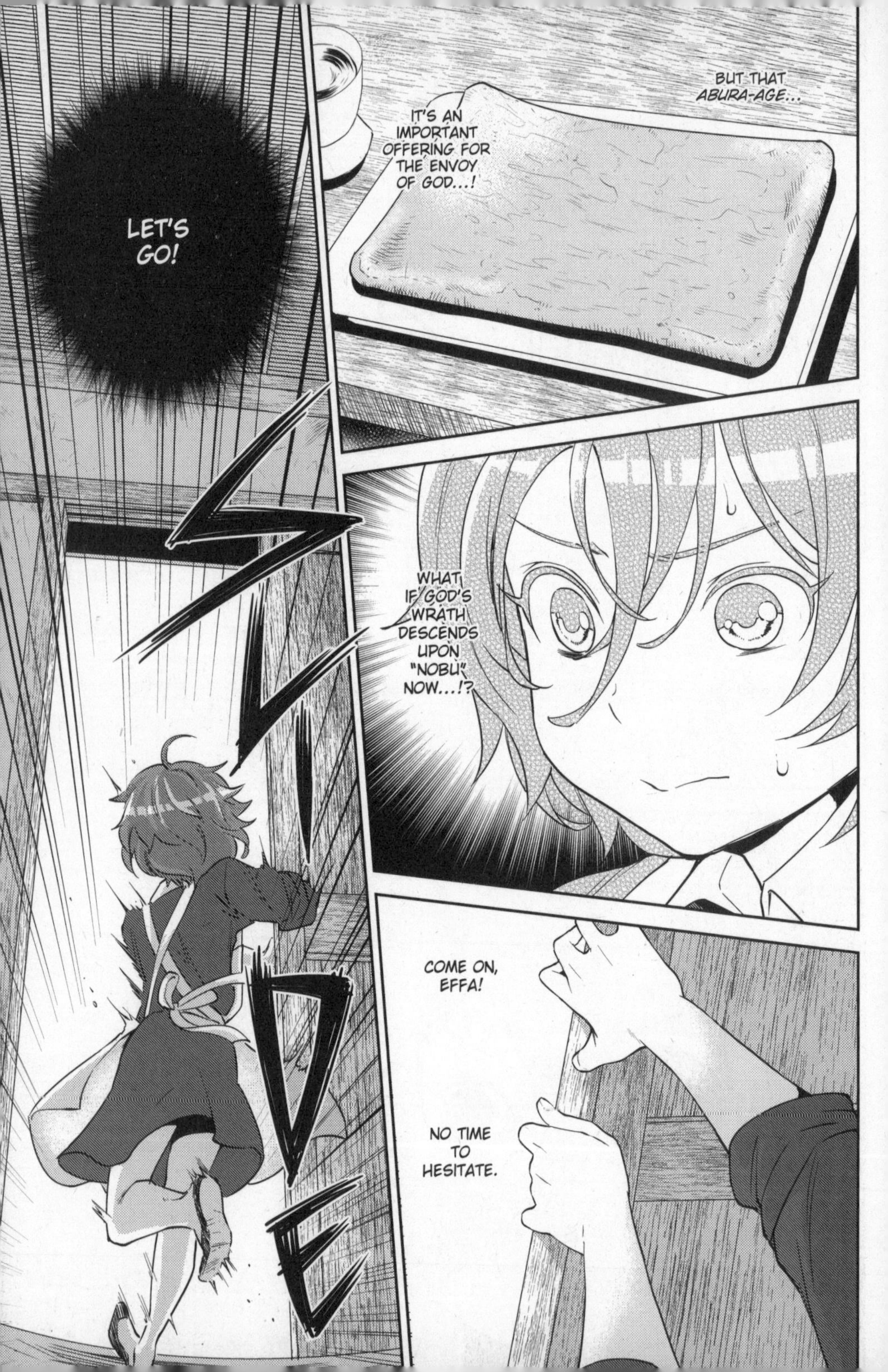
BUT THAT ABURA-AGE...
IT'S AN IMPORTANT OFFERING FOR THE ENVOY OF GOD...!
WHAT IF GOD'S WRATH DESCENDS UPON "NOBU" NOW...!?
COME ON, EFFA!
NO TIME TO HESITATE.
LET'S GO!

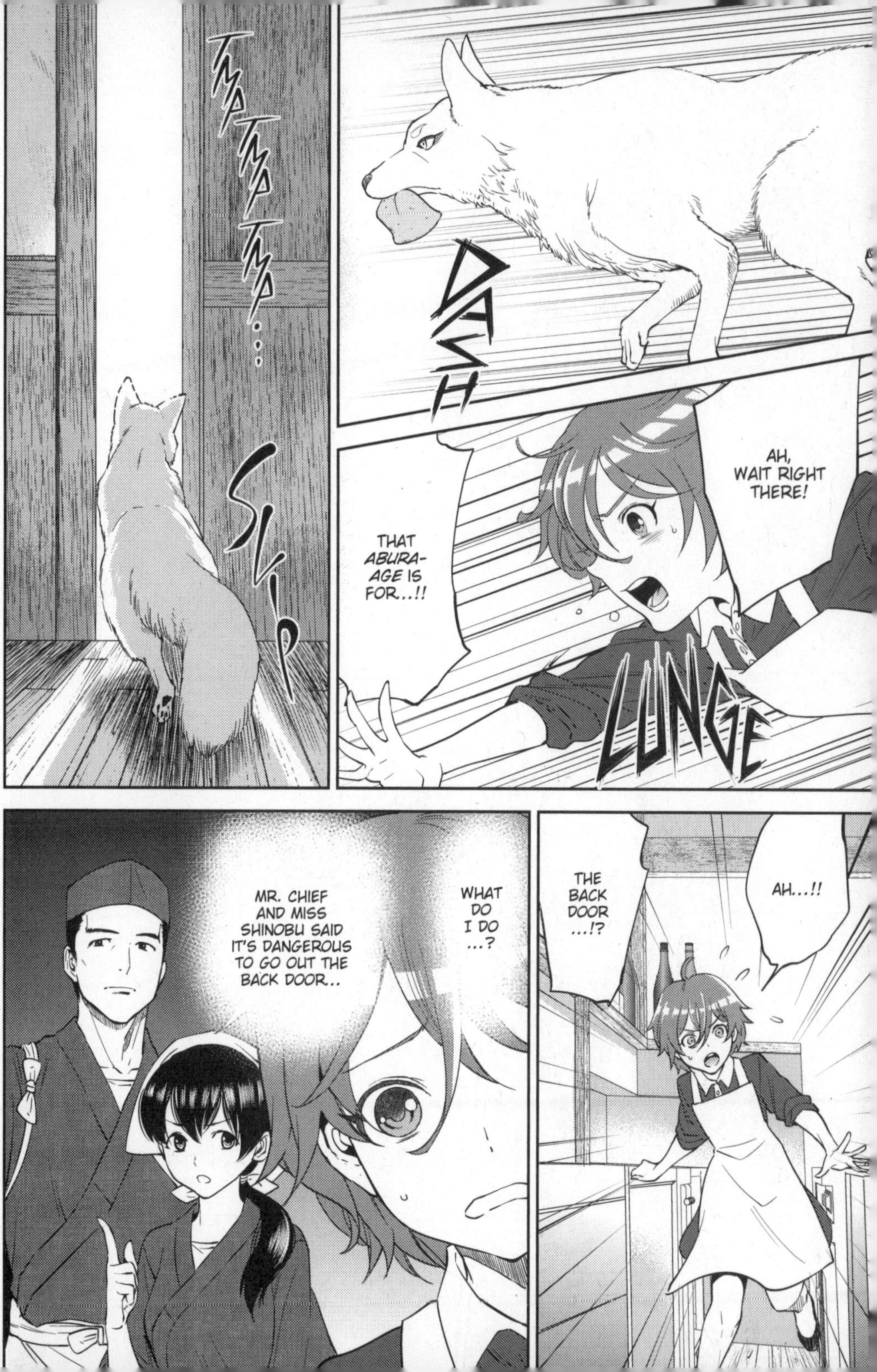
DASH
AH, WAIT RIGHT THERE!
THAT ABURAGE IS FOR...!!
LUNGE
TMPTMPTMP...
SLIP
AH...!!
THE BACK DOOR ...!?
WHAT DO I DO ...?
MR. CHIEF AND MISS SHINOBU SAID IT'S DANGEROUS TO GO OUT THE BACK DOOR...

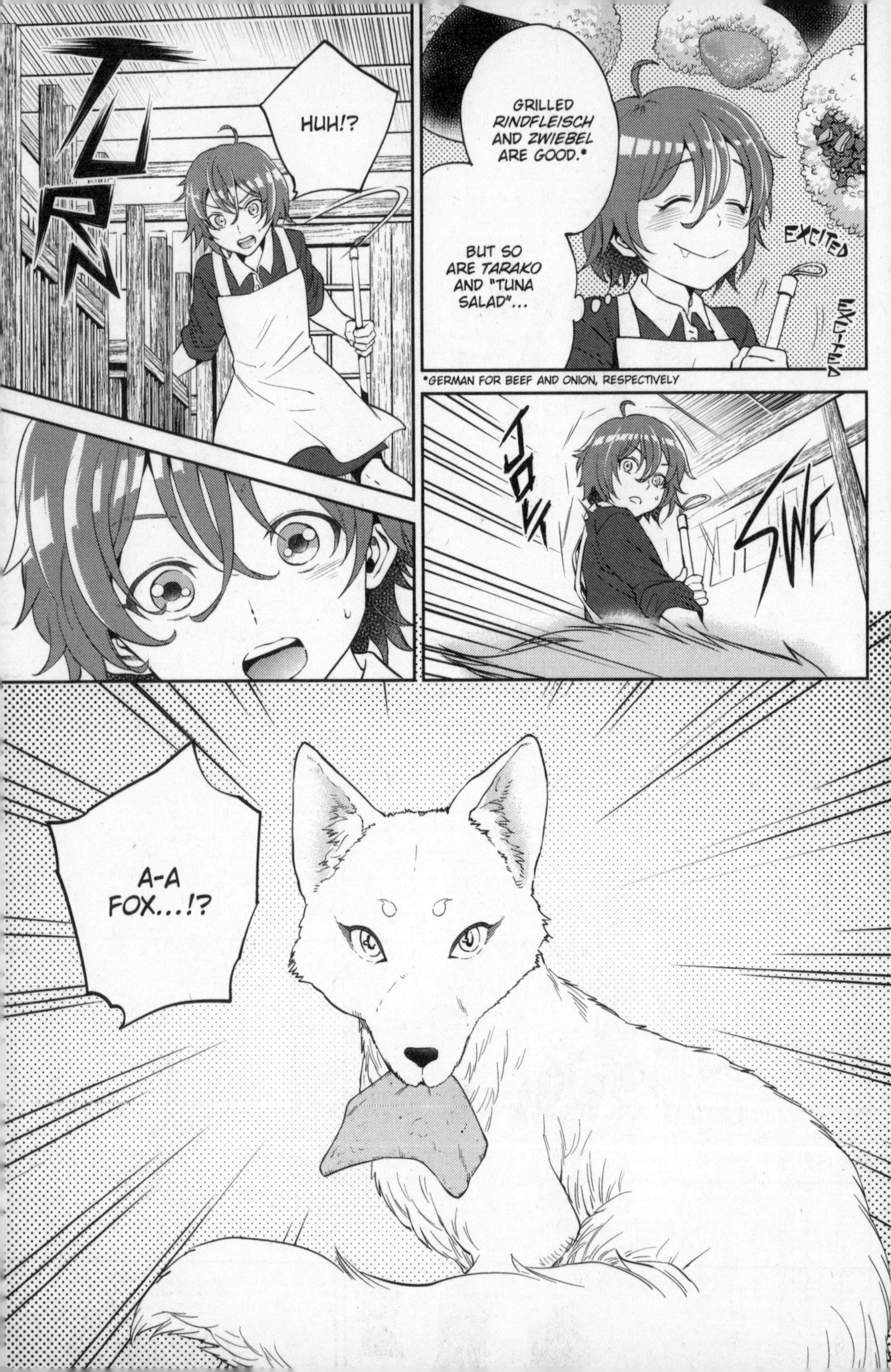
GRILLED RINDFLEISCH AND ZWIEBEL ARE GOOD.*
BUT SO ARE TARAKO AND "TUNA SALAD"...
EXCITED
EXCITED
*GERMAN FOR BEEF AND ONION, RESPECTIVELY
HUH!?
SWF
A-A FOX...!?

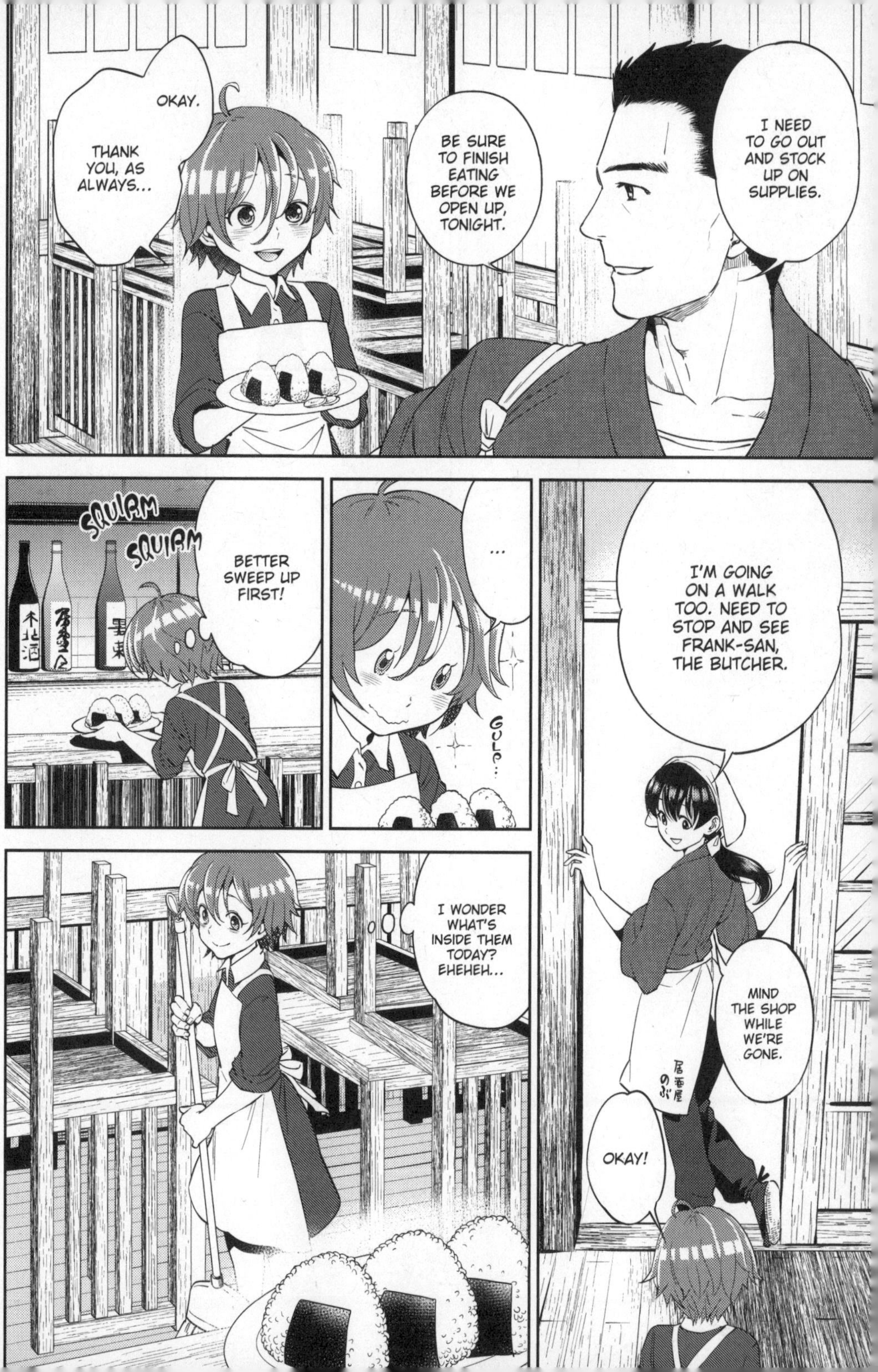
I NEED TO GO OUT AND STOCK UP ON SUPPLIES.
BE SURE TO FINISH EATING BEFORE WE OPEN UP, TONIGHT.
OKAY.
THANK YOU, AS ALWAYS...
I'M GOING ON A WALK TOO. NEED TO STOP AND SEE FRANK-SAN, THE BUTCHER.
MIND THE SHOP WHILE WE'RE GONE.
居酒屋のぶ
OKAY!
...
GULP...
BETTER SWEEP UP FIRST!
SQUIRM
SQUIRM
I WONDER WHAT'S INSIDE THEM TODAY? EHEHEH...

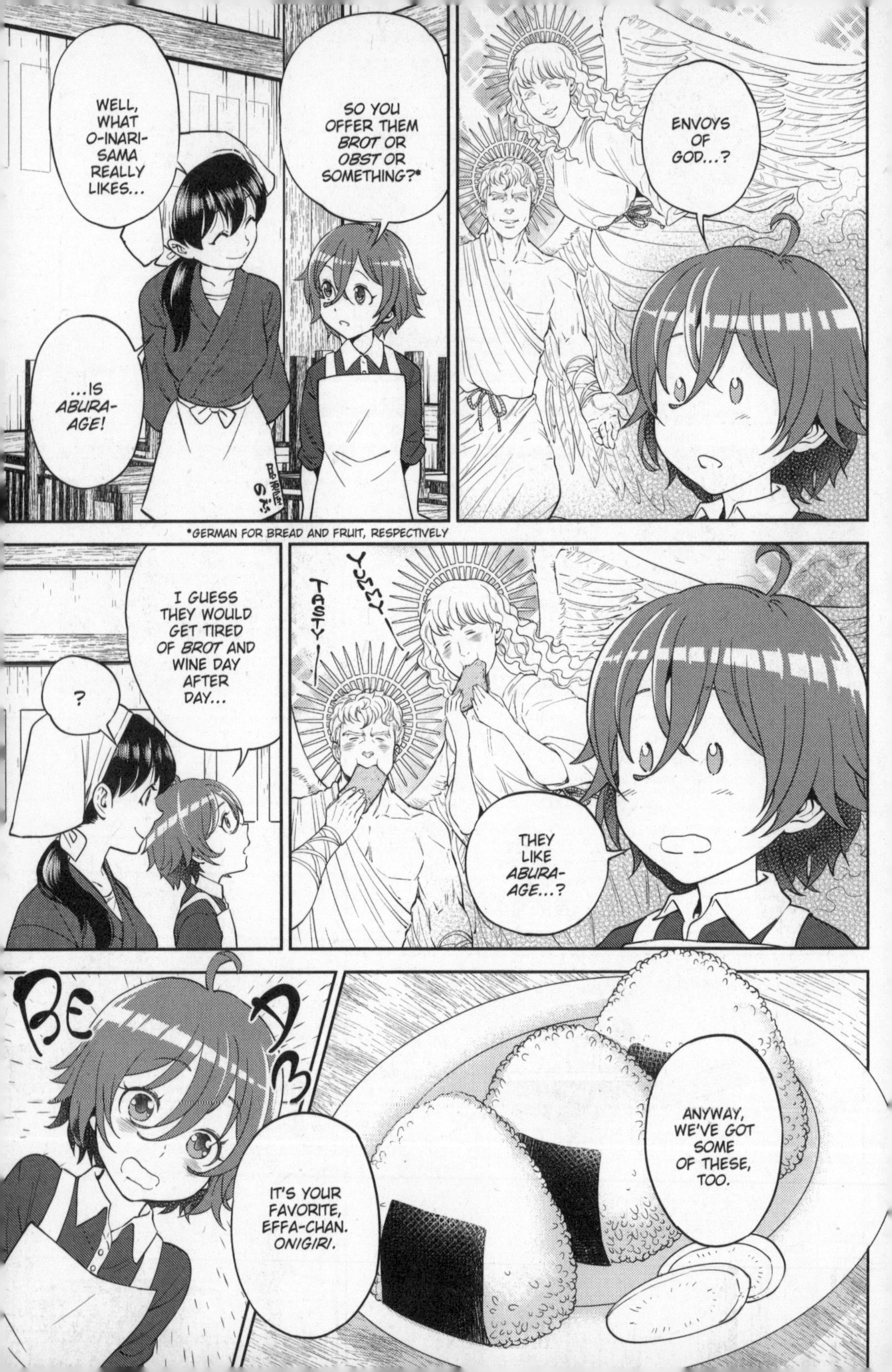
ENVOYS OF GOD...?
SO YOU OFFER THEM *BROT* OR *OBST* OR SOMETHING?*
WELL, WHAT O-INARI-SAMA REALLY LIKES...
...IS *ABURA-AGE!*
YUMMY
TASTY
THEY LIKE *ABURA-AGE*...?
I GUESS THEY WOULD GET TIRED OF *BROT* AND WINE DAY AFTER DAY...
?
ANYWAY, WE'VE GOT SOME OF THESE, TOO.
IT'S YOUR FAVORITE, EFFA-CHAN. *ONIGIRI.*
BEAM

*GERMAN FOR BREAD AND FRUIT, RESPECTIVELY

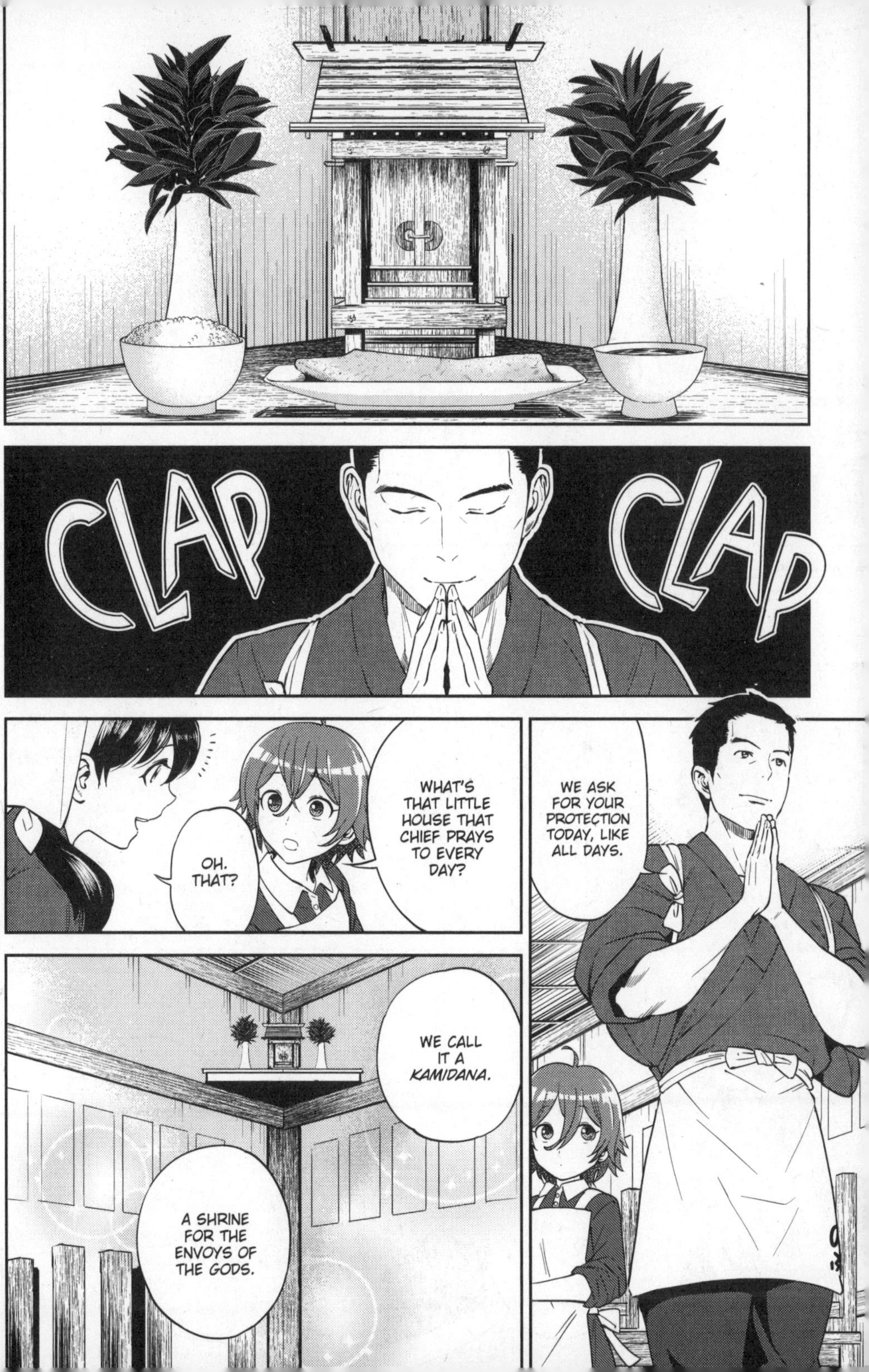
CLAP CLAP
WE ASK FOR YOUR PROTECTION TODAY, LIKE ALL DAYS.
WHAT'S THAT LITTLE HOUSE THAT CHIEF PRAYS TO EVERY DAY?
OH. THAT?
WE CALL IT A *KAMIDANA*.
A SHRINE FOR THE ENVOYS OF THE GODS.

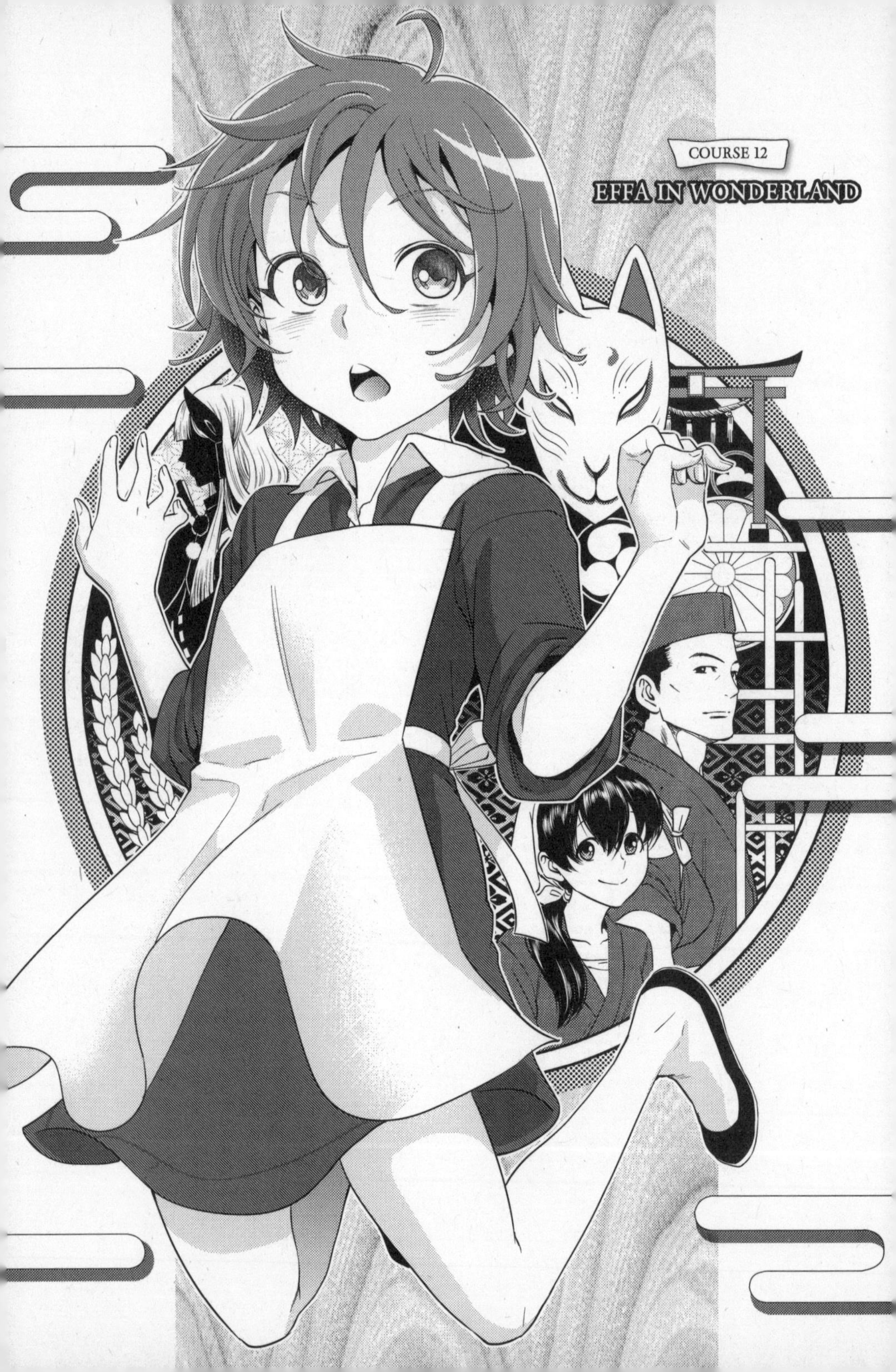
COURSE 12
EFFA IN WONDERLAND

OTHERWORLDLY IZAKAYA

NOBU

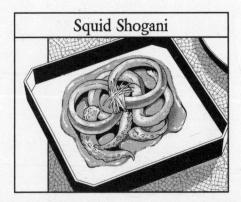
Squid Shogani

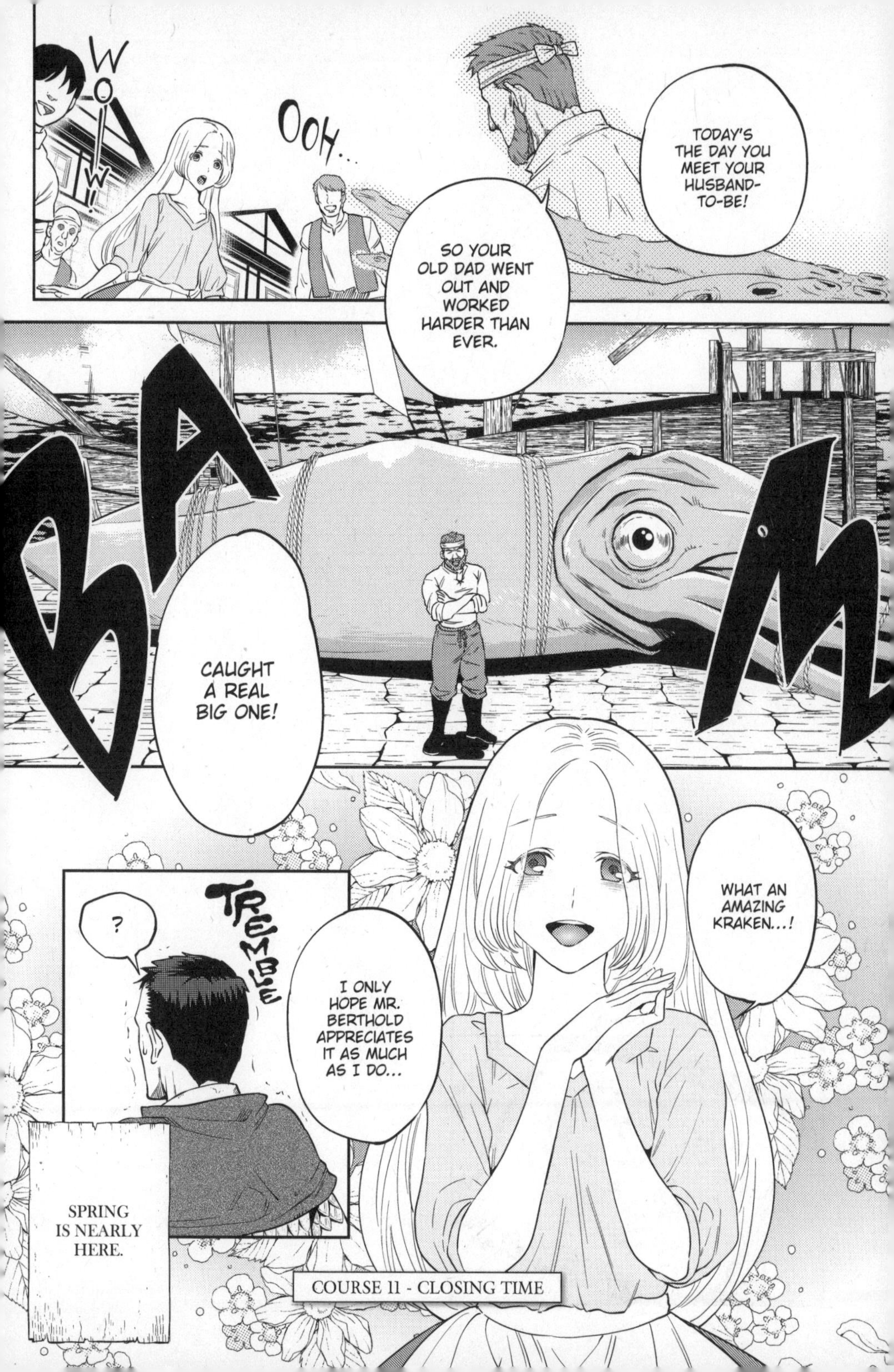
TODAY'S THE DAY YOU MEET YOUR HUSBAND-TO-BE!
SO YOUR OLD DAD WENT OUT AND WORKED HARDER THAN EVER.
OOH...
WOW!
BAM
CAUGHT A REAL BIG ONE!
WHAT AN AMAZING KRAKEN...!
I ONLY HOPE MR. BERTHOLD APPRECIATES IT AS MUCH AS I DO...
TREMBLE
?
SPRING IS NEARLY HERE.
COURSE 11 - CLOSING TIME

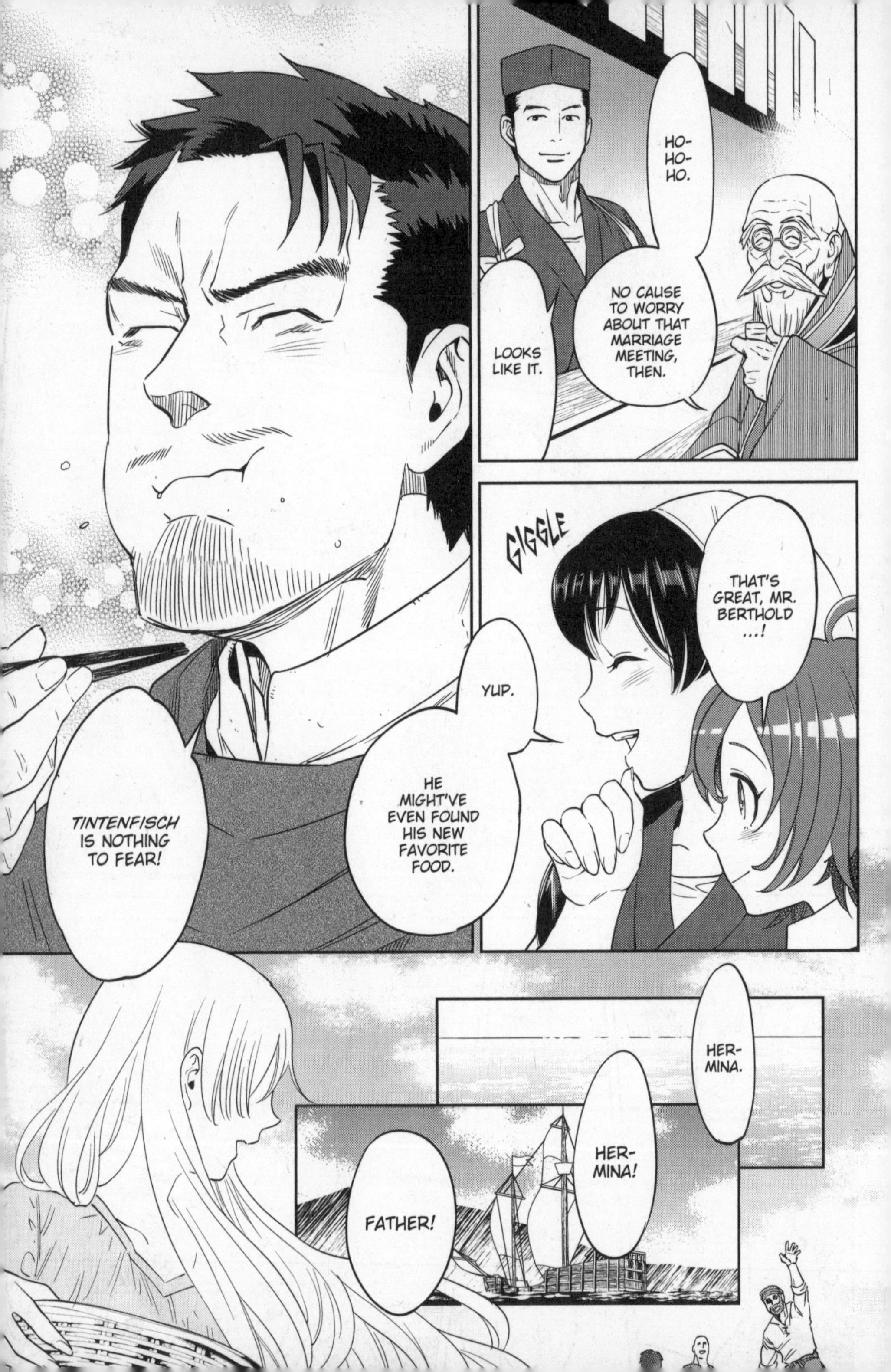
HO-HO-HO.
NO CAUSE TO WORRY ABOUT THAT MARRIAGE MEETING, THEN.
LOOKS LIKE IT.
GIGGLE
THAT'S GREAT, MR. BERTHOLD ...!
YUP.
HE MIGHT'VE EVEN FOUND HIS NEW FAVORITE FOOD.
TINTENFISCH IS NOTHING TO FEAR!
HER-MINA.
HER-MINA!
FATHER!

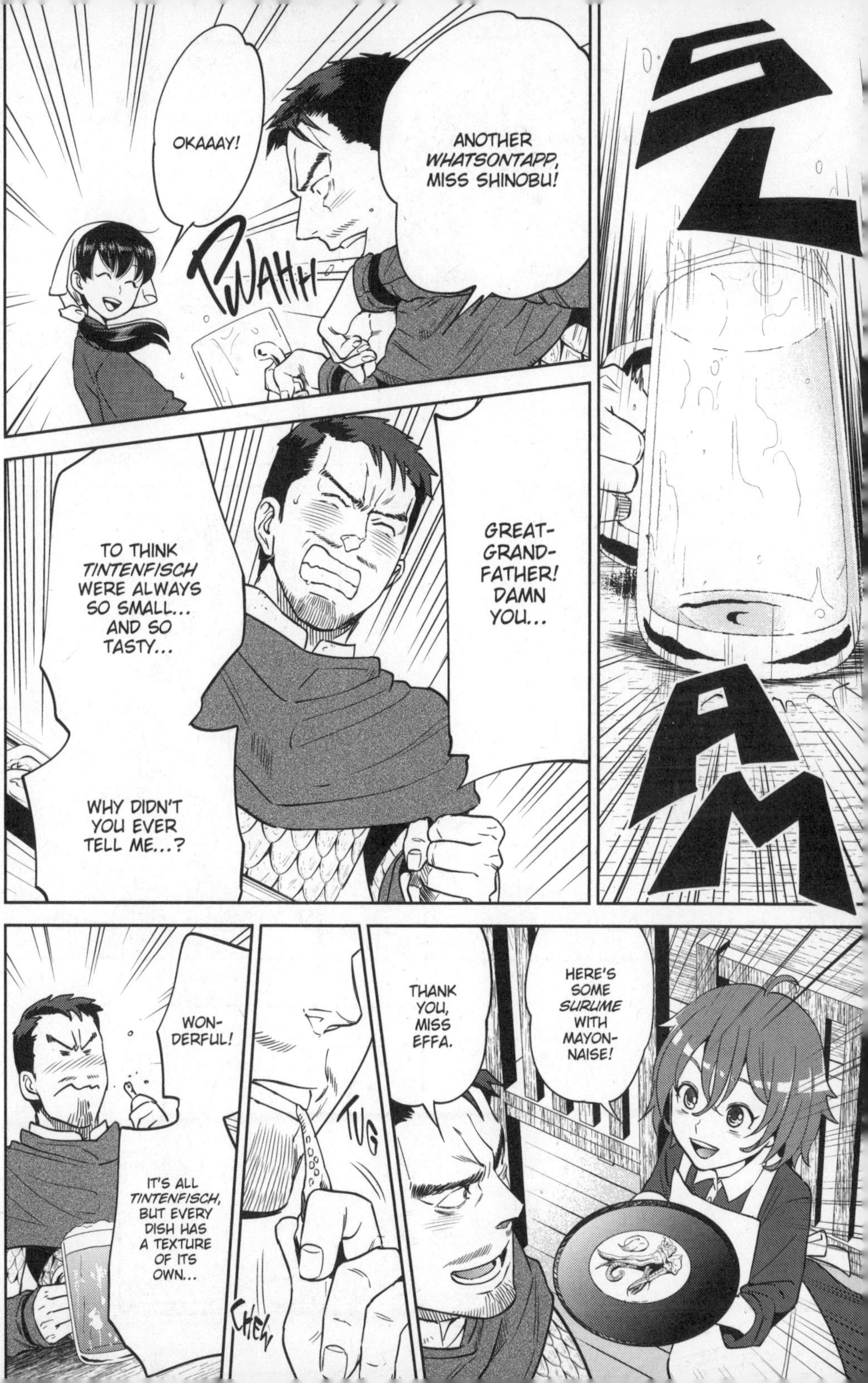
SLAM
ANOTHER *WHATSONTAPP*, MISS SHINOBU!
OKAAAY!
PWAHH
GREAT-GRANDFATHER! DAMN YOU...
TO THINK *TINTENFISCH* WERE ALWAYS SO SMALL... AND SO TASTY...
WHY DIDN'T YOU EVER TELL ME...?
HERE'S SOME *SURUME* WITH MAYONNAISE!
THANK YOU, MISS EFFA.
TUG
WONDERFUL!
IT'S ALL *TINTENFISCH*, BUT EVERY DISH HAS A TEXTURE OF ITS OWN...
CHEW

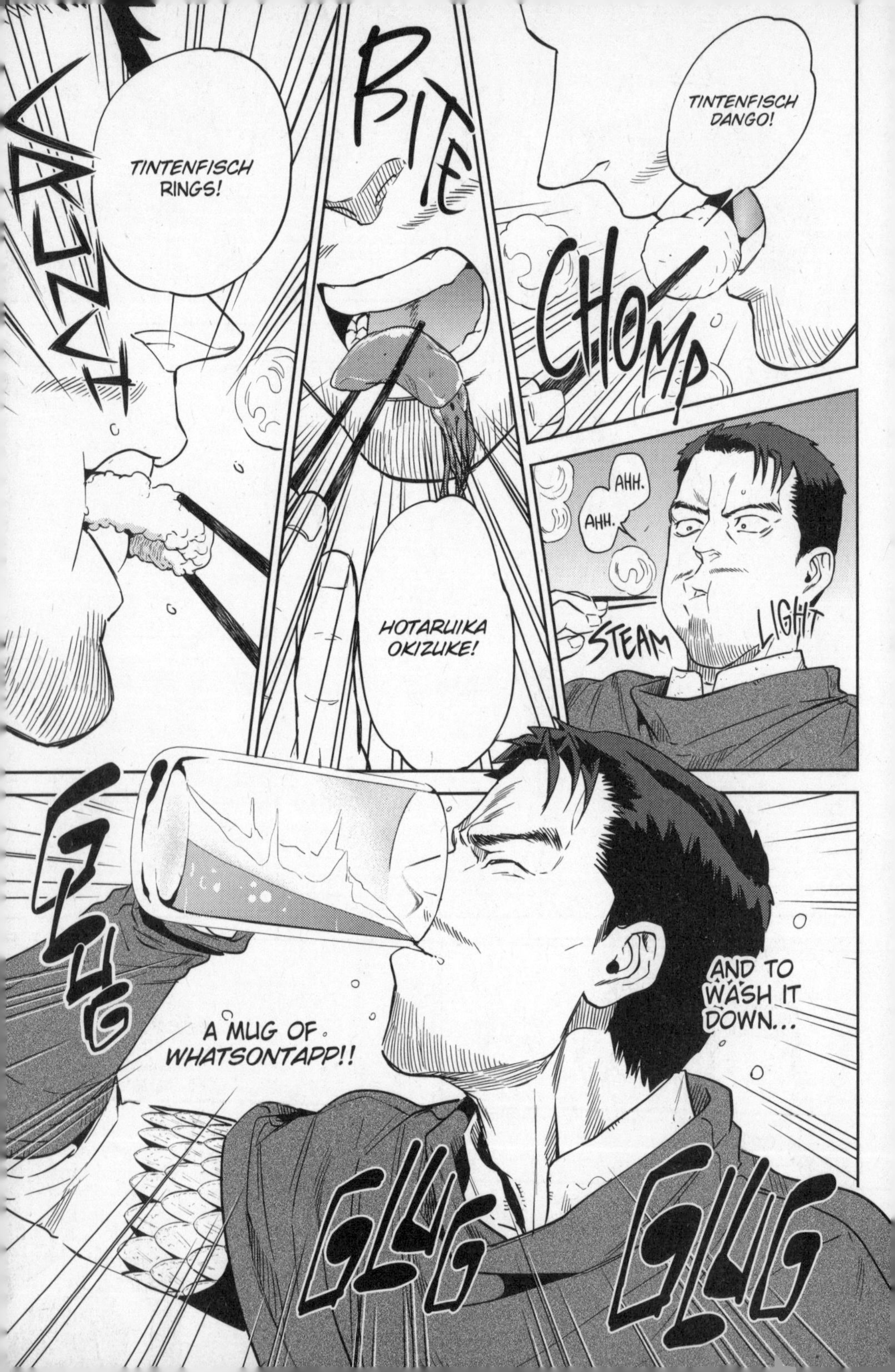
TINTENFISCH DANGO!
CHOMP
AHH.
AHH.
STEAM
LIGHT
BITE
HOTARUIKA OKIZUKE!
CRUNCH
TINTENFISCH RINGS!
AND TO WASH IT DOWN...
A MUG OF WHATSONTAPP!!
GLUG
GLUG
GLUG

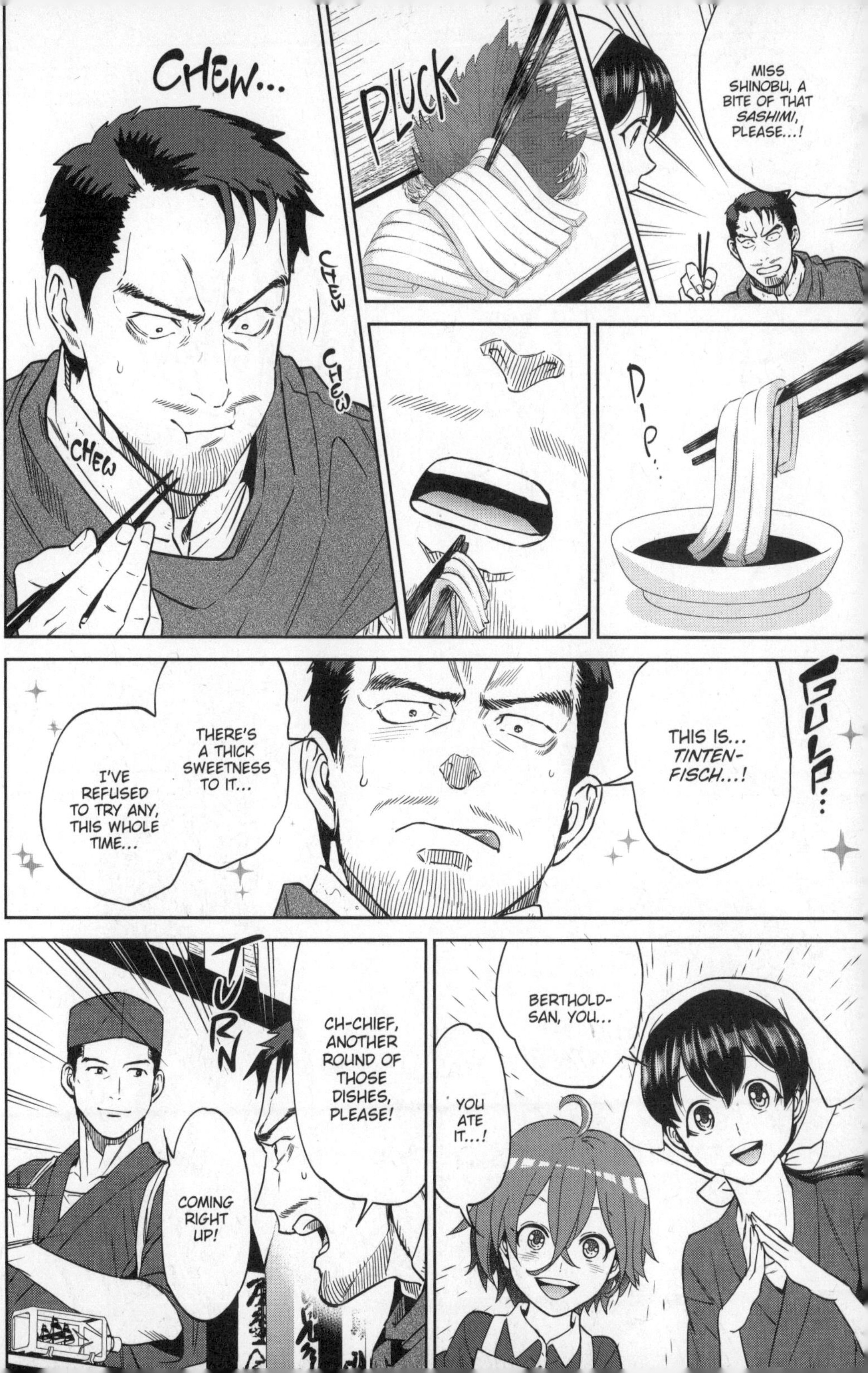
MISS SHINOBU, A BITE OF THAT *SASHIMI*, PLEASE...!
PLUCK
DIP...
CHEW...
CHEW
CHEW
CHEW
GULP...
THIS IS... *TINTEN-FISCH*...!
THERE'S A THICK SWEETNESS TO IT...
I'VE REFUSED TO TRY ANY, THIS WHOLE TIME...
BERTHOLD-SAN, YOU...
YOU ATE IT...!
TURN
CH-CHIEF, ANOTHER ROUND OF THOSE DISHES, PLEASE!
COMING RIGHT UP!

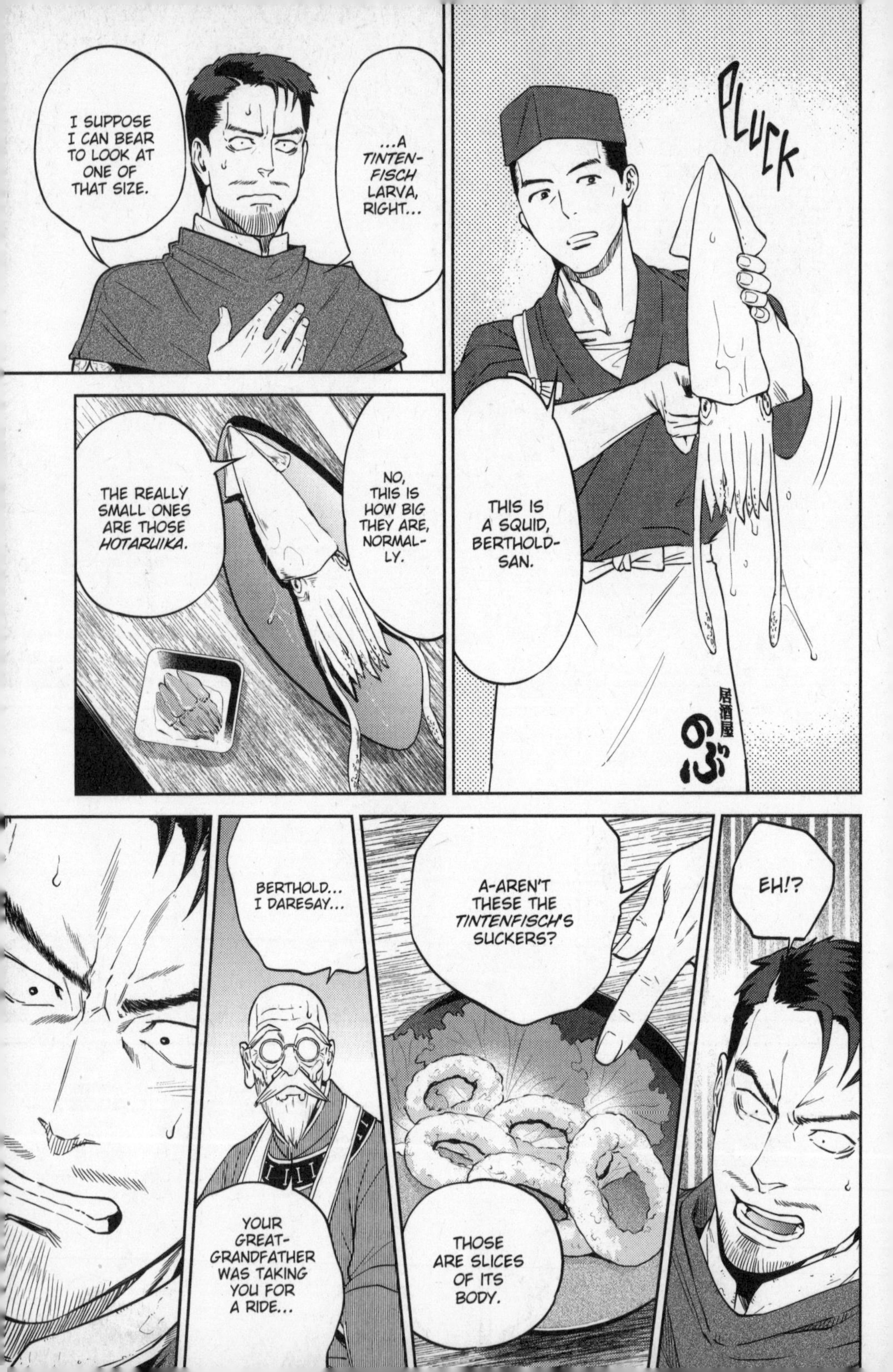
PLUCK
THIS IS A SQUID, BERTHOLD-SAN.
居酒屋のぶ
...A TINTENFISCH LARVA, RIGHT...
I SUPPOSE I CAN BEAR TO LOOK AT ONE OF THAT SIZE.
NO, THIS IS HOW BIG THEY ARE, NORMALLY.
THE REALLY SMALL ONES ARE THOSE HOTARUIKA.
EH!?
A-AREN'T THESE THE TINTENFISCH'S SUCKERS?
THOSE ARE SLICES OF ITS BODY.
BERTHOLD... I DARESAY...
YOUR GREAT-GRANDFATHER WAS TAKING YOU FOR A RIDE...

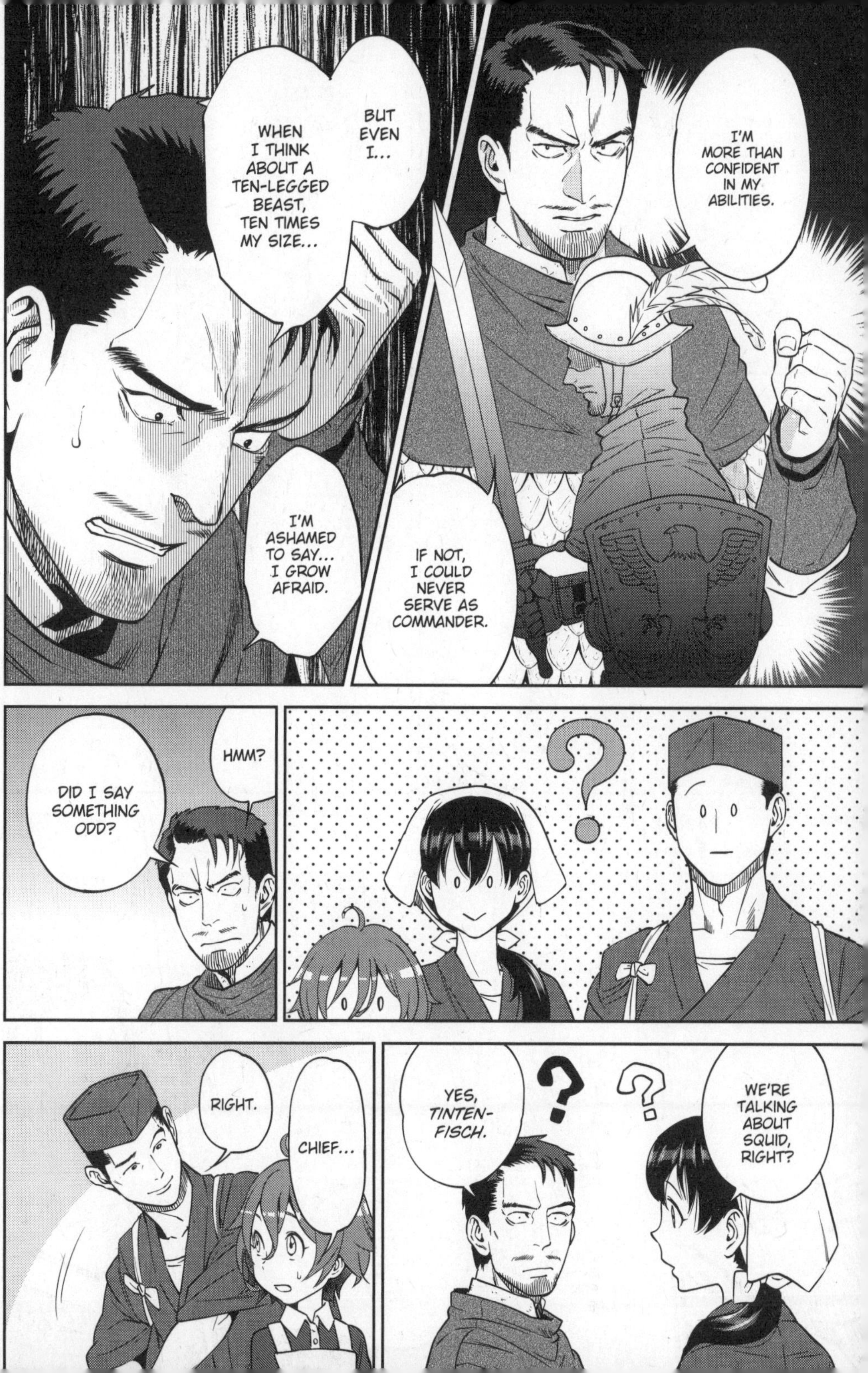
I'M MORE THAN CONFIDENT IN MY ABILITIES.
IF NOT, I COULD NEVER SERVE AS COMMANDER.
BUT EVEN I...
WHEN I THINK ABOUT A TEN-LEGGED BEAST, TEN TIMES MY SIZE...
I'M ASHAMED TO SAY... I GROW AFRAID.
HMM?
DID I SAY SOMETHING ODD?
WE'RE TALKING ABOUT SQUID, RIGHT?
YES, TINTEN-FISCH.
RIGHT.
CHIEF...

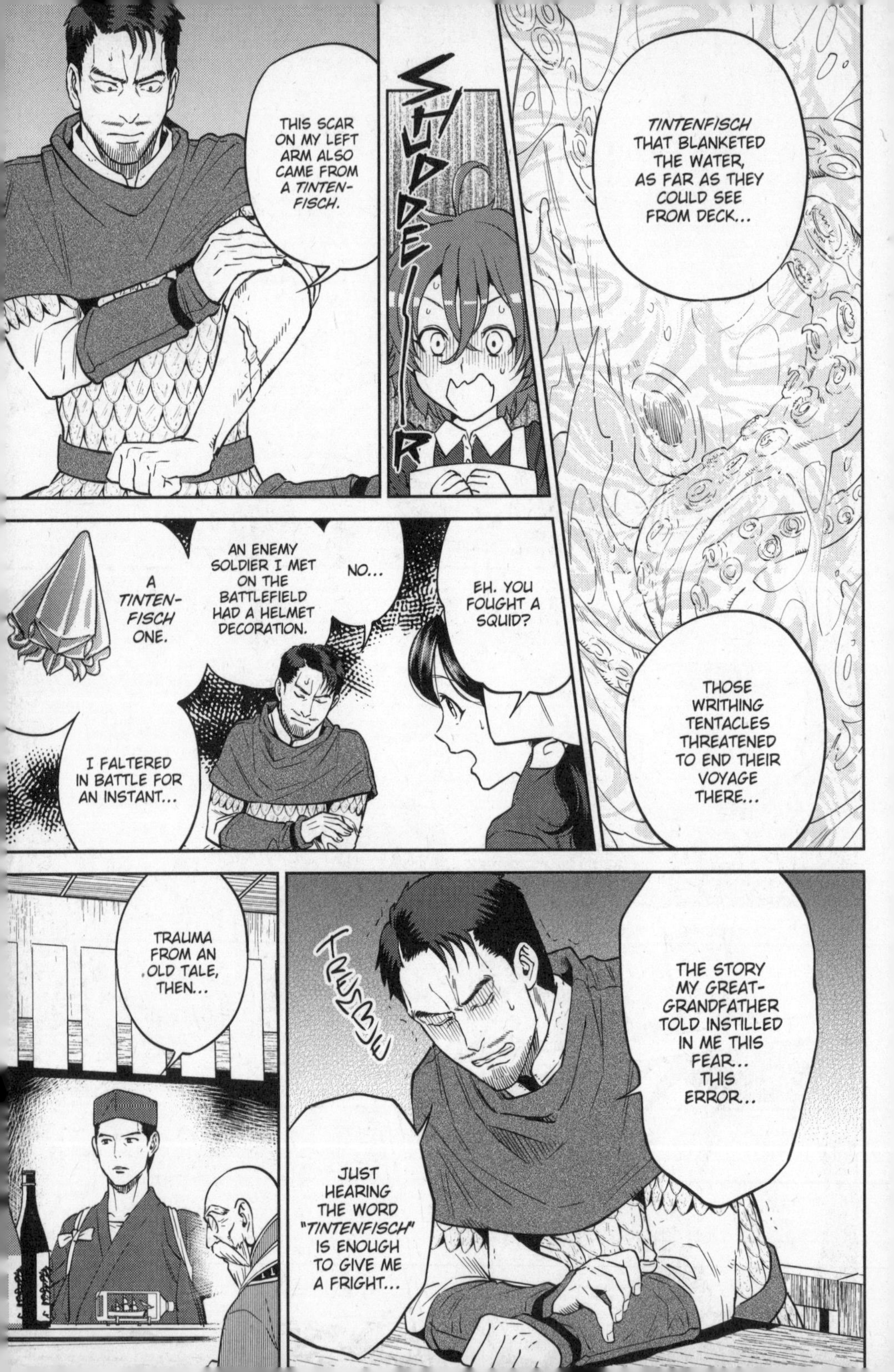
TINTENFISCH THAT BLANKETED THE WATER, AS FAR AS THEY COULD SEE FROM DECK...
THOSE WRITHING TENTACLES THREATENED TO END THEIR VOYAGE THERE...
SHUDDER
THIS SCAR ON MY LEFT ARM ALSO CAME FROM A TINTEN-FISCH.
EH. YOU FOUGHT A SQUID?
NO...
AN ENEMY SOLDIER I MET ON THE BATTLEFIELD HAD A HELMET DECORATION.
A TINTEN-FISCH ONE.
I FALTERED IN BATTLE FOR AN INSTANT...
THE STORY MY GREAT-GRANDFATHER TOLD INSTILLED IN ME THIS FEAR... THIS ERROR...
TREMBLE
JUST HEARING THE WORD "TINTENFISCH" IS ENOUGH TO GIVE ME A FRIGHT...
TRAUMA FROM AN OLD TALE, THEN...

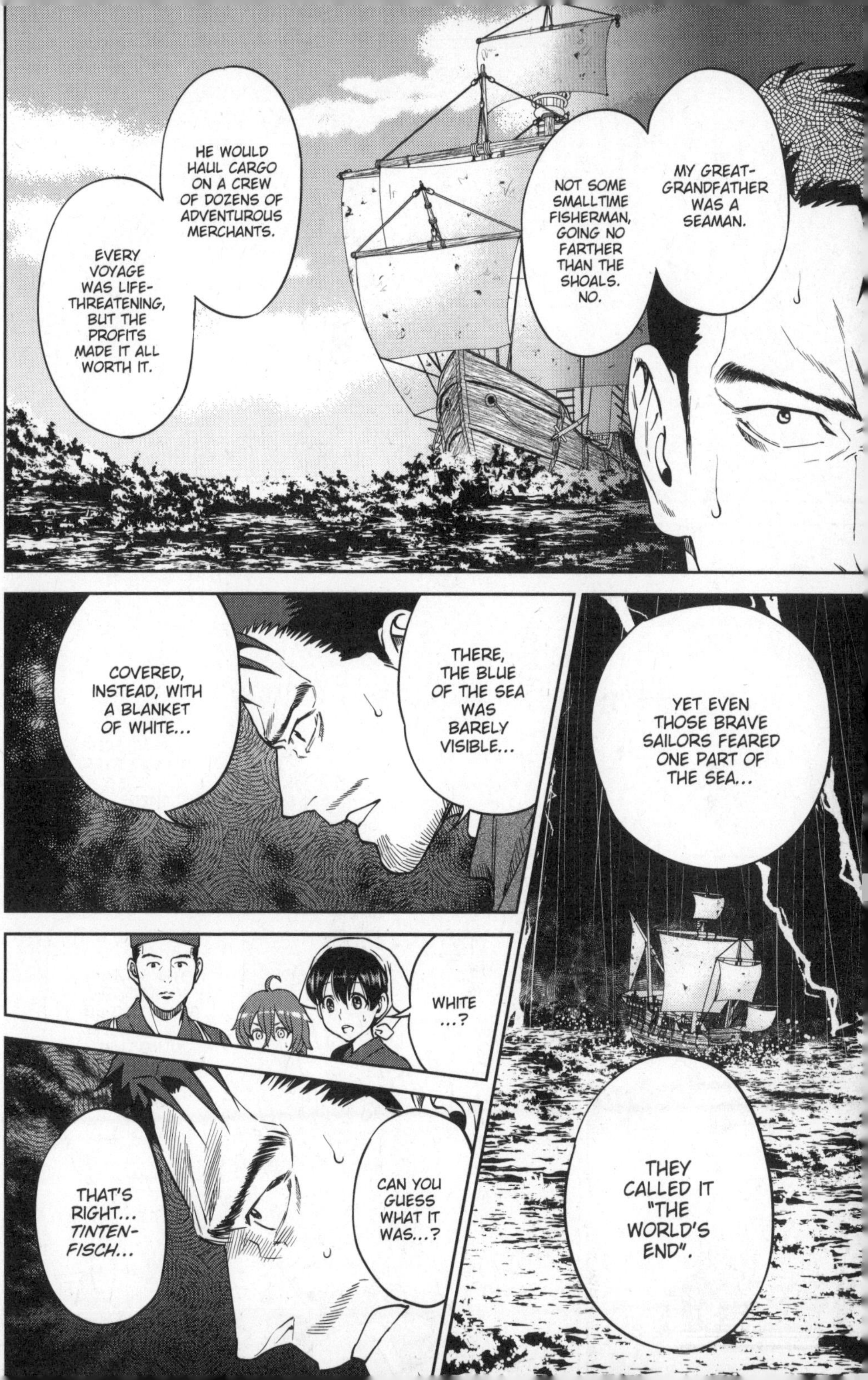
MY GREAT-GRANDFATHER WAS A SEAMAN.
NOT SOME SMALLTIME FISHERMAN, GOING NO FARTHER THAN THE SHOALS. NO.
HE WOULD HAUL CARGO ON A CREW OF DOZENS OF ADVENTUROUS MERCHANTS.
EVERY VOYAGE WAS LIFE-THREATENING, BUT THE PROFITS MADE IT ALL WORTH IT.
YET EVEN THOSE BRAVE SAILORS FEARED ONE PART OF THE SEA...
THEY CALLED IT "THE WORLD'S END".
THERE, THE BLUE OF THE SEA WAS BARELY VISIBLE...
COVERED, INSTEAD, WITH A BLANKET OF WHITE...
WHITE ...?
CAN YOU GUESS WHAT IT WAS...?
THAT'S RIGHT... TINTEN-FISCH...

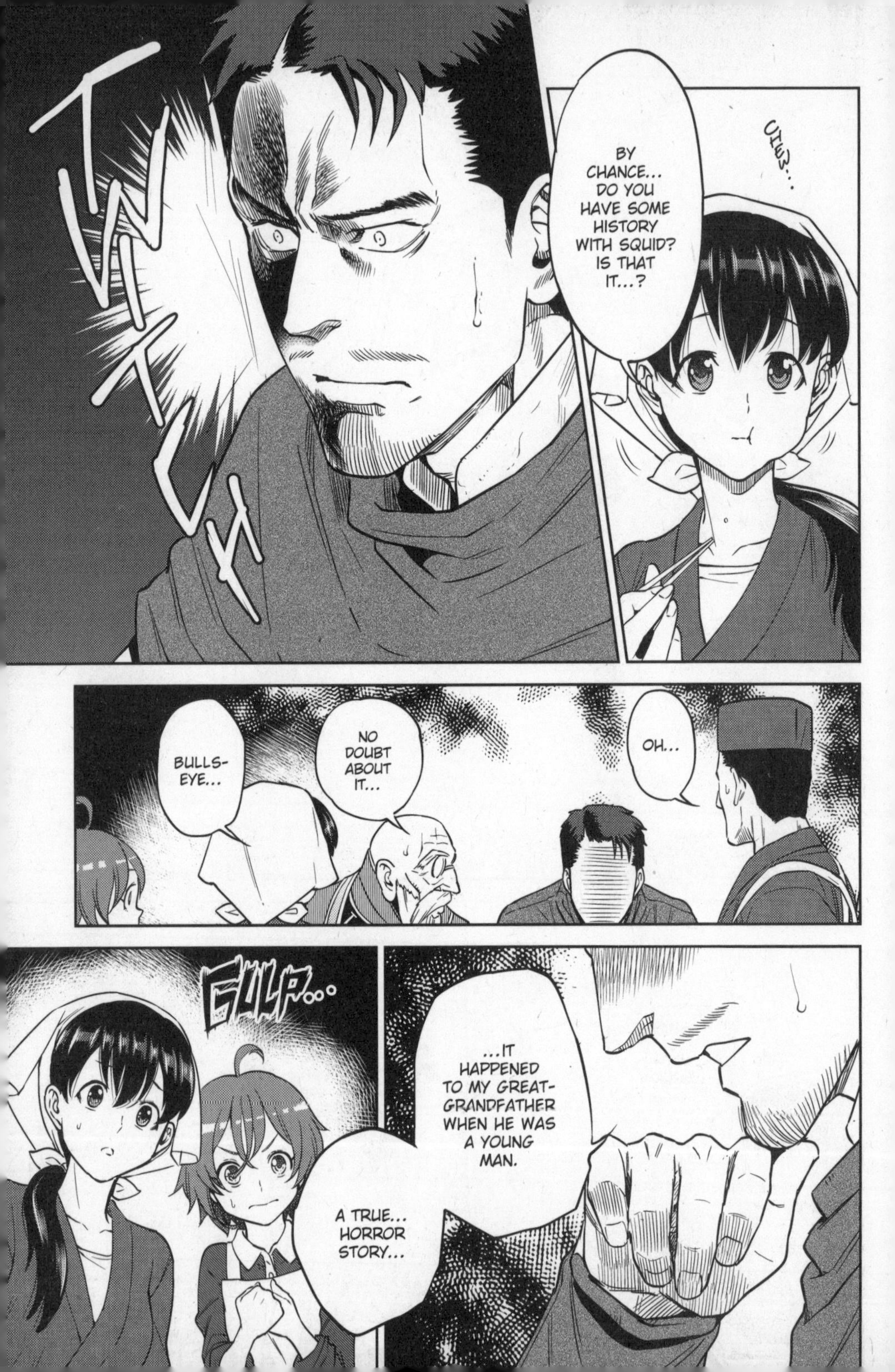
CHEW...
BY CHANCE... DO YOU HAVE SOME HISTORY WITH SQUID? IS THAT IT...?
OH...
NO DOUBT ABOUT IT...
BULLS-EYE...
...IT HAPPENED TO MY GREAT-GRANDFATHER WHEN HE WAS A YOUNG MAN.
A TRUE... HORROR STORY...
GULP...

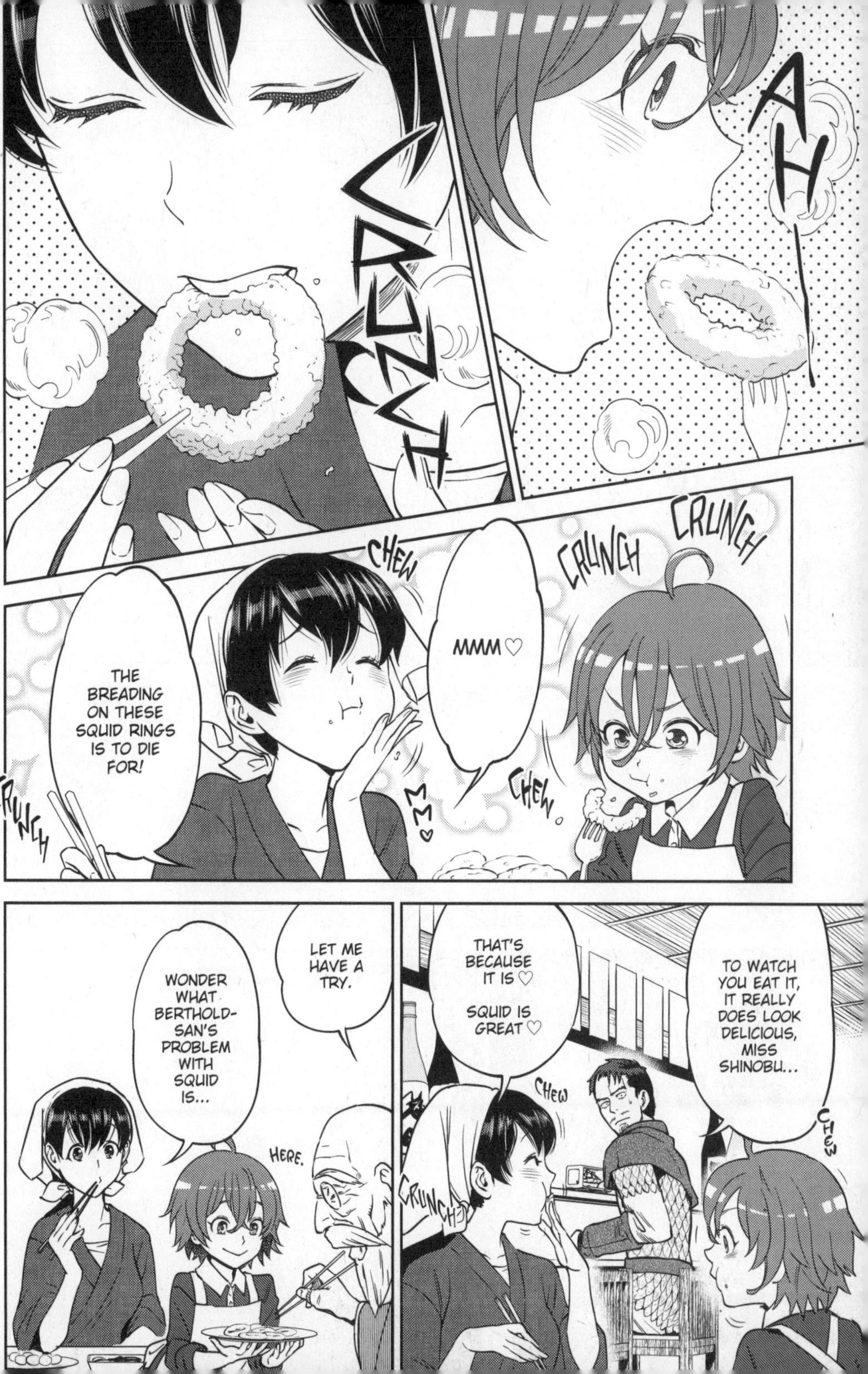
AH
CRUNCH
CRUNCH
CRUNCH
MMM♡
CHEW
MM♡
CHEW
THE BREADING ON THESE SQUID RINGS IS TO DIE FOR!
CRUNCH
TO WATCH YOU EAT IT, IT REALLY DOES LOOK DELICIOUS, MISS SHINOBU...
CHEW
THAT'S BECAUSE IT IS♡
SQUID IS GREAT♡
CHEW
CRUNCH
LET ME HAVE A TRY.
WONDER WHAT BERTHOLD-SAN'S PROBLEM WITH SQUID IS...
HERE.

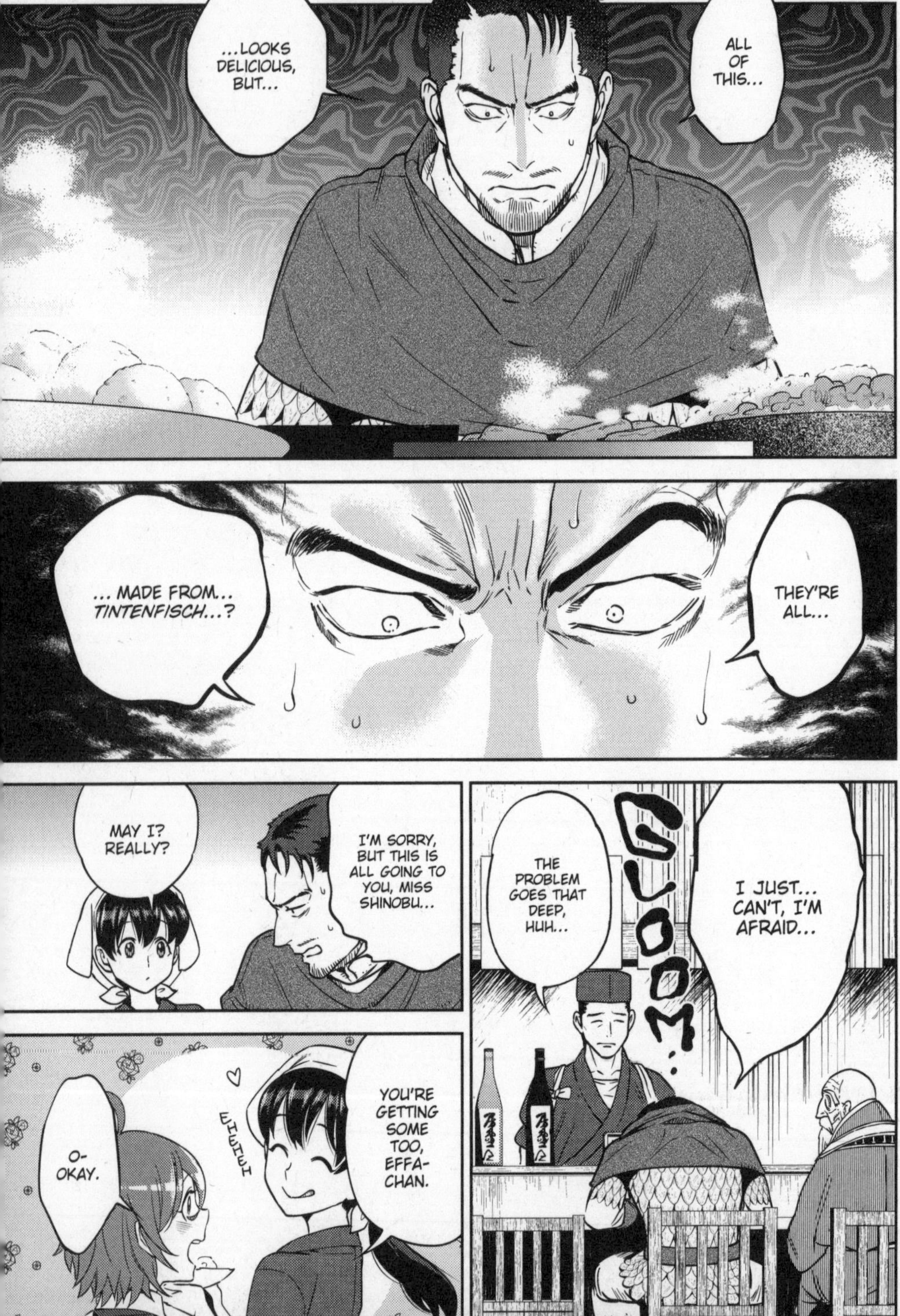
ALL OF THIS...
...LOOKS DELICIOUS, BUT...
THEY'RE ALL...
... MADE FROM... *TINTENFISCH*...?
I JUST... CAN'T, I'M AFRAID...
GLOOM..
THE PROBLEM GOES THAT DEEP, HUH...
I'M SORRY, BUT THIS IS ALL GOING TO YOU, MISS SHINOBU...
MAY I? REALLY?
YOU'RE GETTING SOME TOO, EFFA-CHAN.
EHEHEH
O-OKAY.

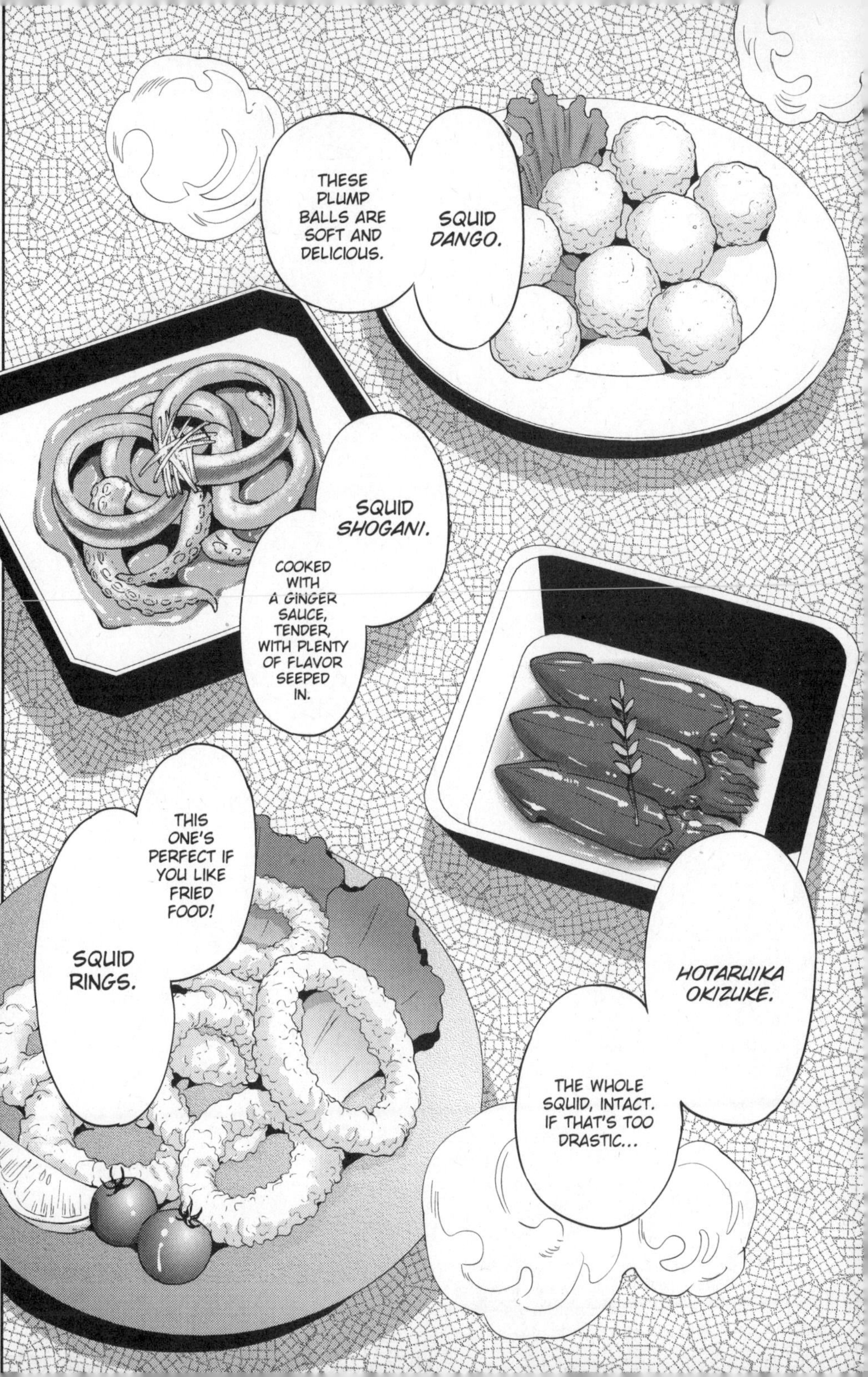
SQUID DANGO.
THESE PLUMP BALLS ARE SOFT AND DELICIOUS.
SQUID SHOGANI.
COOKED WITH A GINGER SAUCE, TENDER, WITH PLENTY OF FLAVOR SEEPED IN.
HOTARUIKA OKIZUKE.
THE WHOLE SQUID, INTACT. IF THAT'S TOO DRASTIC...
THIS ONE'S PERFECT IF YOU LIKE FRIED FOOD!
SQUID RINGS.

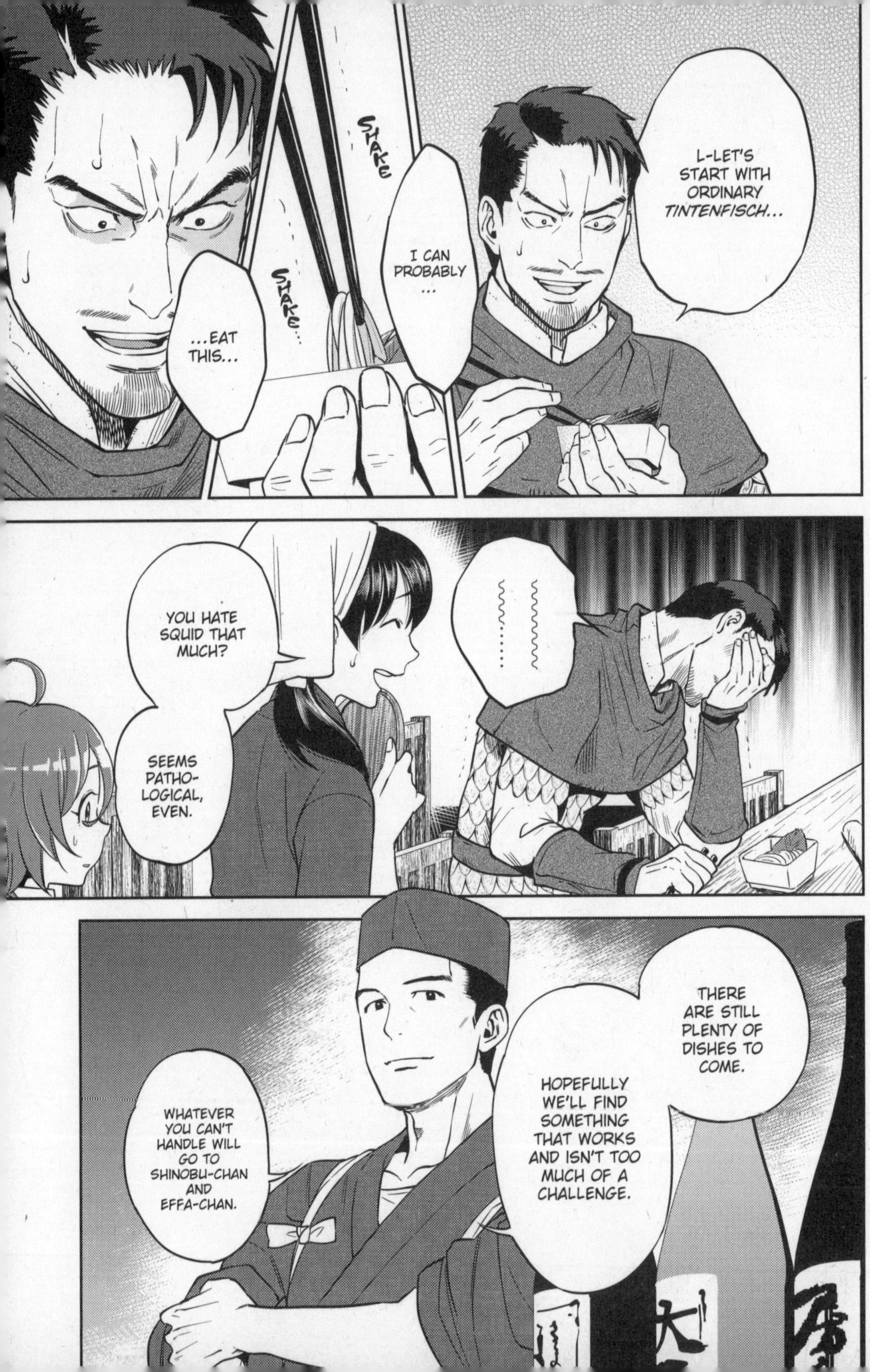
L-LET'S START WITH ORDINARY *TINTENFISCH*...
I CAN PROBABLY ...
SHAKE
SHAKE...
...EAT THIS...
......
YOU HATE SQUID THAT MUCH?
SEEMS PATHO-LOGICAL, EVEN.
THERE ARE STILL PLENTY OF DISHES TO COME.
HOPEFULLY WE'LL FIND SOMETHING THAT WORKS AND ISN'T TOO MUCH OF A CHALLENGE.
WHATEVER YOU CAN'T HANDLE WILL GO TO SHINOBU-CHAN AND EFFA-CHAN.

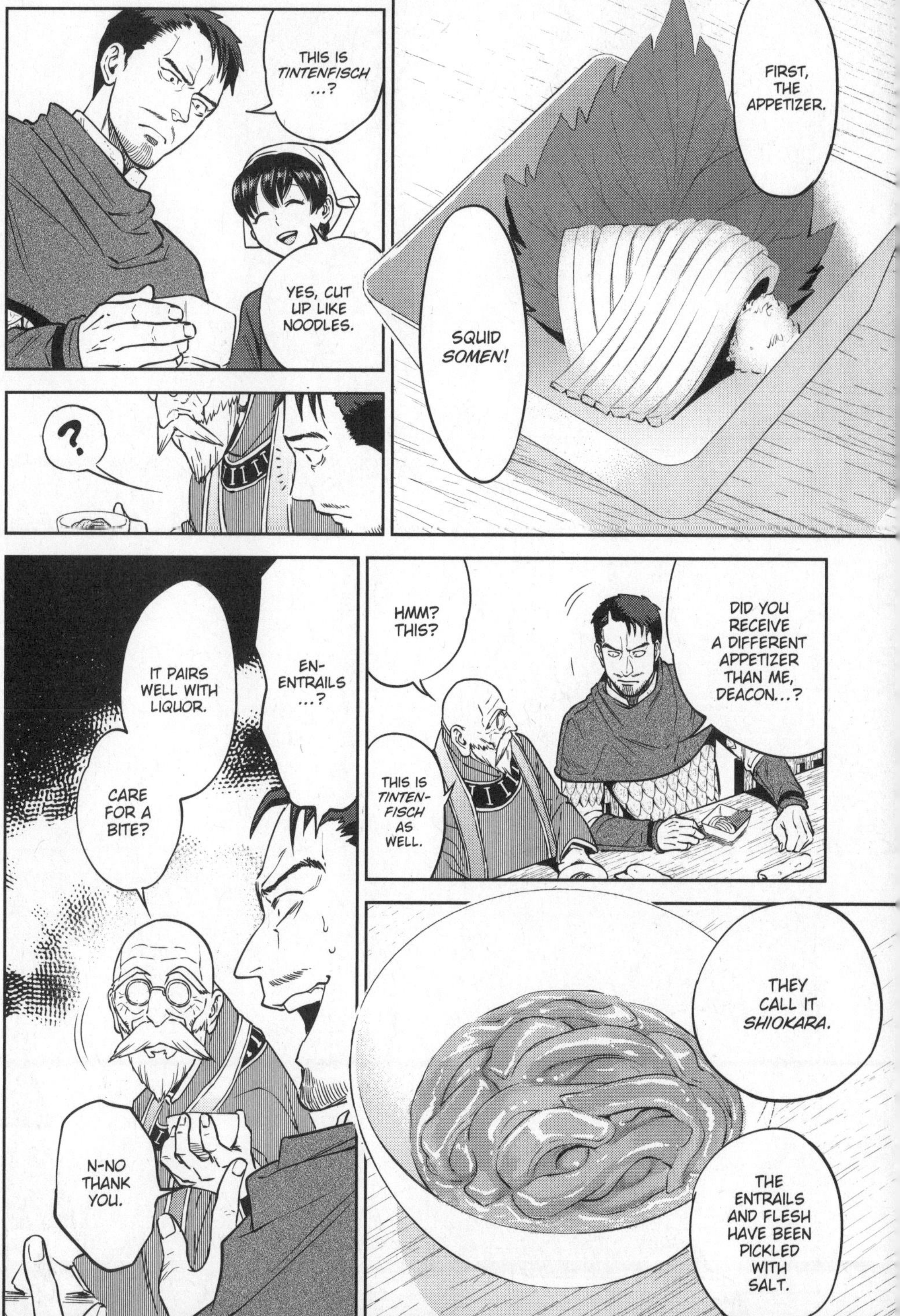
FIRST, THE APPETIZER.
SQUID *SOMEN*!
THIS IS *TINTENFISCH* ...?
YES, CUT UP LIKE NOODLES.
?
DID YOU RECEIVE A DIFFERENT APPETIZER THAN ME, DEACON...?
HMM? THIS?
THIS IS *TINTEN-FISCH* AS WELL.
THEY CALL IT *SHIOKARA*.
THE ENTRAILS AND FLESH HAVE BEEN PICKLED WITH SALT.
EN-ENTRAILS ...?
IT PAIRS WELL WITH LIQUOR.
CARE FOR A BITE?
N-NO THANK YOU.

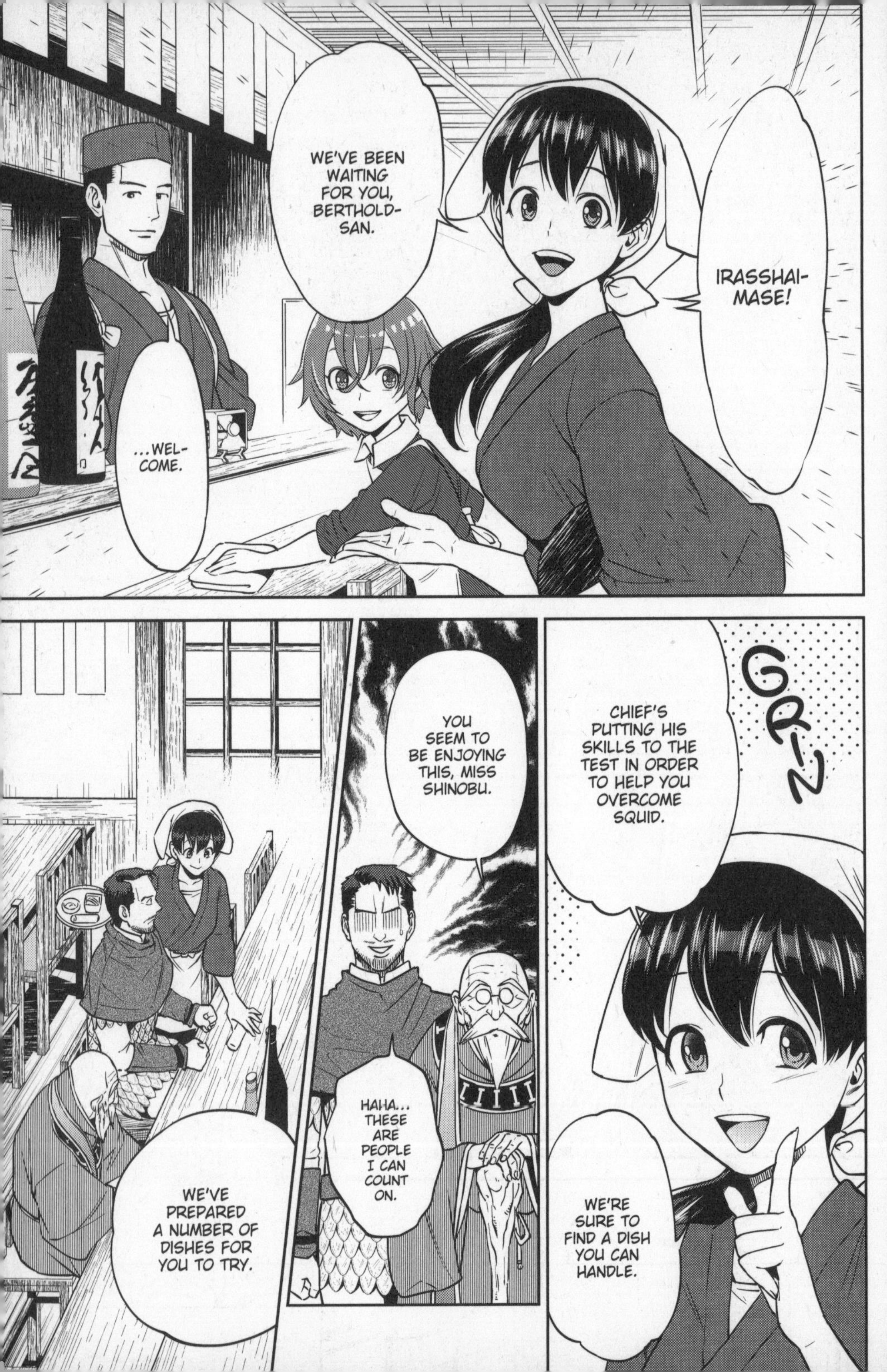
IRASSHAI-MASE!
WE'VE BEEN WAITING FOR YOU, BERTHOLD-SAN.
...WEL-COME.
GRIN
CHIEF'S PUTTING HIS SKILLS TO THE TEST IN ORDER TO HELP YOU OVERCOME SQUID.
WE'RE SURE TO FIND A DISH YOU CAN HANDLE.
YOU SEEM TO BE ENJOYING THIS, MISS SHINOBU.
HAHA... THESE ARE PEOPLE I CAN COUNT ON.
WE'VE PREPARED A NUMBER OF DISHES FOR YOU TO TRY.

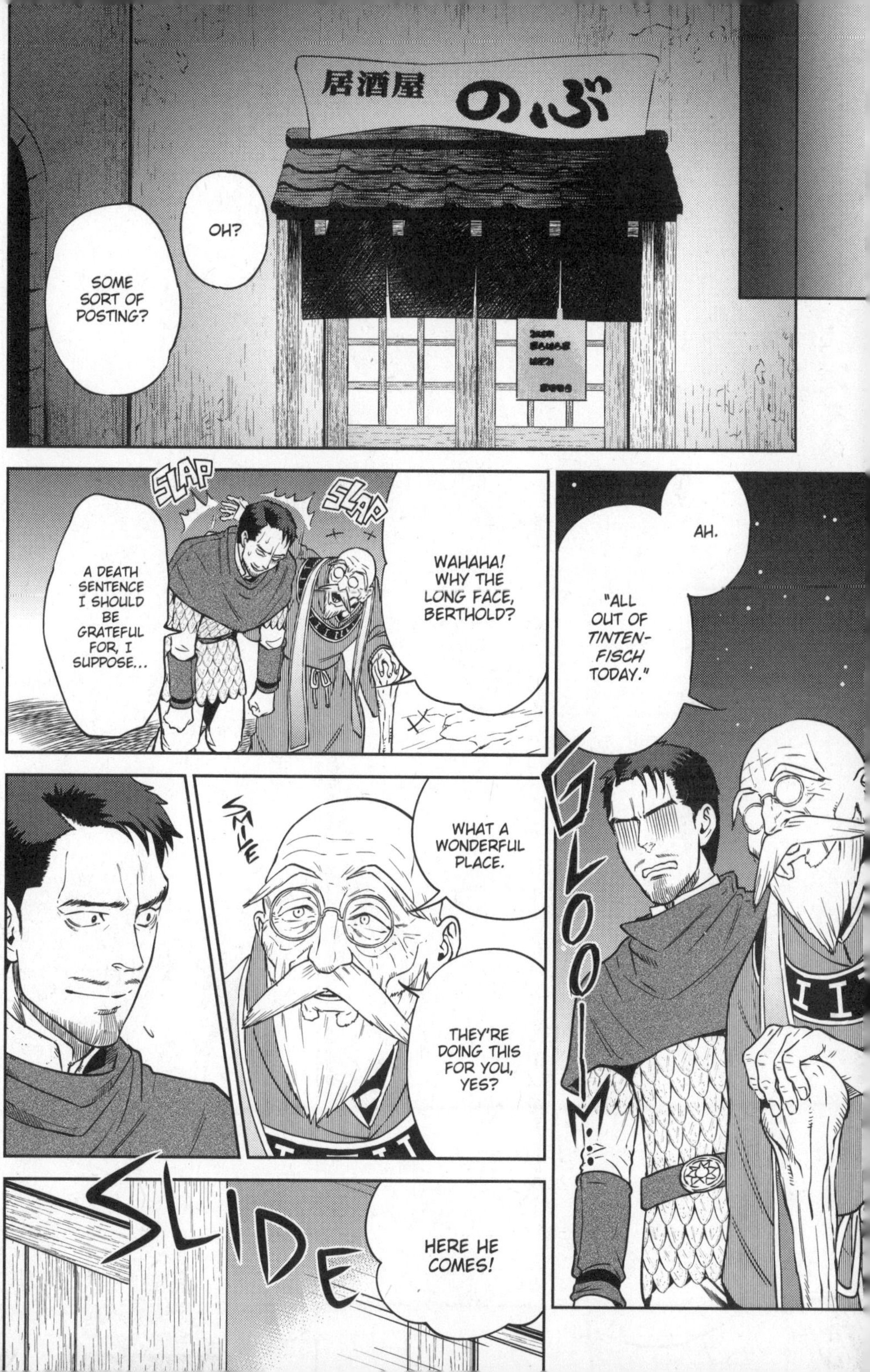
居酒屋 のぶ
OH?
SOME SORT OF POSTING?
AH.
"ALL OUT OF TINTEN-FISCH TODAY."
GLOOOM...
SLAP
SLAP
WAHAHA! WHY THE LONG FACE, BERTHOLD?
A DEATH SENTENCE I SHOULD BE GRATEFUL FOR, I SUPPOSE...
SMILE
WHAT A WONDERFUL PLACE.
THEY'RE DOING THIS FOR YOU, YES?
SLIDE
HERE HE COMES!

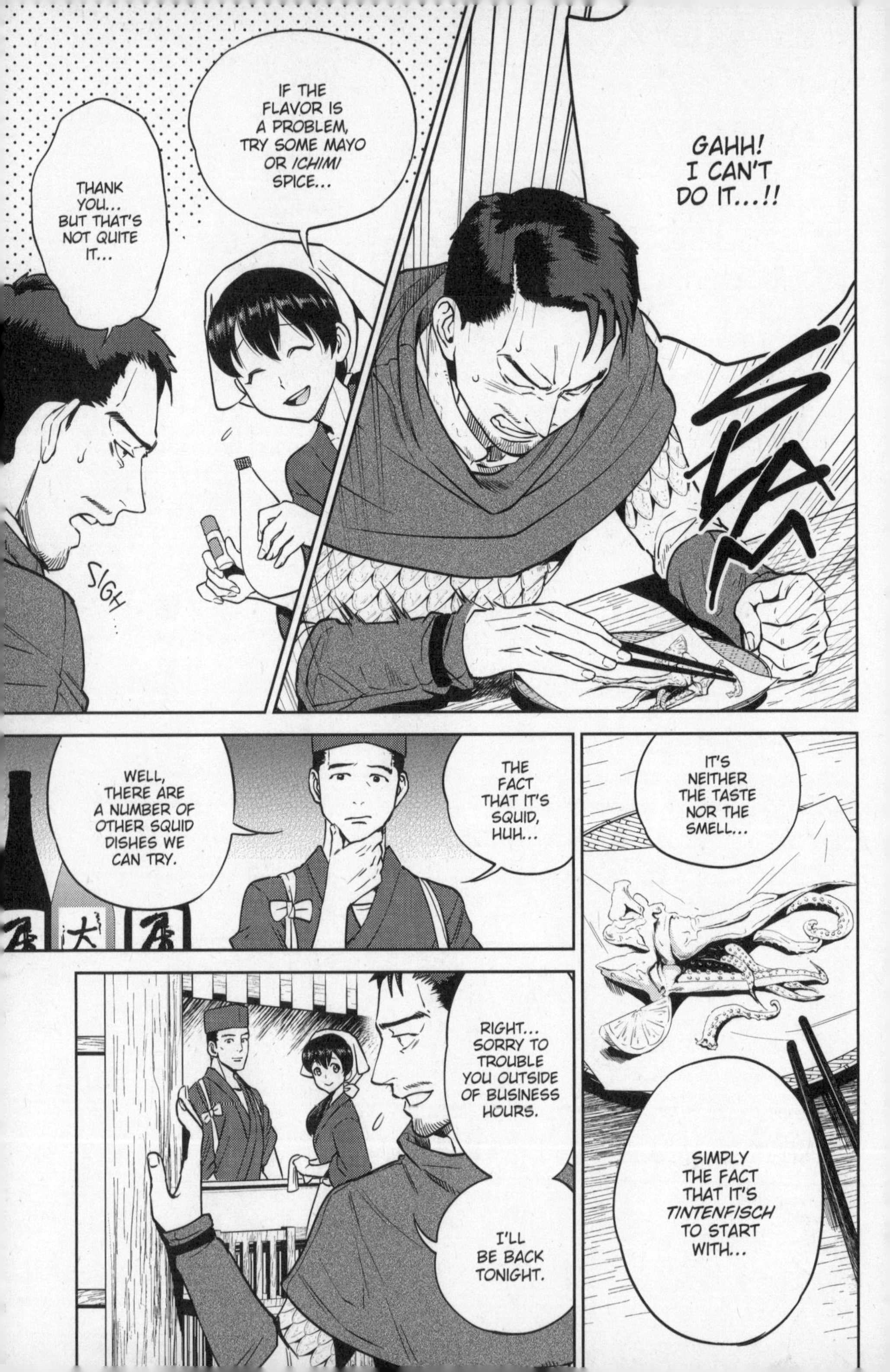
GAHH! I CAN'T DO IT...!!
SLAM
IF THE FLAVOR IS A PROBLEM, TRY SOME MAYO OR *ICHIMI* SPICE...
THANK YOU... BUT THAT'S NOT QUITE IT...
SIGH...
IT'S NEITHER THE TASTE NOR THE SMELL...
SIMPLY THE FACT THAT IT'S *TINTENFISCH* TO START WITH...
THE FACT THAT IT'S SQUID, HUH...
WELL, THERE ARE A NUMBER OF OTHER SQUID DISHES WE CAN TRY.
RIGHT... SORRY TO TROUBLE YOU OUTSIDE OF BUSINESS HOURS.
I'LL BE BACK TONIGHT.

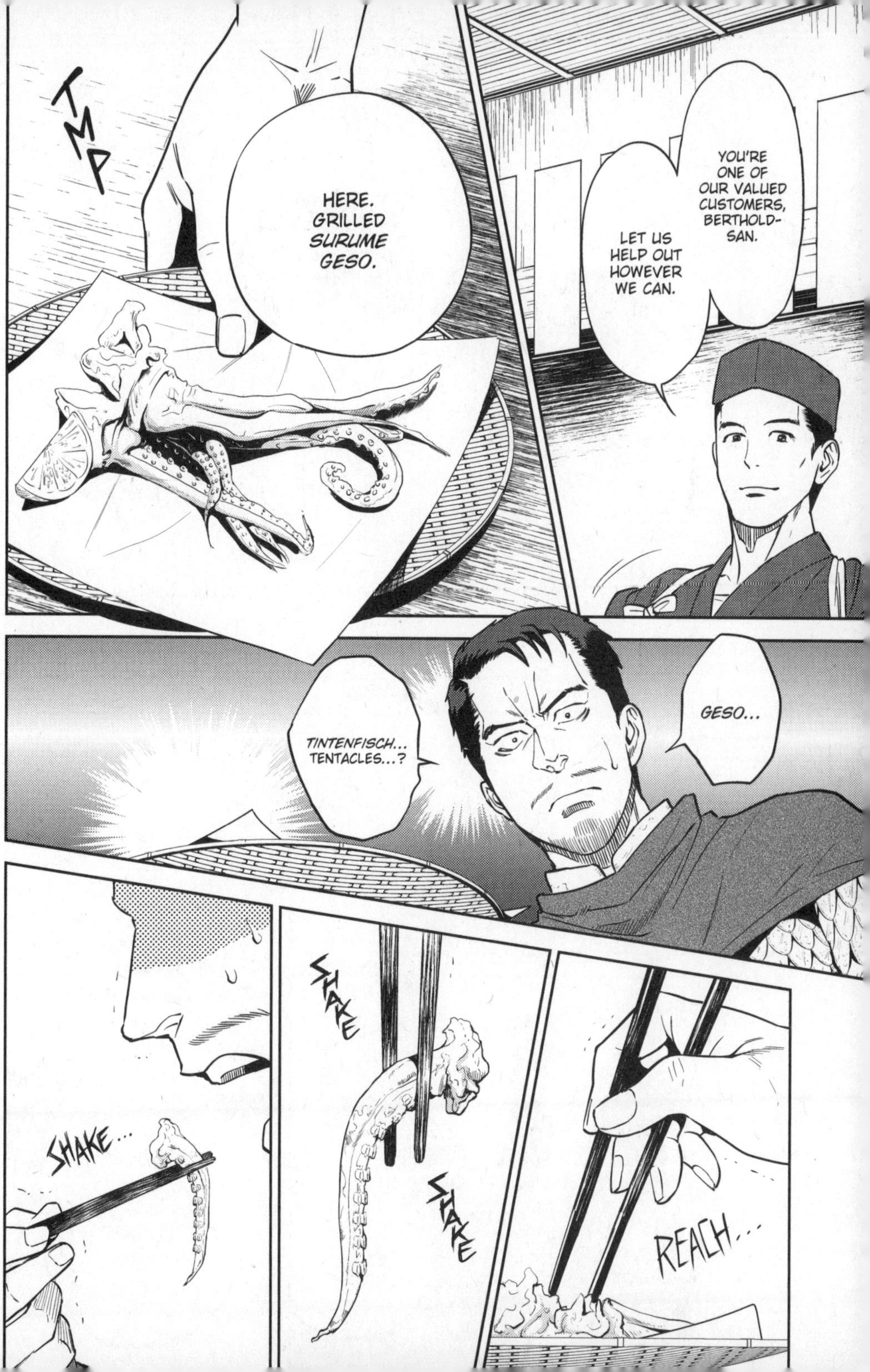
YOU'RE ONE OF OUR VALUED CUSTOMERS, BERTHOLD-SAN.
LET US HELP OUT HOWEVER WE CAN.
TMP
HERE. GRILLED *SURUME GESO.*
GESO...
TINTENFISCH... TENTACLES...?
REACH...
SHAKE
SHAKE
SHAKE...

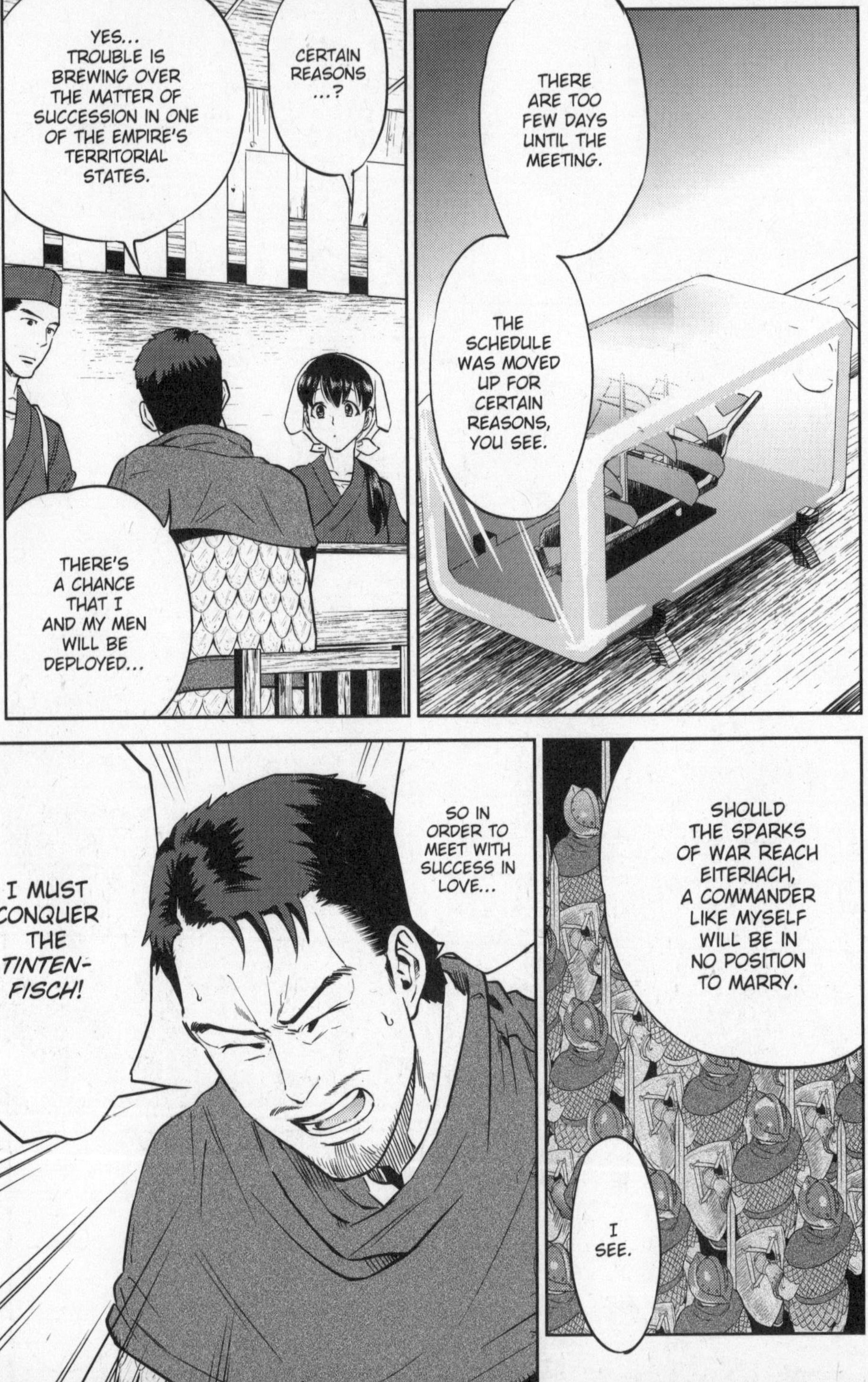
THERE ARE TOO FEW DAYS UNTIL THE MEETING.
THE SCHEDULE WAS MOVED UP FOR CERTAIN REASONS, YOU SEE.
CERTAIN REASONS ...?
YES... TROUBLE IS BREWING OVER THE MATTER OF SUCCESSION IN ONE OF THE EMPIRE'S TERRITORIAL STATES.
THERE'S A CHANCE THAT I AND MY MEN WILL BE DEPLOYED...
SHOULD THE SPARKS OF WAR REACH EITERIACH, A COMMANDER LIKE MYSELF WILL BE IN NO POSITION TO MARRY.
I SEE.
SO IN ORDER TO MEET WITH SUCCESS IN LOVE...
I MUST CONQUER THE *TINTEN-FISCH*!

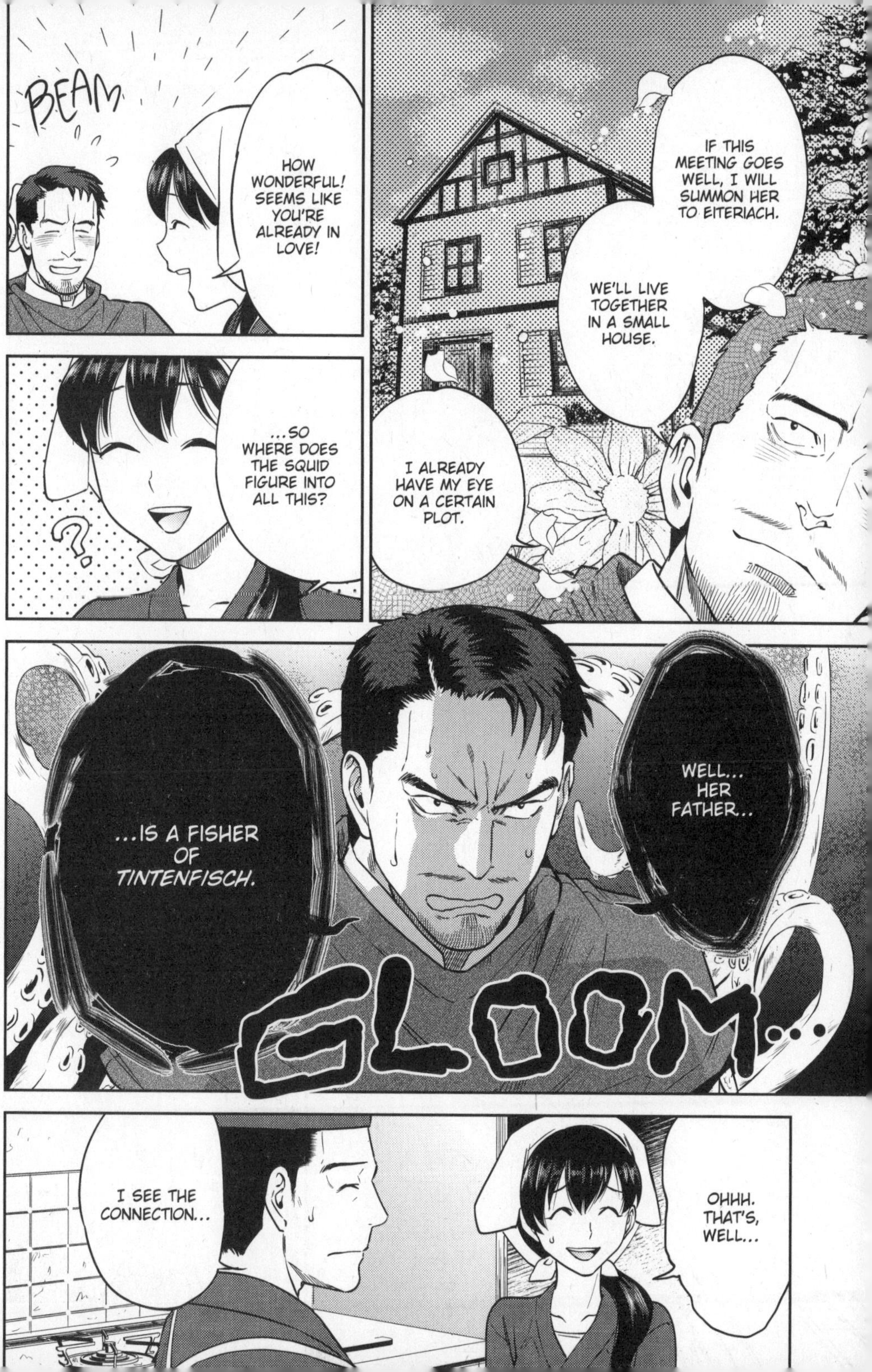
IF THIS MEETING GOES WELL, I WILL SUMMON HER TO EITERIACH.
WE'LL LIVE TOGETHER IN A SMALL HOUSE.
I ALREADY HAVE MY EYE ON A CERTAIN PLOT.
HOW WONDERFUL! SEEMS LIKE YOU'RE ALREADY IN LOVE!
BEAM
...SO WHERE DOES THE SQUID FIGURE INTO ALL THIS?
?
WELL... HER FATHER...
...IS A FISHER OF TINTENFISCH.
GLOOM...
OHHH. THAT'S, WELL...
I SEE THE CONNECTION...

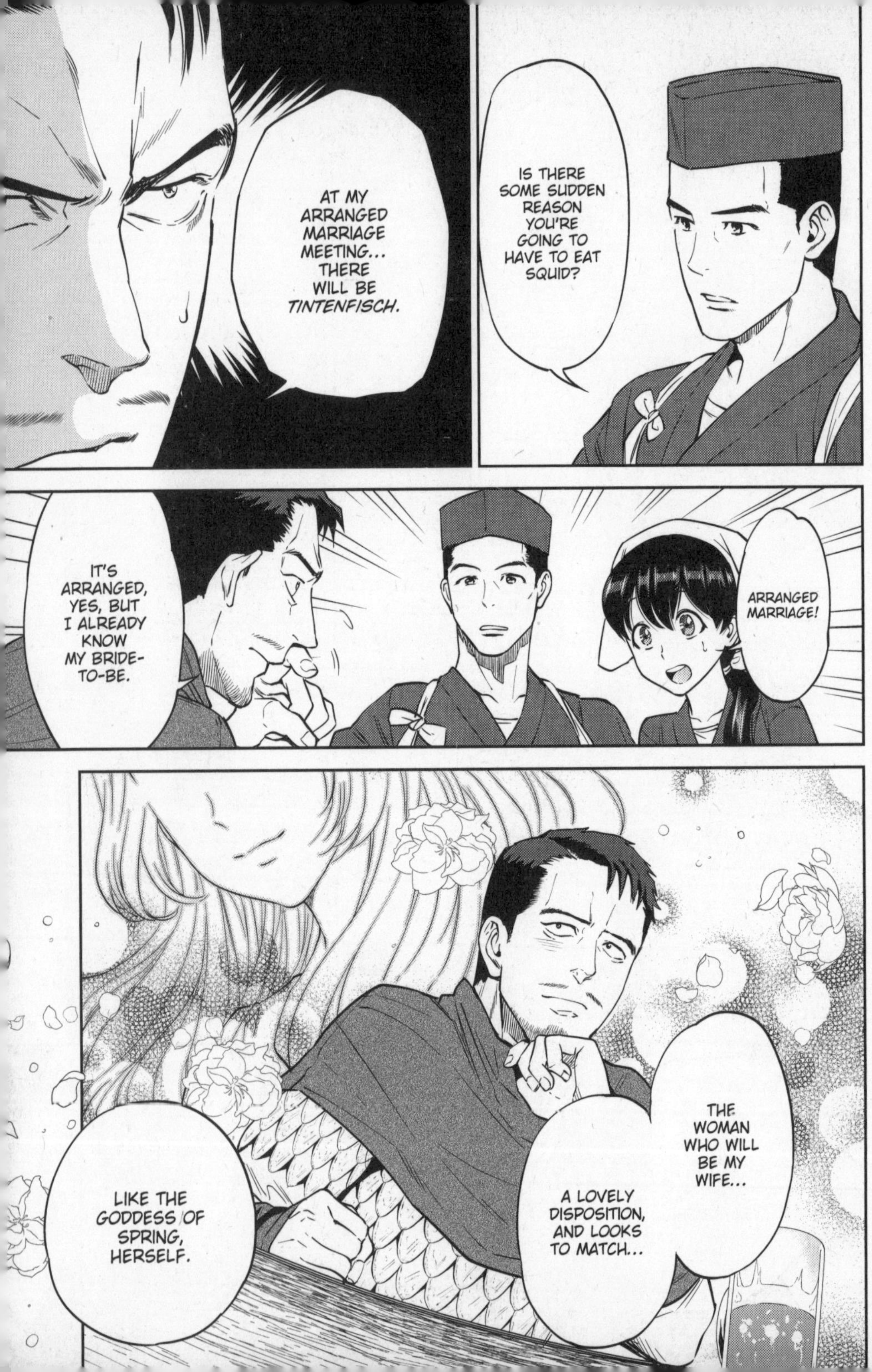

IS THERE SOME SUDDEN REASON YOU'RE GOING TO HAVE TO EAT SQUID?
AT MY ARRANGED MARRIAGE MEETING... THERE WILL BE *TINTENFISCH*.
ARRANGED MARRIAGE!
IT'S ARRANGED, YES, BUT I ALREADY KNOW MY BRIDE-TO-BE.
THE WOMAN WHO WILL BE MY WIFE...
A LOVELY DISPOSITION, AND LOOKS TO MATCH...
LIKE THE GODDESS OF SPRING, HERSELF.

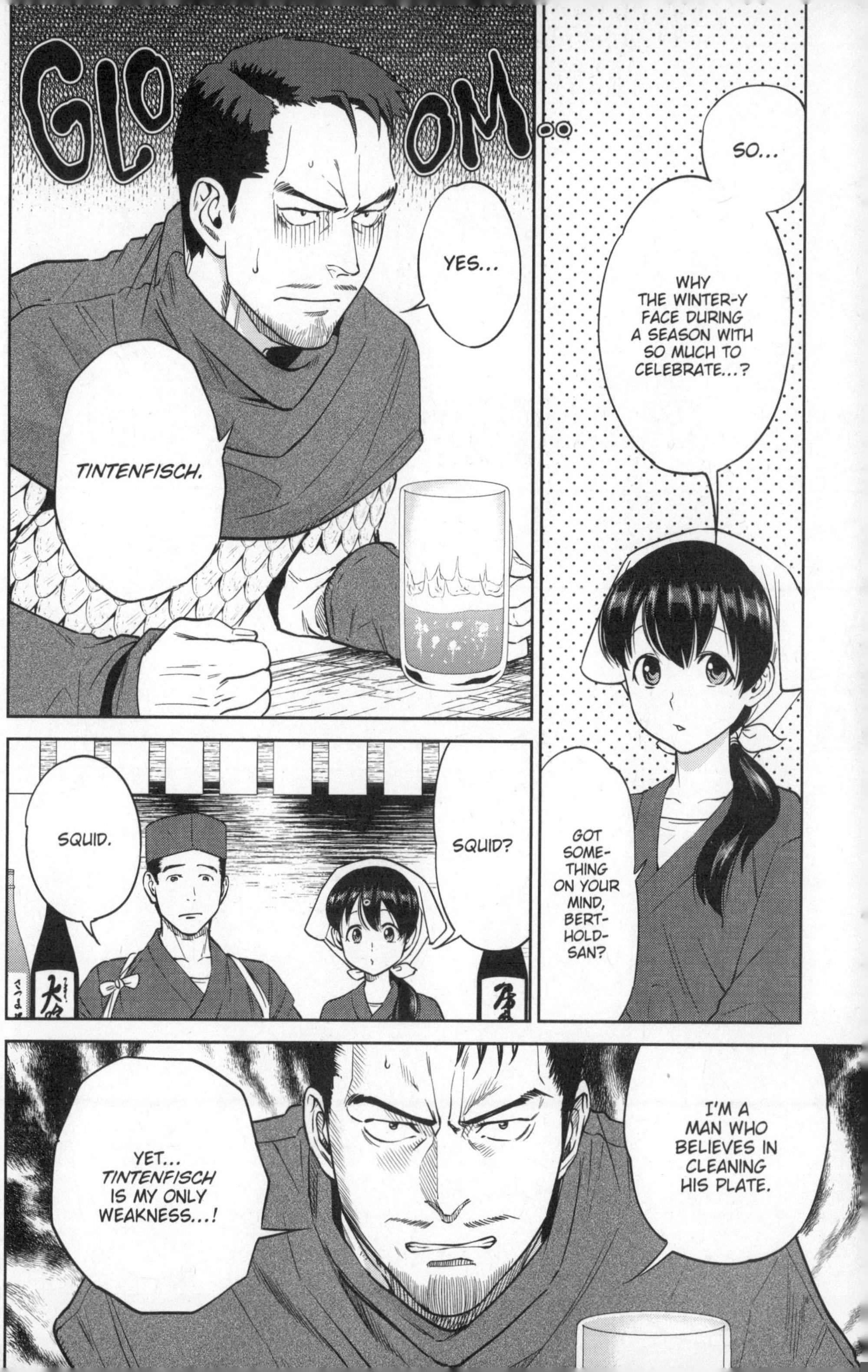
SO...
WHY THE WINTER-Y FACE DURING A SEASON WITH SO MUCH TO CELEBRATE...?
GOT SOMETHING ON YOUR MIND, BERTHOLD-SAN?
GLOOM...
YES...
TINTENFISCH.
SQUID?
SQUID.
I'M A MAN WHO BELIEVES IN CLEANING HIS PLATE.
YET... *TINTENFISCH* IS MY ONLY WEAKNESS...!

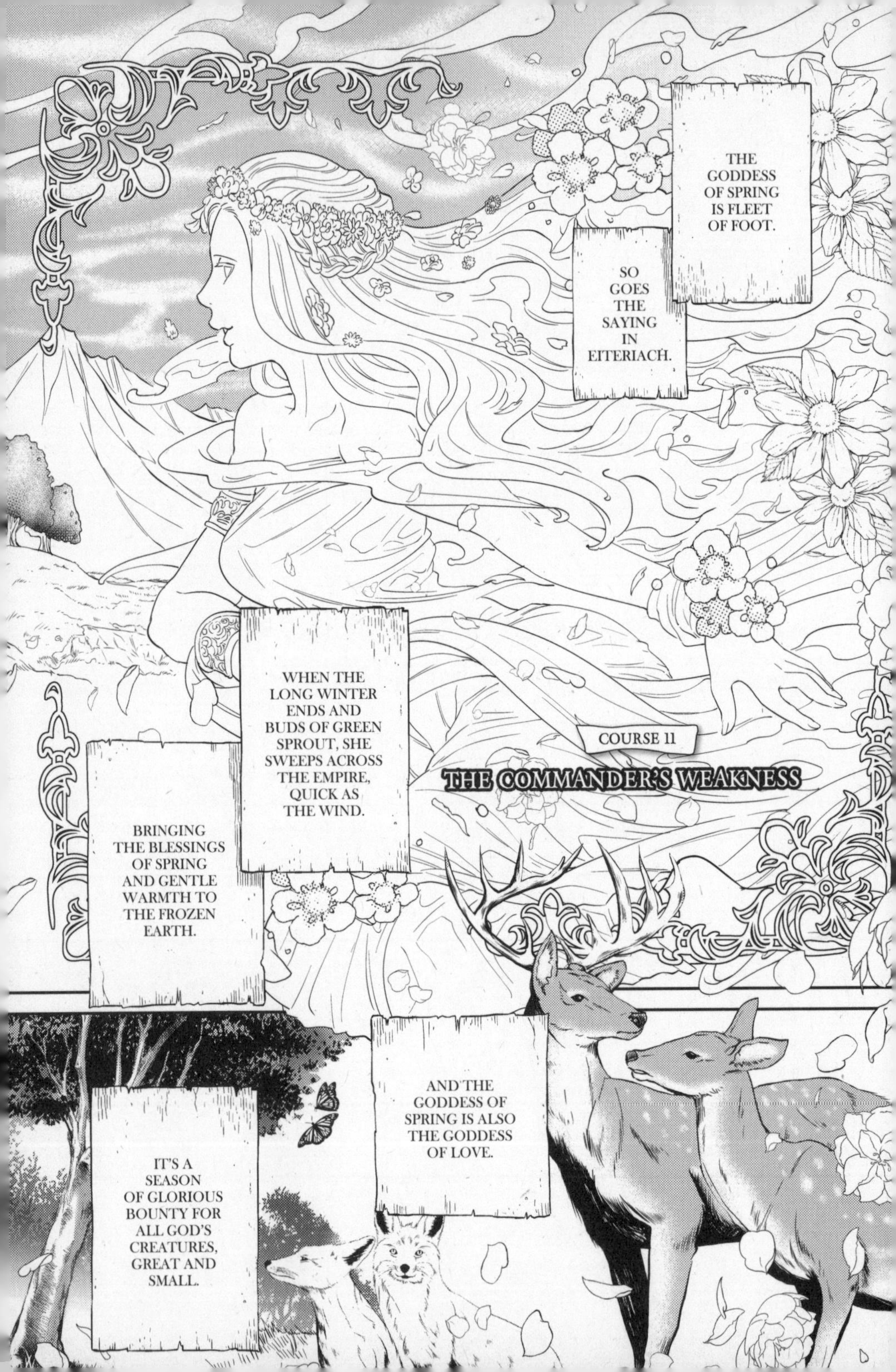
THE GODDESS OF SPRING IS FLEET OF FOOT.
SO GOES THE SAYING IN EITERIACH.
COURSE 11
THE COMMANDER'S WEAKNESS
WHEN THE LONG WINTER ENDS AND BUDS OF GREEN SPROUT, SHE SWEEPS ACROSS THE EMPIRE, QUICK AS THE WIND.
BRINGING THE BLESSINGS OF SPRING AND GENTLE WARMTH TO THE FROZEN EARTH.
AND THE GODDESS OF SPRING IS ALSO THE GODDESS OF LOVE.
IT'S A SEASON OF GLORIOUS BOUNTY FOR ALL GOD'S CREATURES, GREAT AND SMALL.

OTHERWORLDLY IZAKAYA

NOBU

Omusoba

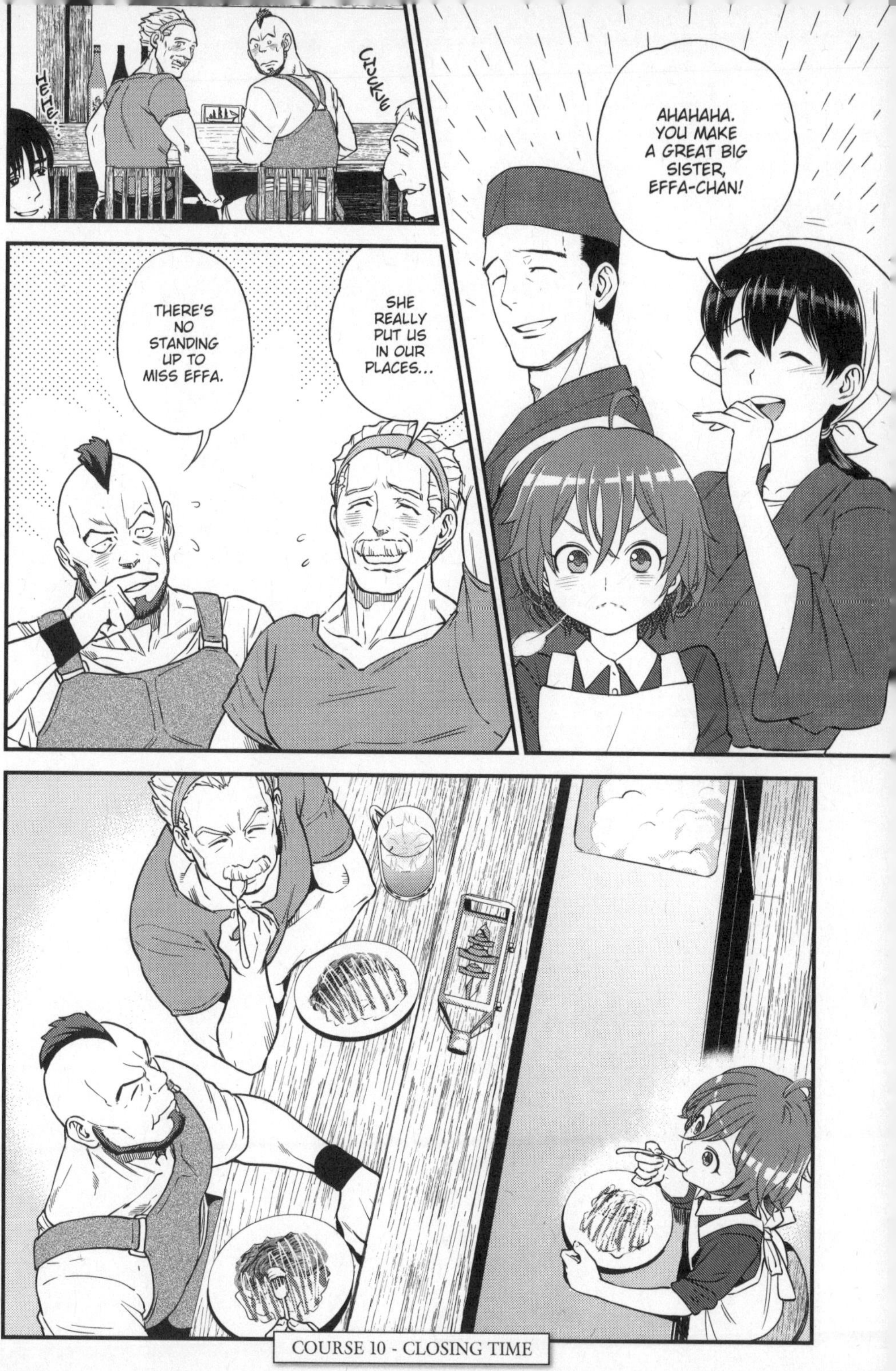
AHAHAHA. YOU MAKE A GREAT BIG SISTER, EFFA-CHAN!
CHUCKLE
HEHE...
SHE REALLY PUT US IN OUR PLACES...
THERE'S NO STANDING UP TO MISS EFFA.

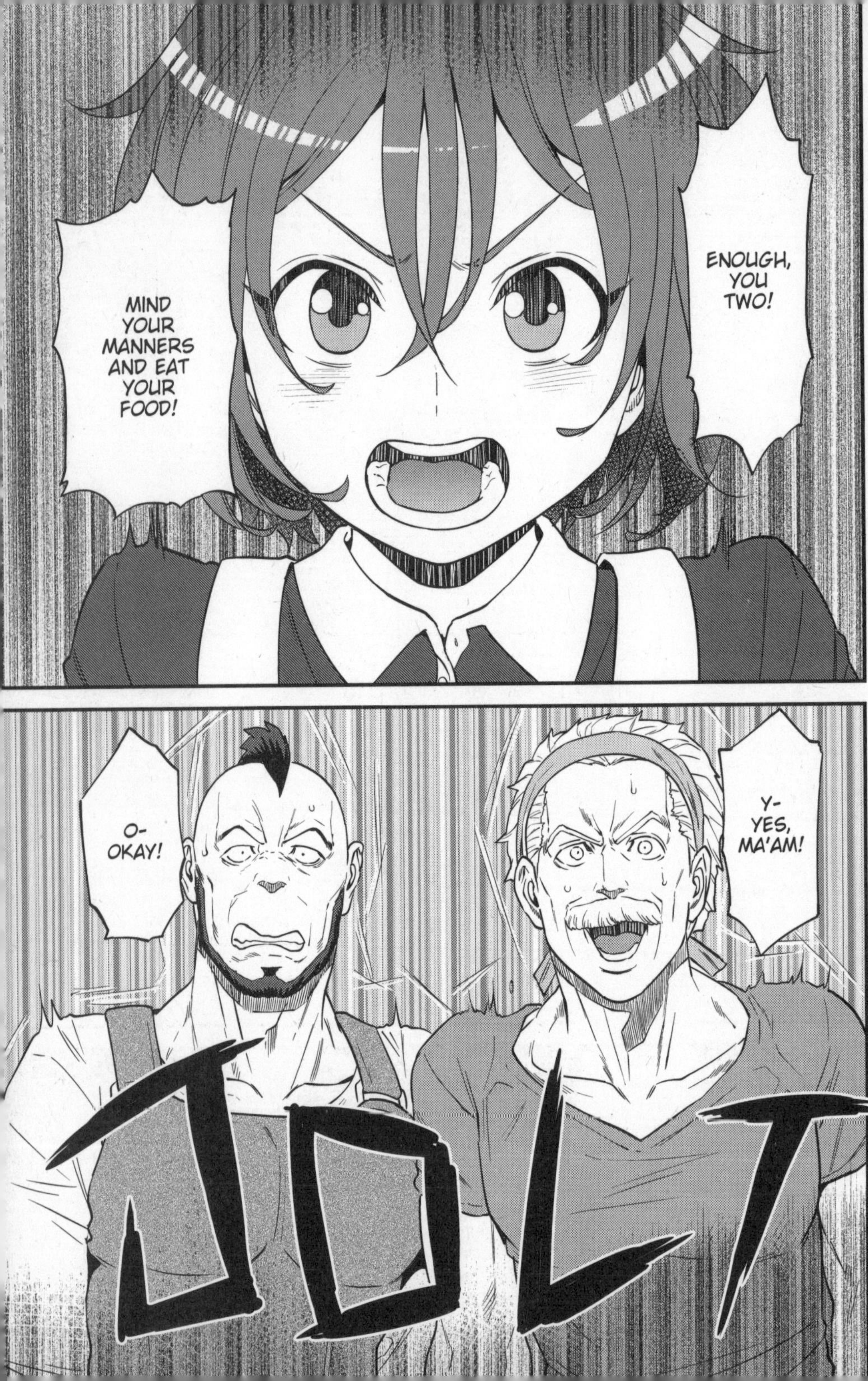
ENOUGH, YOU TWO!
MIND YOUR MANNERS AND EAT YOUR FOOD!
Y-YES, MA'AM!
O-OKAY!
JOLT

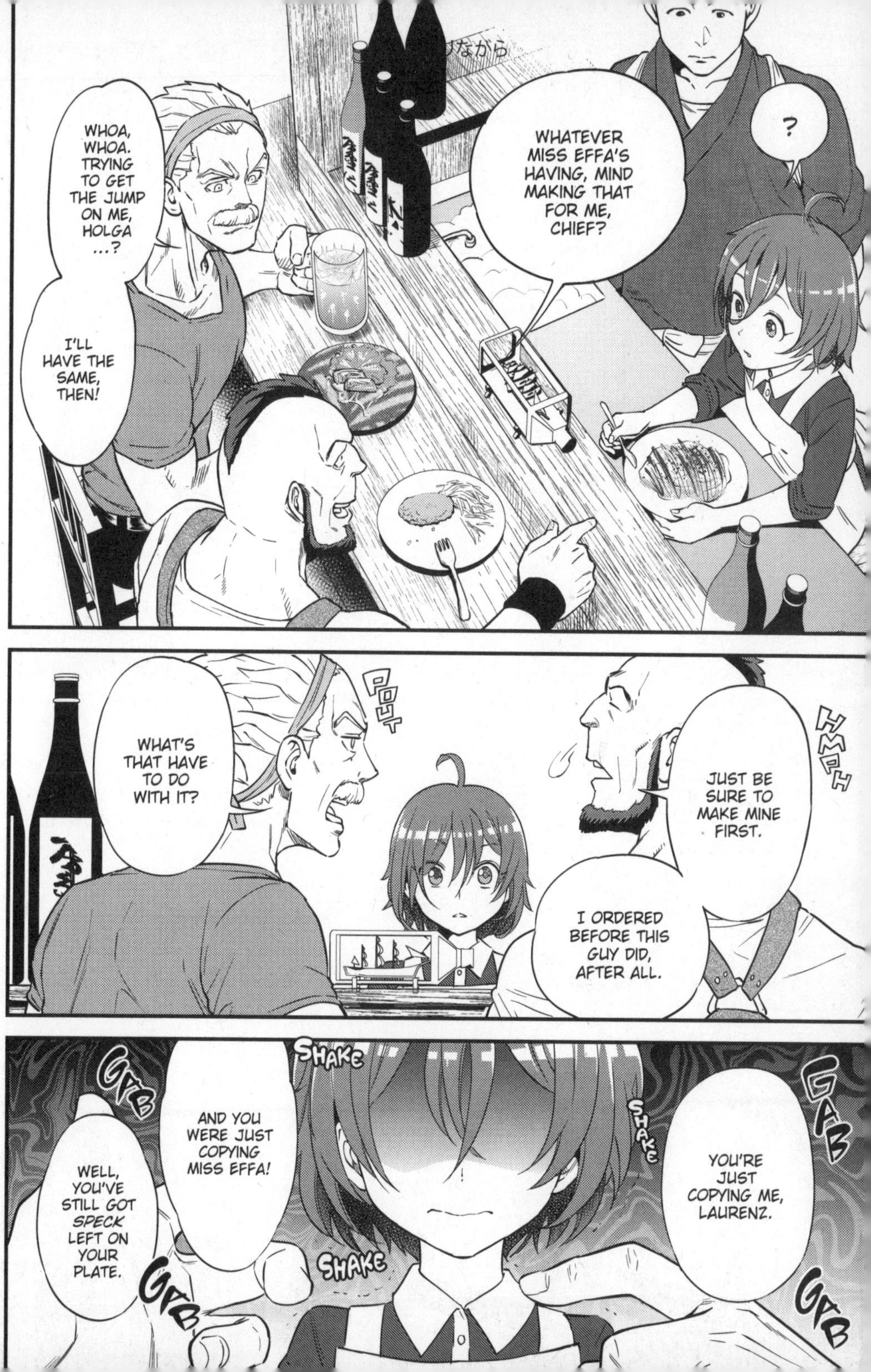
?
WHATEVER MISS EFFA'S HAVING, MIND MAKING THAT FOR ME, CHIEF?
WHOA, WHOA. TRYING TO GET THE JUMP ON ME, HOLGA ...?
I'LL HAVE THE SAME, THEN!
HMPH
JUST BE SURE TO MAKE MINE FIRST.
I ORDERED BEFORE THIS GUY DID, AFTER ALL.
POUT
WHAT'S THAT HAVE TO DO WITH IT?
GAB
GAB
YOU'RE JUST COPYING ME, LAURENZ.
SHAKE
SHAKE
AND YOU WERE JUST COPYING MISS EFFA!
SHAKE
GAB
WELL, YOU'VE STILL GOT *SPECK* LEFT ON YOUR PLATE.
GAB

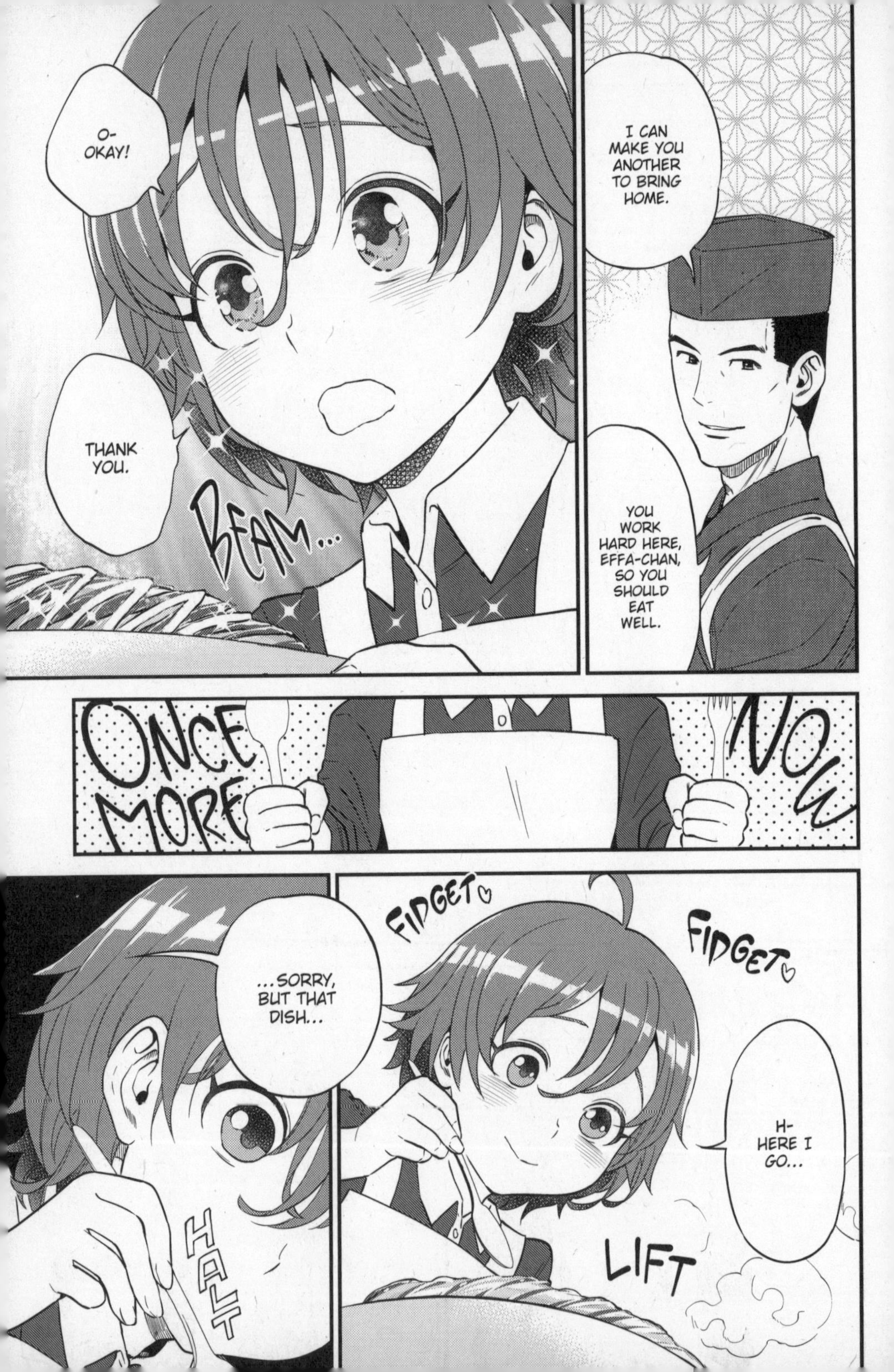

I CAN MAKE YOU ANOTHER TO BRING HOME.
YOU WORK HARD HERE, EFFA-CHAN, SO YOU SHOULD EAT WELL.
O-OKAY!
THANK YOU.
BEAM...
NOW
ONCE MORE
FIDGET♡
FIDGET♡
H-HERE I GO...
LIFT
...SORRY, BUT THAT DISH...
HALT

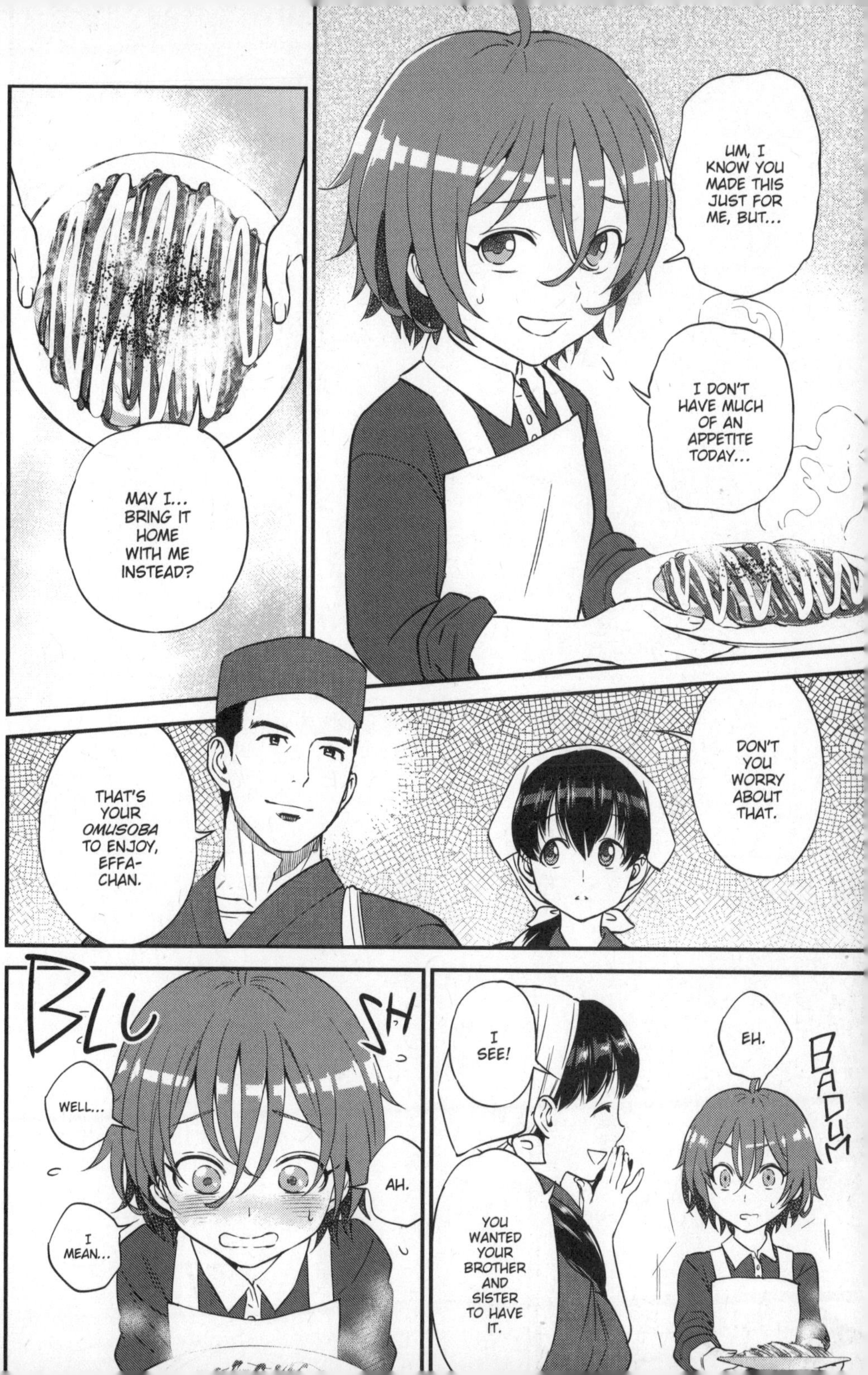
UM, I KNOW YOU MADE THIS JUST FOR ME, BUT...
I DON'T HAVE MUCH OF AN APPETITE TODAY...
MAY I... BRING IT HOME WITH ME INSTEAD?
DON'T YOU WORRY ABOUT THAT.
THAT'S YOUR *OMUSOBA* TO ENJOY, EFFA-CHAN.
EH.
BADUM
I SEE!
YOU WANTED YOUR BROTHER AND SISTER TO HAVE IT.
BLUSH
AH.
WELL...
I MEAN...

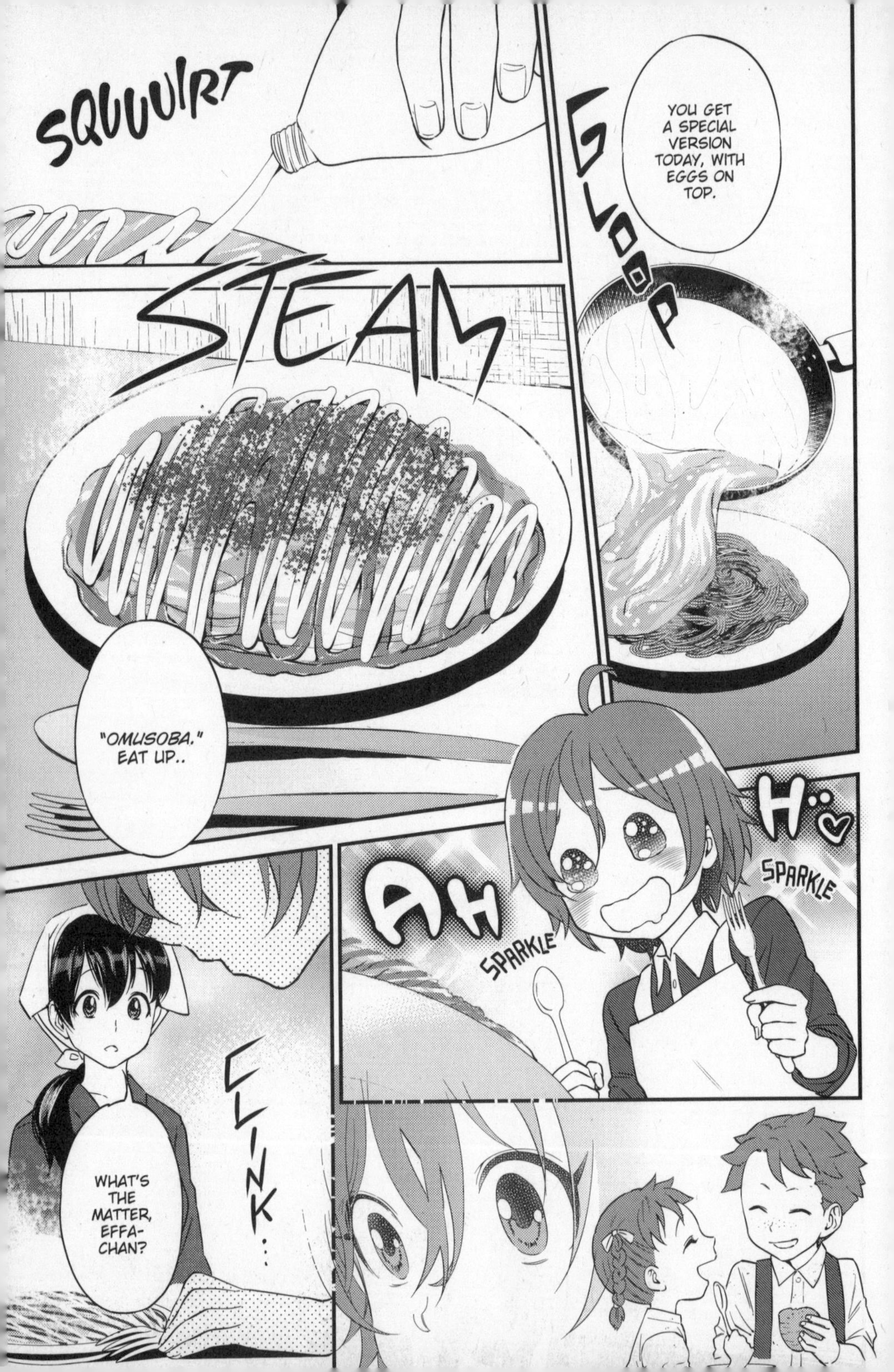
GLOOP
YOU GET A SPECIAL VERSION TODAY, WITH EGGS ON TOP.
SQUUUIRT
STEAM
"OMUSOBA." EAT UP..
H♥
SPARKLE
AH
SPARKLE
CLINK...
WHAT'S THE MATTER, EFFA-CHAN?

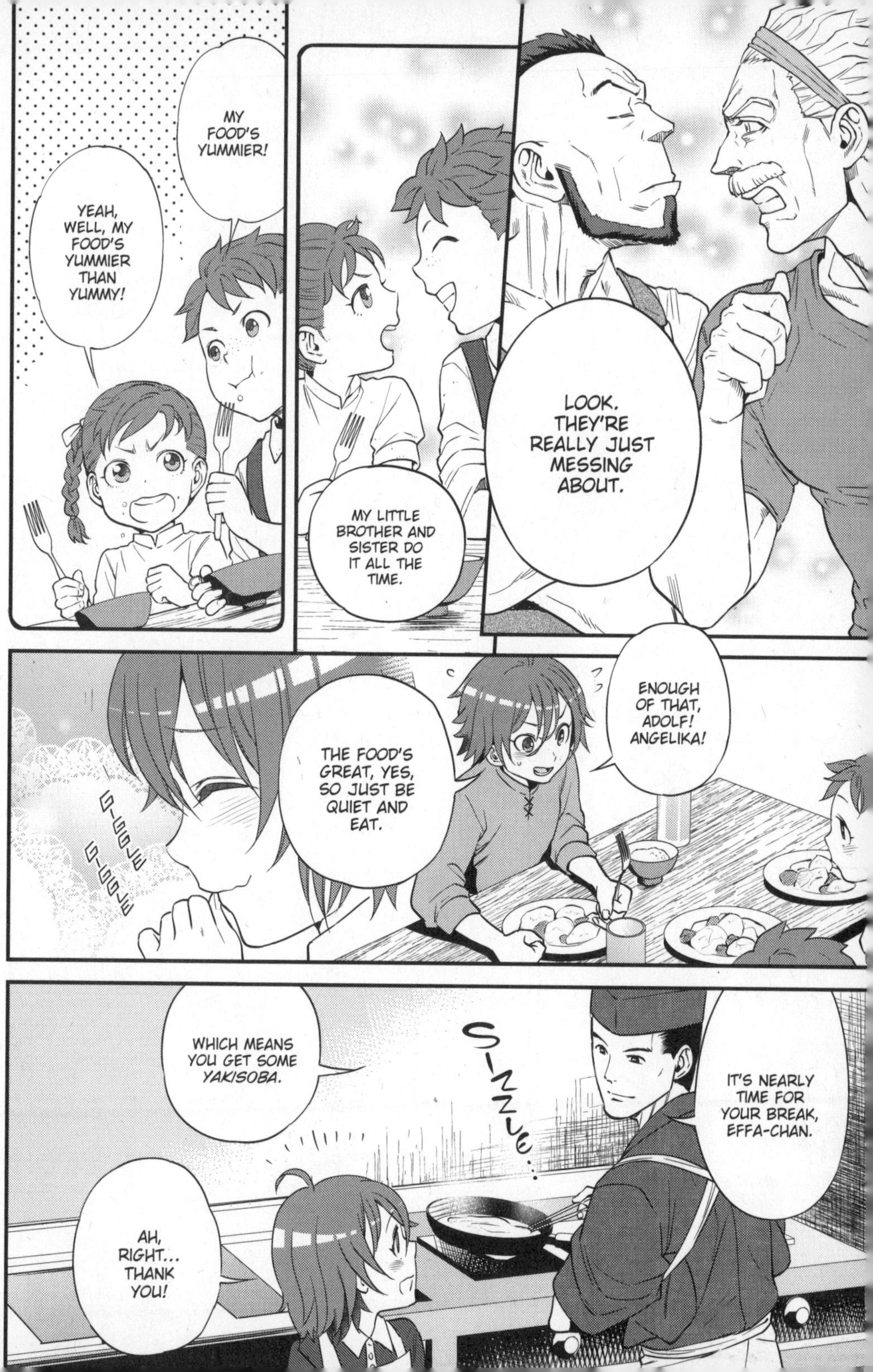
LOOK. THEY'RE REALLY JUST MESSING ABOUT.
MY LITTLE BROTHER AND SISTER DO IT ALL THE TIME.
MY FOOD'S YUMMIER!
YEAH, WELL, MY FOOD'S YUMMIER THAN YUMMY!
ENOUGH OF THAT, ADOLF! ANGELIKA!
THE FOOD'S GREAT, YES, SO JUST BE QUIET AND EAT.
GIGGLE GIGGLE
IT'S NEARLY TIME FOR YOUR BREAK, EFFA-CHAN.
SIZZLE...
WHICH MEANS YOU GET SOME *YAKISOBA*.
AH, RIGHT... THANK YOU!

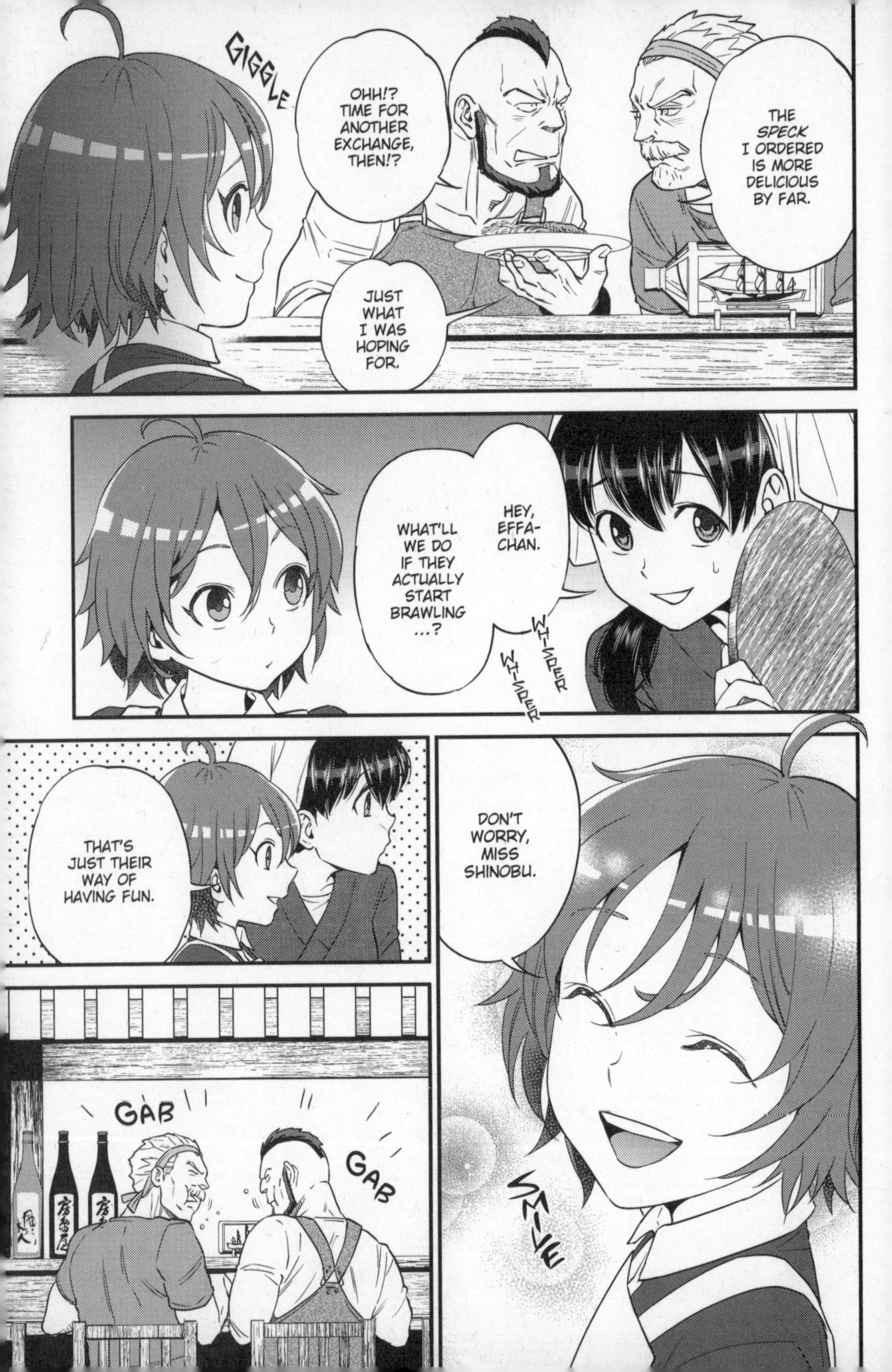
THE SPECK I ORDERED IS MORE DELICIOUS BY FAR.
OHH!? TIME FOR ANOTHER EXCHANGE, THEN!?
GIGGLE
JUST WHAT I WAS HOPING FOR.
HEY, EFFA-CHAN.
WHAT'LL WE DO IF THEY ACTUALLY START BRAWLING ...?
WHISPER
WHISPER
DON'T WORRY, MISS SHINOBU.
SMILE
THAT'S JUST THEIR WAY OF HAVING FUN.
GAB
GAB

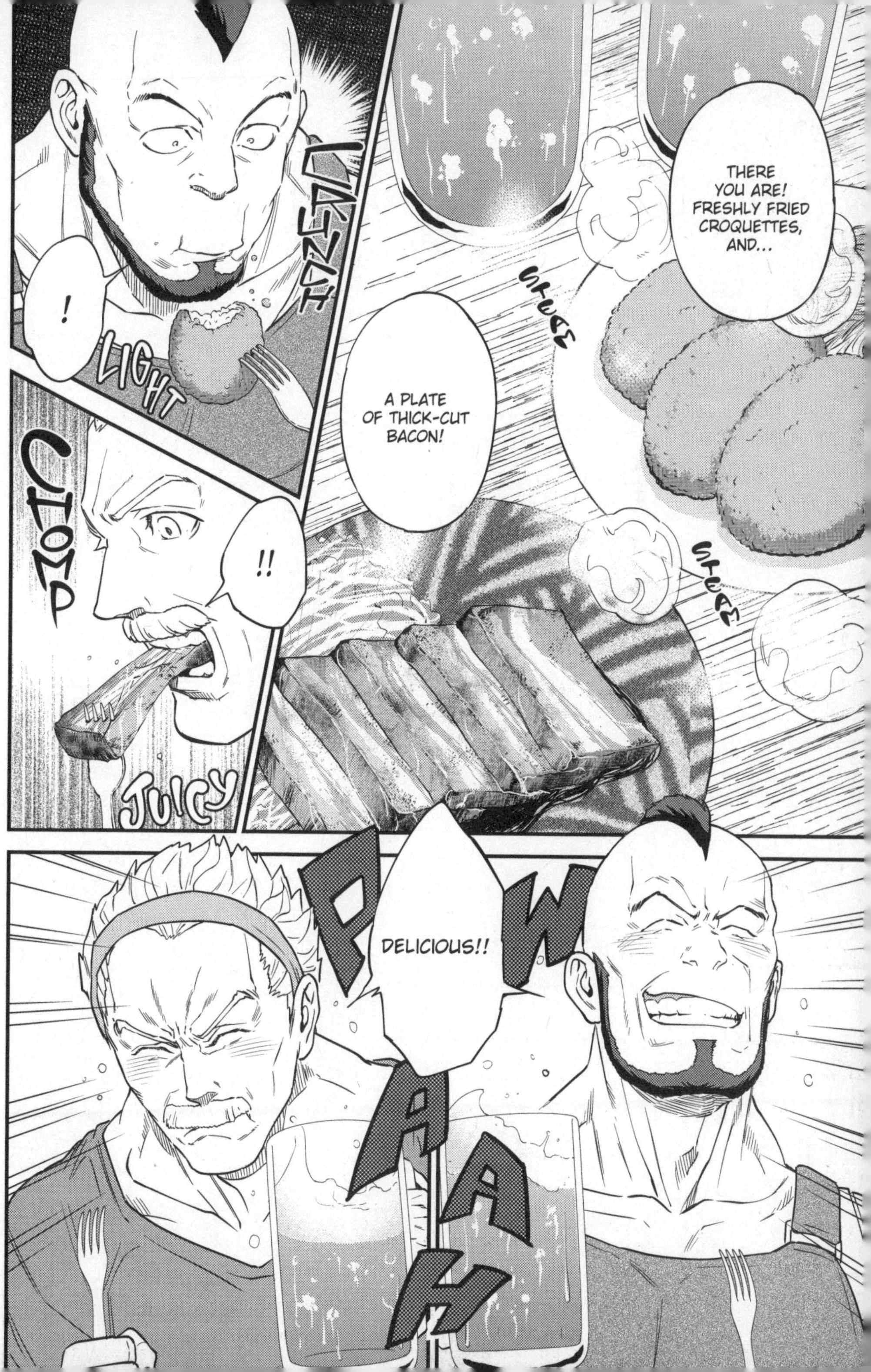
THERE YOU ARE! FRESHLY FRIED CROQUETTES, AND...
STEAM
A PLATE OF THICK-CUT BACON!
STEAM
CRUNCH
!
LIGHT
CHOMP
!!
JUICY
PWAAH
DELICIOUS!!

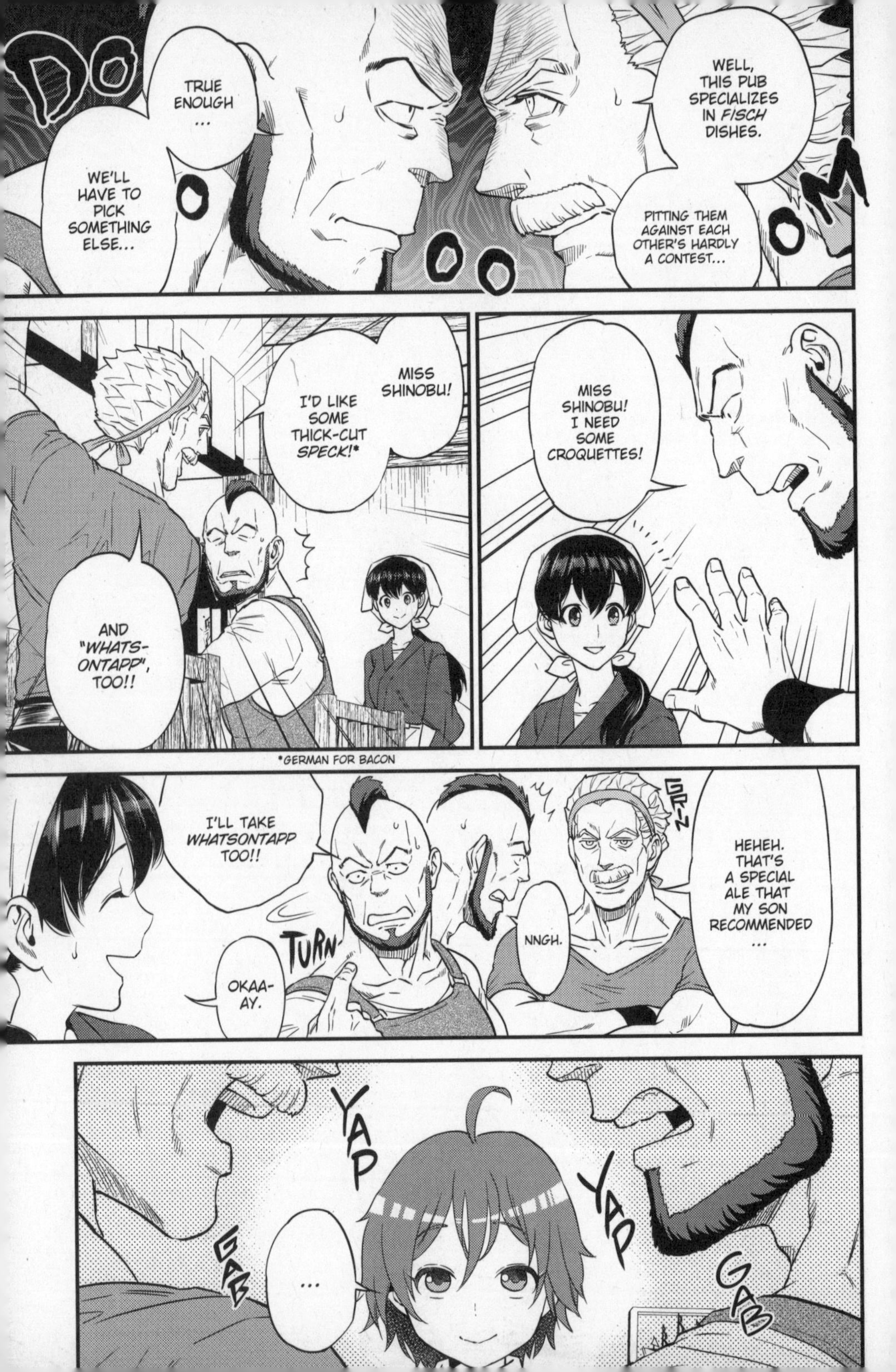
WELL, THIS PUB SPECIALIZES IN *FISCH* DISHES.
PITTING THEM AGAINST EACH OTHER'S HARDLY A CONTEST...
DOOOOOM
TRUE ENOUGH ...
WE'LL HAVE TO PICK SOMETHING ELSE...
MISS SHINOBU! I NEED SOME CROQUETTES!
MISS SHINOBU!
I'D LIKE SOME THICK-CUT *SPECK!**
AND "WHATSONTAPP", TOO!!
*GERMAN FOR BACON
GRIN
HEHEH. THAT'S A SPECIAL ALE THAT MY SON RECOMMENDED ...
NNGH.
I'LL TAKE *WHATSONTAPP* TOO!!
TURN
OKAA-AY.
YAP
YAP
GAB
GAB
...

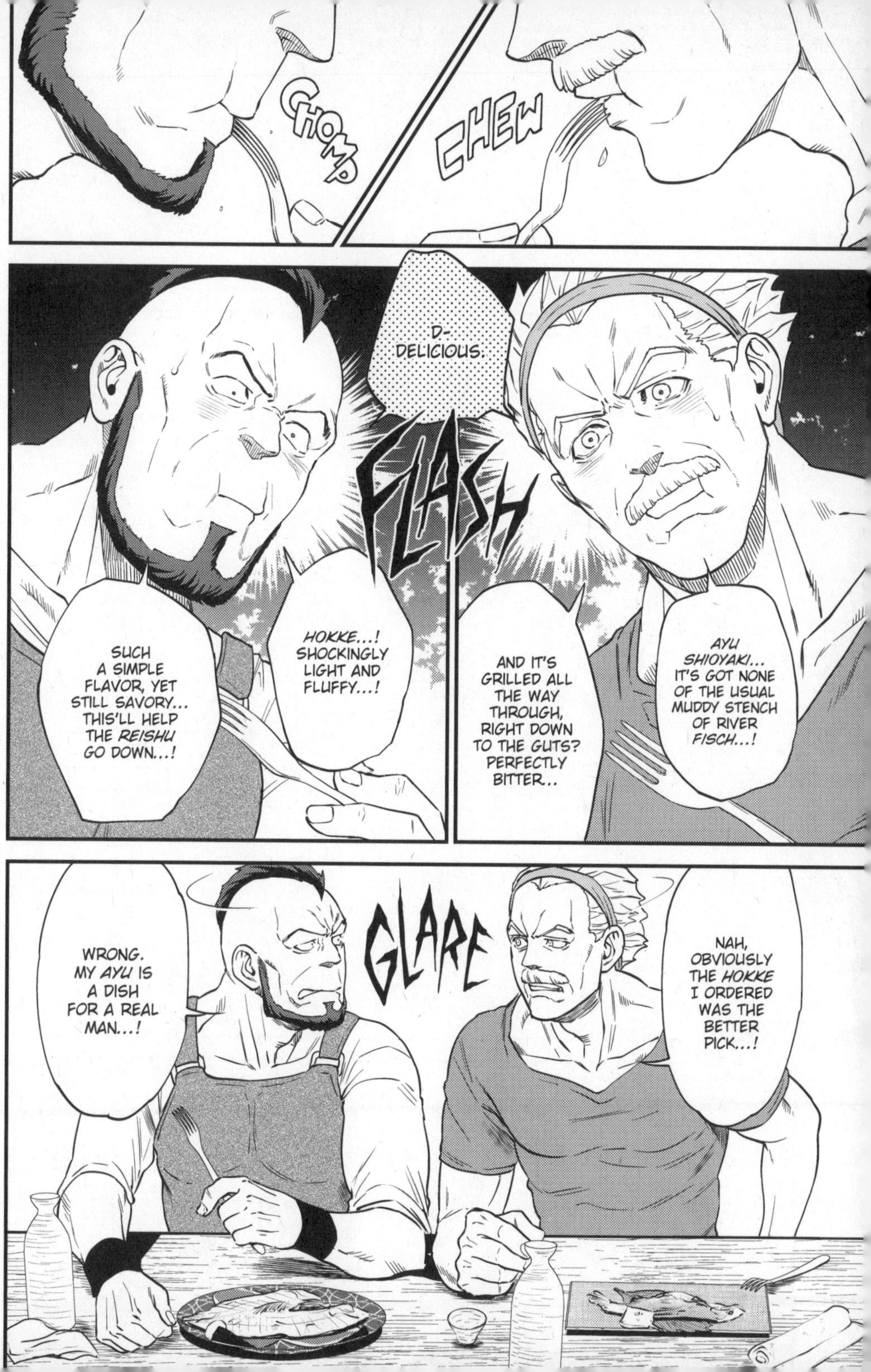

CHEW
CHOMP
D- DELICIOUS.
FLASH
AYU SHIOYAKI... IT'S GOT NONE OF THE USUAL MUDDY STENCH OF RIVER FISCH...!
AND IT'S GRILLED ALL THE WAY THROUGH, RIGHT DOWN TO THE GUTS? PERFECTLY BITTER...
HOKKE...! SHOCKINGLY LIGHT AND FLUFFY...!
SUCH A SIMPLE FLAVOR, YET STILL SAVORY... THIS'LL HELP THE REISHU GO DOWN...!
NAH, OBVIOUSLY THE HOKKE I ORDERED WAS THE BETTER PICK...!
GLARE
WRONG. MY AYU IS A DISH FOR A REAL MAN...!

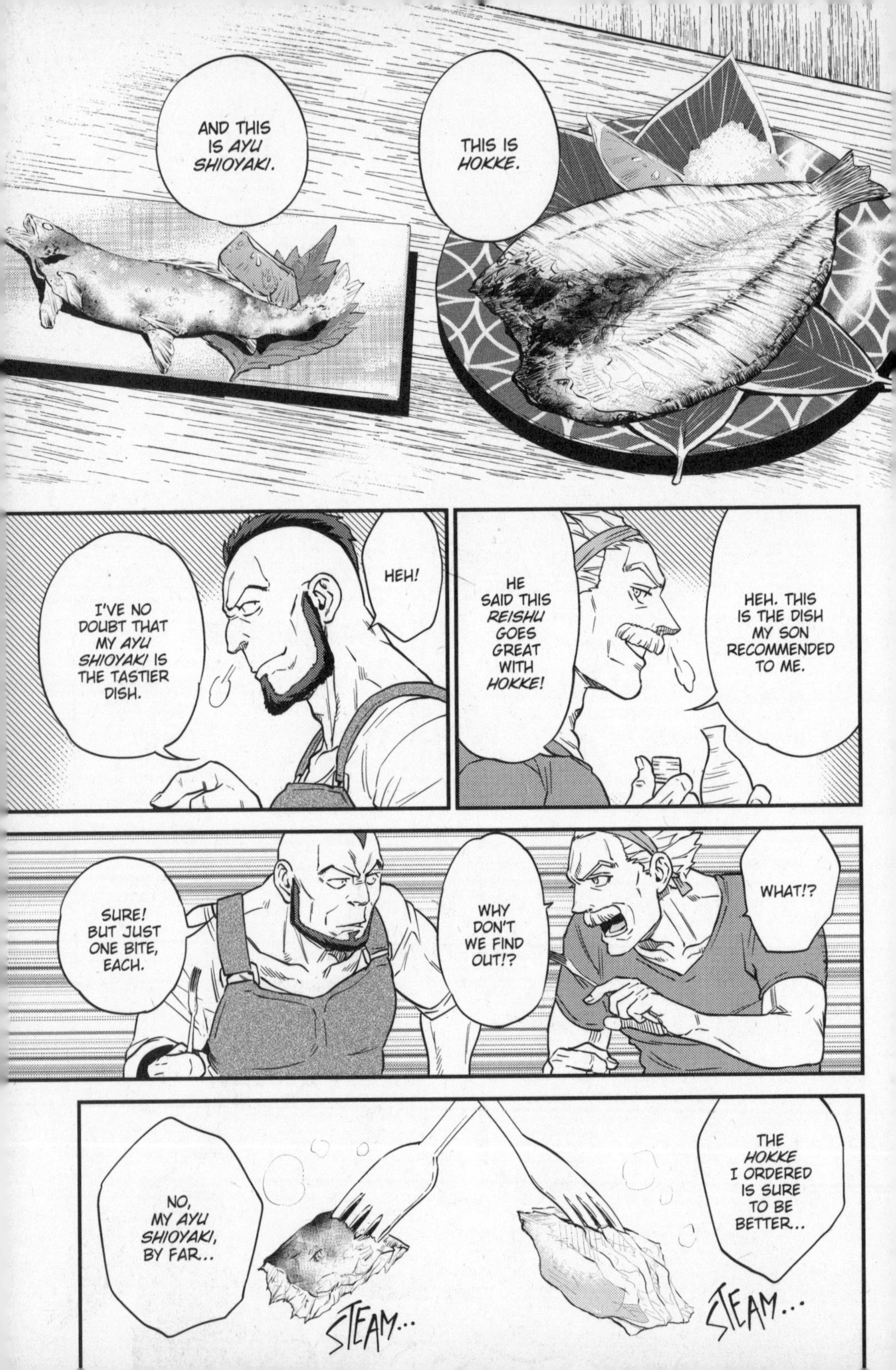
THIS IS HOKKE.
AND THIS IS AYU SHIOYAKI.
HEH. THIS IS THE DISH MY SON RECOMMENDED TO ME.
HE SAID THIS REISHU GOES GREAT WITH HOKKE!
HEH!
I'VE NO DOUBT THAT MY AYU SHIOYAKI IS THE TASTIER DISH.
WHAT!?
WHY DON'T WE FIND OUT!?
SURE! BUT JUST ONE BITE, EACH.
THE HOKKE I ORDERED IS SURE TO BE BETTER...
STEAM...
NO, MY AYU SHIOYAKI, BY FAR...
STEAM...

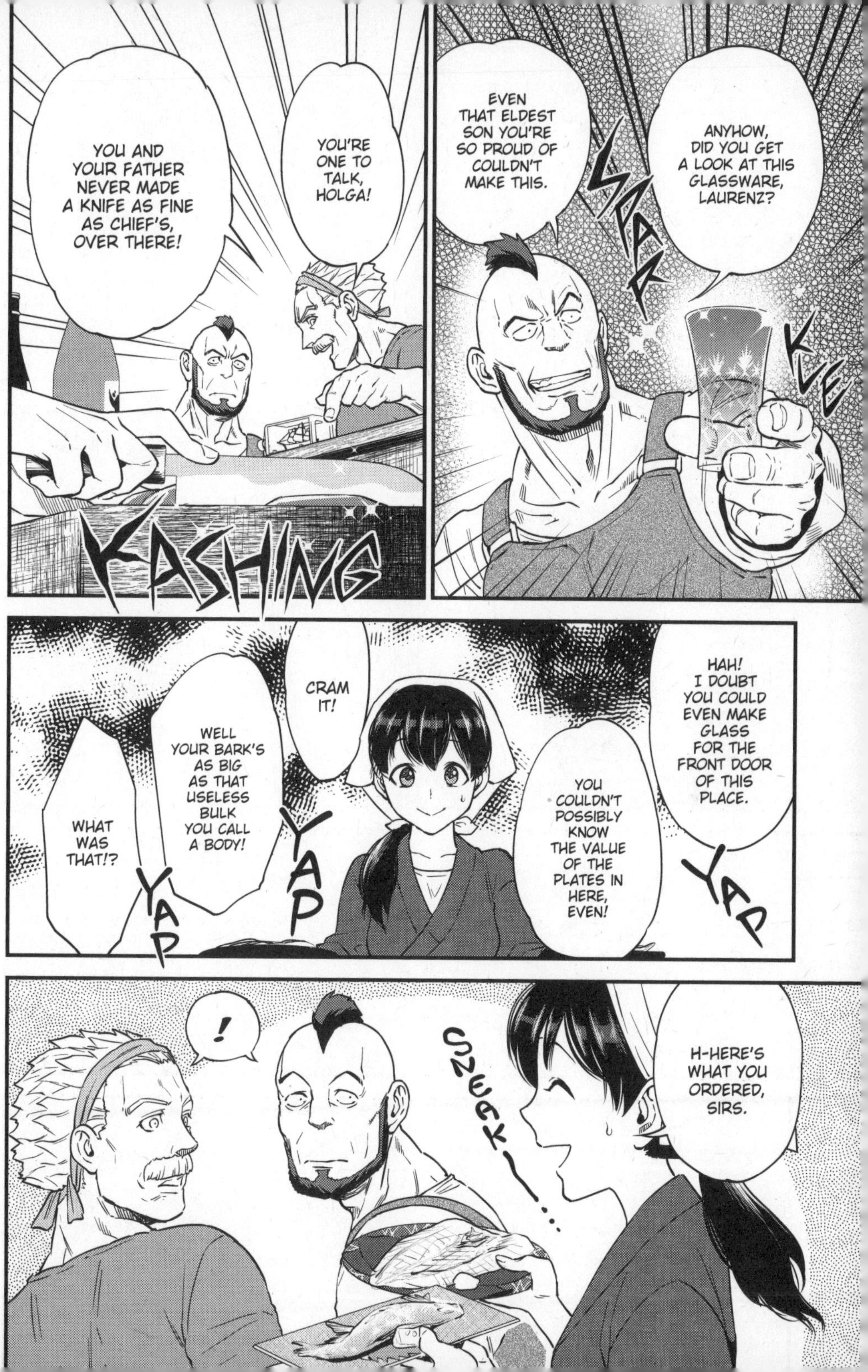
ANYHOW, DID YOU GET A LOOK AT THIS GLASSWARE, LAURENZ?
EVEN THAT ELDEST SON YOU'RE SO PROUD OF COULDN'T MAKE THIS.
YOU'RE ONE TO TALK, HOLGA!
YOU AND YOUR FATHER NEVER MADE A KNIFE AS FINE AS CHIEF'S, OVER THERE!
KASHING
HAH! I DOUBT YOU COULD EVEN MAKE GLASS FOR THE FRONT DOOR OF THIS PLACE.
YAP
YOU COULDN'T POSSIBLY KNOW THE VALUE OF THE PLATES IN HERE, EVEN!
CRAM IT!
YAP
WELL YOUR BARK'S AS BIG AS THAT USELESS BULK YOU CALL A BODY!
WHAT WAS THAT!?
YAP
H-HERE'S WHAT YOU ORDERED, SIRS.
SNEAK...
!

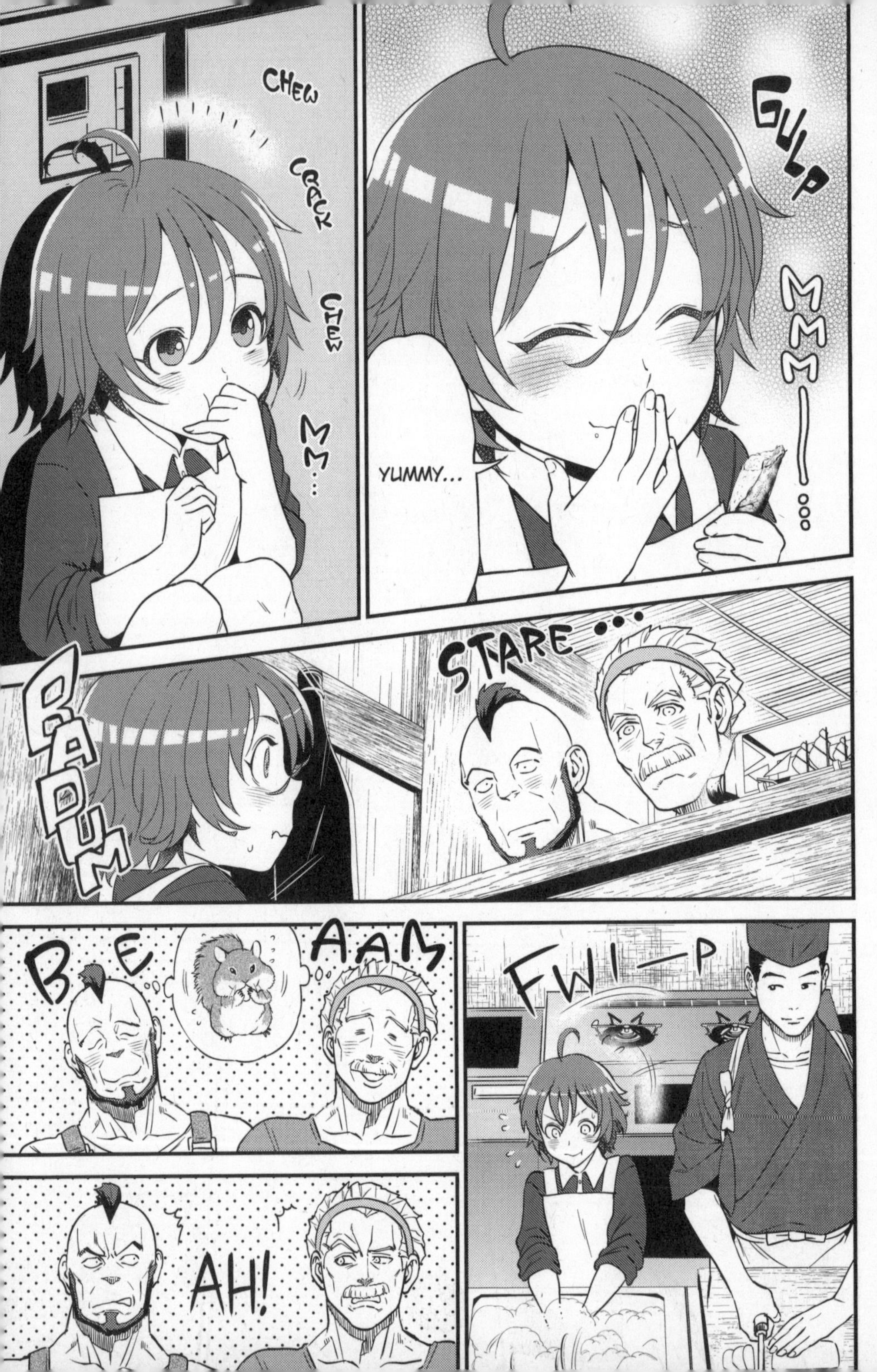
GULP
MMM—I...
YUMMY...
CHEW
CRACK
CHEW
MM...
STARE...
BADUM
FWI—P
B E AAM
AH!

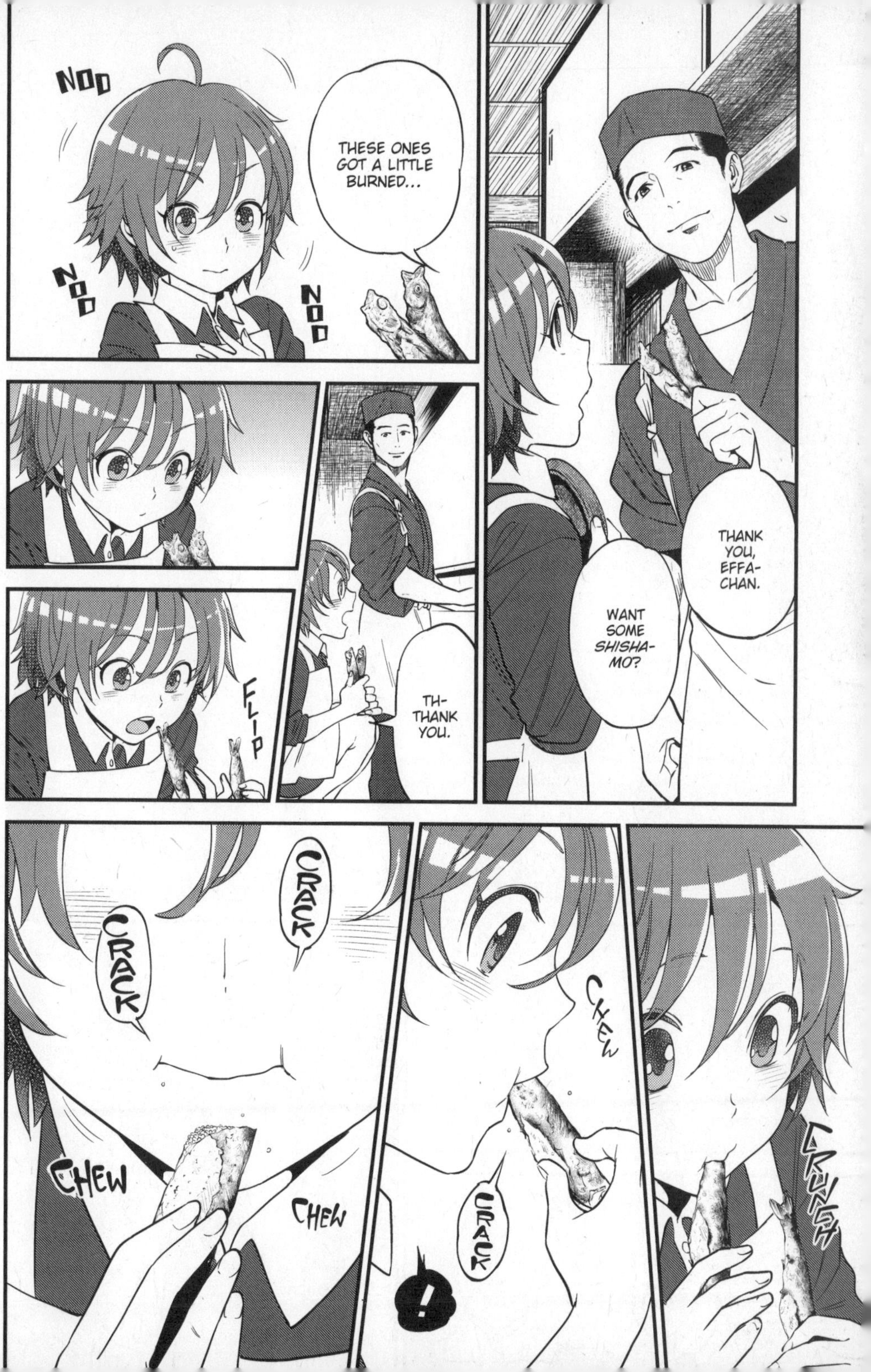
THANK YOU, EFFA-CHAN.
WANT SOME SHISHAMO?
THESE ONES GOT A LITTLE BURNED...
NOD
NOD
NOD
TH-THANK YOU.
FLIP
CRUNCH
CHEW
CRACK
!
CRACK
CRACK
CHEW
CHEW

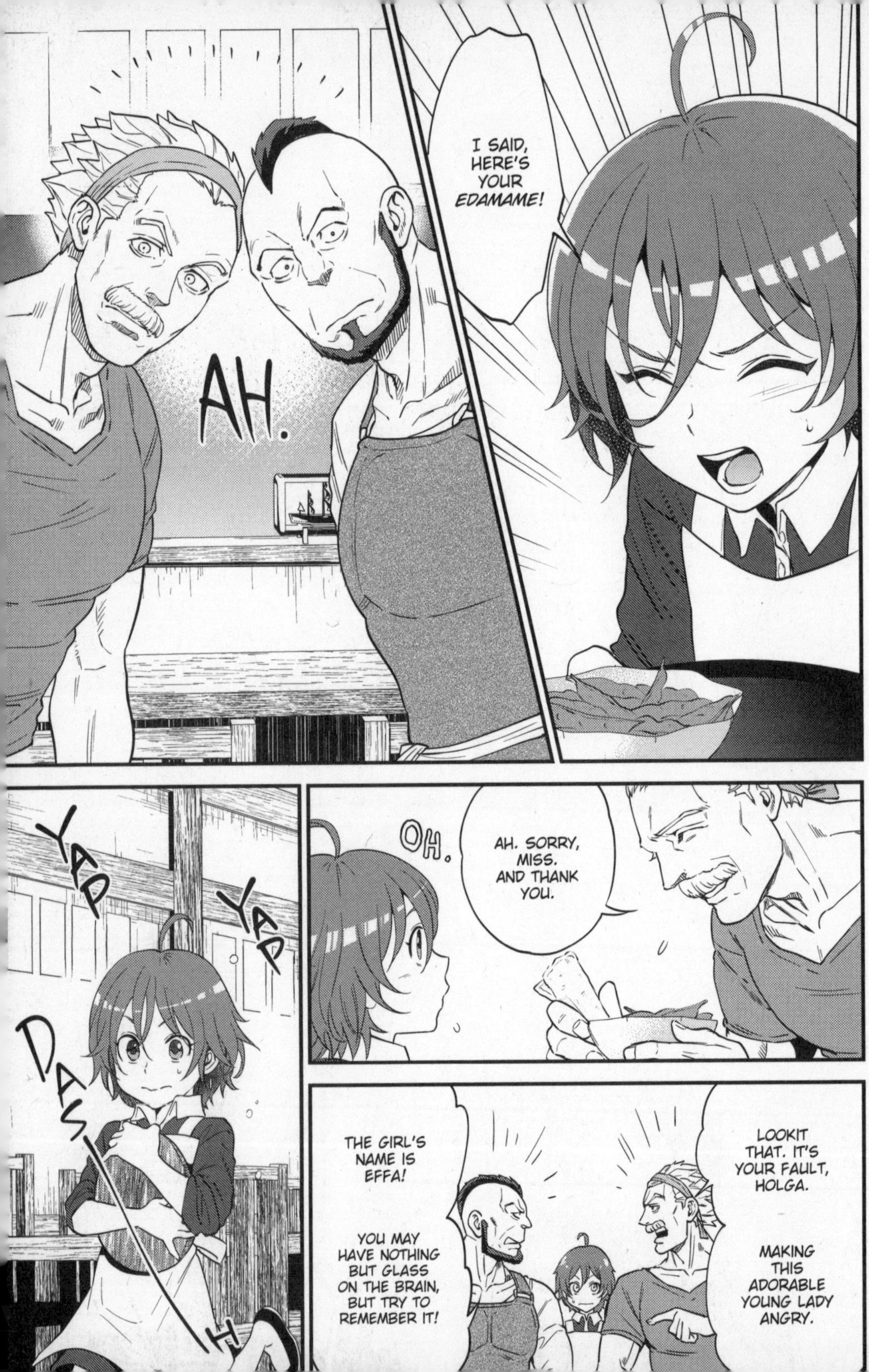
I SAID, HERE'S YOUR *EDAMAME!*
AH.
AH. SORRY, MISS. AND THANK YOU.
OH.
LOOKIT THAT. IT'S YOUR FAULT, HOLGA.
MAKING THIS ADORABLE YOUNG LADY ANGRY.
THE GIRL'S NAME IS EFFA!
YOU MAY HAVE NOTHING BUT GLASS ON THE BRAIN, BUT TRY TO REMEMBER IT!
YAP
YAP
DASH

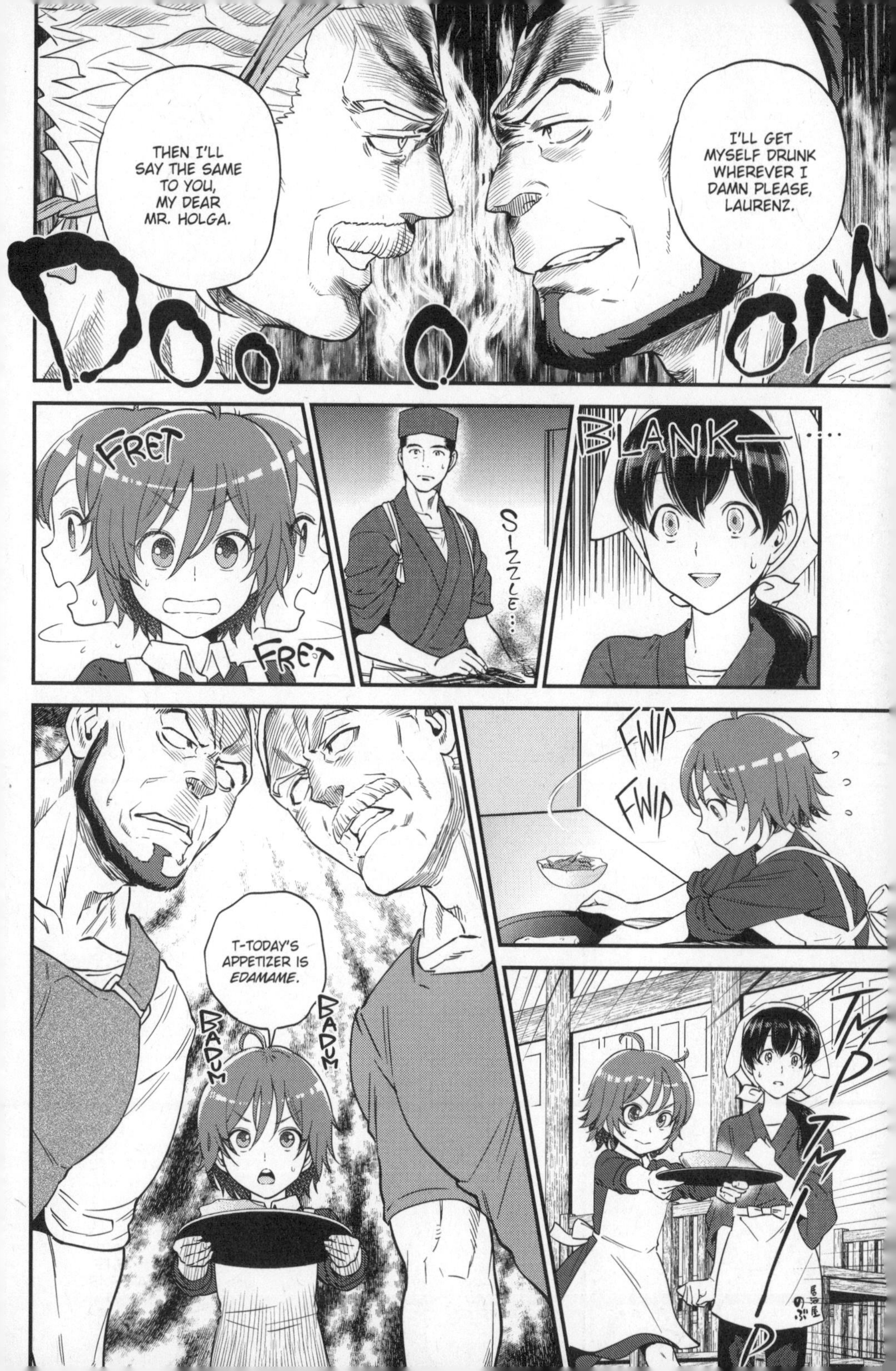
I'LL GET MYSELF DRUNK WHEREVER I DAMN PLEASE, LAURENZ.
THEN I'LL SAY THE SAME TO YOU, MY DEAR MR. HOLGA.
DOOOOM
BLANK—...
SIZZLE...
FRET
FRET
FWIP
FWIP
TMP
TMP
TMP
居酒屋のぶ
T-TODAY'S APPETIZER IS *EDAMAME*.
BADUM
BADUM

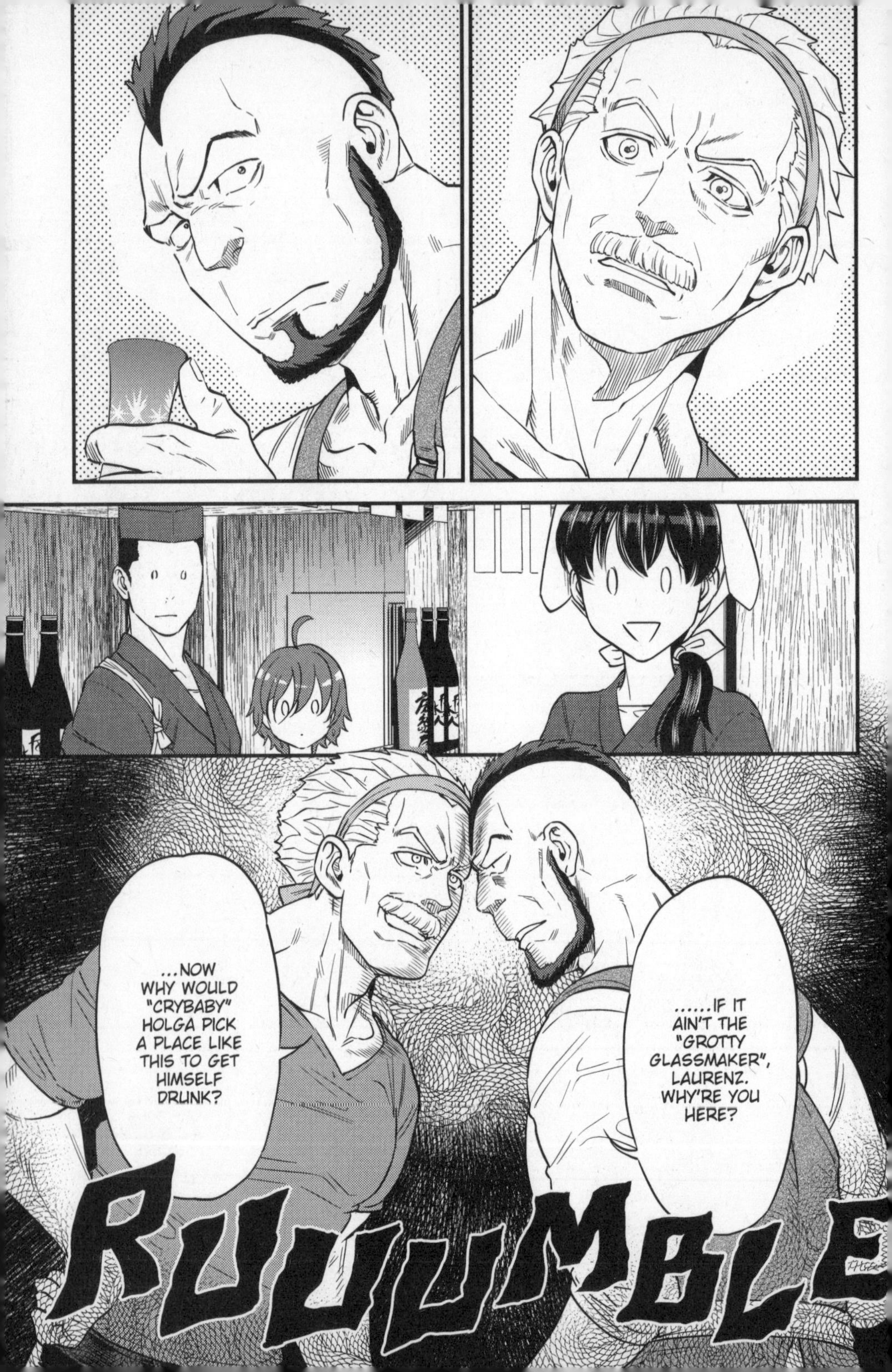
......IF IT AIN'T THE "GROTTY GLASSMAKER", LAURENZ. WHY'RE YOU HERE?
...NOW WHY WOULD "CRYBABY" HOLGA PICK A PLACE LIKE THIS TO GET HIMSELF DRUNK?
RUUUMBLE

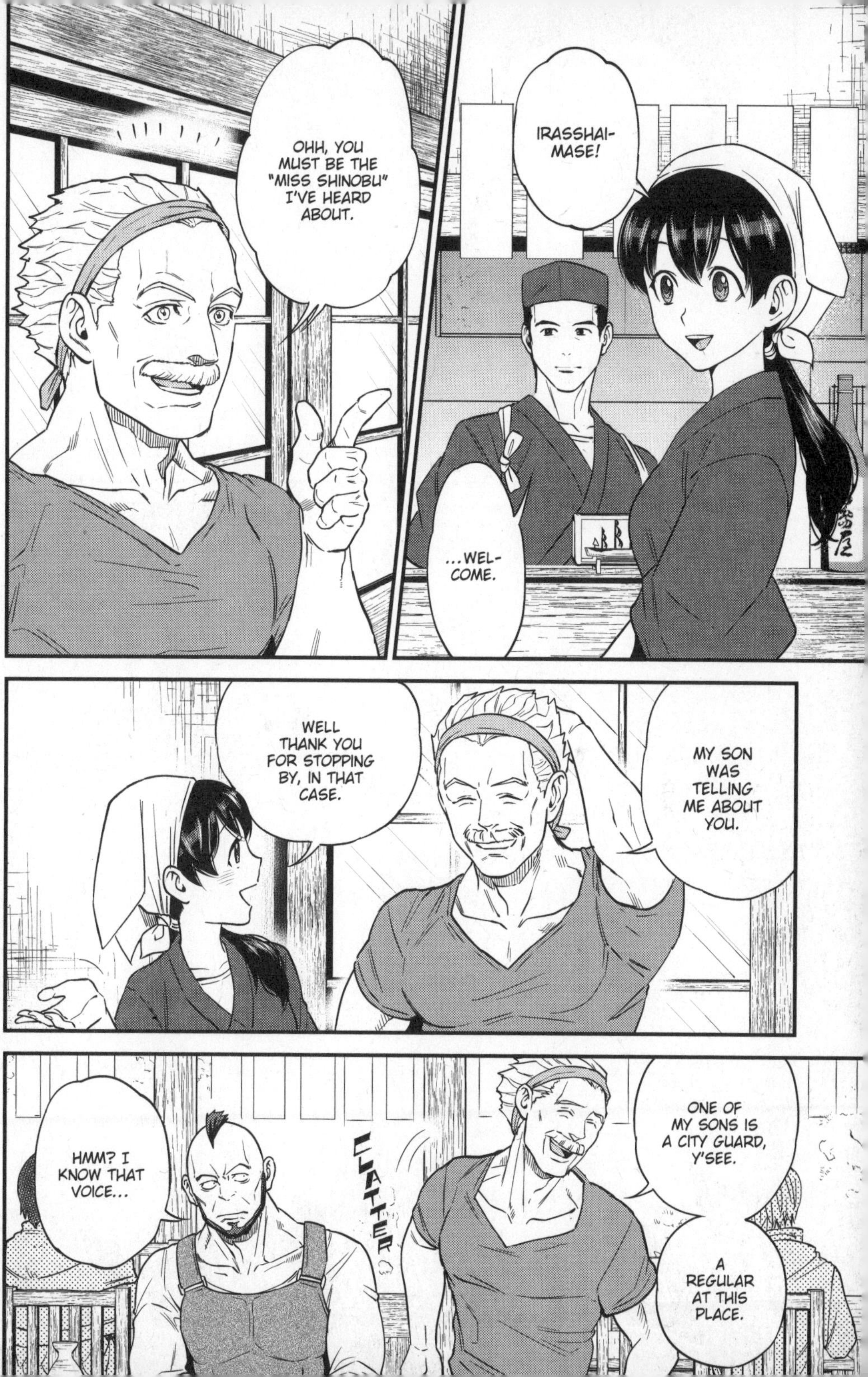
IRASSHAI-MASE!
...WEL-COME.
OHH, YOU MUST BE THE "MISS SHINOBU" I'VE HEARD ABOUT.
MY SON WAS TELLING ME ABOUT YOU.
WELL THANK YOU FOR STOPPING BY, IN THAT CASE.
ONE OF MY SONS IS A CITY GUARD, Y'SEE.
A REGULAR AT THIS PLACE.
CLATTER
HMM? I KNOW THAT VOICE...

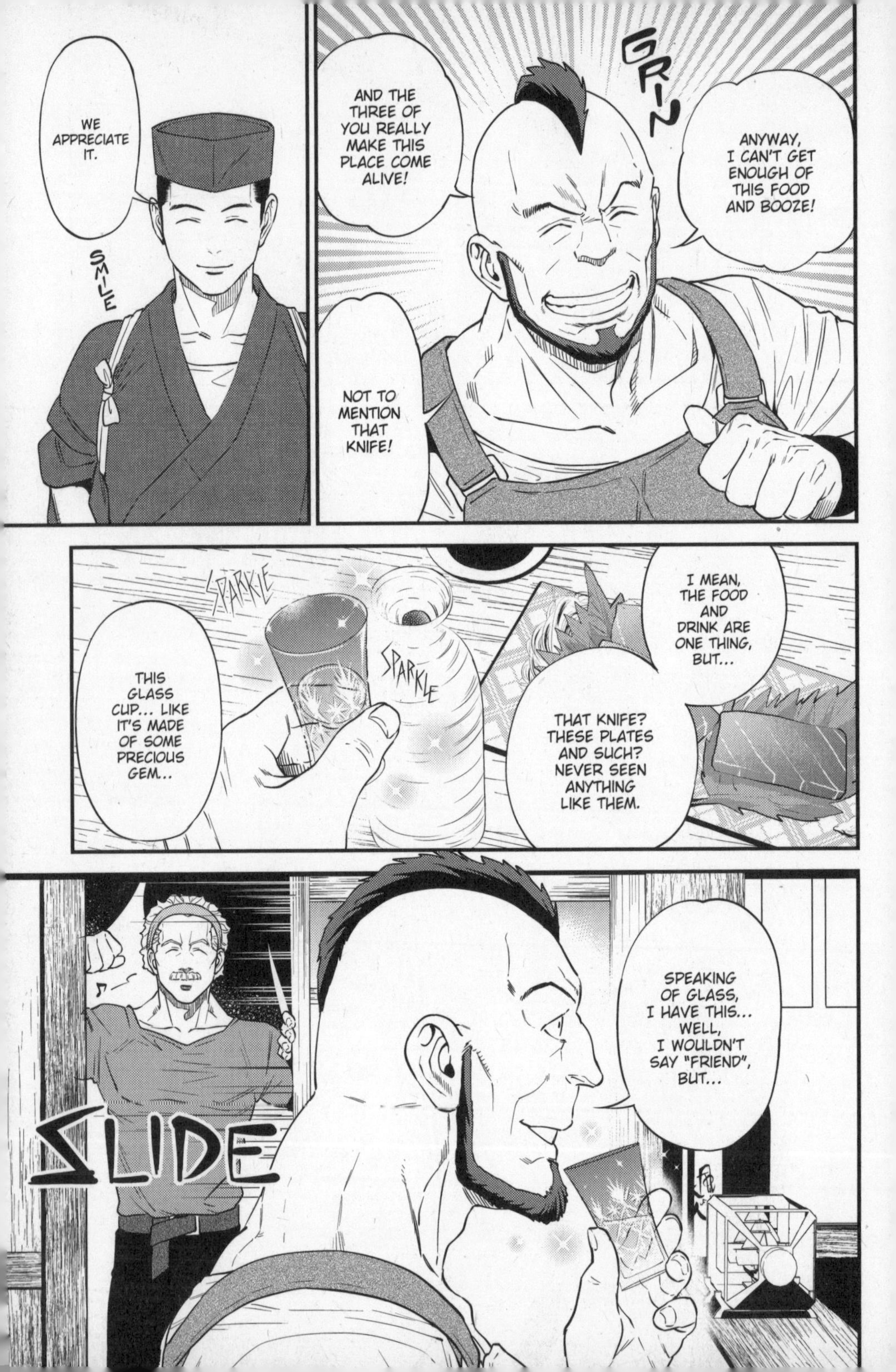
GRIN
ANYWAY, I CAN'T GET ENOUGH OF THIS FOOD AND BOOZE!
AND THE THREE OF YOU REALLY MAKE THIS PLACE COME ALIVE!
NOT TO MENTION THAT KNIFE!
WE APPRECIATE IT.
SMILE
I MEAN, THE FOOD AND DRINK ARE ONE THING, BUT...
THAT KNIFE? THESE PLATES AND SUCH? NEVER SEEN ANYTHING LIKE THEM.
SPARKLE
SPARKLE
THIS GLASS CUP... LIKE IT'S MADE OF SOME PRECIOUS GEM...
SPEAKING OF GLASS, I HAVE THIS... WELL, I WOULDN'T SAY "FRIEND", BUT...
SLIDE

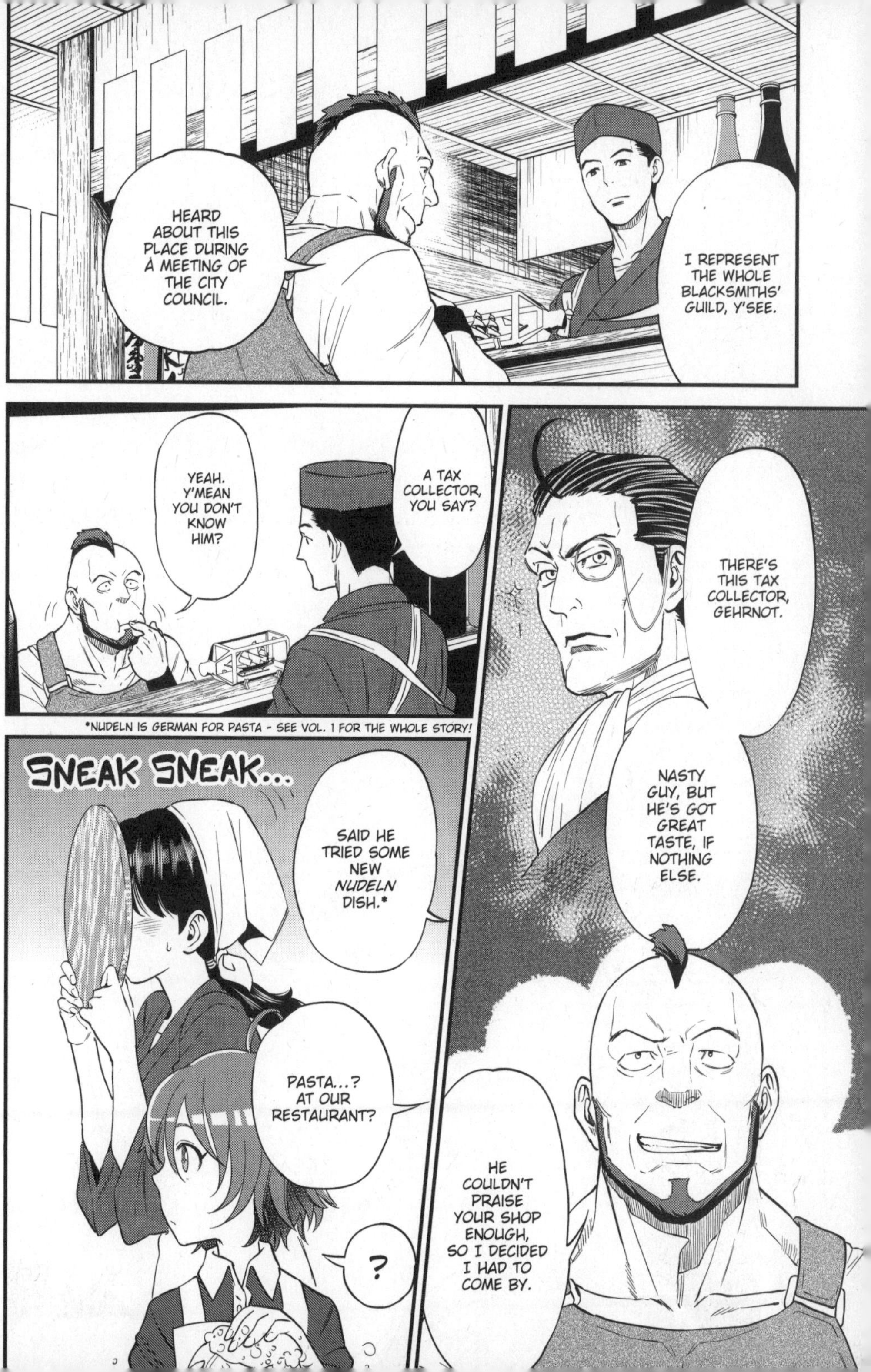
I REPRESENT THE WHOLE BLACKSMITHS' GUILD, Y'SEE.
HEARD ABOUT THIS PLACE DURING A MEETING OF THE CITY COUNCIL.
THERE'S THIS TAX COLLECTOR, GEHRNOT.
NASTY GUY, BUT HE'S GOT GREAT TASTE, IF NOTHING ELSE.
HE COULDN'T PRAISE YOUR SHOP ENOUGH, SO I DECIDED I HAD TO COME BY.
A TAX COLLECTOR, YOU SAY?
YEAH. Y'MEAN YOU DON'T KNOW HIM?
SNEAK SNEAK...
SAID HE TRIED SOME NEW *NUDELN* DISH.*
PASTA...? AT OUR RESTAURANT?
?
*NUDELN IS GERMAN FOR PASTA - SEE VOL. 1 FOR THE WHOLE STORY!

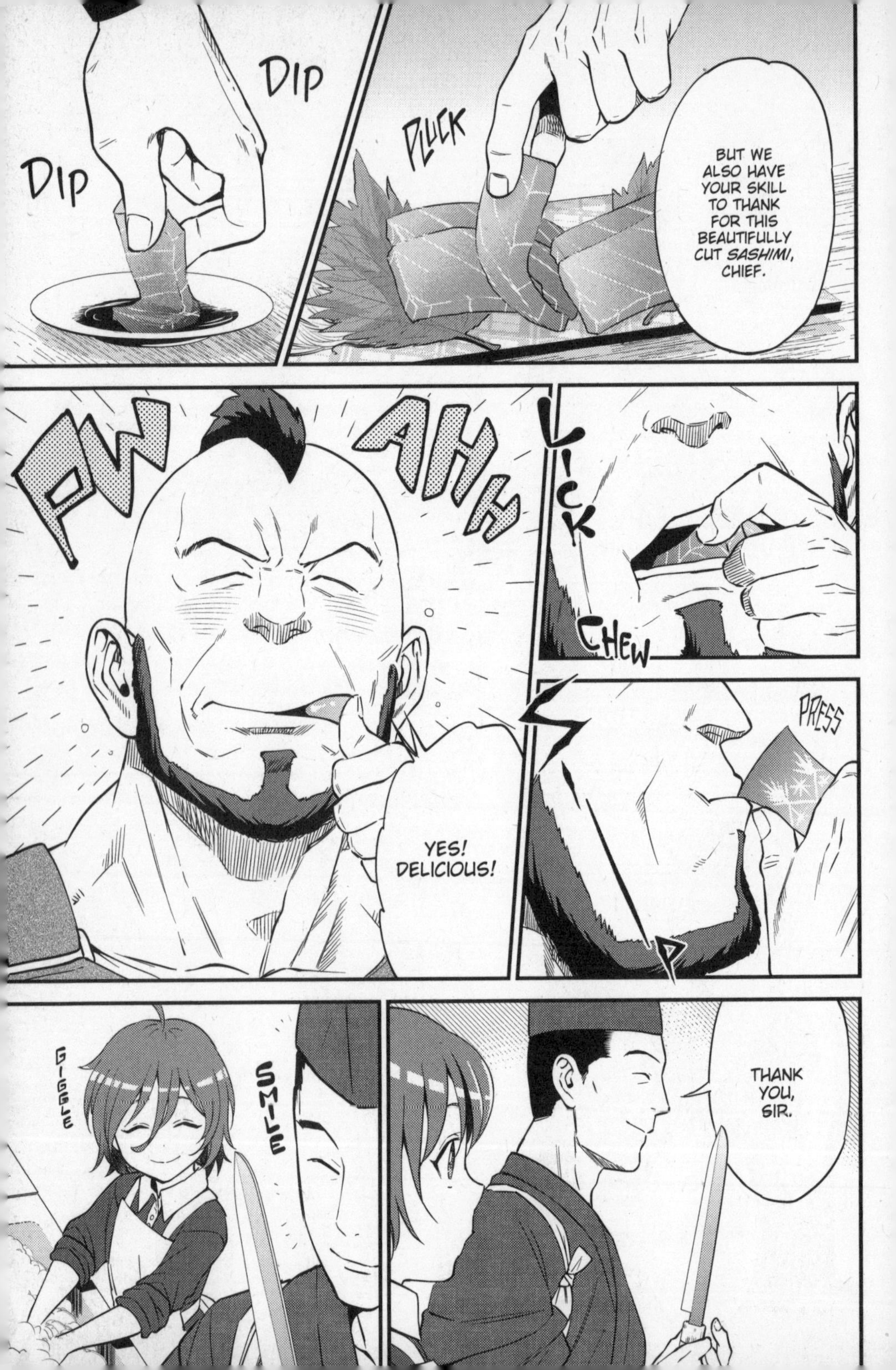
PLUCK
BUT WE ALSO HAVE YOUR SKILL TO THANK FOR THIS BEAUTIFULLY CUT *SASHIMI*, CHIEF.
Dip
Dip
LICK
CHEW
PRESS
PWAHH
YES! DELICIOUS!
THANK YOU, SIR.
SMILE
GIGGLE

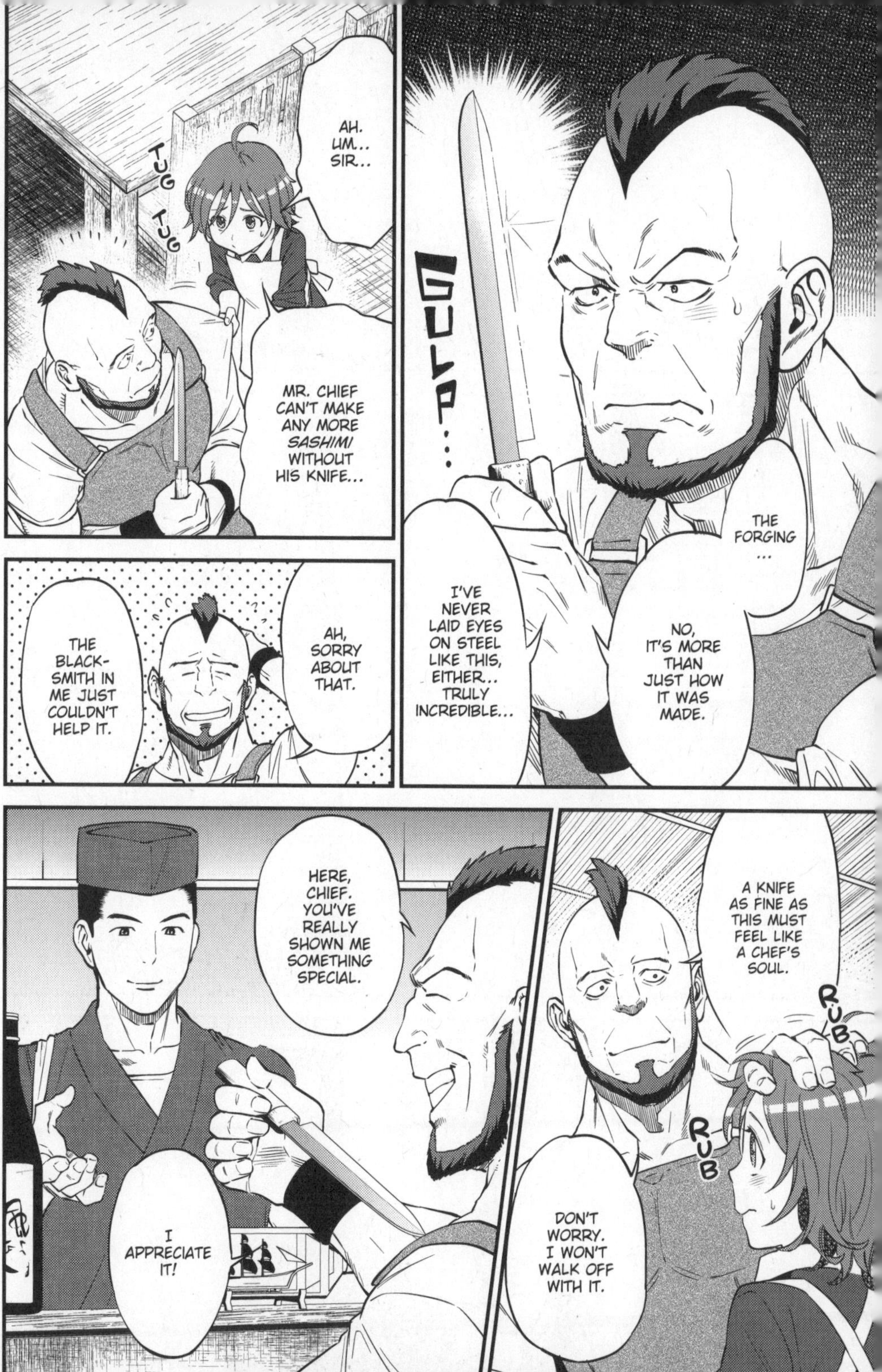
GULP...
THE FORGING...
NO, IT'S MORE THAN JUST HOW IT WAS MADE.
I'VE NEVER LAID EYES ON STEEL LIKE THIS, EITHER... TRULY INCREDIBLE...
TUG TUG
AH. UM... SIR...
MR. CHIEF CAN'T MAKE ANY MORE *SASHIMI* WITHOUT HIS KNIFE...
AH, SORRY ABOUT THAT.
THE BLACK-SMITH IN ME JUST COULDN'T HELP IT.
A KNIFE AS FINE AS THIS MUST FEEL LIKE A CHEF'S SOUL.
RUB RUB
DON'T WORRY. I WON'T WALK OFF WITH IT.
HERE, CHIEF. YOU'VE REALLY SHOWN ME SOMETHING SPECIAL.
I APPRECIATE IT!

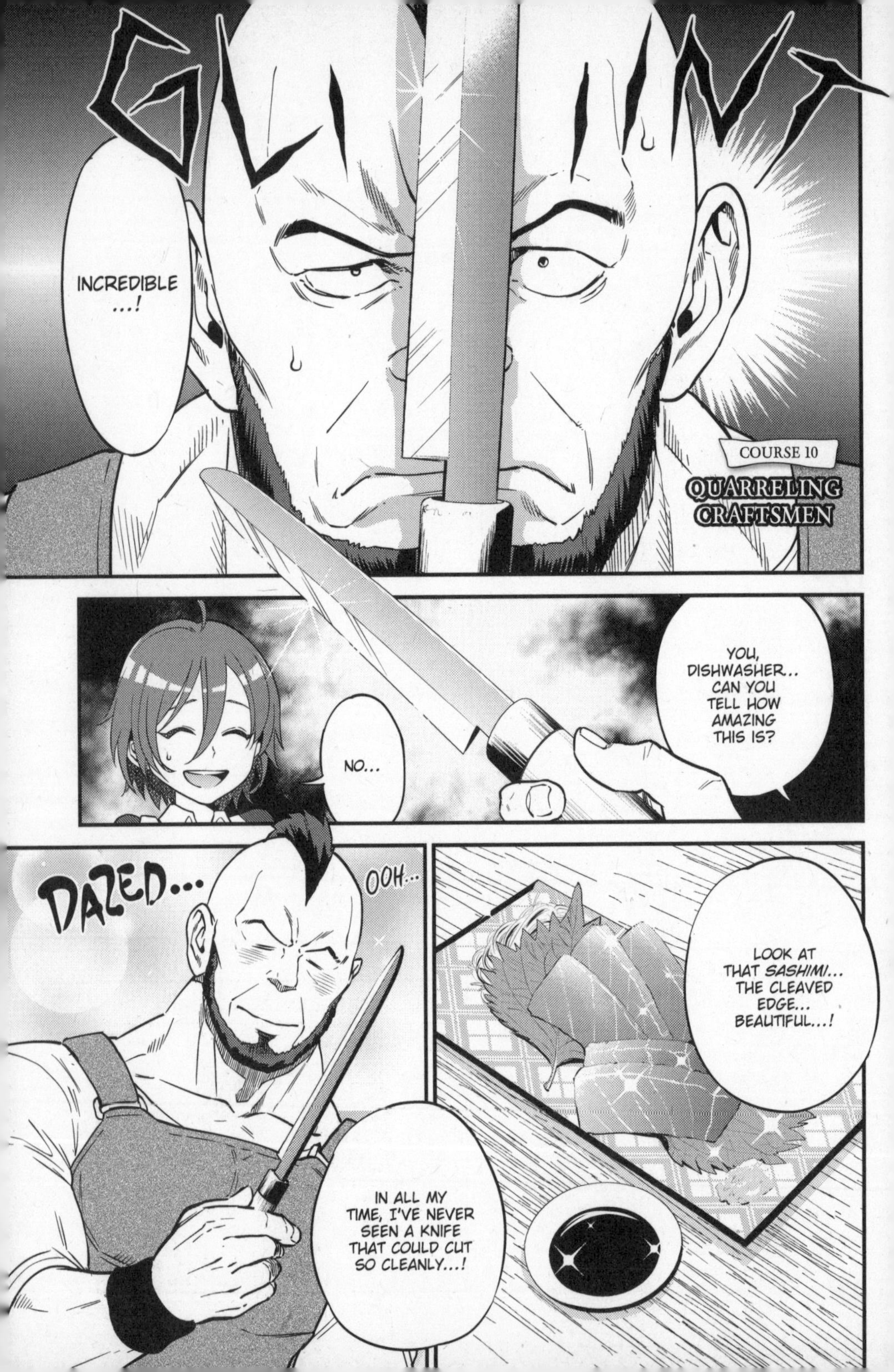
GLINT
COURSE 10
QUARRELING CRAFTSMEN
INCREDIBLE ...!
YOU, DISHWASHER... CAN YOU TELL HOW AMAZING THIS IS?
NO...
LOOK AT THAT SASHIMI... THE CLEAVED EDGE... BEAUTIFUL...!
OOH...
DAZED...
IN ALL MY TIME, I'VE NEVER SEEN A KNIFE THAT COULD CUT SO CLEANLY...!

Hirekatsu Sandwich

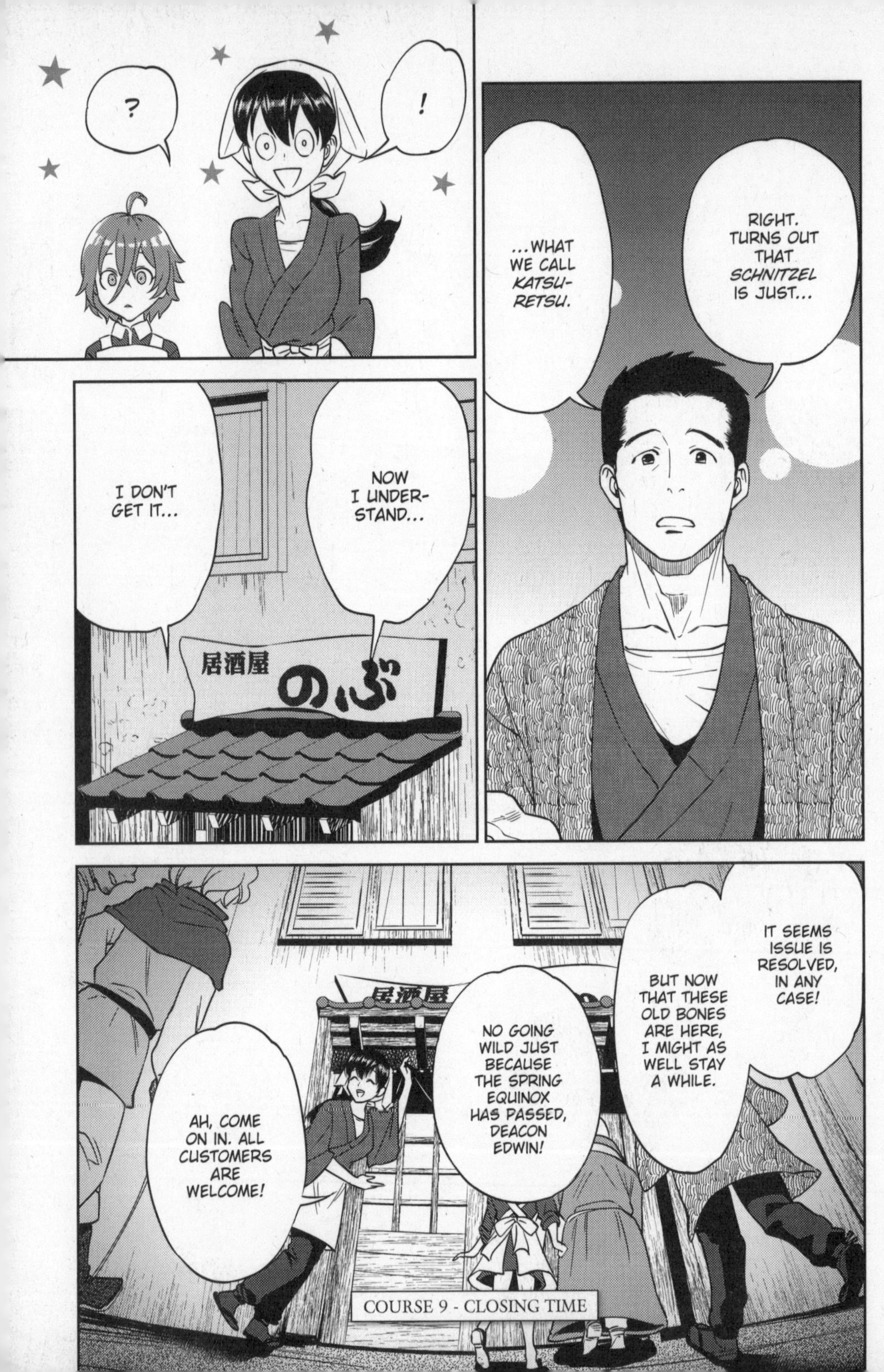
RIGHT. TURNS OUT THAT *SCHNITZEL* IS JUST...
...WHAT WE CALL *KATSU-RETSU.*
!
?
NOW I UNDER-STAND...
I DON'T GET IT...
居酒屋 のぶ
IT SEEMS ISSUE IS RESOLVED, IN ANY CASE!
BUT NOW THAT THESE OLD BONES ARE HERE, I MIGHT AS WELL STAY A WHILE.
NO GOING WILD JUST BECAUSE THE SPRING EQUINOX HAS PASSED, DEACON EDWIN!
AH, COME ON IN. ALL CUSTOMERS ARE WELCOME!
COURSE 9 - CLOSING TIME

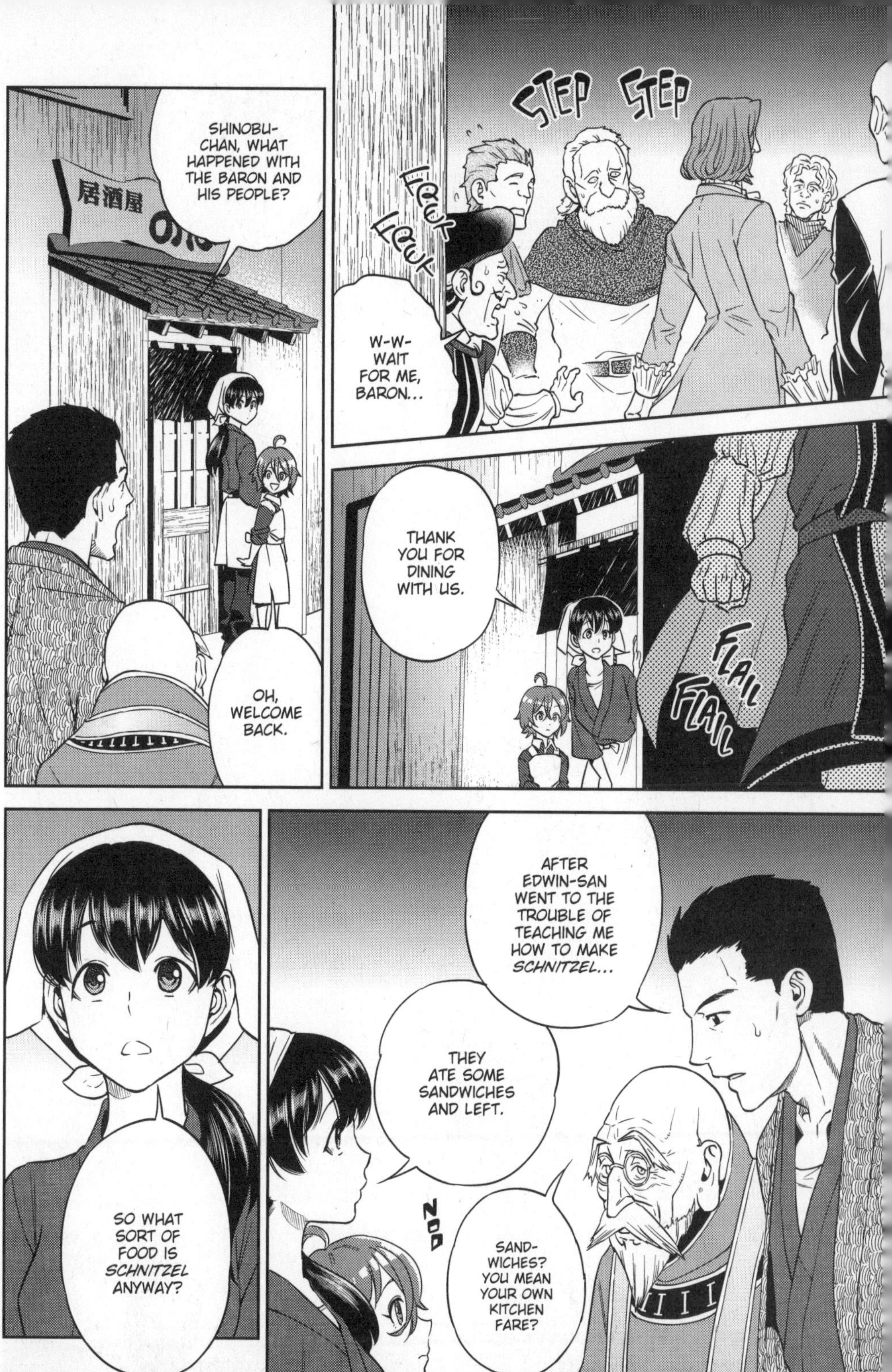
STEP STEP
FRET FRET
W-W-WAIT FOR ME, BARON...
THANK YOU FOR DINING WITH US.
FLAIL FLAIL
SHINOBU-CHAN, WHAT HAPPENED WITH THE BARON AND HIS PEOPLE?
居酒屋
OH, WELCOME BACK.
AFTER EDWIN-SAN WENT TO THE TROUBLE OF TEACHING ME HOW TO MAKE *SCHNITZEL*...
THEY ATE SOME SANDWICHES AND LEFT.
NOD
SAND-WICHES? YOU MEAN YOUR OWN KITCHEN FARE?
SO WHAT SORT OF FOOD IS *SCHNITZEL* ANYWAY?

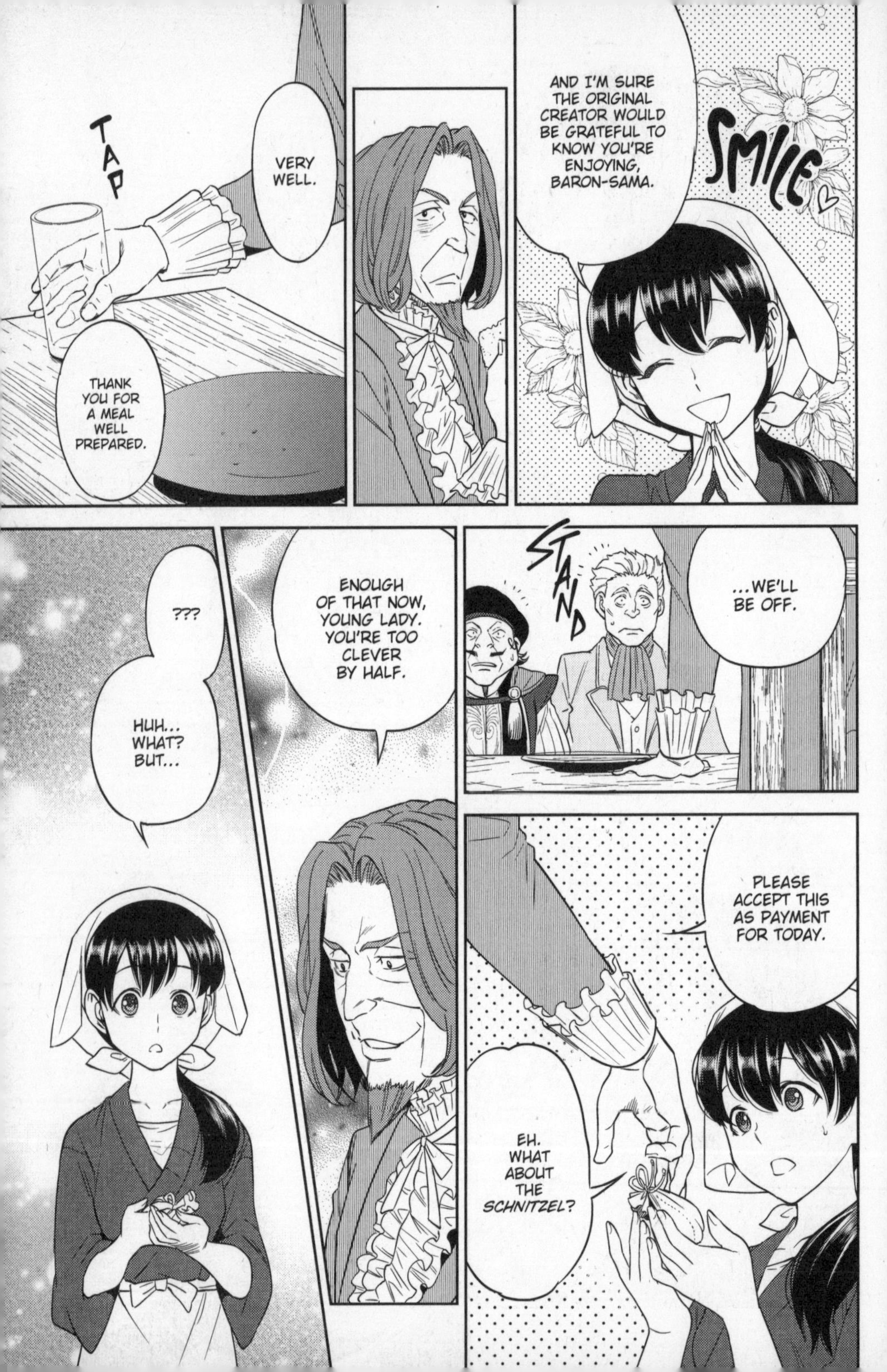
AND I'M SURE THE ORIGINAL CREATOR WOULD BE GRATEFUL TO KNOW YOU'RE ENJOYING, BARON-SAMA.
SMILE
VERY WELL.
TAP
THANK YOU FOR A MEAL WELL PREPARED.
STAND
...WE'LL BE OFF.
PLEASE ACCEPT THIS AS PAYMENT FOR TODAY.
EH. WHAT ABOUT THE *SCHNITZEL*?
ENOUGH OF THAT NOW, YOUNG LADY. YOU'RE TOO CLEVER BY HALF.
???
HUH... WHAT? BUT...

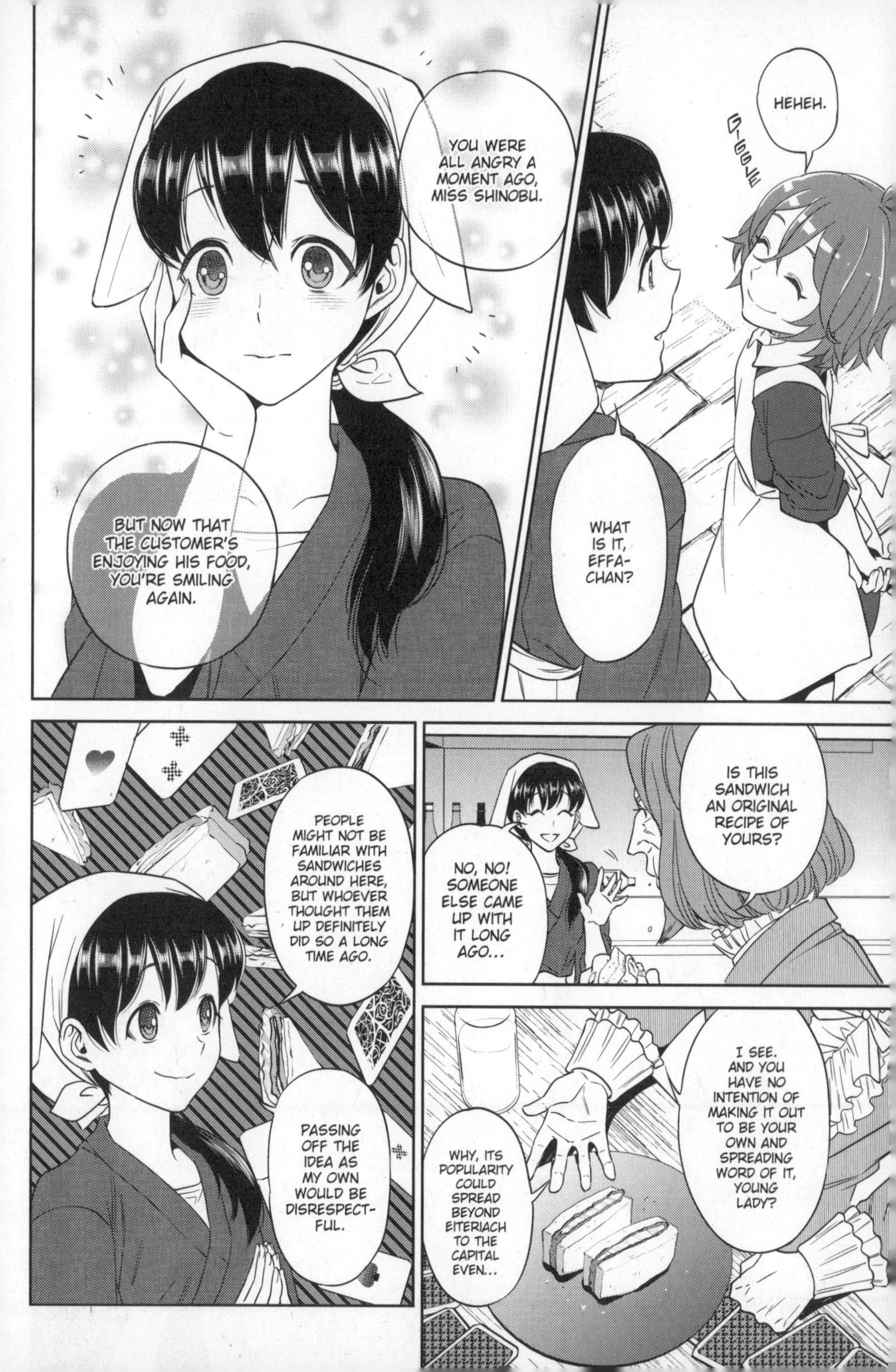
HEHEH.
GIGGLE
WHAT IS IT, EFFA-CHAN?
YOU WERE ALL ANGRY A MOMENT AGO, MISS SHINOBU.
BUT NOW THAT THE CUSTOMER'S ENJOYING HIS FOOD, YOU'RE SMILING AGAIN.
IS THIS SANDWICH AN ORIGINAL RECIPE OF YOURS?
NO, NO! SOMEONE ELSE CAME UP WITH IT LONG AGO...
I SEE. AND YOU HAVE NO INTENTION OF MAKING IT OUT TO BE YOUR OWN AND SPREADING WORD OF IT, YOUNG LADY?
WHY, ITS POPULARITY COULD SPREAD BEYOND EITERIACH TO THE CAPITAL EVEN...
PEOPLE MIGHT NOT BE FAMILIAR WITH SANDWICHES AROUND HERE, BUT WHOEVER THOUGHT THEM UP DEFINITELY DID SO A LONG TIME AGO.
PASSING OFF THE IDEA AS MY OWN WOULD BE DISRESPECT-FUL.

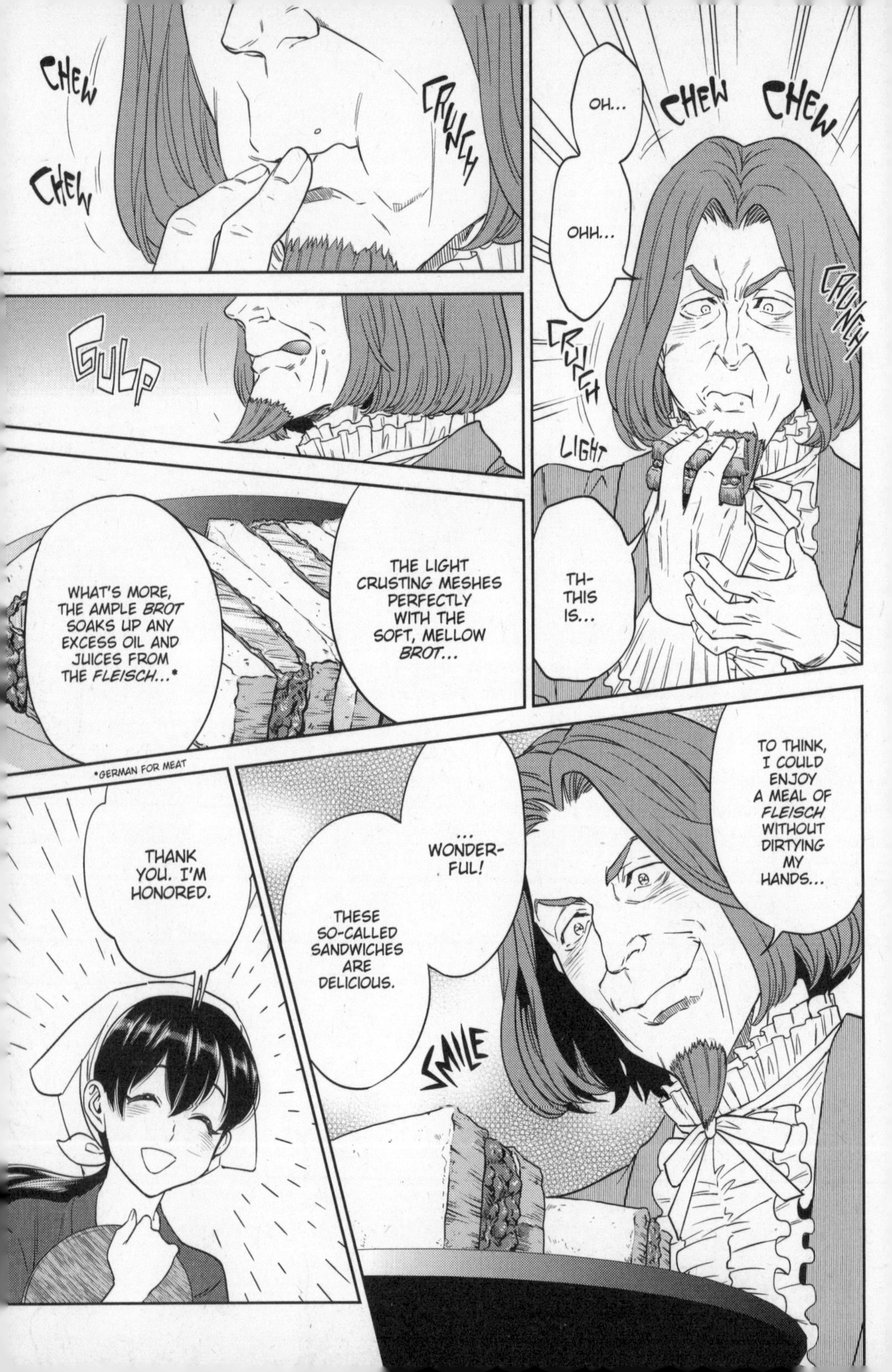

OH...
CHEW
CHEW
OHH...
CRUNCH
CRUNCH
LIGHT
TH-THIS IS...
CHEW
CRUNCH
CHEW
GULP
THE LIGHT CRUSTING MESHES PERFECTLY WITH THE SOFT, MELLOW *BROT*...
WHAT'S MORE, THE AMPLE *BROT* SOAKS UP ANY EXCESS OIL AND JUICES FROM THE *FLEISCH*...*
TO THINK, I COULD ENJOY A MEAL OF *FLEISCH* WITHOUT DIRTYING MY HANDS...
... WONDERFUL!
THESE SO-CALLED SANDWICHES ARE DELICIOUS.
SMILE
THANK YOU. I'M HONORED.

*GERMAN FOR MEAT

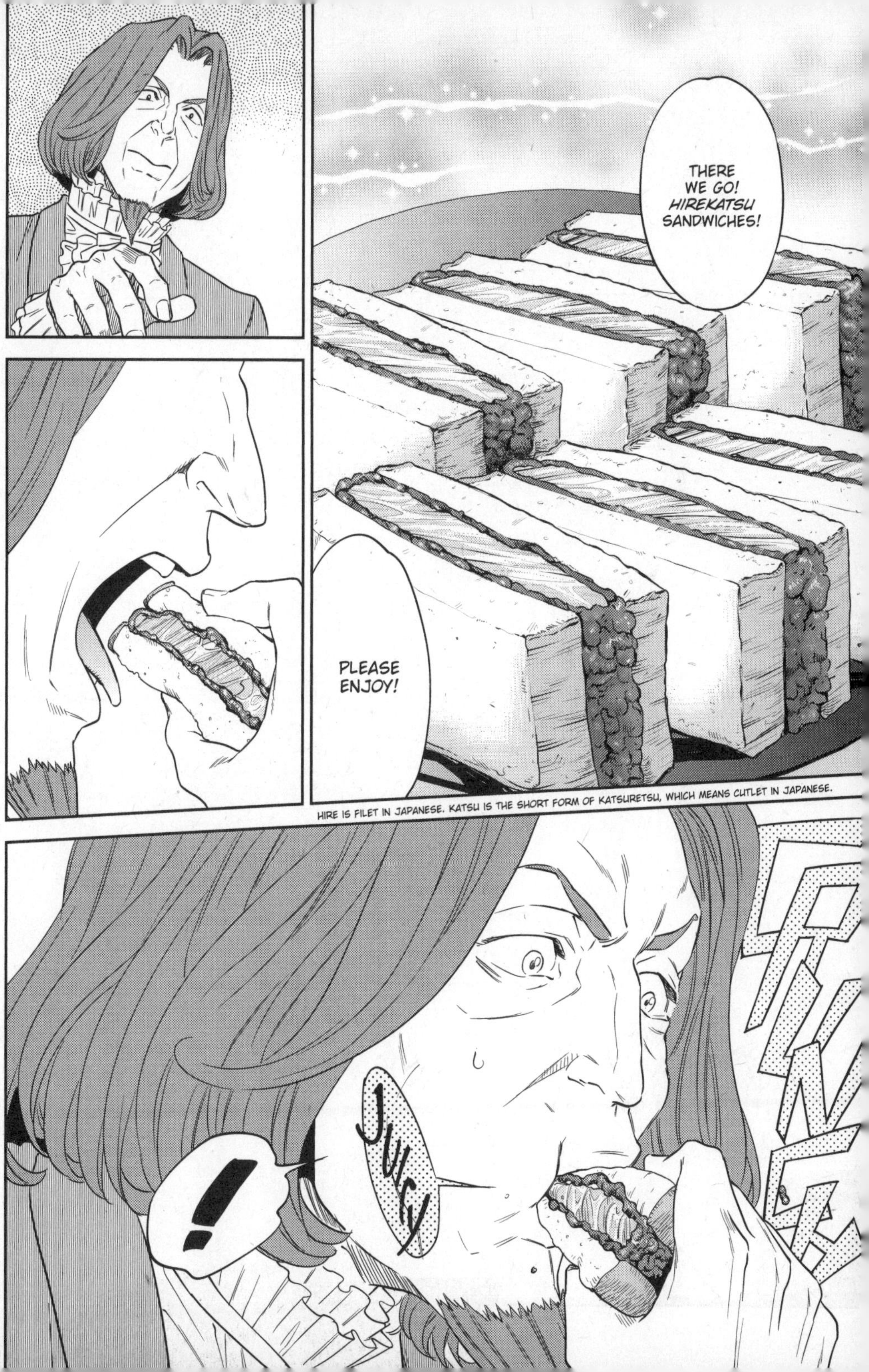
THERE WE GO! HIREKATSU SANDWICHES!
PLEASE ENJOY!
JUICY
!

HIRE IS FILET IN JAPANESE. KATSU IS THE SHORT FORM OF KATSURETSU, WHICH MEANS CUTLET IN JAPANESE.

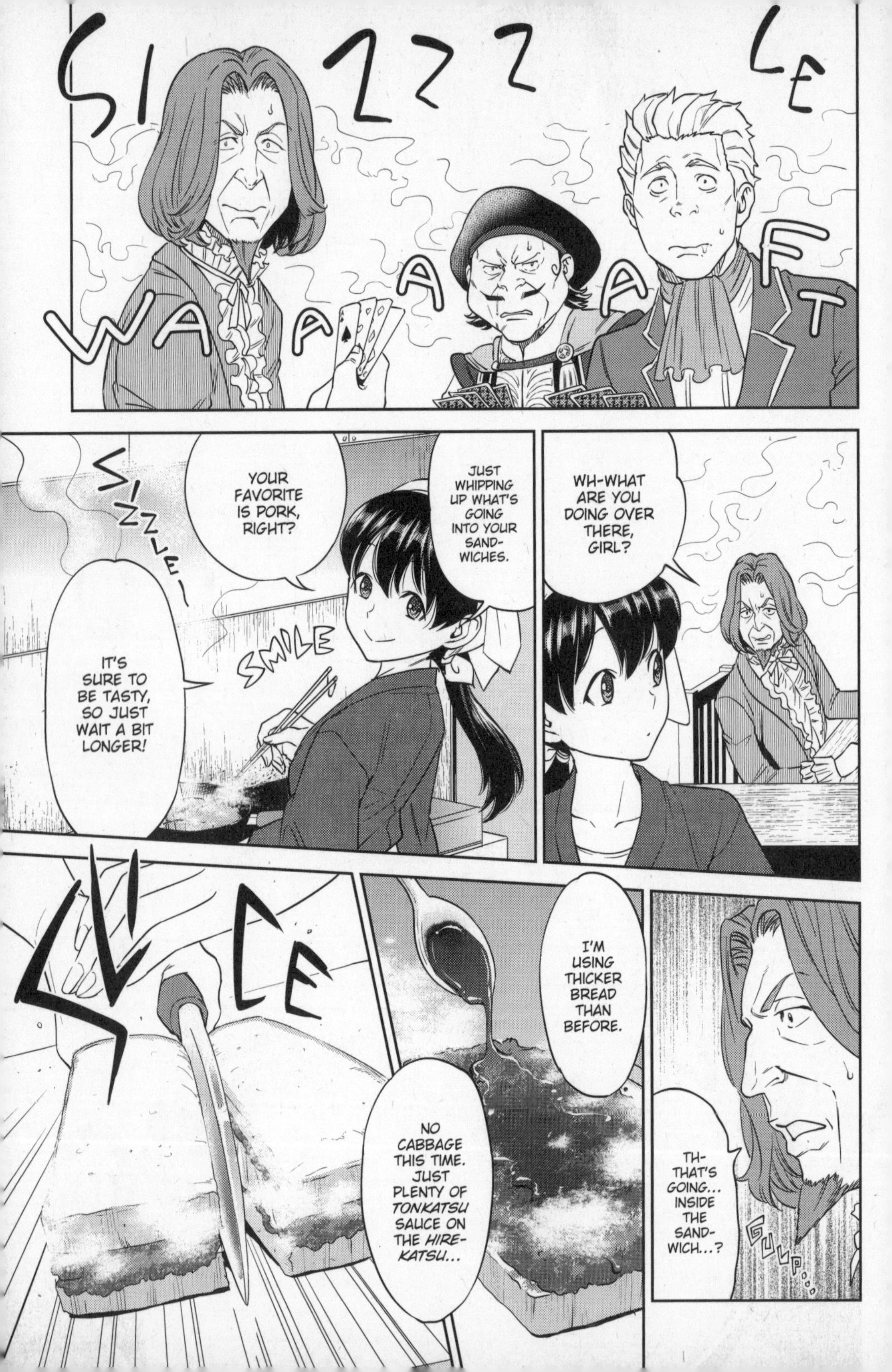
SIZZZZLE
WAAAAFT
WH-WHAT ARE YOU DOING OVER THERE, GIRL?
JUST WHIPPING UP WHAT'S GOING INTO YOUR SANDWICHES.
YOUR FAVORITE IS PORK, RIGHT?
SIZZLE
SMILE
IT'S SURE TO BE TASTY, SO JUST WAIT A BIT LONGER!
TH-THAT'S GOING... INSIDE THE SANDWICH...?
GULP...
I'M USING THICKER BREAD THAN BEFORE.
NO CABBAGE THIS TIME. JUST PLENTY OF *TONKATSU* SAUCE ON THE *HIRE-KATSU*...
SLICE

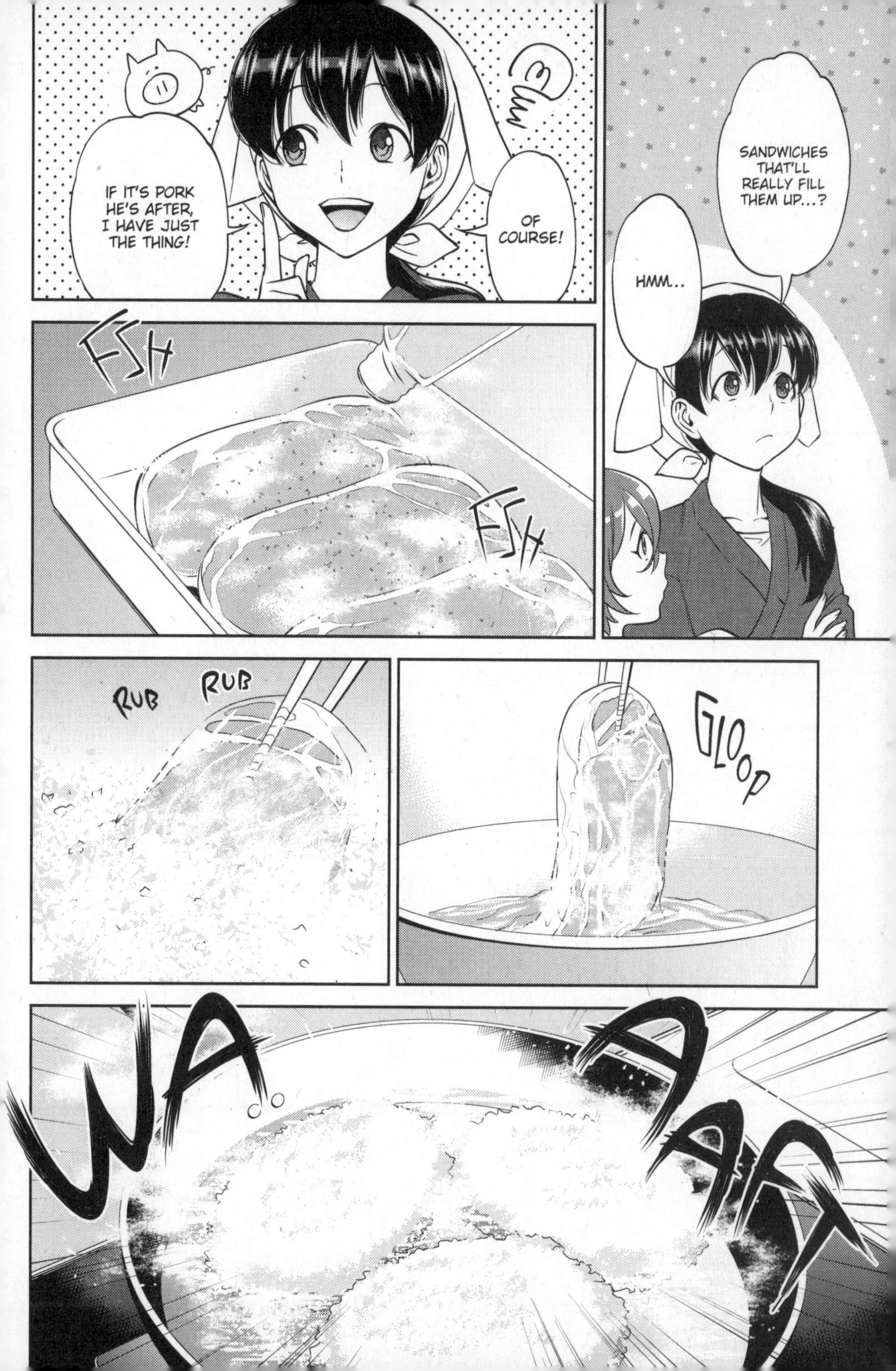

SANDWICHES THAT'LL REALLY FILL THEM UP...?
HMM...
OF COURSE!
IF IT'S PORK HE'S AFTER, I HAVE JUST THE THING!
FSH
FSH
GLOOP
RUB RUB
WA
AAA

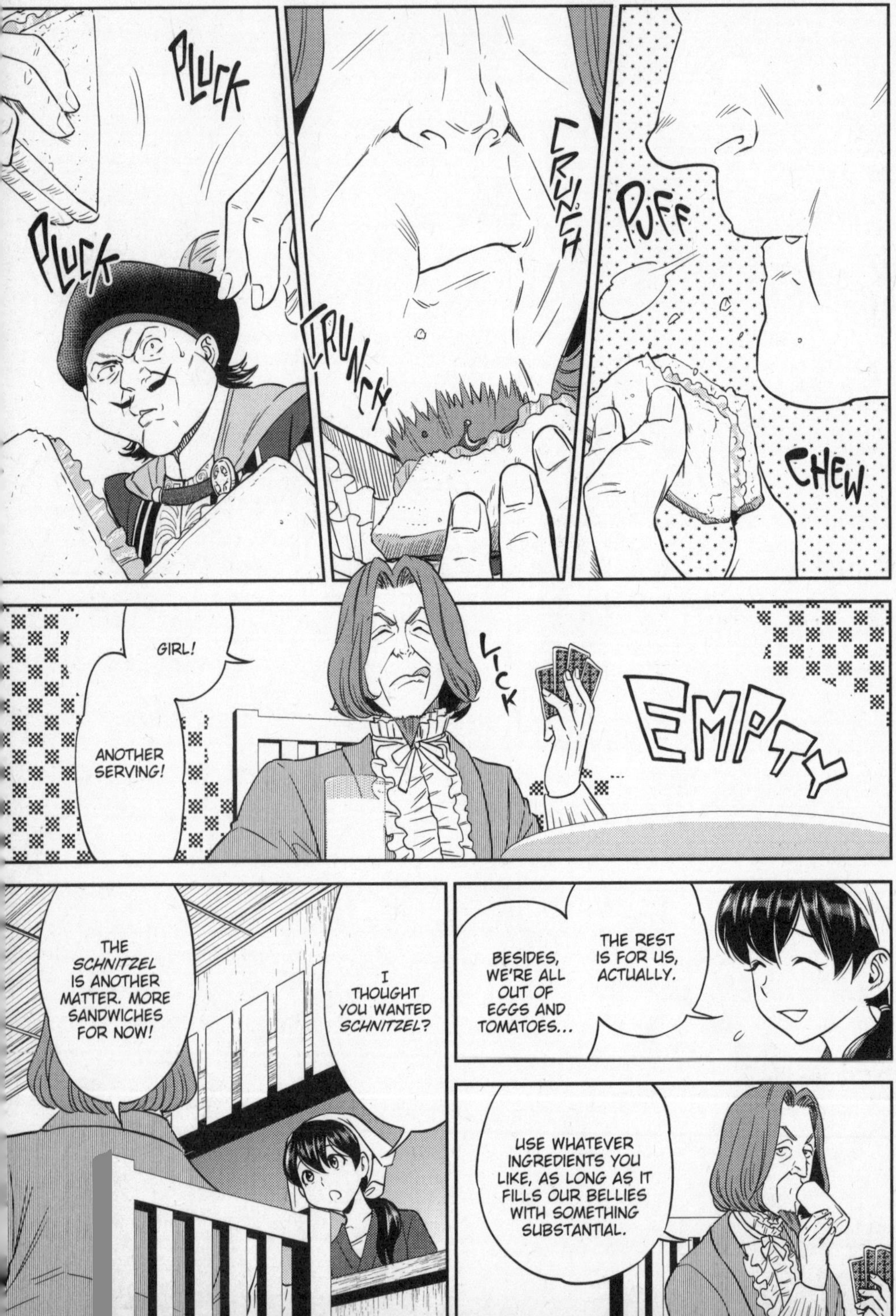
PLUCK
PLUCK
CRUNCH
CRUNCH
PUFF
CHEW
GIRL!
ANOTHER SERVING!
LICK
EMPTY
I THOUGHT YOU WANTED *SCHNITZEL*?
THE *SCHNITZEL* IS ANOTHER MATTER. MORE SANDWICHES FOR NOW!
THE REST IS FOR US, ACTUALLY.
BESIDES, WE'RE ALL OUT OF EGGS AND TOMATOES...
USE WHATEVER INGREDIENTS YOU LIKE, AS LONG AS IT FILLS OUR BELLIES WITH SOMETHING SUBSTANTIAL.

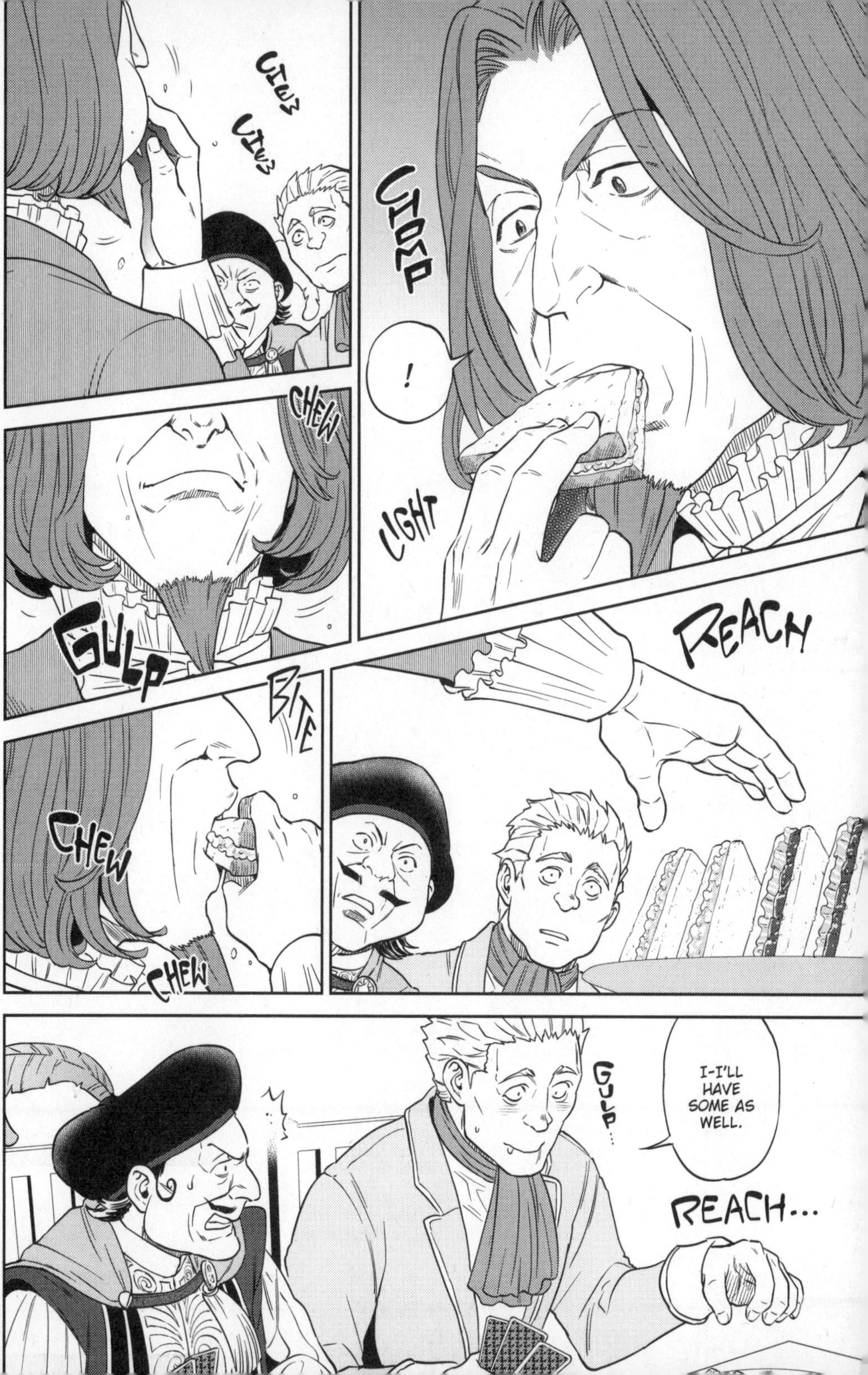
CHOMP
!
LIGHT
CHEW
CHEW
CHEW
GULP
REACH
BITE
CHEW
CHEW
GULP...
I-I'LL HAVE SOME AS WELL.
REACH...

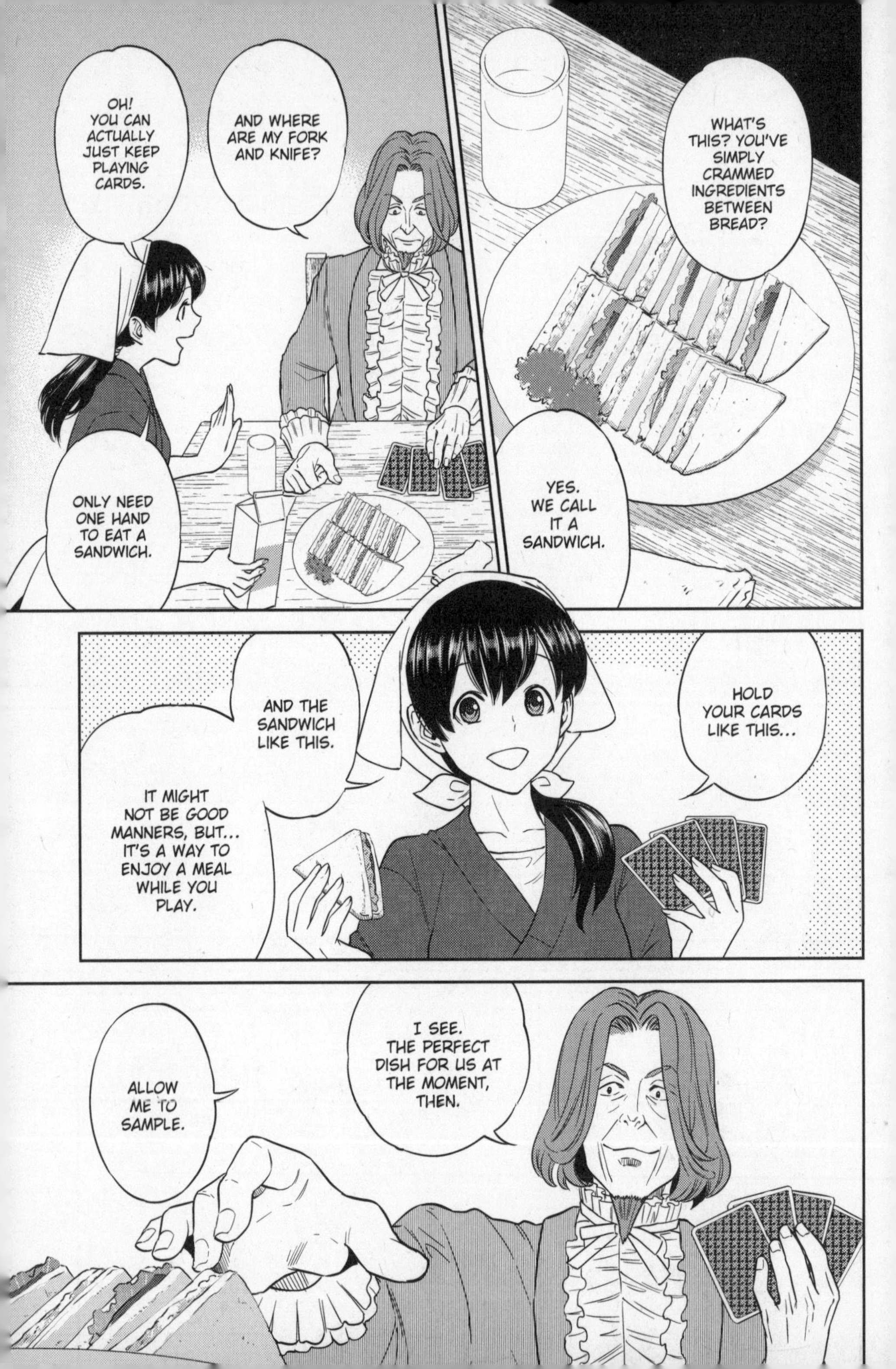
WHAT'S THIS? YOU'VE SIMPLY CRAMMED INGREDIENTS BETWEEN BREAD?
YES. WE CALL IT A SANDWICH.
AND WHERE ARE MY FORK AND KNIFE?
OH! YOU CAN ACTUALLY JUST KEEP PLAYING CARDS.
ONLY NEED ONE HAND TO EAT A SANDWICH.
HOLD YOUR CARDS LIKE THIS...
AND THE SANDWICH LIKE THIS.
IT MIGHT NOT BE GOOD MANNERS, BUT... IT'S A WAY TO ENJOY A MEAL WHILE YOU PLAY.
I SEE. THE PERFECT DISH FOR US AT THE MOMENT, THEN.
ALLOW ME TO SAMPLE.

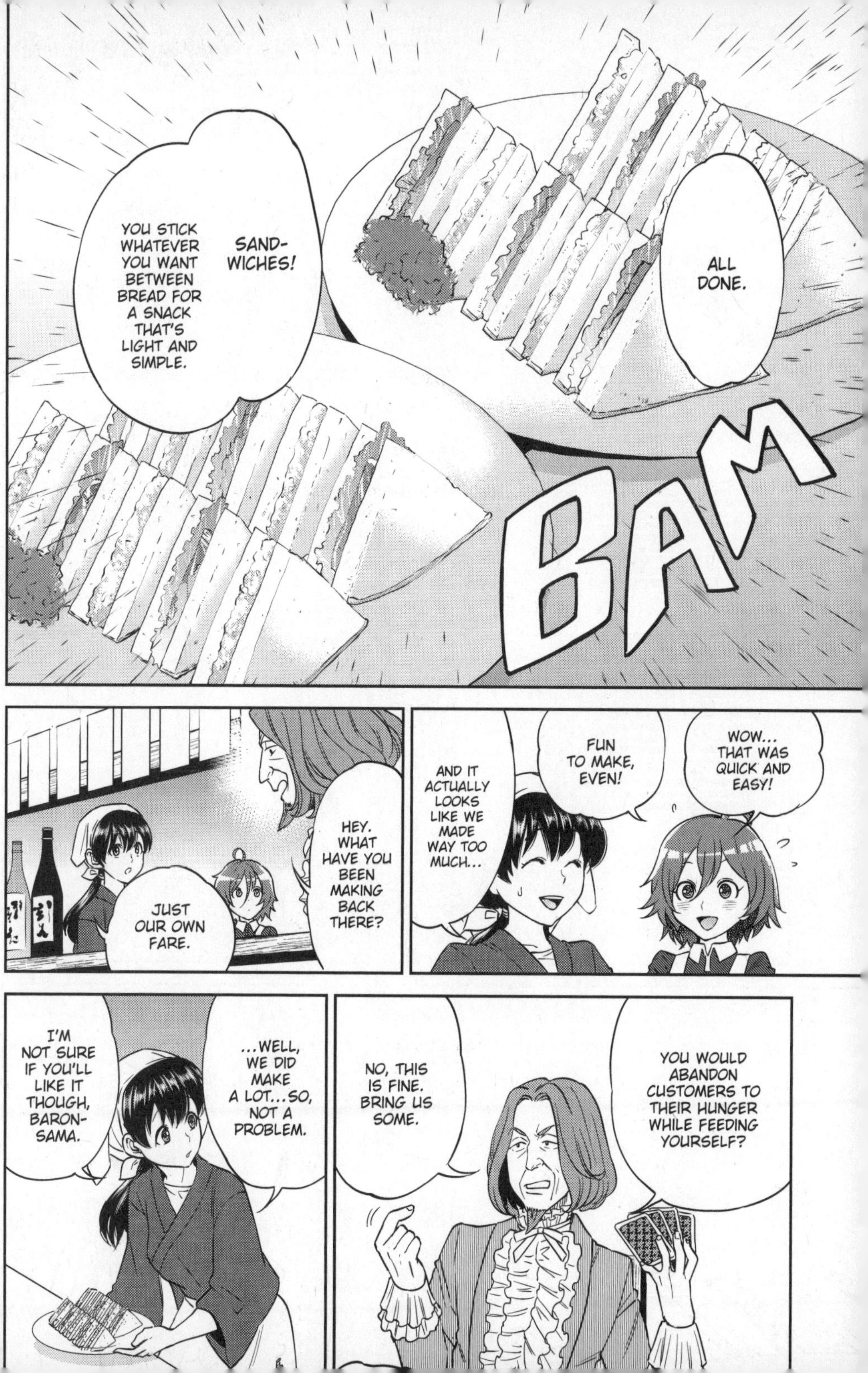
ALL DONE.
SANDWICHES!
YOU STICK WHATEVER YOU WANT BETWEEN BREAD FOR A SNACK THAT'S LIGHT AND SIMPLE.
BAM
WOW... THAT WAS QUICK AND EASY!
FUN TO MAKE, EVEN!
AND IT ACTUALLY LOOKS LIKE WE MADE WAY TOO MUCH...
HEY. WHAT HAVE YOU BEEN MAKING BACK THERE?
JUST OUR OWN FARE.
YOU WOULD ABANDON CUSTOMERS TO THEIR HUNGER WHILE FEEDING YOURSELF?
NO, THIS IS FINE. BRING US SOME.
...WELL, WE DID MAKE A LOT...SO, NOT A PROBLEM.
I'M NOT SURE IF YOU'LL LIKE IT THOUGH, BARON-SAMA.

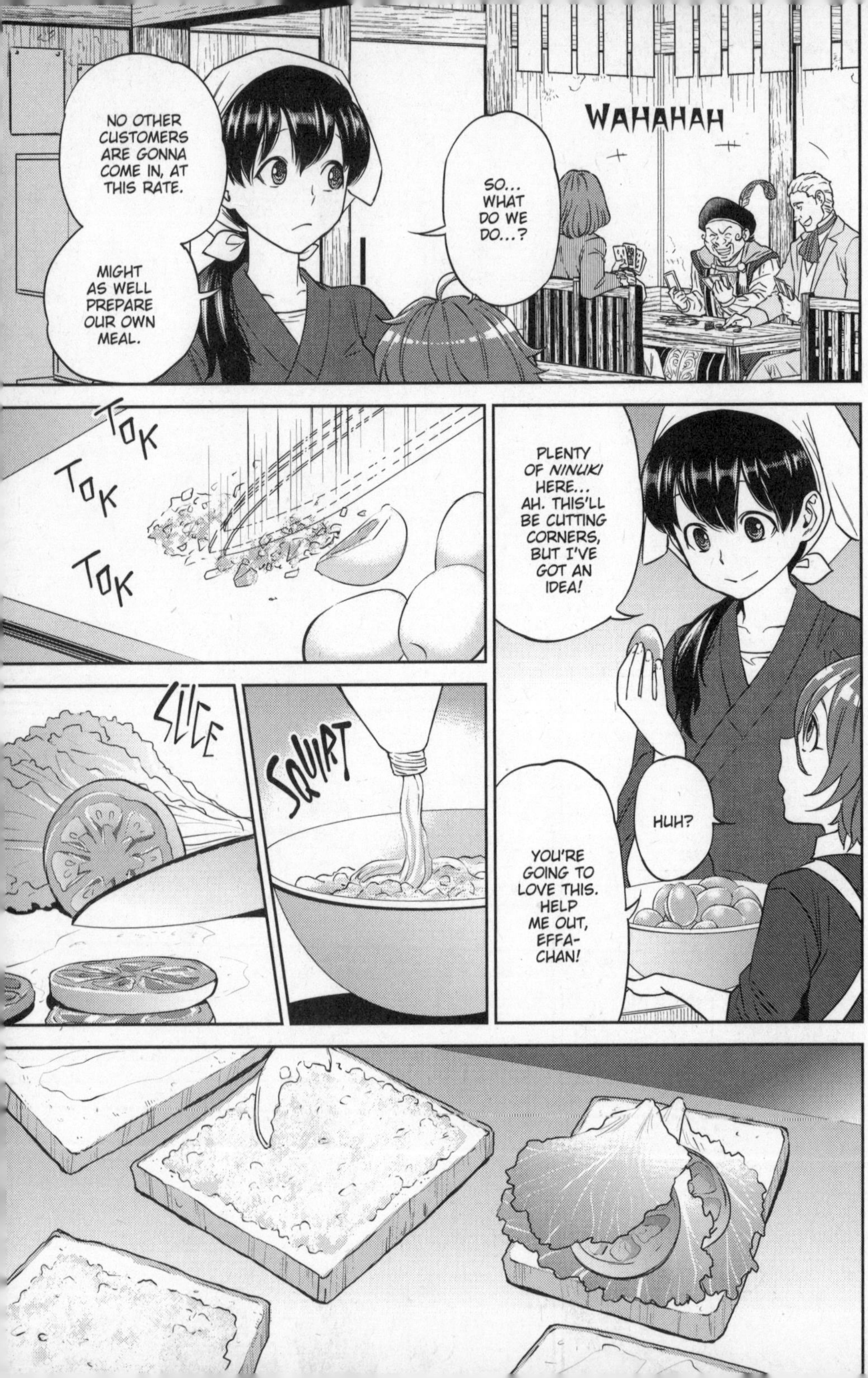
WAHAHAH
SO... WHAT DO WE DO...?
NO OTHER CUSTOMERS ARE GONNA COME IN, AT THIS RATE.
MIGHT AS WELL PREPARE OUR OWN MEAL.
PLENTY OF *NINUKI* HERE... AH. THIS'LL BE CUTTING CORNERS, BUT I'VE GOT AN IDEA!
HUH?
YOU'RE GOING TO LOVE THIS. HELP ME OUT, EFFA-CHAN!
TOK TOK TOK
SQUIRT
SLICE

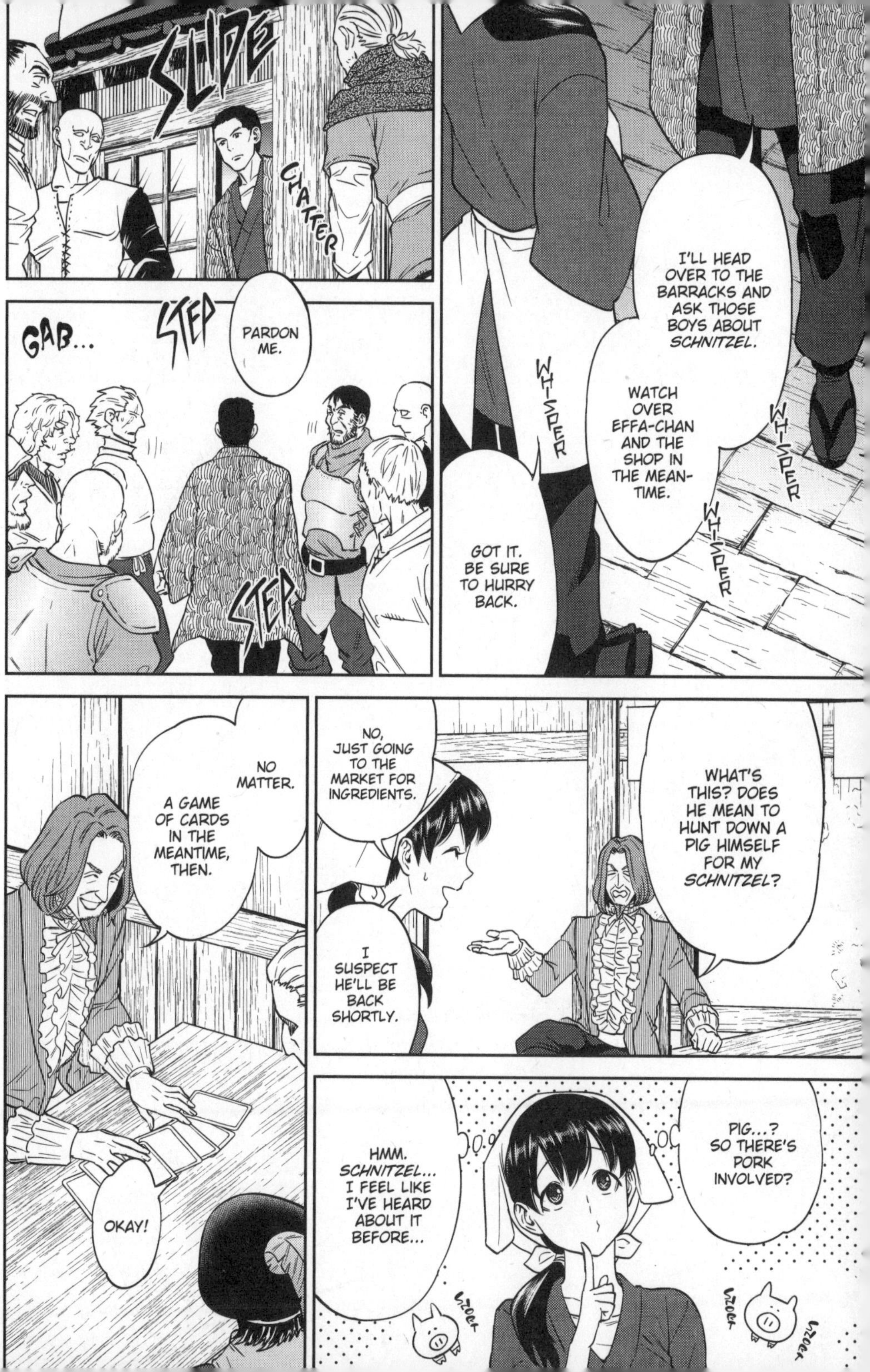
I'LL HEAD OVER TO THE BARRACKS AND ASK THOSE BOYS ABOUT SCHNITZEL.
WATCH OVER EFFA-CHAN AND THE SHOP IN THE MEAN-TIME.
WHISPER
WHISPER
WHISPER
GOT IT. BE SURE TO HURRY BACK.
SLIDE
CHATTER
STEP
PARDON ME.
GAB...
STEP
WHAT'S THIS? DOES HE MEAN TO HUNT DOWN A PIG HIMSELF FOR MY SCHNITZEL?
NO, JUST GOING TO THE MARKET FOR INGREDIENTS.
I SUSPECT HE'LL BE BACK SHORTLY.
PIG...? SO THERE'S PORK INVOLVED?
HMM. SCHNITZEL... I FEEL LIKE I'VE HEARD ABOUT IT BEFORE...
NO MATTER.
A GAME OF CARDS IN THE MEANTIME, THEN.
OKAY!

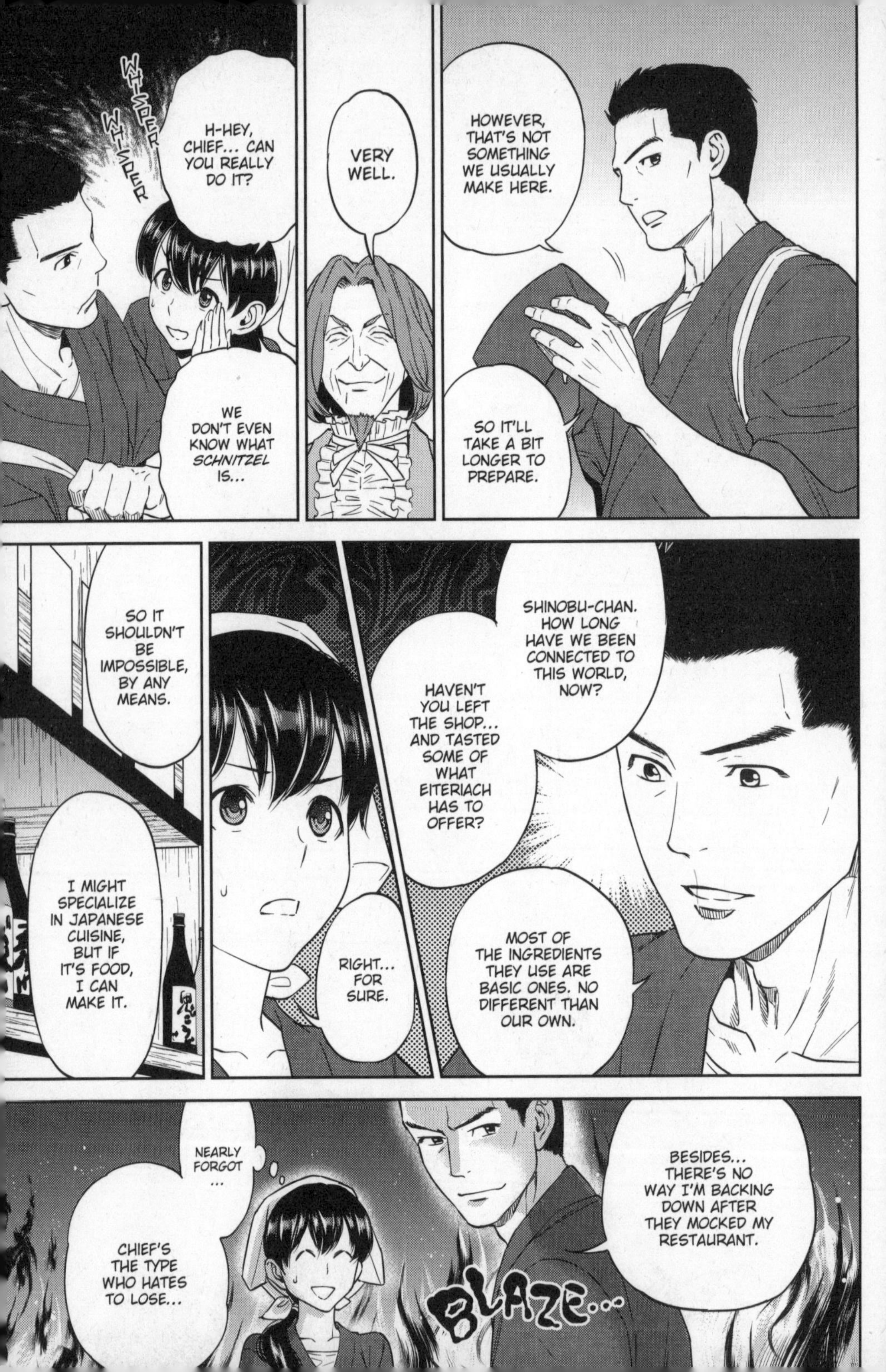
HOWEVER, THAT'S NOT SOMETHING WE USUALLY MAKE HERE.
SO IT'LL TAKE A BIT LONGER TO PREPARE.
VERY WELL.
WHISPER WHISPER
H-HEY, CHIEF... CAN YOU REALLY DO IT?
WE DON'T EVEN KNOW WHAT *SCHNITZEL* IS...
SHINOBU-CHAN. HOW LONG HAVE WE BEEN CONNECTED TO THIS WORLD, NOW?
HAVEN'T YOU LEFT THE SHOP... AND TASTED SOME OF WHAT EITERIACH HAS TO OFFER?
MOST OF THE INGREDIENTS THEY USE ARE BASIC ONES. NO DIFFERENT THAN OUR OWN.
RIGHT... FOR SURE.
SO IT SHOULDN'T BE IMPOSSIBLE, BY ANY MEANS.
I MIGHT SPECIALIZE IN JAPANESE CUISINE, BUT IF IT'S FOOD, I CAN MAKE IT.
BESIDES... THERE'S NO WAY I'M BACKING DOWN AFTER THEY MOCKED MY RESTAURANT.
BLAZE...
NEARLY FORGOT...
CHIEF'S THE TYPE WHO HATES TO LOSE...

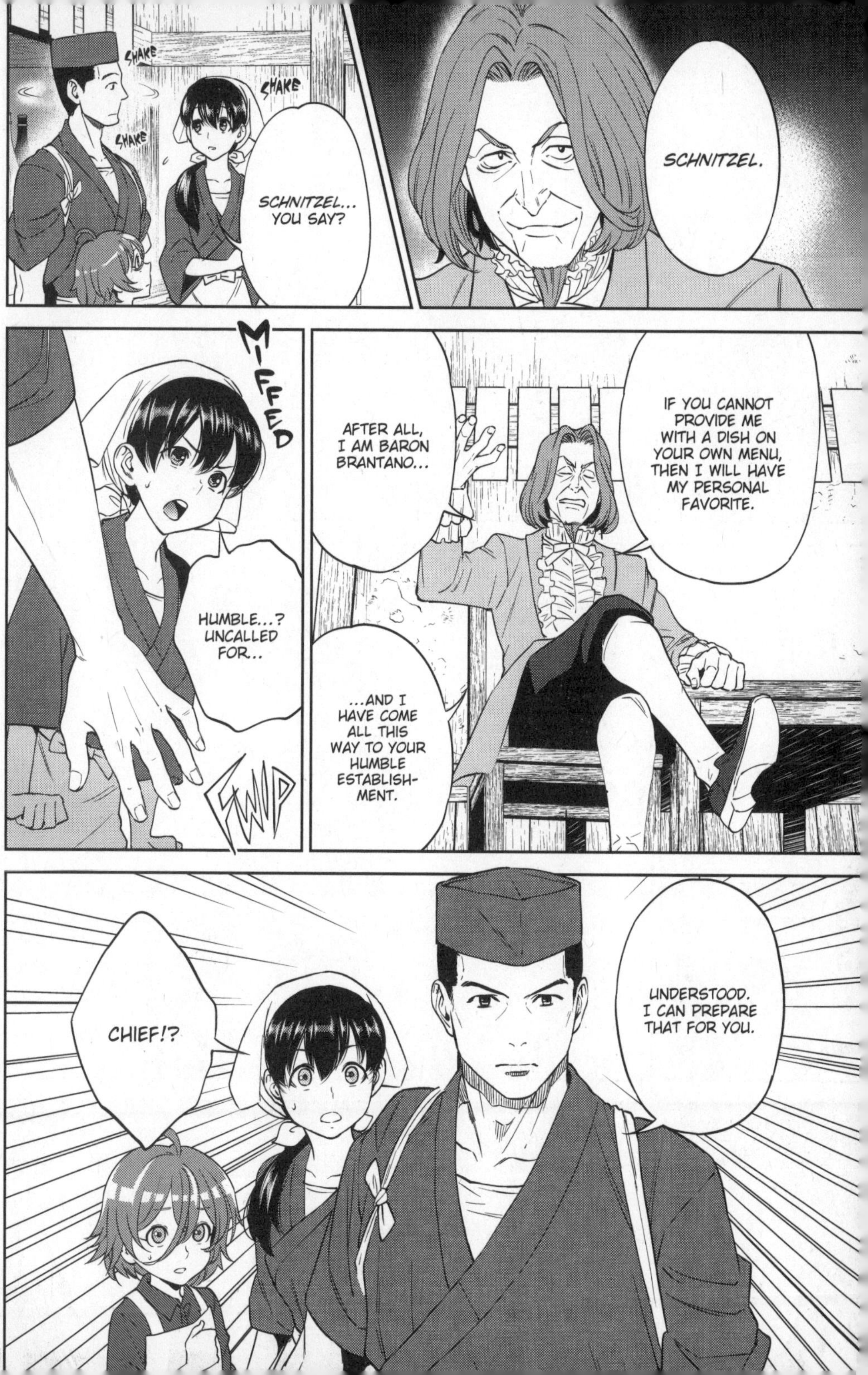
SCHNITZEL.
SHAKE
SHAKE
SHAKE
SCHNITZEL... YOU SAY?
IF YOU CANNOT PROVIDE ME WITH A DISH ON YOUR OWN MENU, THEN I WILL HAVE MY PERSONAL FAVORITE.
AFTER ALL, I AM BARON BRANTANO...
...AND I HAVE COME ALL THIS WAY TO YOUR HUMBLE ESTABLISH-MENT.
MIFFED
HUMBLE...? UNCALLED FOR...
SWIP
UNDERSTOOD. I CAN PREPARE THAT FOR YOU.
CHIEF!?

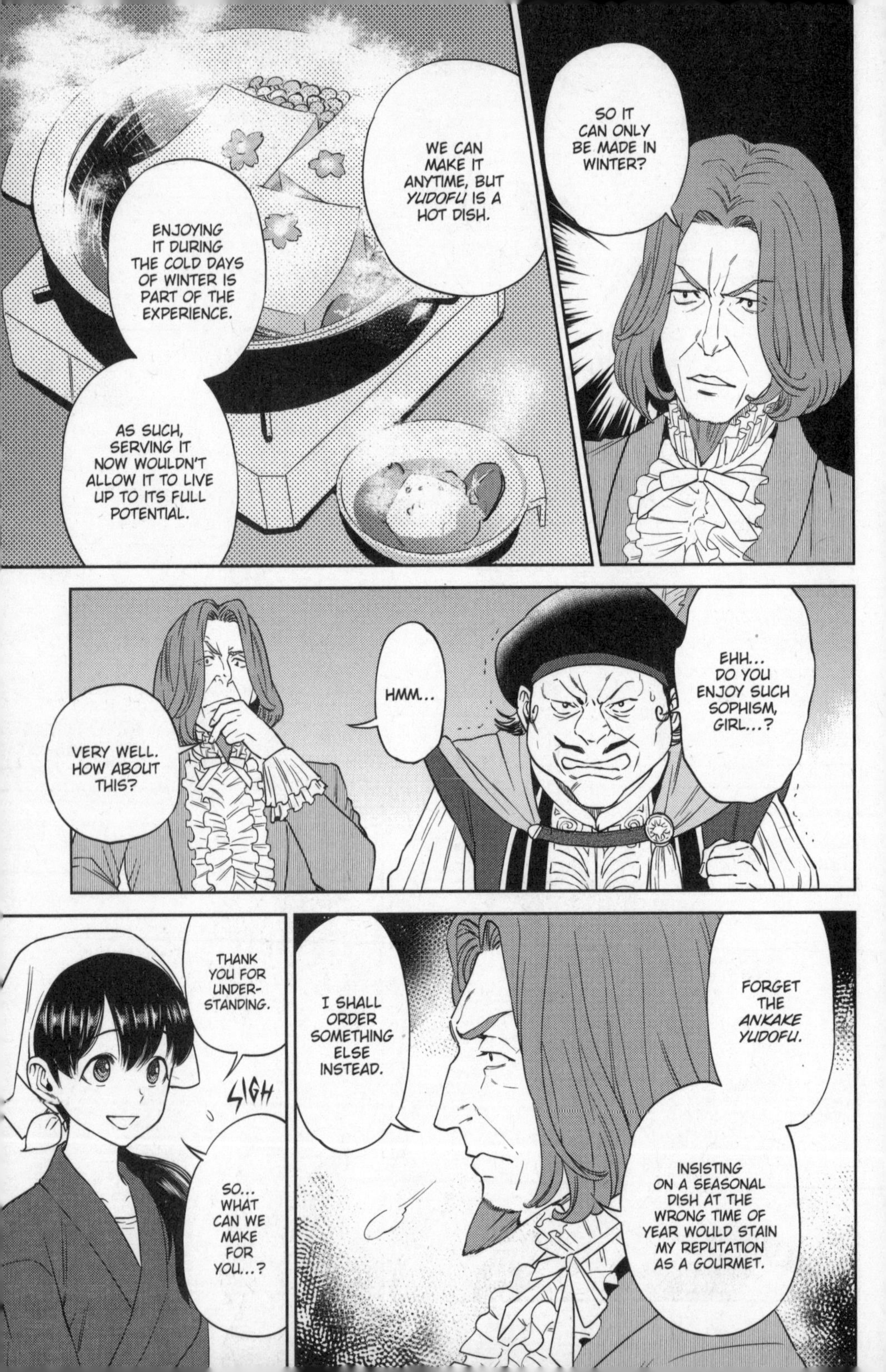
SO IT CAN ONLY BE MADE IN WINTER?
WE CAN MAKE IT ANYTIME, BUT *YUDOFU* IS A HOT DISH.
ENJOYING IT DURING THE COLD DAYS OF WINTER IS PART OF THE EXPERIENCE.
AS SUCH, SERVING IT NOW WOULDN'T ALLOW IT TO LIVE UP TO ITS FULL POTENTIAL.
EHH... DO YOU ENJOY SUCH SOPHISM, GIRL...?
HMM...
VERY WELL. HOW ABOUT THIS?
FORGET THE *ANKAKE YUDOFU.*
INSISTING ON A SEASONAL DISH AT THE WRONG TIME OF YEAR WOULD STAIN MY REPUTATION AS A GOURMET.
I SHALL ORDER SOMETHING ELSE INSTEAD.
THANK YOU FOR UNDER-STANDING.
SIGH
SO... WHAT CAN WE MAKE FOR YOU...?

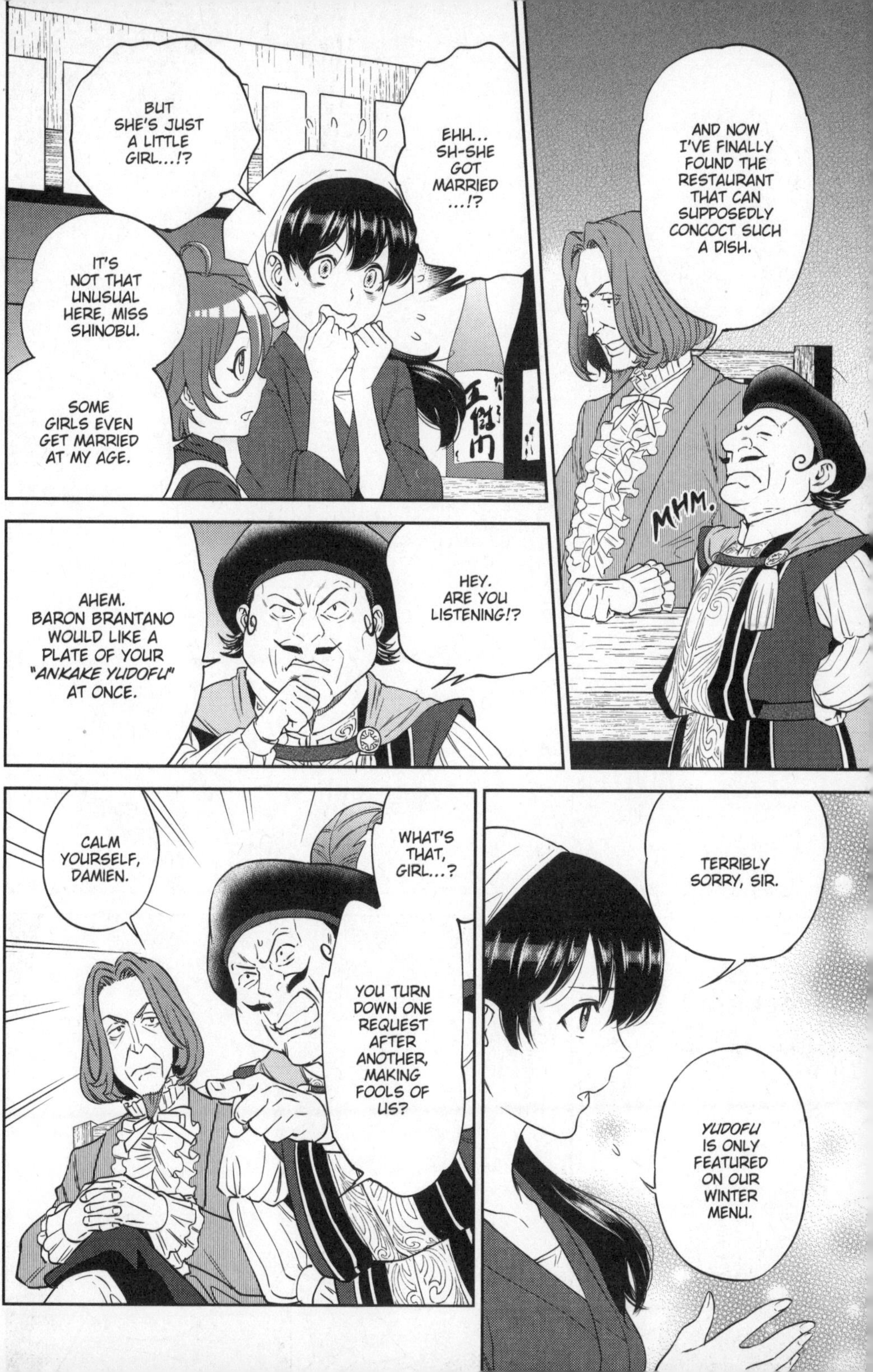
AND NOW I'VE FINALLY FOUND THE RESTAURANT THAT CAN SUPPOSEDLY CONCOCT SUCH A DISH.
MHM.
EHH... SH-SHE GOT MARRIED ...!?
BUT SHE'S JUST A LITTLE GIRL...!?
IT'S NOT THAT UNUSUAL HERE, MISS SHINOBU.
SOME GIRLS EVEN GET MARRIED AT MY AGE.
HEY. ARE YOU LISTENING!?
AHEM. BARON BRANTANO WOULD LIKE A PLATE OF YOUR "*ANKAKE YUDOFU*" AT ONCE.
TERRIBLY SORRY, SIR.
YUDOFU IS ONLY FEATURED ON OUR WINTER MENU.
WHAT'S THAT, GIRL...?
YOU TURN DOWN ONE REQUEST AFTER ANOTHER, MAKING FOOLS OF US?
CALM YOURSELF, DAMIEN.

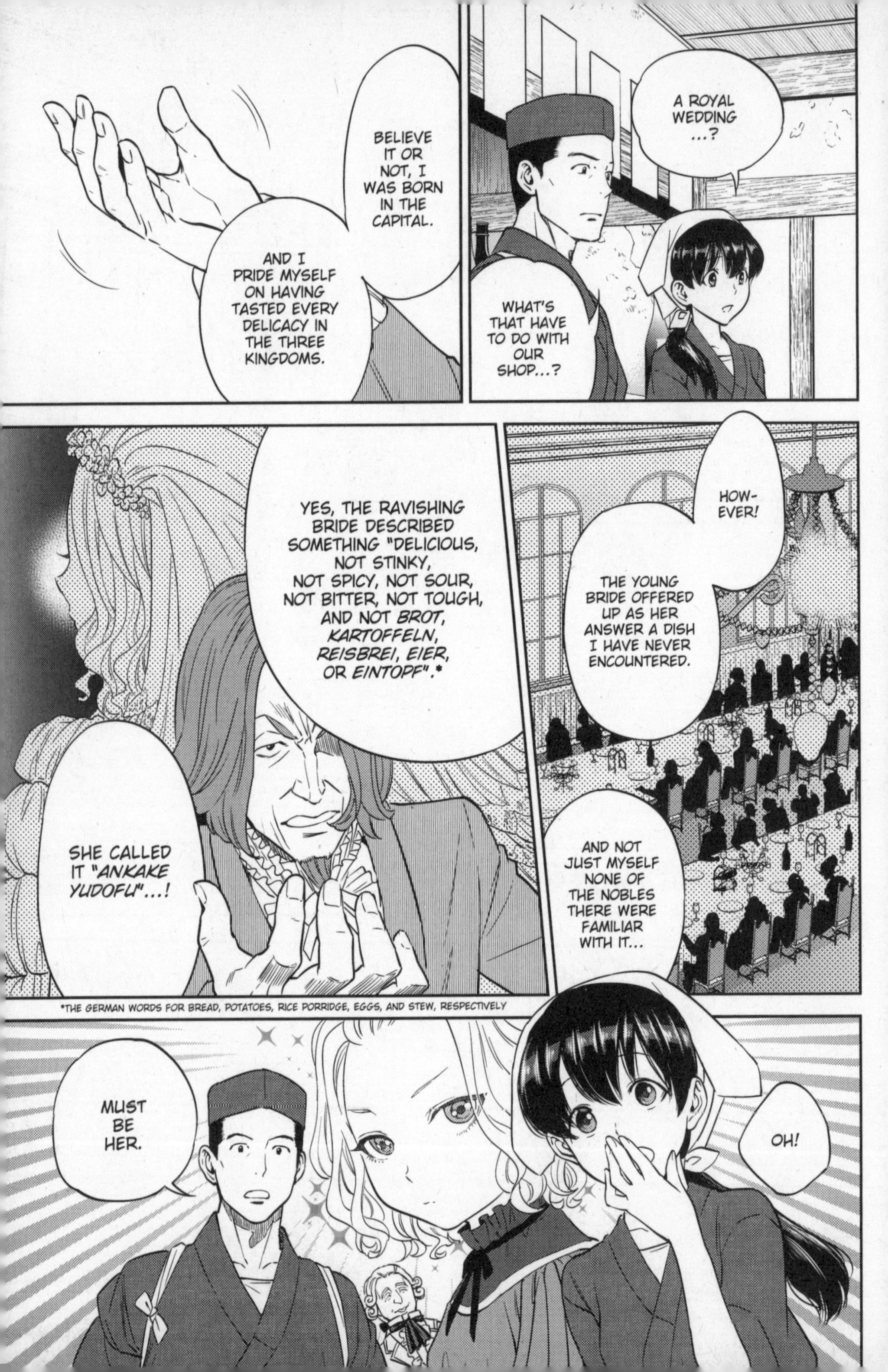
A ROYAL WEDDING ...?
WHAT'S THAT HAVE TO DO WITH OUR SHOP...?
BELIEVE IT OR NOT, I WAS BORN IN THE CAPITAL.
AND I PRIDE MYSELF ON HAVING TASTED EVERY DELICACY IN THE THREE KINGDOMS.
HOW-EVER!
THE YOUNG BRIDE OFFERED UP AS HER ANSWER A DISH I HAVE NEVER ENCOUNTERED.
AND NOT JUST MYSELF NONE OF THE NOBLES THERE WERE FAMILIAR WITH IT...
YES, THE RAVISHING BRIDE DESCRIBED SOMETHING "DELICIOUS, NOT STINKY, NOT SPICY, NOT SOUR, NOT BITTER, NOT TOUGH, AND NOT *BROT, KARTOFFELN, REISBREI, EIER,* OR *EINTOPF*".*
SHE CALLED IT "*ANKAKE YUDOFU*"...!
OH!
MUST BE HER.

*THE GERMAN WORDS FOR BREAD, POTATOES, RICE PORRIDGE, EGGS, AND STEW, RESPECTIVELY

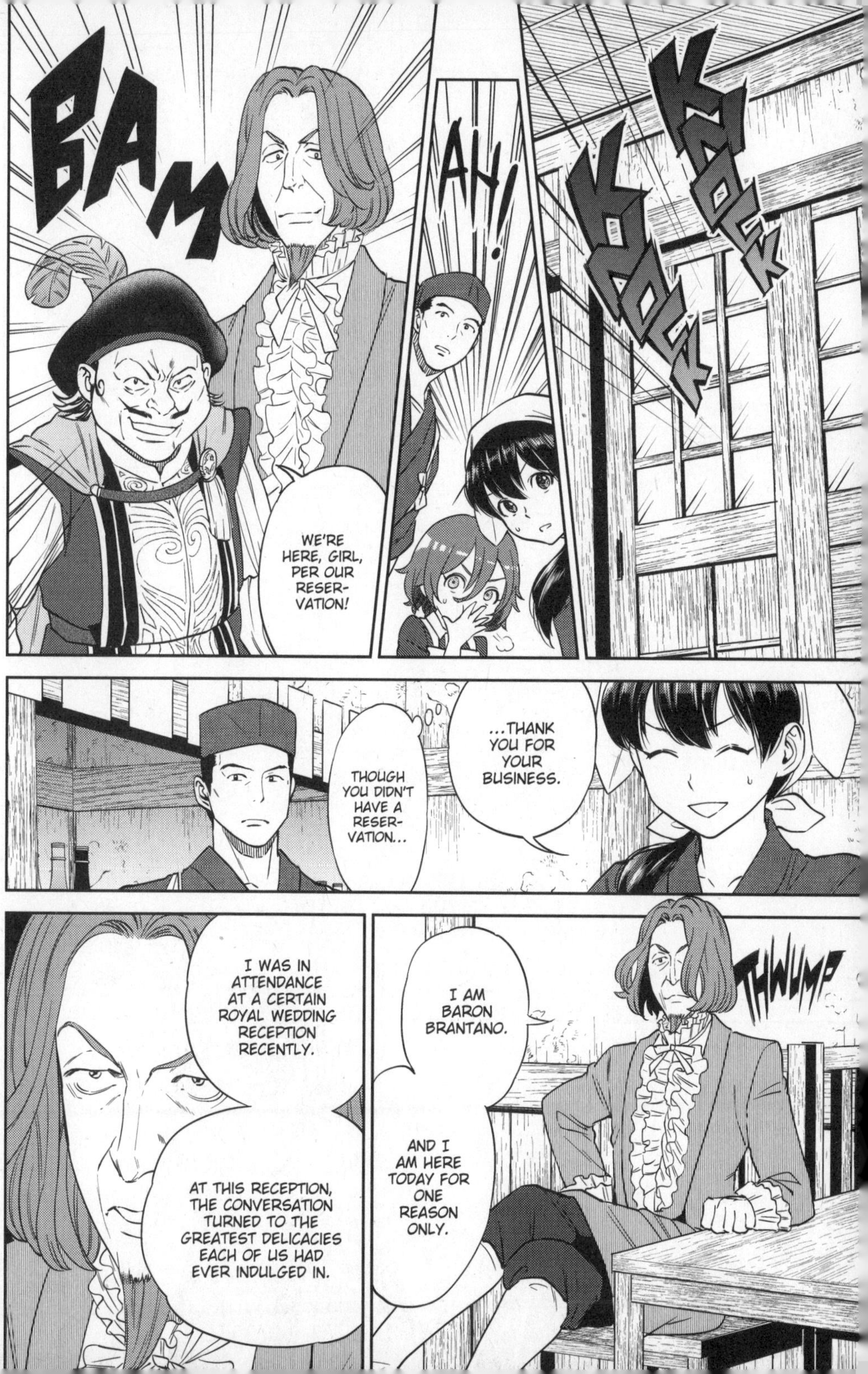
KNOCK KNOCK
AH!
BAM
WE'RE HERE, GIRL, PER OUR RESER-VATION!
...THANK YOU FOR YOUR BUSINESS.
THOUGH YOU DIDN'T HAVE A RESER-VATION...
THWUMP
I AM BARON BRANTANO.
AND I AM HERE TODAY FOR ONE REASON ONLY.
I WAS IN ATTENDANCE AT A CERTAIN ROYAL WEDDING RECEPTION RECENTLY.
AT THIS RECEPTION, THE CONVERSATION TURNED TO THE GREATEST DELICACIES EACH OF US HAD EVER INDULGED IN.

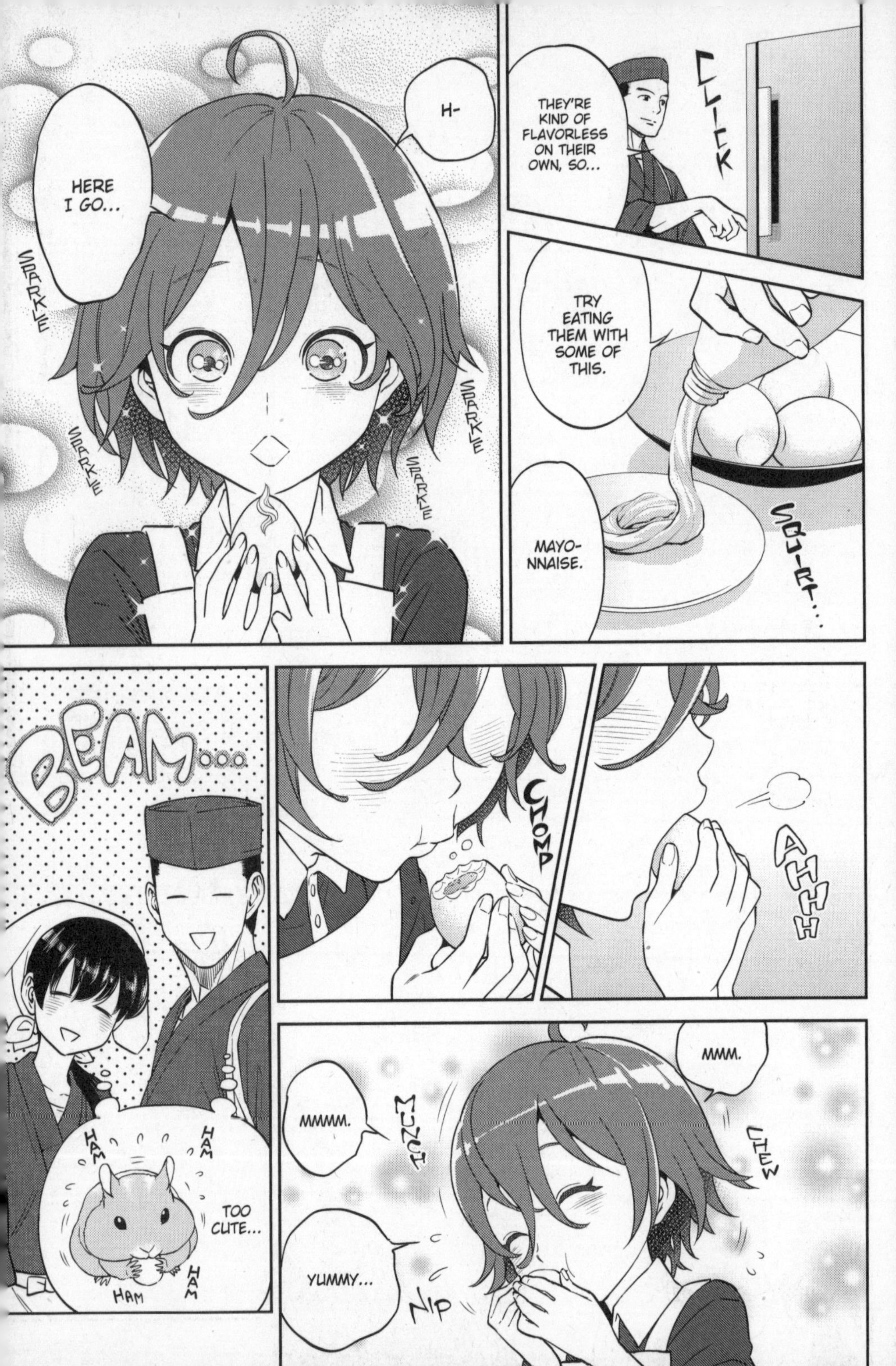

CLICK
THEY'RE KIND OF FLAVORLESS ON THEIR OWN, SO...
TRY EATING THEM WITH SOME OF THIS.
SQUIRT...
MAYONNAISE.
H-
HERE I GO...
SPARKLE
SPARKLE
SPARKLE
SPARKLE
AHHH
CHOMP
MMM.
CHEW
MUNCH
MMMM.
YUMMY...
NIP
BEAM...
HAM
HAM
TOO CUTE...
HAM
HAM

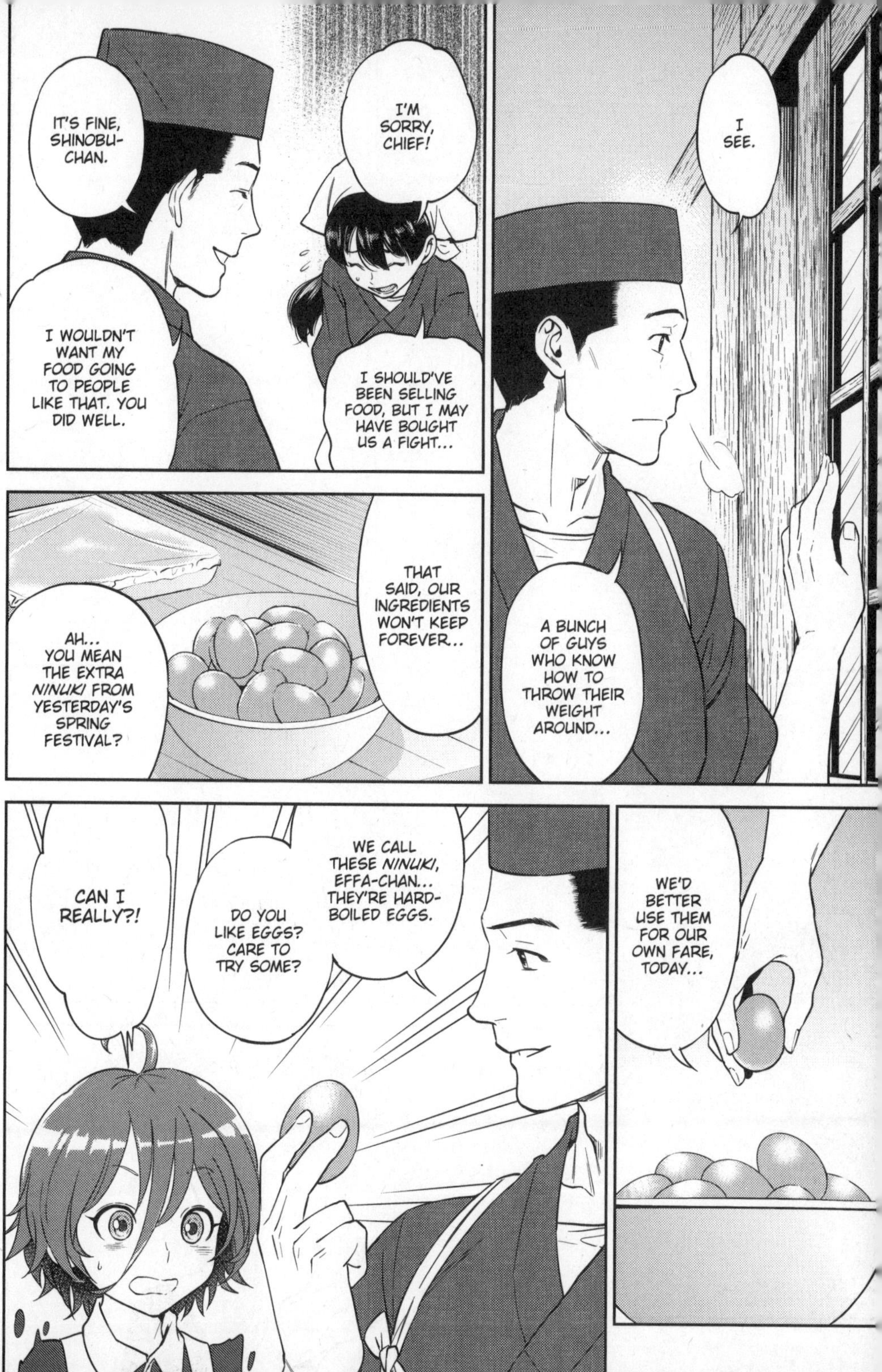
I SEE.
A BUNCH OF GUYS WHO KNOW HOW TO THROW THEIR WEIGHT AROUND...
I'M SORRY, CHIEF!
I SHOULD'VE BEEN SELLING FOOD, BUT I MAY HAVE BOUGHT US A FIGHT...
IT'S FINE, SHINOBU-CHAN.
I WOULDN'T WANT MY FOOD GOING TO PEOPLE LIKE THAT. YOU DID WELL.
THAT SAID, OUR INGREDIENTS WON'T KEEP FOREVER...
AH... YOU MEAN THE EXTRA *NINUKI* FROM YESTERDAY'S SPRING FESTIVAL?
WE'D BETTER USE THEM FOR OUR OWN FARE, TODAY...
WE CALL THESE *NINUKI*, EFFA-CHAN... THEY'RE HARD-BOILED EGGS.
DO YOU LIKE EGGS? CARE TO TRY SOME?
CAN I REALLY?!

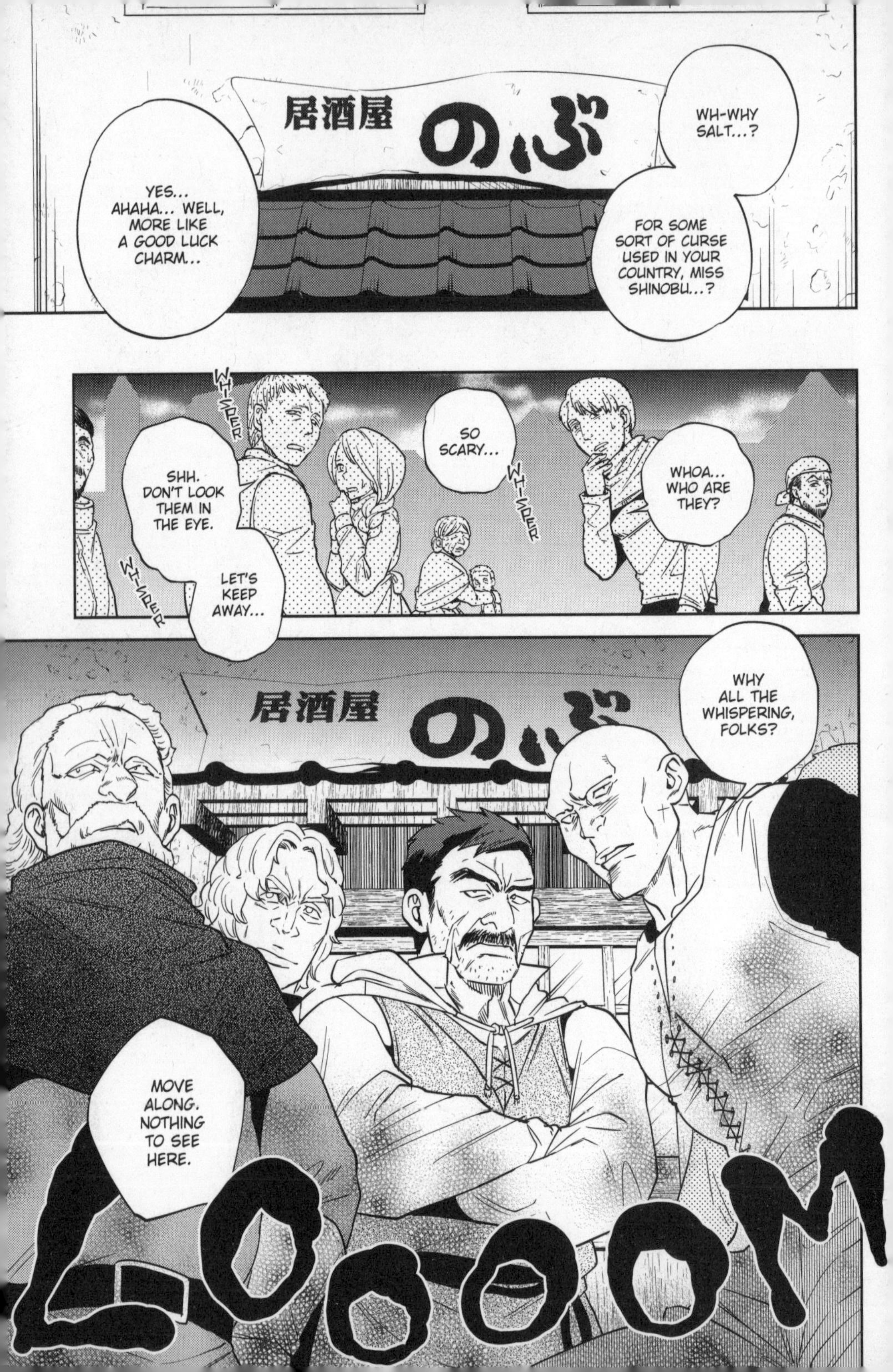
居酒屋 のぶ
WH-WHY SALT...?
FOR SOME SORT OF CURSE USED IN YOUR COUNTRY, MISS SHINOBU...?
YES... AHAHA... WELL, MORE LIKE A GOOD LUCK CHARM...
WHOA... WHO ARE THEY?
WHISPER
SO SCARY...
WHISPER
SHH. DON'T LOOK THEM IN THE EYE.
WHISPER
LET'S KEEP AWAY...
居酒屋 のぶ
WHY ALL THE WHISPERING, FOLKS?
MOVE ALONG. NOTHING TO SEE HERE.
LOOOOOM

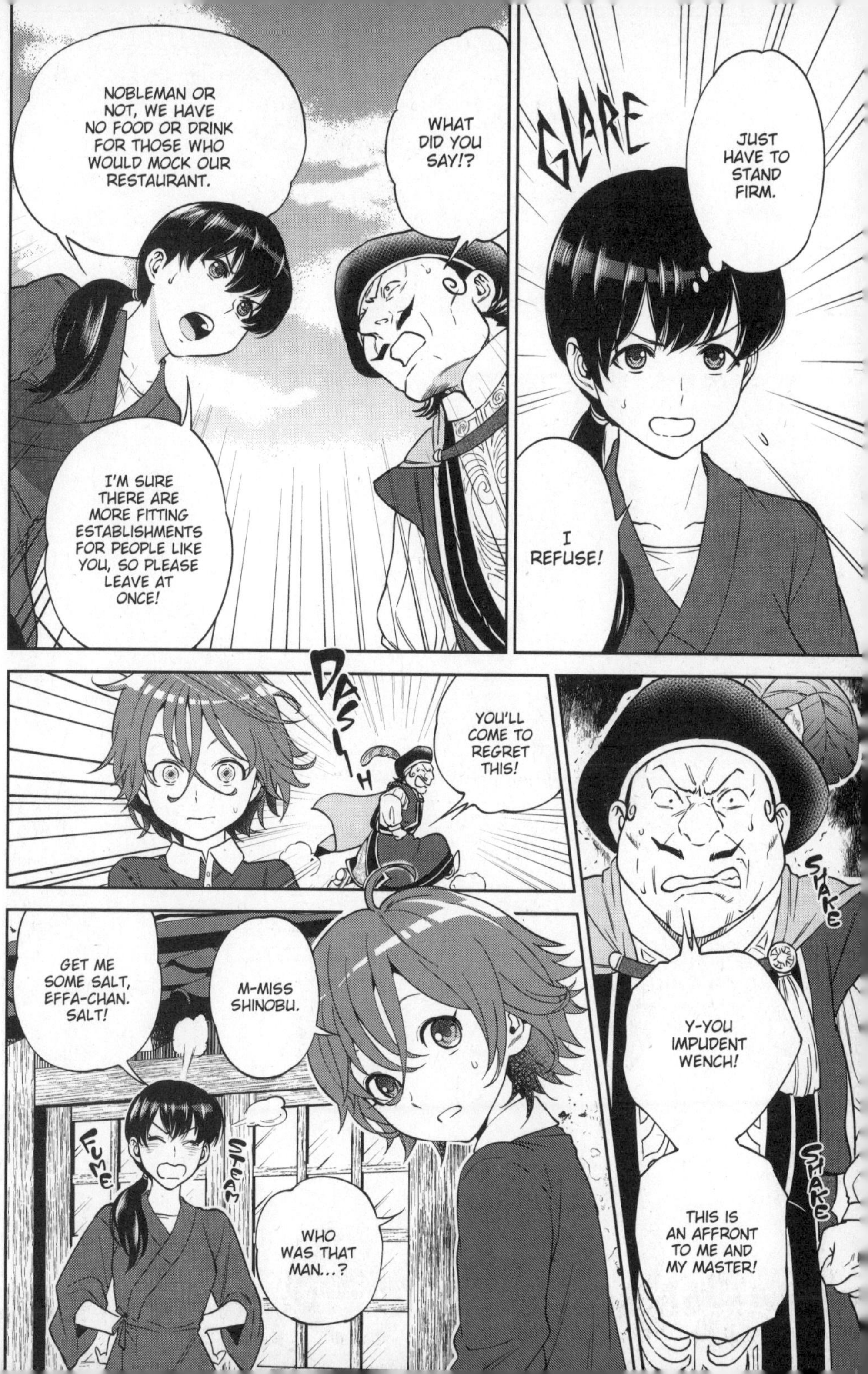
JUST HAVE TO STAND FIRM.
GLARE
I REFUSE!
WHAT DID YOU SAY!?
NOBLEMAN OR NOT, WE HAVE NO FOOD OR DRINK FOR THOSE WHO WOULD MOCK OUR RESTAURANT.
I'M SURE THERE ARE MORE FITTING ESTABLISHMENTS FOR PEOPLE LIKE YOU, SO PLEASE LEAVE AT ONCE!
SHAKE
Y-YOU IMPUDENT WENCH!
SHAKE
THIS IS AN AFFRONT TO ME AND MY MASTER!
YOU'LL COME TO REGRET THIS!
DASH
M-MISS SHINOBU.
GET ME SOME SALT, EFFA-CHAN. SALT!
STEAM
FUME
WHO WAS THAT MAN...?

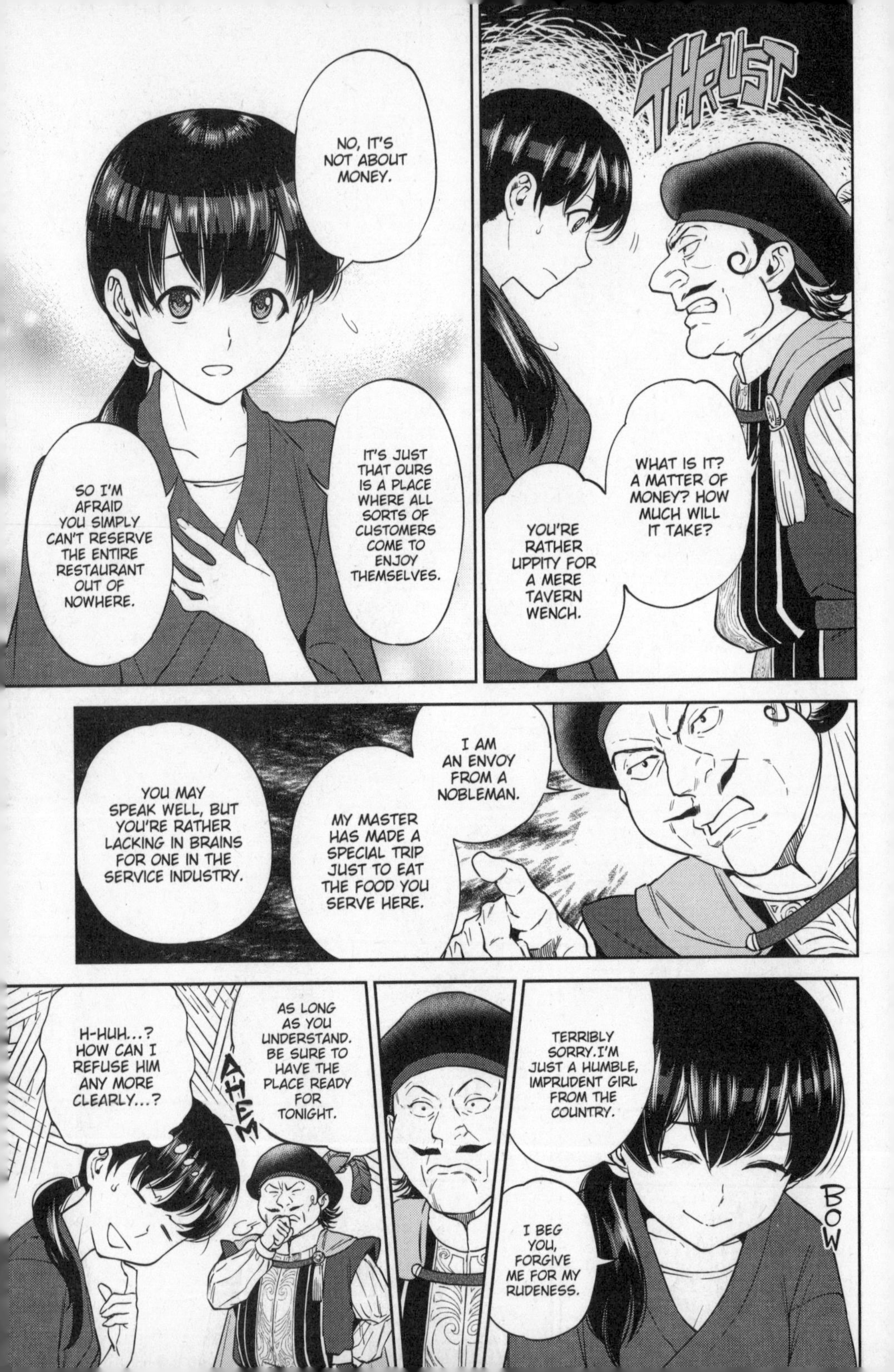
THRUST
WHAT IS IT? A MATTER OF MONEY? HOW MUCH WILL IT TAKE?
YOU'RE RATHER UPPITY FOR A MERE TAVERN WENCH.
NO, IT'S NOT ABOUT MONEY.
IT'S JUST THAT OURS IS A PLACE WHERE ALL SORTS OF CUSTOMERS COME TO ENJOY THEMSELVES.
SO I'M AFRAID YOU SIMPLY CAN'T RESERVE THE ENTIRE RESTAURANT OUT OF NOWHERE.
I AM AN ENVOY FROM A NOBLEMAN.
MY MASTER HAS MADE A SPECIAL TRIP JUST TO EAT THE FOOD YOU SERVE HERE.
YOU MAY SPEAK WELL, BUT YOU'RE RATHER LACKING IN BRAINS FOR ONE IN THE SERVICE INDUSTRY.
TERRIBLY SORRY. I'M JUST A HUMBLE, IMPRUDENT GIRL FROM THE COUNTRY.
BOW
I BEG YOU, FORGIVE ME FOR MY RUDENESS.
AS LONG AS YOU UNDERSTAND. BE SURE TO HAVE THE PLACE READY FOR TONIGHT.
AHEM
H-HUH...? HOW CAN I REFUSE HIM ANY MORE CLEARLY...?

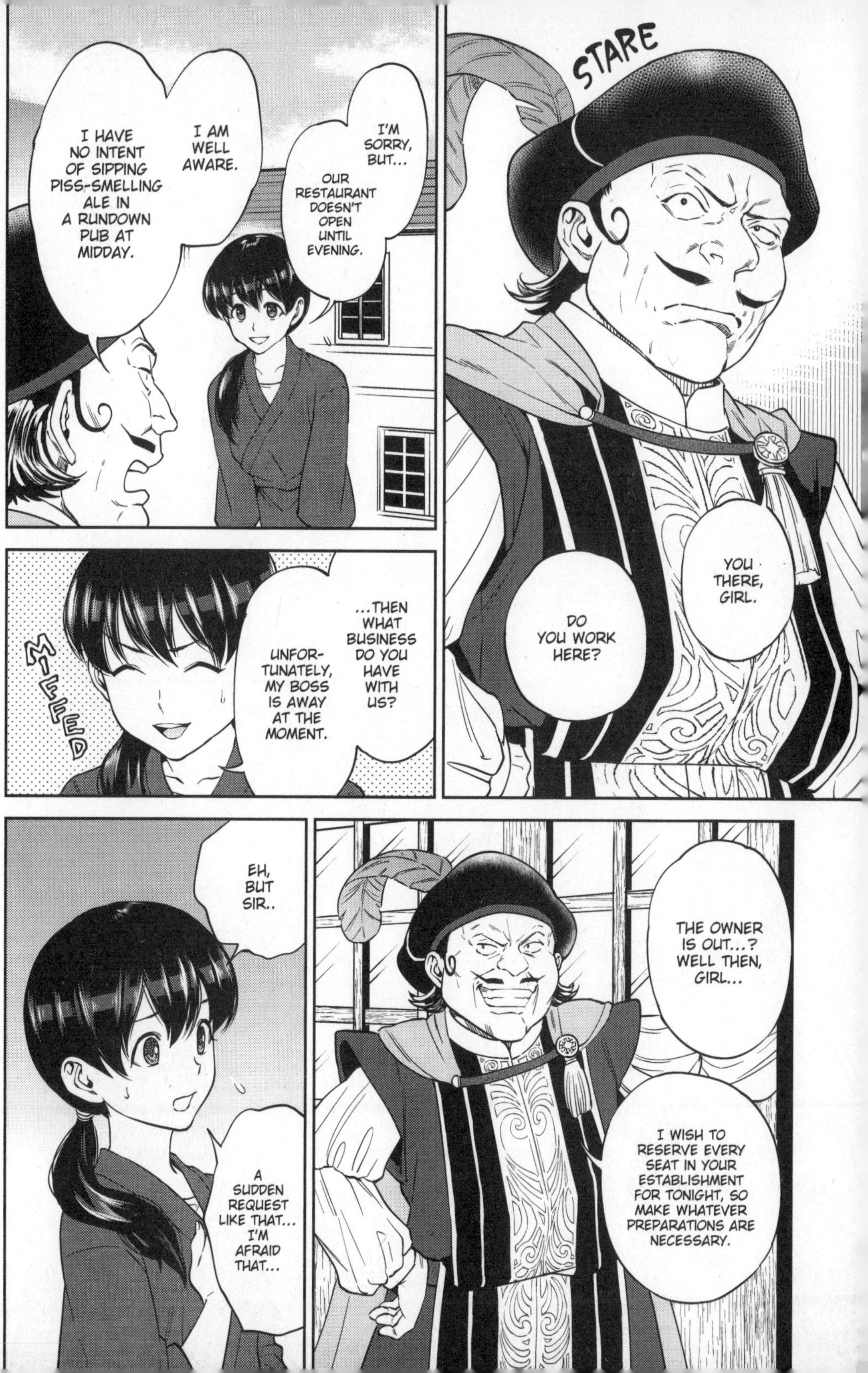
STARE
YOU THERE, GIRL.
DO YOU WORK HERE?
I'M SORRY, BUT...
OUR RESTAURANT DOESN'T OPEN UNTIL EVENING.
I AM WELL AWARE.
I HAVE NO INTENT OF SIPPING PISS-SMELLING ALE IN A RUNDOWN PUB AT MIDDAY.
...THEN WHAT BUSINESS DO YOU HAVE WITH US?
UNFOR-TUNATELY, MY BOSS IS AWAY AT THE MOMENT.
MIFFED
THE OWNER IS OUT...? WELL THEN, GIRL...
I WISH TO RESERVE EVERY SEAT IN YOUR ESTABLISHMENT FOR TONIGHT, SO MAKE WHATEVER PREPARATIONS ARE NECESSARY.
EH, BUT SIR..
A SUDDEN REQUEST LIKE THAT... I'M AFRAID THAT...

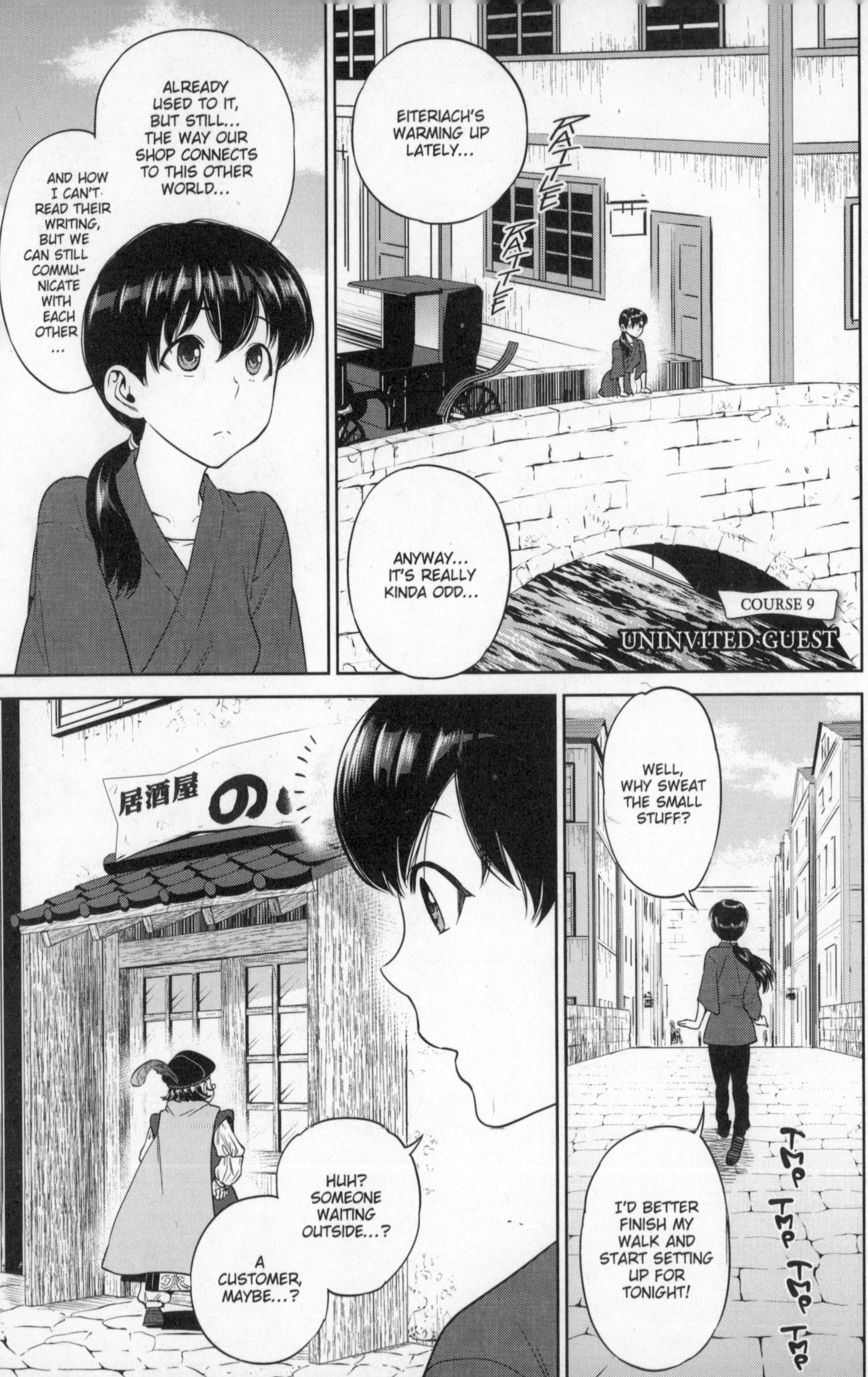
EITERIACH'S WARMING UP LATELY...
RATTLE RATTLE
ANYWAY... IT'S REALLY KINDA ODD...
COURSE 9
UNINVITED GUEST
ALREADY USED TO IT, BUT STILL... THE WAY OUR SHOP CONNECTS TO THIS OTHER WORLD...
AND HOW I CAN'T READ THEIR WRITING, BUT WE CAN STILL COMMUNICATE WITH EACH OTHER...
WELL, WHY SWEAT THE SMALL STUFF?
I'D BETTER FINISH MY WALK AND START SETTING UP FOR TONIGHT!
TMP TMP TMP TMP
居酒屋 の
HUH? SOMEONE WAITING OUTSIDE...?
A CUSTOMER, MAYBE...?

OTHERWORLDLY IZAKAYA
NOBU

Shuto

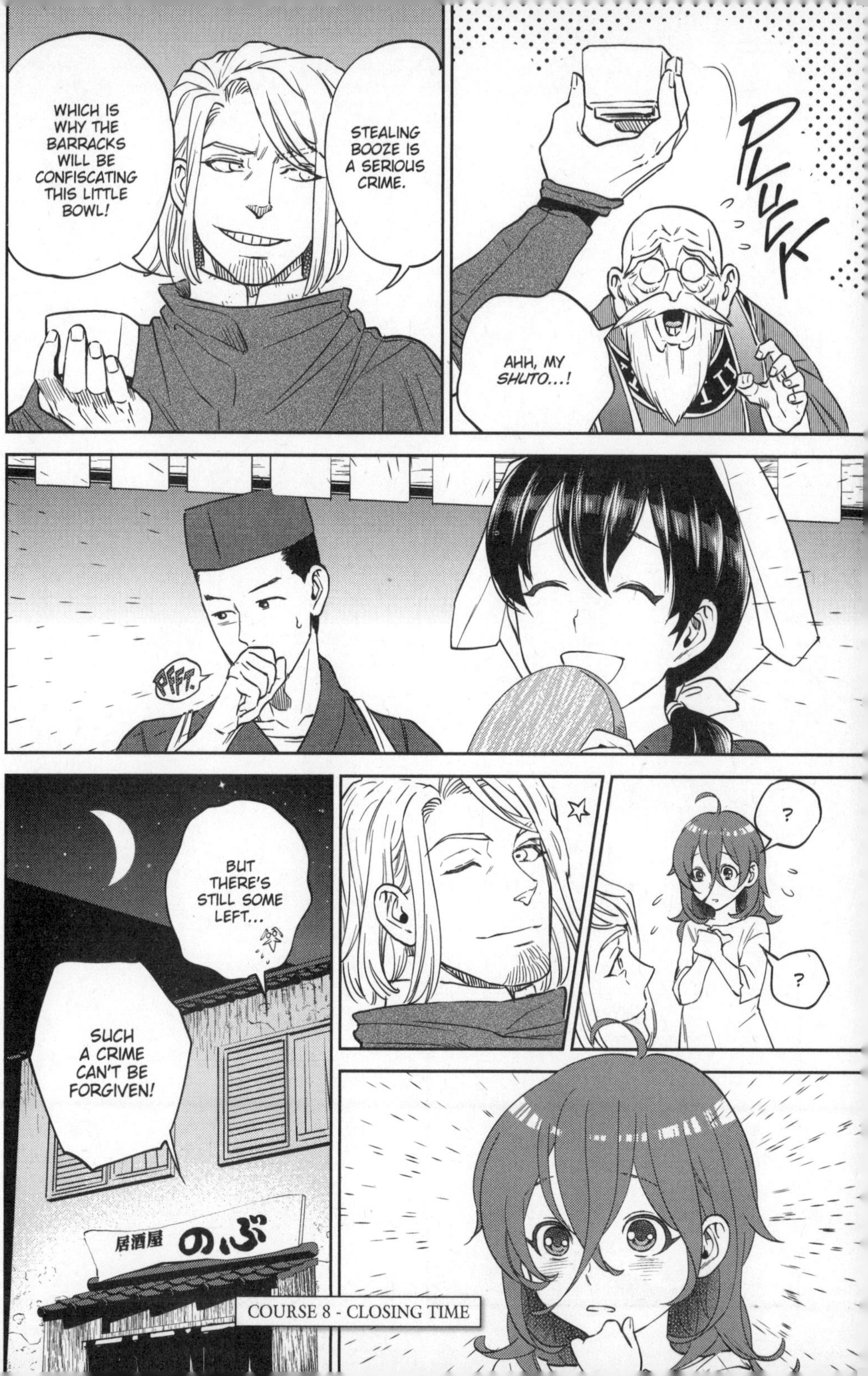
PLUCK
AHH, MY SHUTO...!
STEALING BOOZE IS A SERIOUS CRIME.
WHICH IS WHY THE BARRACKS WILL BE CONFISCATING THIS LITTLE BOWL!
PFFT.
?
?
BUT THERE'S STILL SOME LEFT...
SUCH A CRIME CAN'T BE FORGIVEN!
居酒屋 のぶ
COURSE 8 - CLOSING TIME

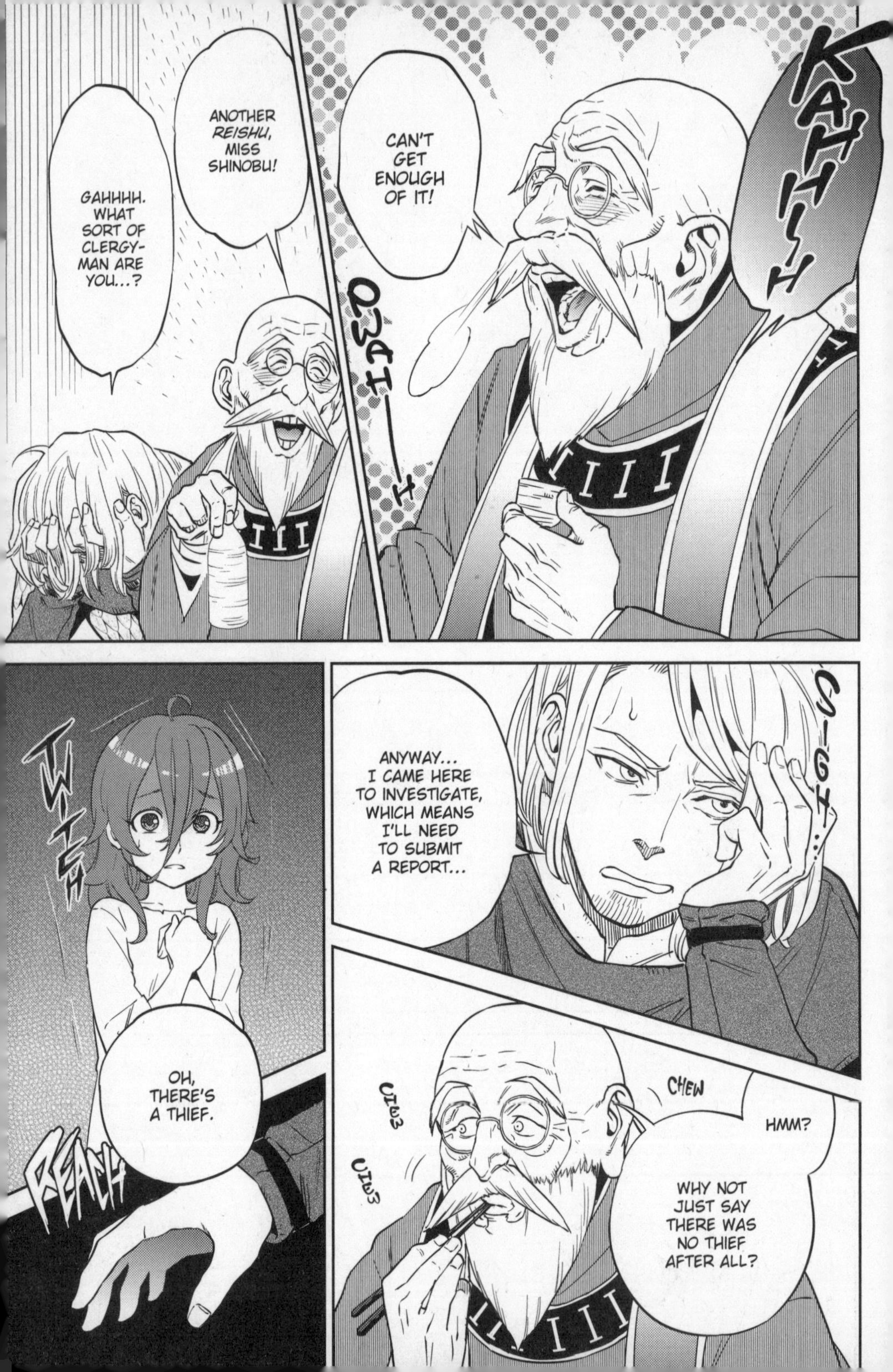
KAHHHH
CAN'T GET ENOUGH OF IT!
QWAH—H
ANOTHER *REISHU*, MISS SHINOBU!
GAHHHH. WHAT SORT OF CLERGY-MAN ARE YOU...?
SIGH...
ANYWAY... I CAME HERE TO INVESTIGATE, WHICH MEANS I'LL NEED TO SUBMIT A REPORT...
CHEW
HMM?
WHY NOT JUST SAY THERE WAS NO THIEF AFTER ALL?
TWITCH
OH, THERE'S A THIEF.
REACH

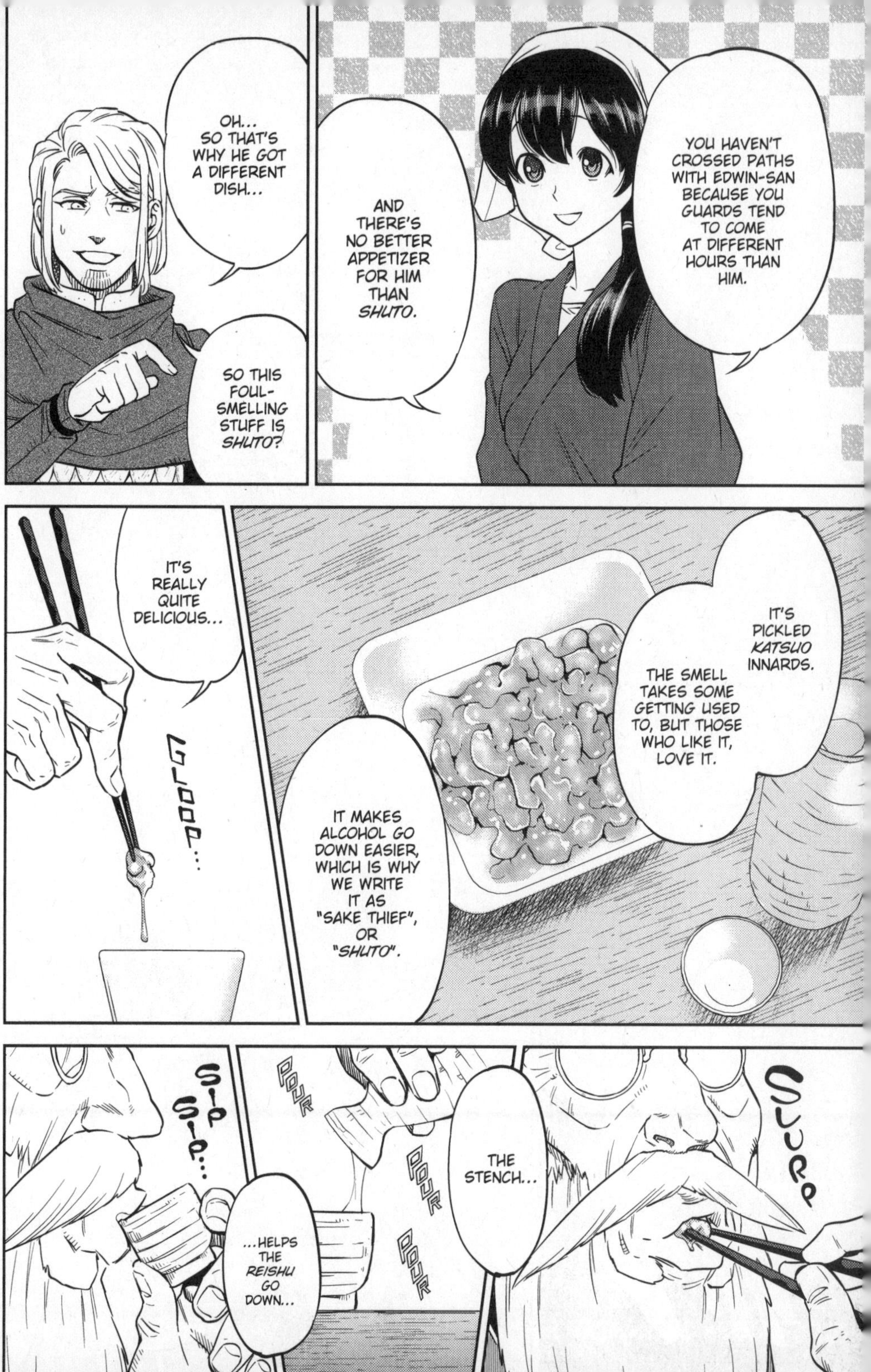
YOU HAVEN'T CROSSED PATHS WITH EDWIN-SAN BECAUSE YOU GUARDS TEND TO COME AT DIFFERENT HOURS THAN HIM.
AND THERE'S NO BETTER APPETIZER FOR HIM THAN SHUTO.
OH... SO THAT'S WHY HE GOT A DIFFERENT DISH...
SO THIS FOUL-SMELLING STUFF IS SHUTO?
IT'S PICKLED KATSUO INNARDS.
THE SMELL TAKES SOME GETTING USED TO, BUT THOSE WHO LIKE IT, LOVE IT.
IT MAKES ALCOHOL GO DOWN EASIER, WHICH IS WHY WE WRITE IT AS "SAKE THIEF", OR "SHUTO".
IT'S REALLY QUITE DELICIOUS...
GLOOP...
SLURP
THE STENCH...
POUR
POUR
POUR
...HELPS THE REISHU GO DOWN...
SIP SIP...

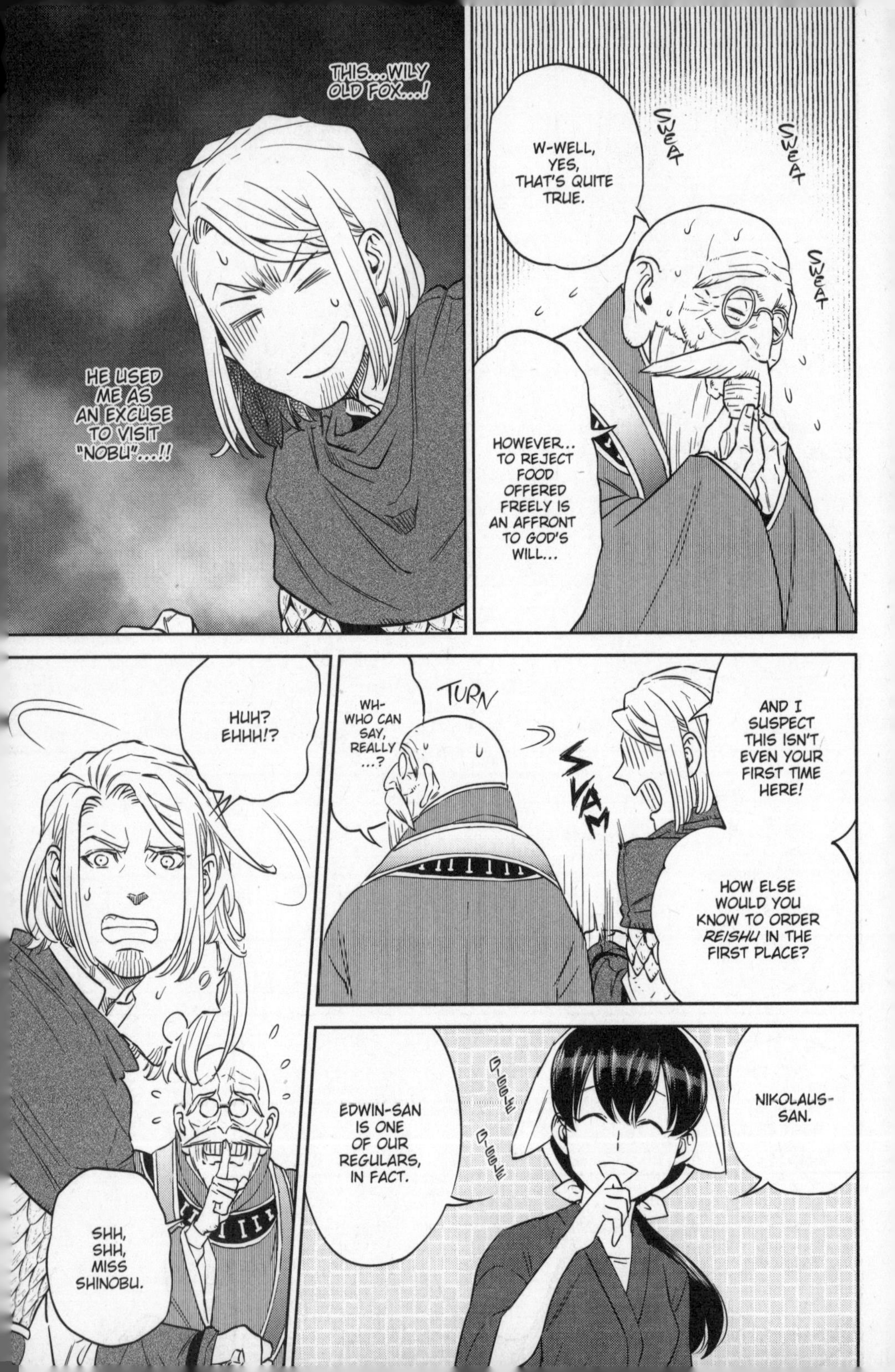
W-WELL, YES, THAT'S QUITE TRUE.
SWEAT
SWEAT
SWEAT
HOWEVER.. TO REJECT FOOD OFFERED FREELY IS AN AFFRONT TO GOD'S WILL...
THIS...WILY OLD FOX...!
HE USED ME AS AN EXCUSE TO VISIT "NOBU"...!!
AND I SUSPECT THIS ISN'T EVEN YOUR FIRST TIME HERE!
SWAM
TURN
WH-WHO CAN SAY, REALLY...?
HOW ELSE WOULD YOU KNOW TO ORDER *REISHU* IN THE FIRST PLACE?
NIKOLAUS-SAN.
EDWIN-SAN IS ONE OF OUR REGULARS, IN FACT.
GIGGLE
GIGGLE
HUH? EHHH!?
SHH, SHH, MISS SHINOBU.

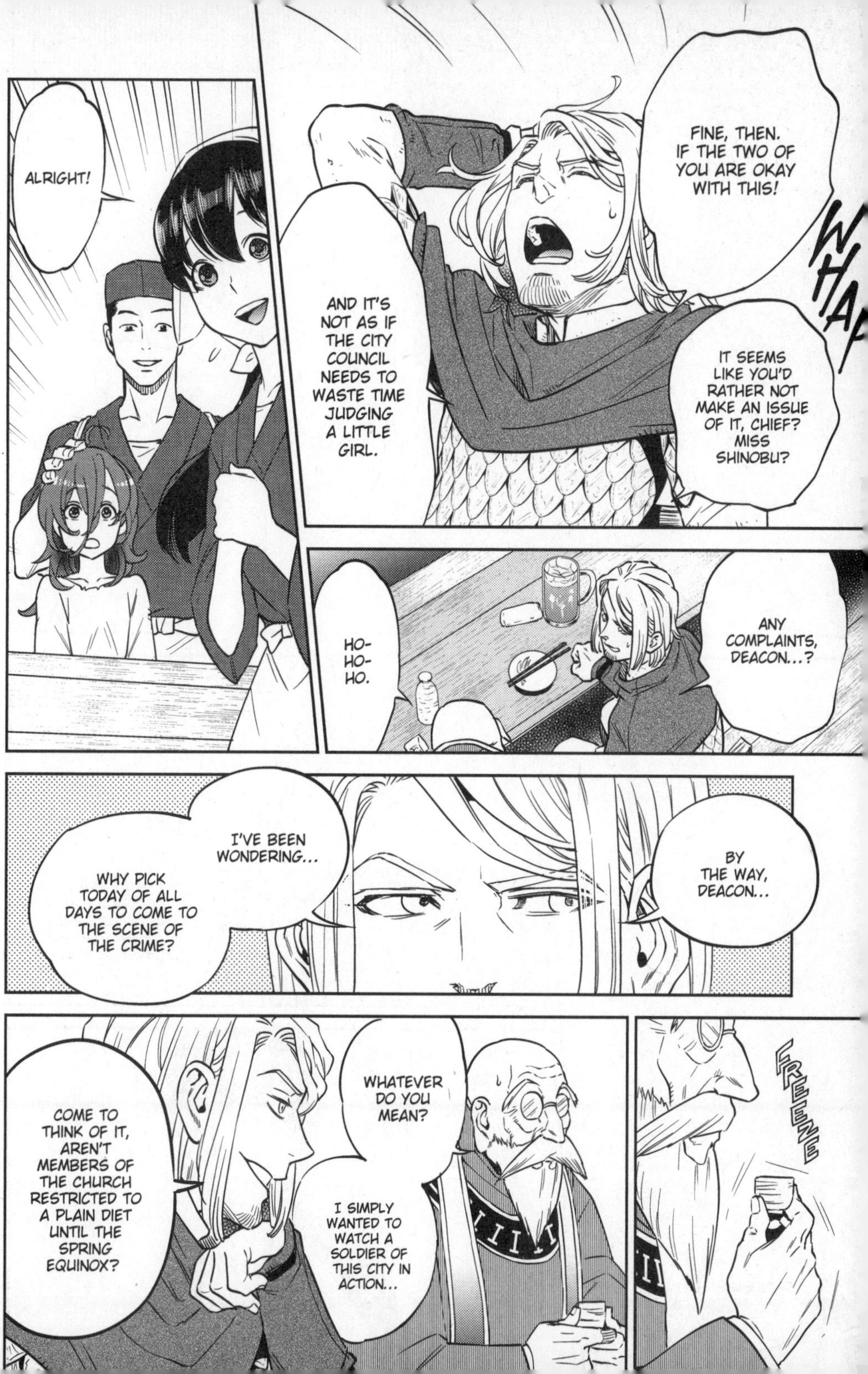
FINE, THEN. IF THE TWO OF YOU ARE OKAY WITH THIS!
WHAP
IT SEEMS LIKE YOU'D RATHER NOT MAKE AN ISSUE OF IT, CHIEF? MISS SHINOBU?
AND IT'S NOT AS IF THE CITY COUNCIL NEEDS TO WASTE TIME JUDGING A LITTLE GIRL.
ANY COMPLAINTS, DEACON...?
HO-HO-HO.
ALRIGHT!
BY THE WAY, DEACON...
I'VE BEEN WONDERING...
WHY PICK TODAY OF ALL DAYS TO COME TO THE SCENE OF THE CRIME?
FREEZE
WHATEVER DO YOU MEAN?
COME TO THINK OF IT, AREN'T MEMBERS OF THE CHURCH RESTRICTED TO A PLAIN DIET UNTIL THE SPRING EQUINOX?
I SIMPLY WANTED TO WATCH A SOLDIER OF THIS CITY IN ACTION...

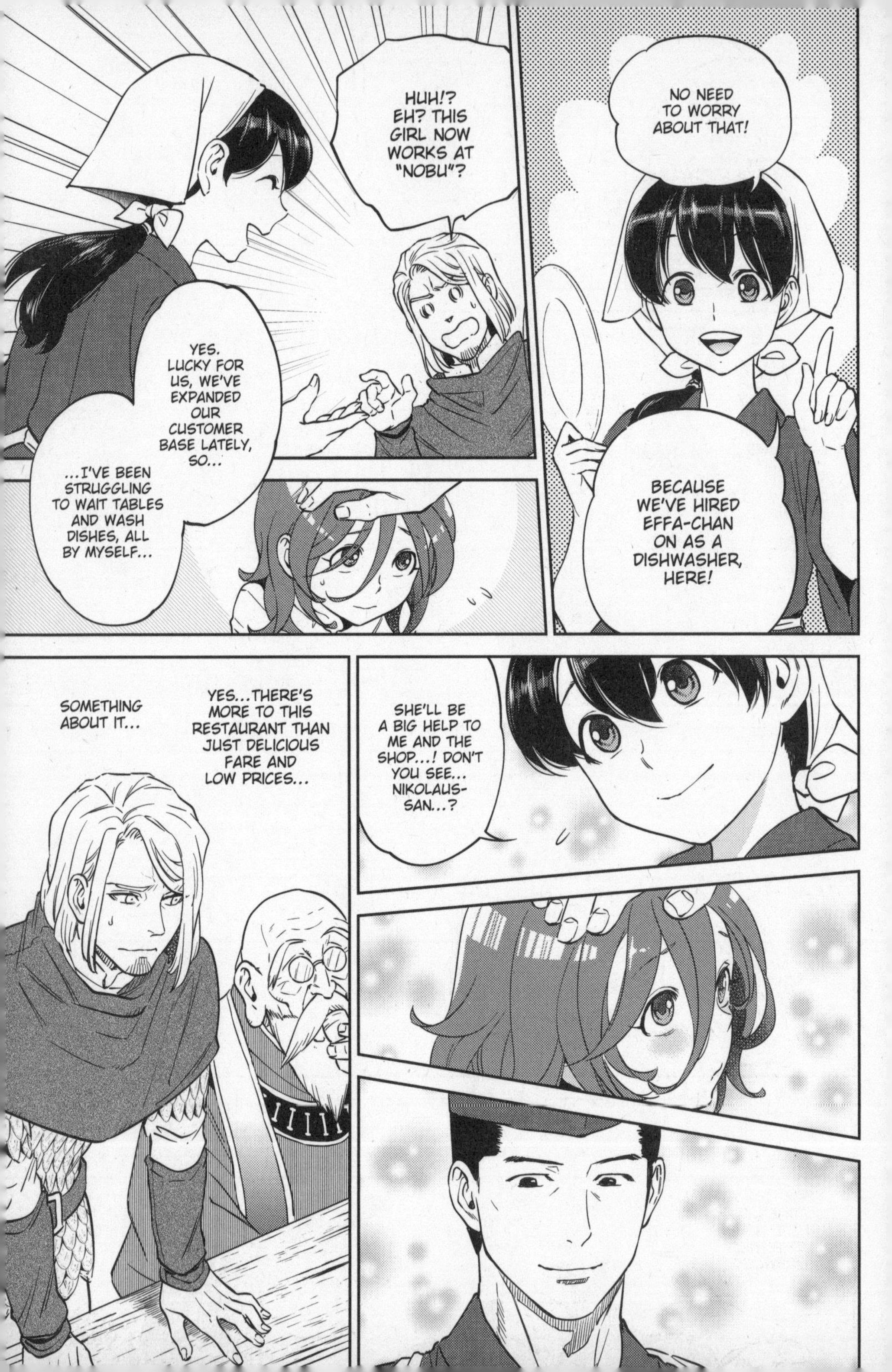
NO NEED TO WORRY ABOUT THAT!
BECAUSE WE'VE HIRED EFFA-CHAN ON AS A DISHWASHER, HERE!
HUH!? EH? THIS GIRL NOW WORKS AT "NOBU"?
YES. LUCKY FOR US, WE'VE EXPANDED OUR CUSTOMER BASE LATELY, SO...
...I'VE BEEN STRUGGLING TO WAIT TABLES AND WASH DISHES, ALL BY MYSELF...
SHE'LL BE A BIG HELP TO ME AND THE SHOP...! DON'T YOU SEE... NIKOLAUS-SAN...?
YES...THERE'S MORE TO THIS RESTAURANT THAN JUST DELICIOUS FARE AND LOW PRICES...
SOMETHING ABOUT IT...

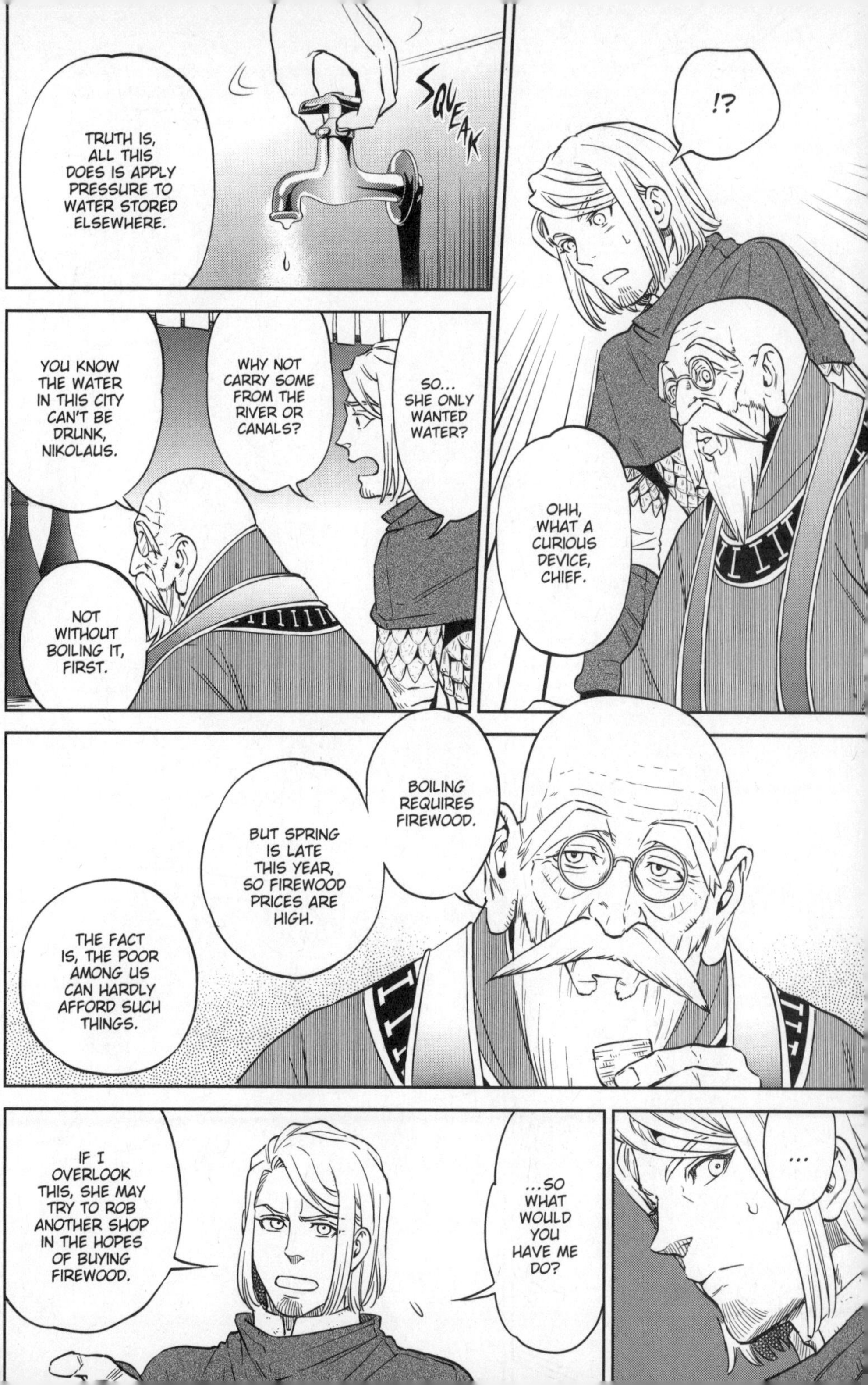
!?
OHH, WHAT A CURIOUS DEVICE, CHIEF.
SQUEAK
TRUTH IS, ALL THIS DOES IS APPLY PRESSURE TO WATER STORED ELSEWHERE.
SO... SHE ONLY WANTED WATER?
YOU KNOW THE WATER IN THIS CITY CAN'T BE DRUNK, NIKOLAUS.
WHY NOT CARRY SOME FROM THE RIVER OR CANALS?
NOT WITHOUT BOILING IT, FIRST.
BOILING REQUIRES FIREWOOD.
BUT SPRING IS LATE THIS YEAR, SO FIREWOOD PRICES ARE HIGH.
THE FACT IS, THE POOR AMONG US CAN HARDLY AFFORD SUCH THINGS.
...
...SO WHAT WOULD YOU HAVE ME DO?
IF I OVERLOOK THIS, SHE MAY TRY TO ROB ANOTHER SHOP IN THE HOPES OF BUYING FIREWOOD.

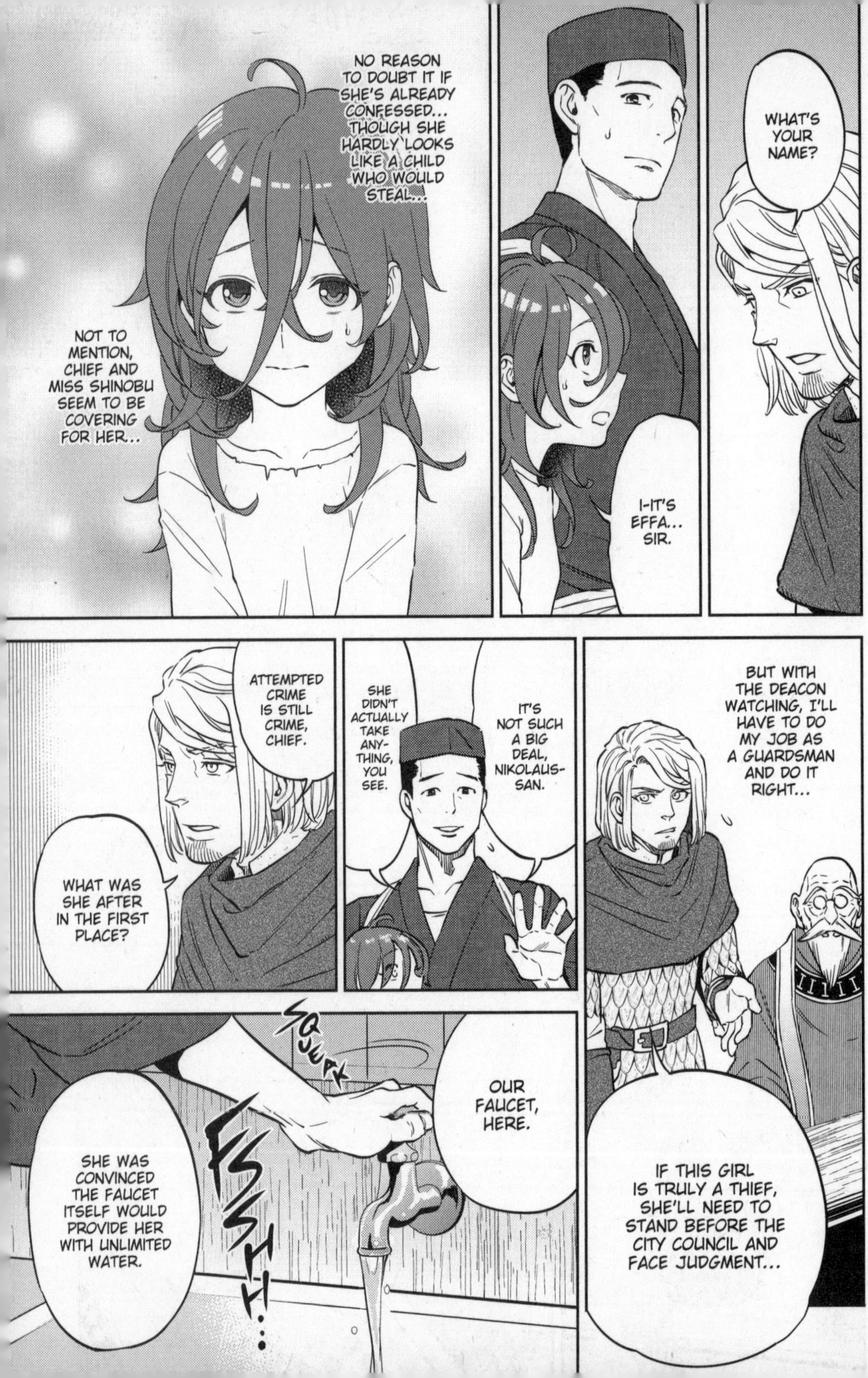
WHAT'S YOUR NAME?
I-IT'S EFFA... SIR.
NO REASON TO DOUBT IT IF SHE'S ALREADY CONFESSED... THOUGH SHE HARDLY LOOKS LIKE A CHILD WHO WOULD STEAL...
NOT TO MENTION, CHIEF AND MISS SHINOBU SEEM TO BE COVERING FOR HER...
BUT WITH THE DEACON WATCHING, I'LL HAVE TO DO MY JOB AS A GUARDSMAN AND DO IT RIGHT...
IF THIS GIRL IS TRULY A THIEF, SHE'LL NEED TO STAND BEFORE THE CITY COUNCIL AND FACE JUDGMENT...
IT'S NOT SUCH A BIG DEAL, NIKOLAUS-SAN.
SHE DIDN'T ACTUALLY TAKE ANYTHING, YOU SEE.
ATTEMPTED CRIME IS STILL CRIME, CHIEF.
WHAT WAS SHE AFTER IN THE FIRST PLACE?
OUR FAUCET, HERE.
SQUEAK
SHE WAS CONVINCED THE FAUCET ITSELF WOULD PROVIDE HER WITH UNLIMITED WATER.
FSSHH!...

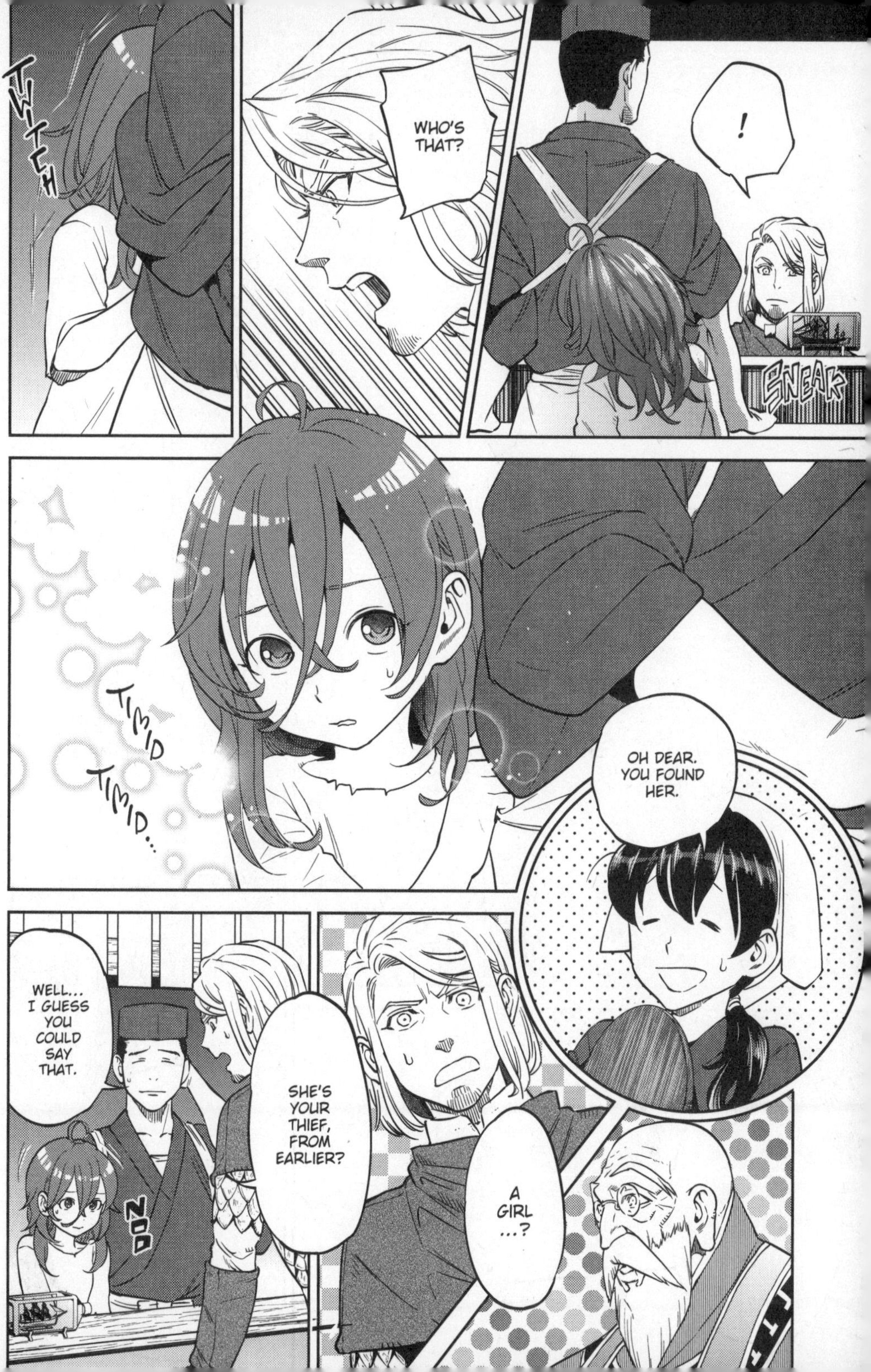
!
SNEAK
WHO'S THAT?
TWITCH
TIMID TIMID...
OH DEAR. YOU FOUND HER.
A GIRL ...?
SHE'S YOUR THIEF, FROM EARLIER?
WELL... I GUESS YOU COULD SAY THAT.
NOD

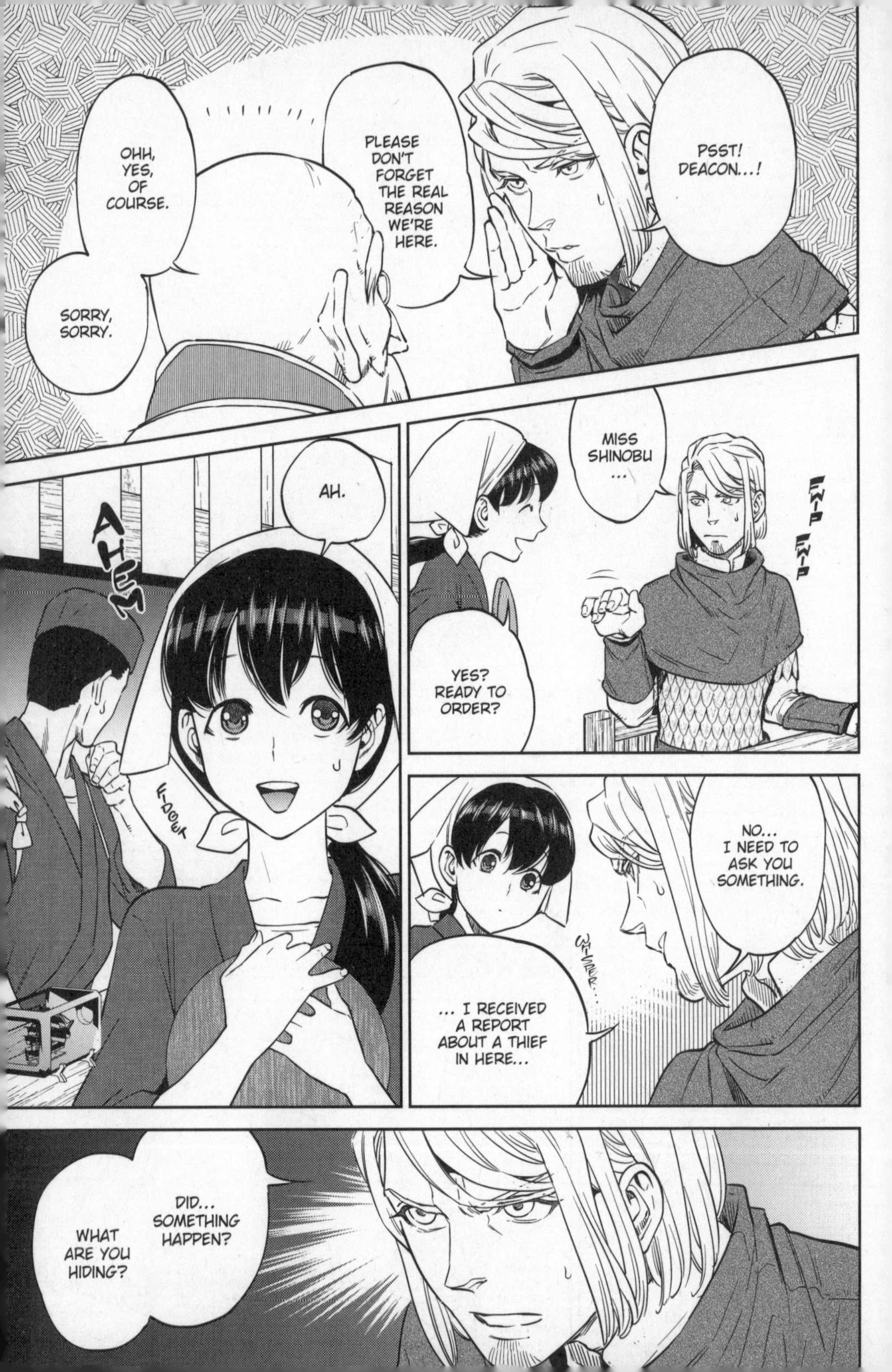
PSST! DEACON...!
PLEASE DON'T FORGET THE REAL REASON WE'RE HERE.
OHH, YES, OF COURSE.
SORRY, SORRY.
FWIP FWIP
MISS SHINOBU ...
YES? READY TO ORDER?
NO... I NEED TO ASK YOU SOMETHING.
WHISPER...
... I RECEIVED A REPORT ABOUT A THIEF IN HERE...
AH.
AHEM
FIDGET
DID... SOMETHING HAPPEN?
WHAT ARE YOU HIDING?

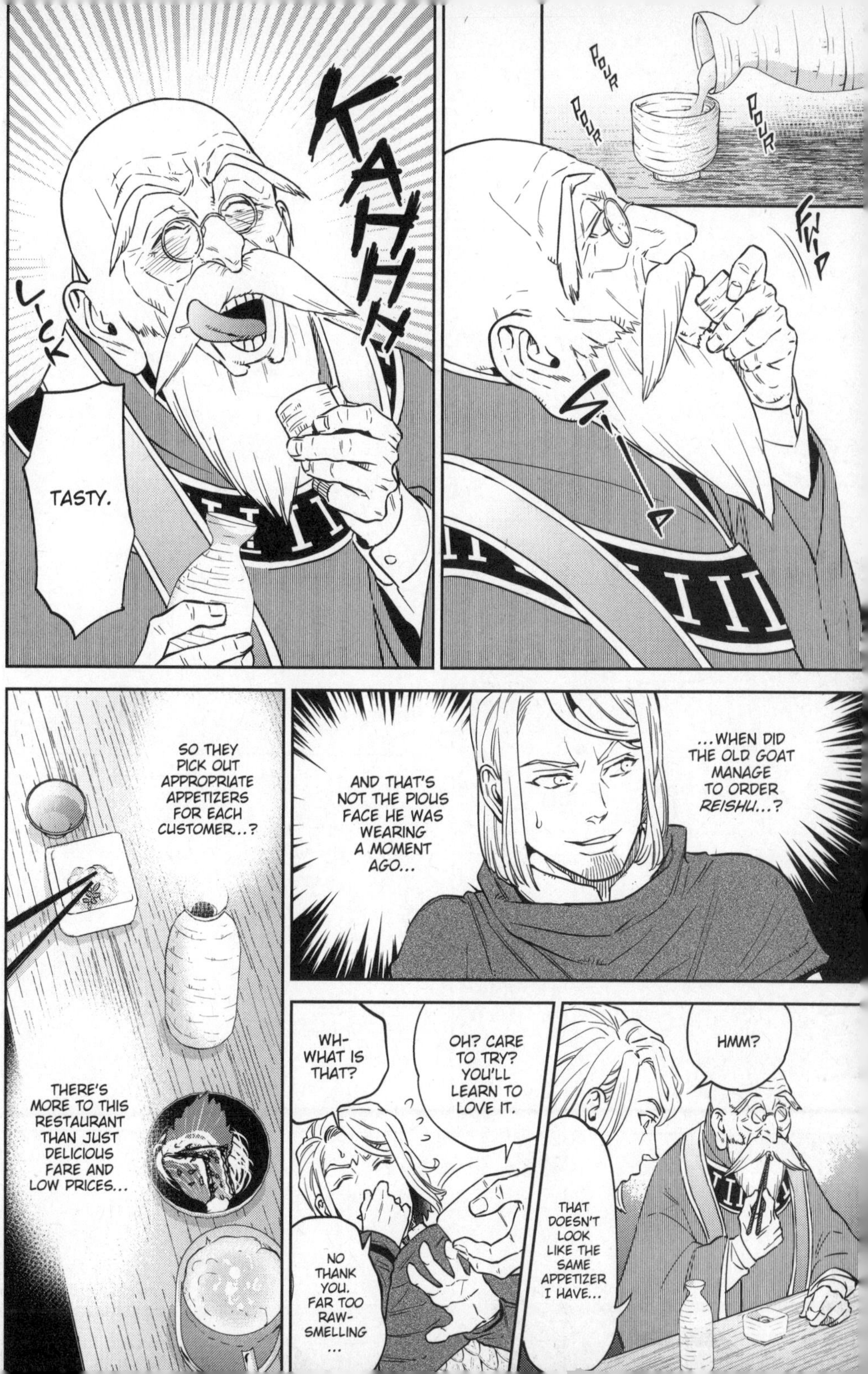
POUR
POUR
POUR
FWIP
SIP
KAHHH
LICK
TASTY.
...WHEN DID THE OLD GOAT MANAGE TO ORDER *REISHU*...?
AND THAT'S NOT THE PIOUS FACE HE WAS WEARING A MOMENT AGO...
HMM?
THAT DOESN'T LOOK LIKE THE SAME APPETIZER I HAVE...
WH-WHAT IS THAT?
OH? CARE TO TRY? YOU'LL LEARN TO LOVE IT.
NO THANK YOU. FAR TOO RAW-SMELLING...
SO THEY PICK OUT APPROPRIATE APPETIZERS FOR EACH CUSTOMER...?
THERE'S MORE TO THIS RESTAURANT THAN JUST DELICIOUS FARE AND LOW PRICES...

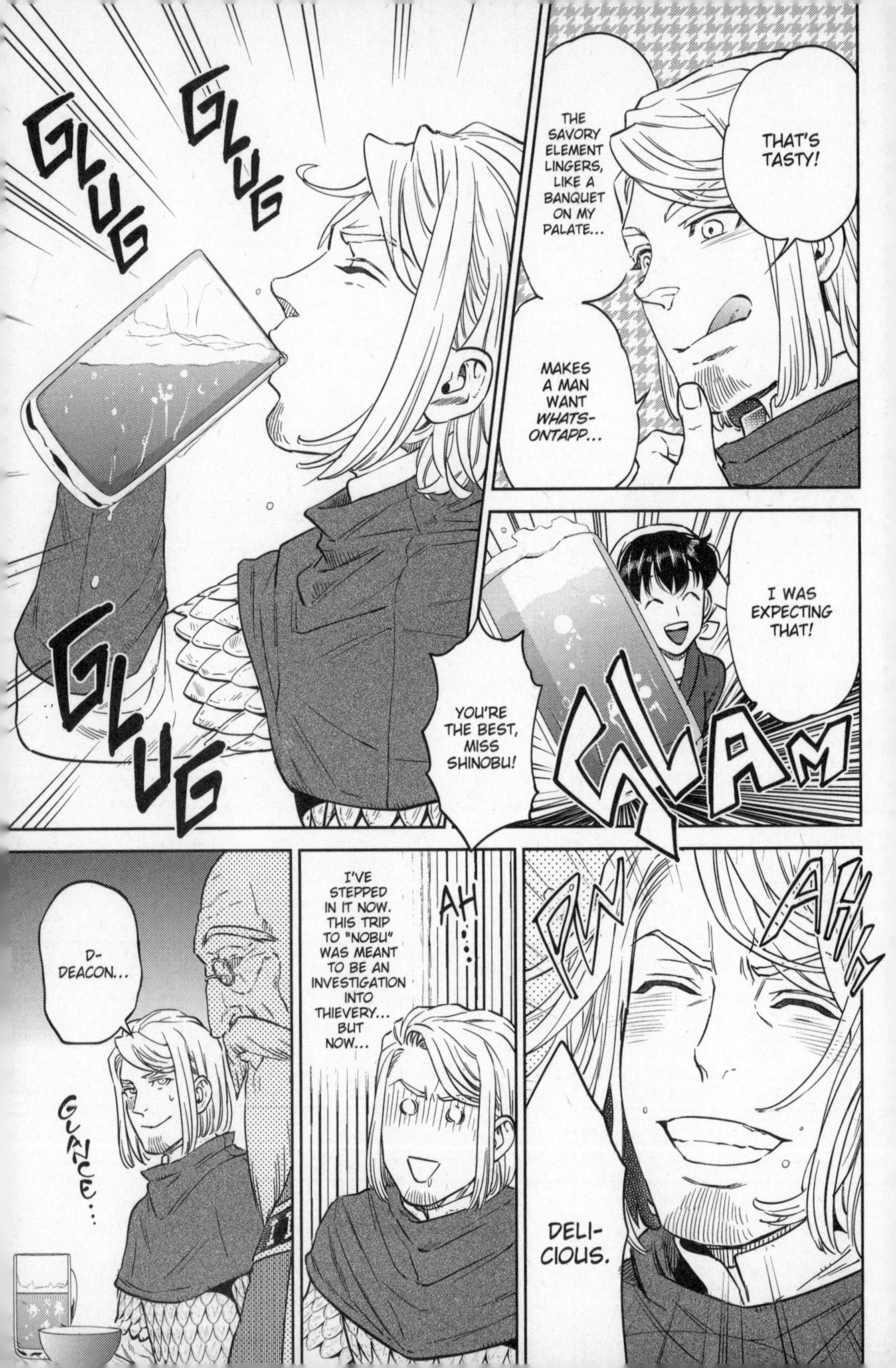
THAT'S TASTY!
THE SAVORY ELEMENT LINGERS, LIKE A BANQUET ON MY PALATE...
MAKES A MAN WANT *WHATS-ONTAPP*...
I WAS EXPECTING THAT!
WHAM
YOU'RE THE BEST, MISS SHINOBU!
GLUG GLUG
GLUG
AHH
DELI-CIOUS.
AH...
I'VE STEPPED IN IT NOW. THIS TRIP TO "NOBU" WAS MEANT TO BE AN INVESTIGATION INTO THIEVERY... BUT NOW...
D-DEACON...
GLANCE...

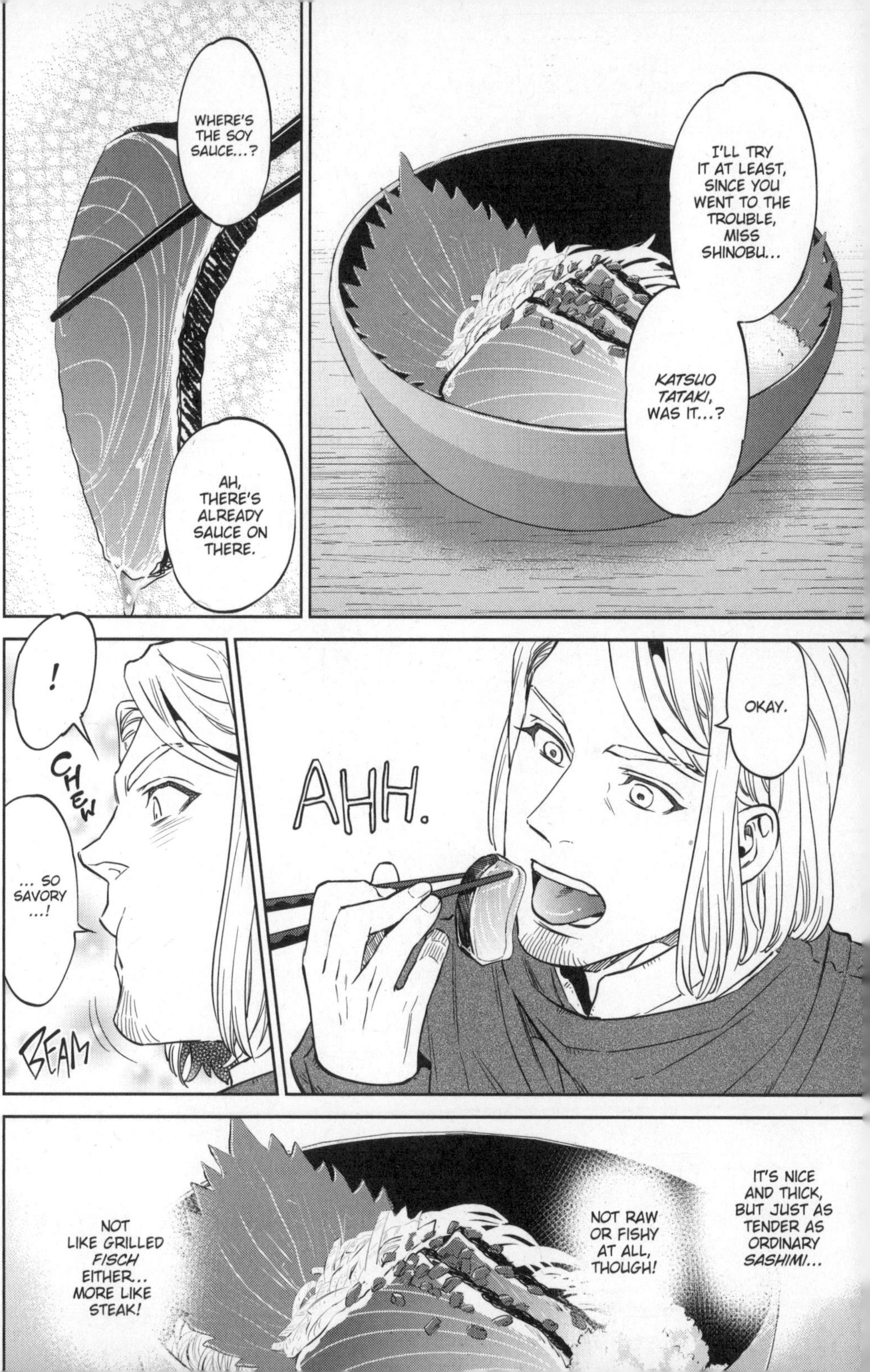
I'LL TRY IT AT LEAST, SINCE YOU WENT TO THE TROUBLE, MISS SHINOBU...
KATSUO TATAKI, WAS IT...?
WHERE'S THE SOY SAUCE...?
AH, THERE'S ALREADY SAUCE ON THERE.
OKAY.
AHH.
!
CHEW
... SO SAVORY ...!
BEAM
IT'S NICE AND THICK, BUT JUST AS TENDER AS ORDINARY *SASHIMI*...
NOT RAW OR FISHY AT ALL, THOUGH!
NOT LIKE GRILLED *FISCH* EITHER... MORE LIKE STEAK!

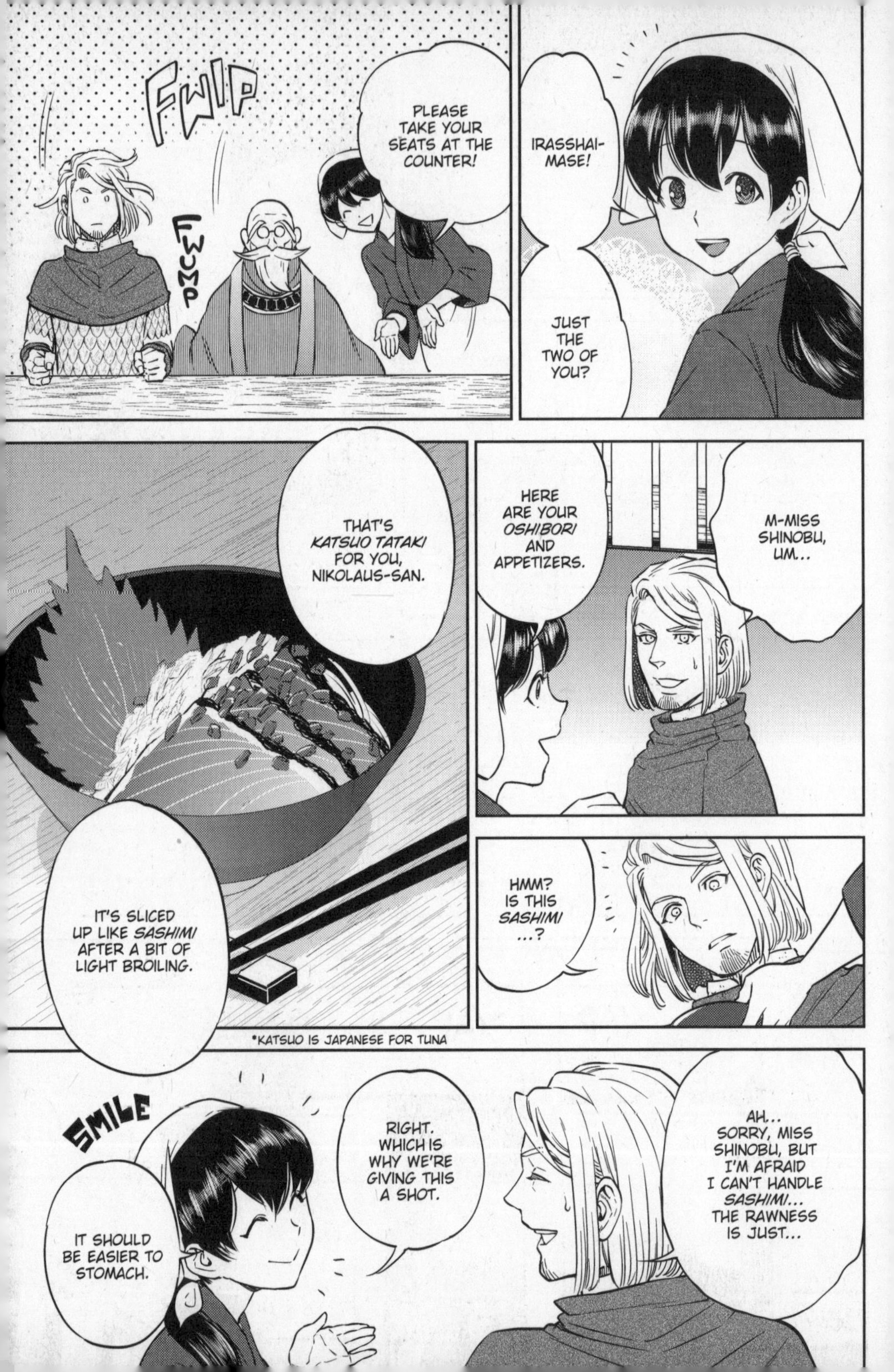
IRASSHAI-MASE!
JUST THE TWO OF YOU?
PLEASE TAKE YOUR SEATS AT THE COUNTER!
FWIP
FWUMP
M-MISS SHINOBU, UM...
HERE ARE YOUR *OSHIBORI* AND APPETIZERS.
HMM? IS THIS *SASHIMI* ...?
THAT'S *KATSUO TATAKI* FOR YOU, NIKOLAUS-SAN.
IT'S SLICED UP LIKE *SASHIMI* AFTER A BIT OF LIGHT BROILING.
AH... SORRY, MISS SHINOBU, BUT I'M AFRAID I CAN'T HANDLE *SASHIMI*... THE RAWNESS IS JUST...
RIGHT. WHICH IS WHY WE'RE GIVING THIS A SHOT.
SMILE
IT SHOULD BE EASIER TO STOMACH.

*KATSUO IS JAPANESE FOR TUNA

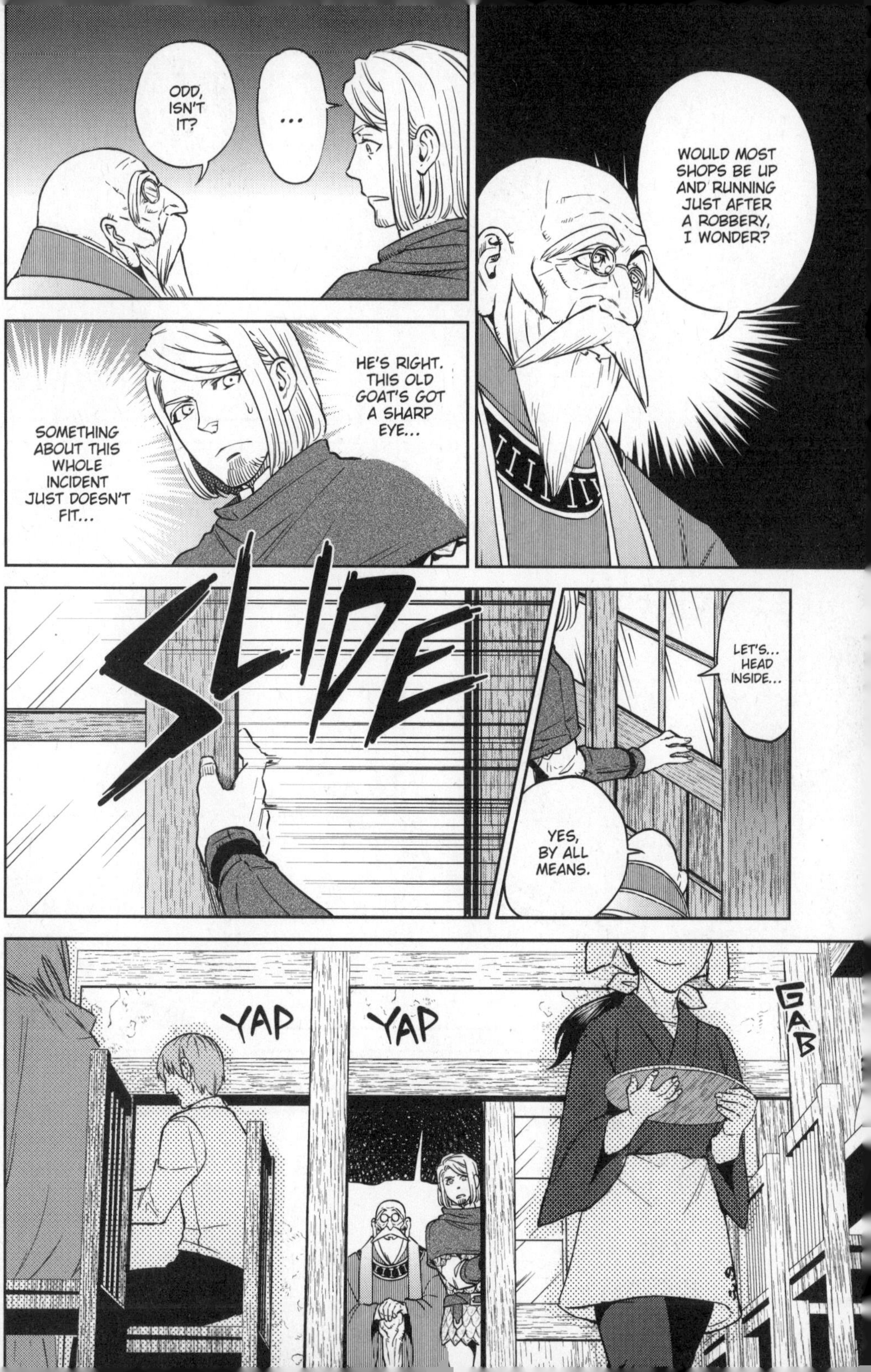
WOULD MOST SHOPS BE UP AND RUNNING JUST AFTER A ROBBERY, I WONDER?
...
ODD, ISN'T IT?
HE'S RIGHT. THIS OLD GOAT'S GOT A SHARP EYE...
SOMETHING ABOUT THIS WHOLE INCIDENT JUST DOESN'T FIT...
LET'S... HEAD INSIDE...
YES, BY ALL MEANS.
SLIDE
GAB
YAP
YAP

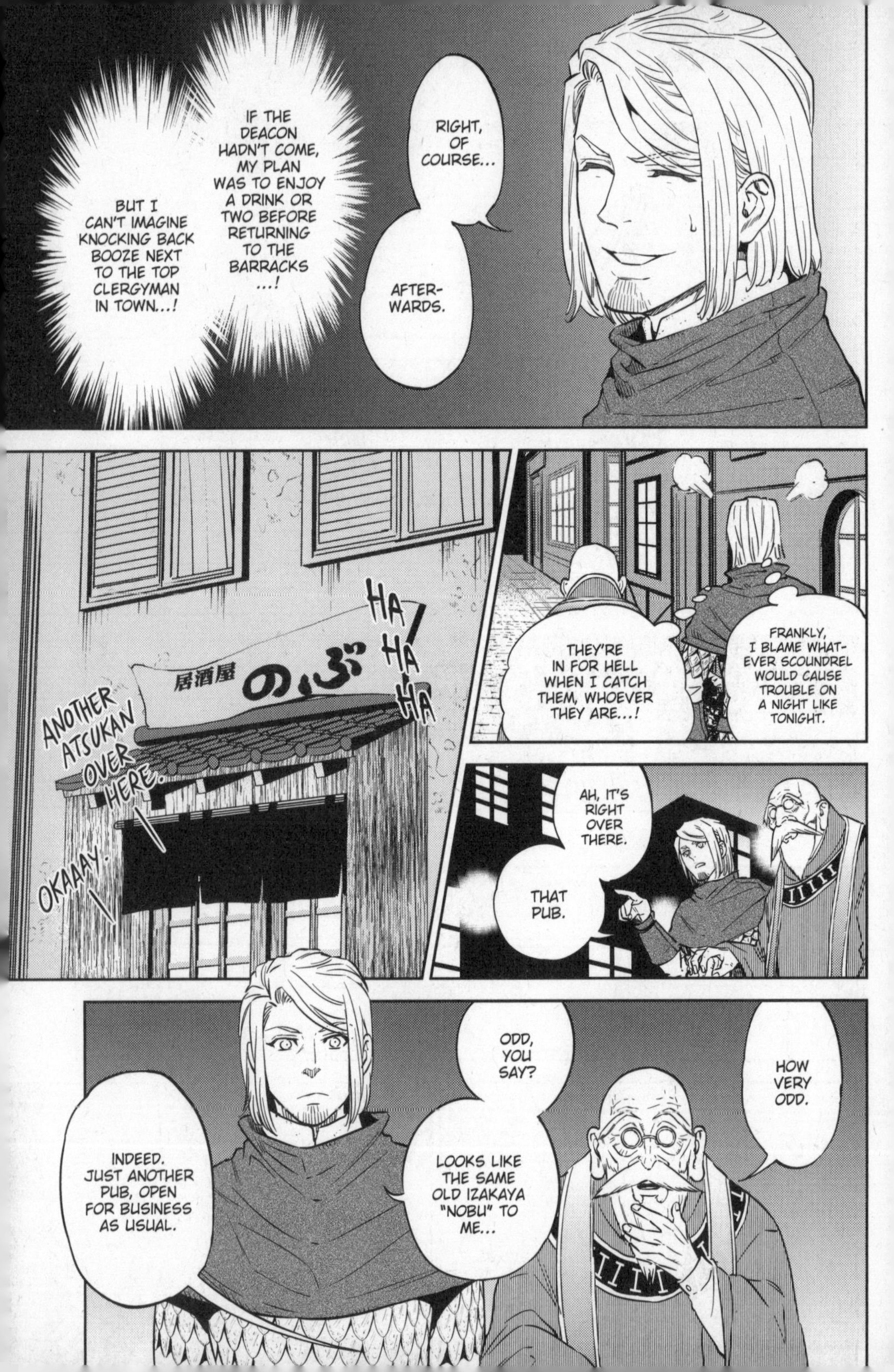
RIGHT, OF COURSE...
AFTER-WARDS.
IF THE DEACON HADN'T COME, MY PLAN WAS TO ENJOY A DRINK OR TWO BEFORE RETURNING TO THE BARRACKS ...!
BUT I CAN'T IMAGINE KNOCKING BACK BOOZE NEXT TO THE TOP CLERGYMAN IN TOWN...!
FRANKLY, I BLAME WHATEVER SCOUNDREL WOULD CAUSE TROUBLE ON A NIGHT LIKE TONIGHT.
THEY'RE IN FOR HELL WHEN I CATCH THEM, WHOEVER THEY ARE...!
AH, IT'S RIGHT OVER THERE.
THAT PUB.
HA HA HA HA
居酒屋 のぶ
ANOTHER ATSUKAN OVER HERE!
OKAAAY!
HOW VERY ODD.
ODD, YOU SAY?
LOOKS LIKE THE SAME OLD IZAKAYA "NOBU" TO ME...
INDEED. JUST ANOTHER PUB, OPEN FOR BUSINESS AS USUAL.

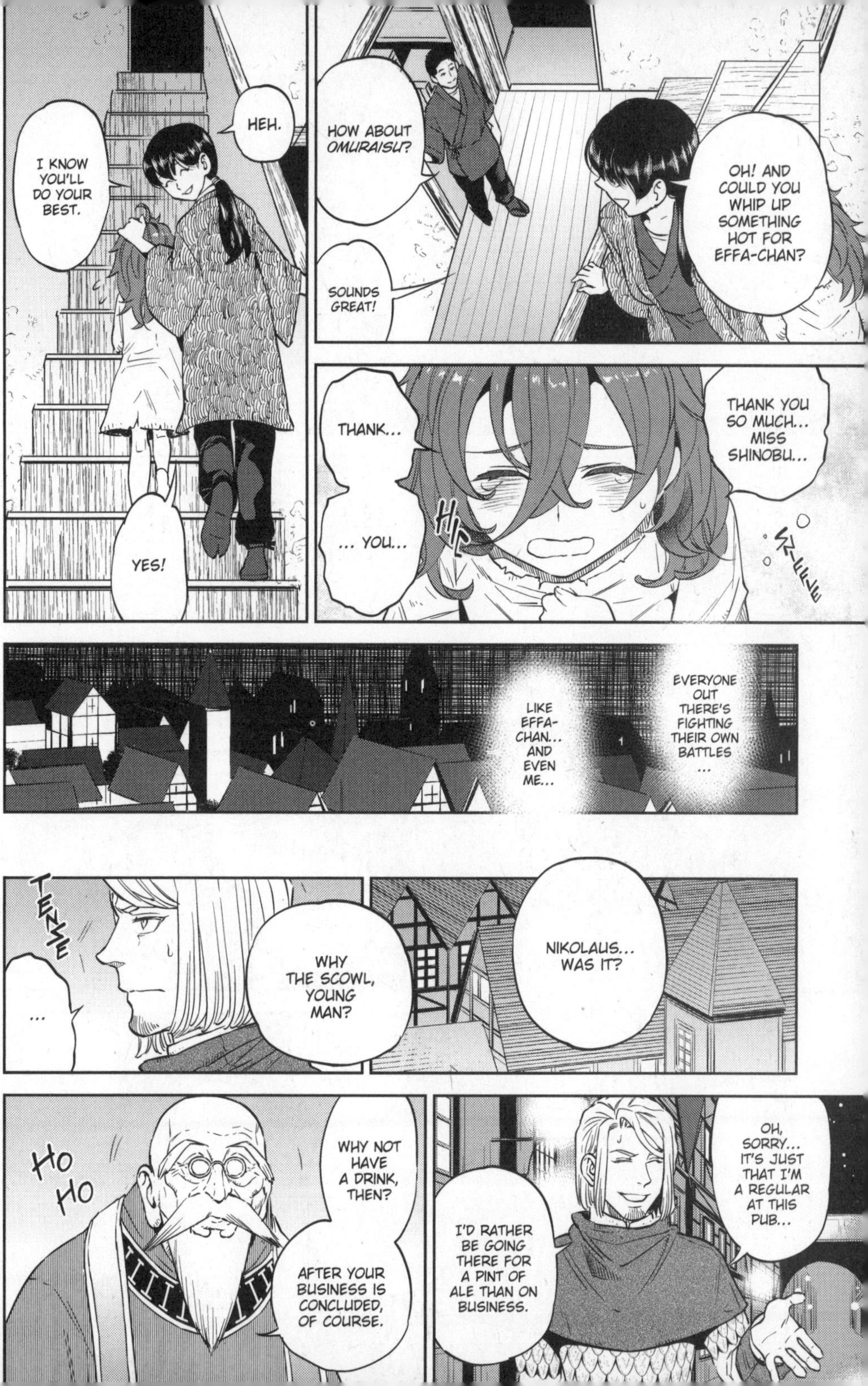
OH! AND COULD YOU WHIP UP SOMETHING HOT FOR EFFA-CHAN?
HOW ABOUT *OMURAISU*?
SOUNDS GREAT!
THANK YOU SO MUCH... MISS SHINOBU...
HIC
THANK...
... YOU...
HEH.
I KNOW YOU'LL DO YOUR BEST.
YES!
EVERYONE OUT THERE'S FIGHTING THEIR OWN BATTLES ...
LIKE EFFA-CHAN... AND EVEN ME...
NIKOLAUS... WAS IT?
WHY THE SCOWL, YOUNG MAN?
TENSE
...
OH, SORRY... IT'S JUST THAT I'M A REGULAR AT THIS PUB...
I'D RATHER BE GOING THERE FOR A PINT OF ALE THAN ON BUSINESS.
HO HO
WHY NOT HAVE A DRINK, THEN?
AFTER YOUR BUSINESS IS CONCLUDED, OF COURSE.

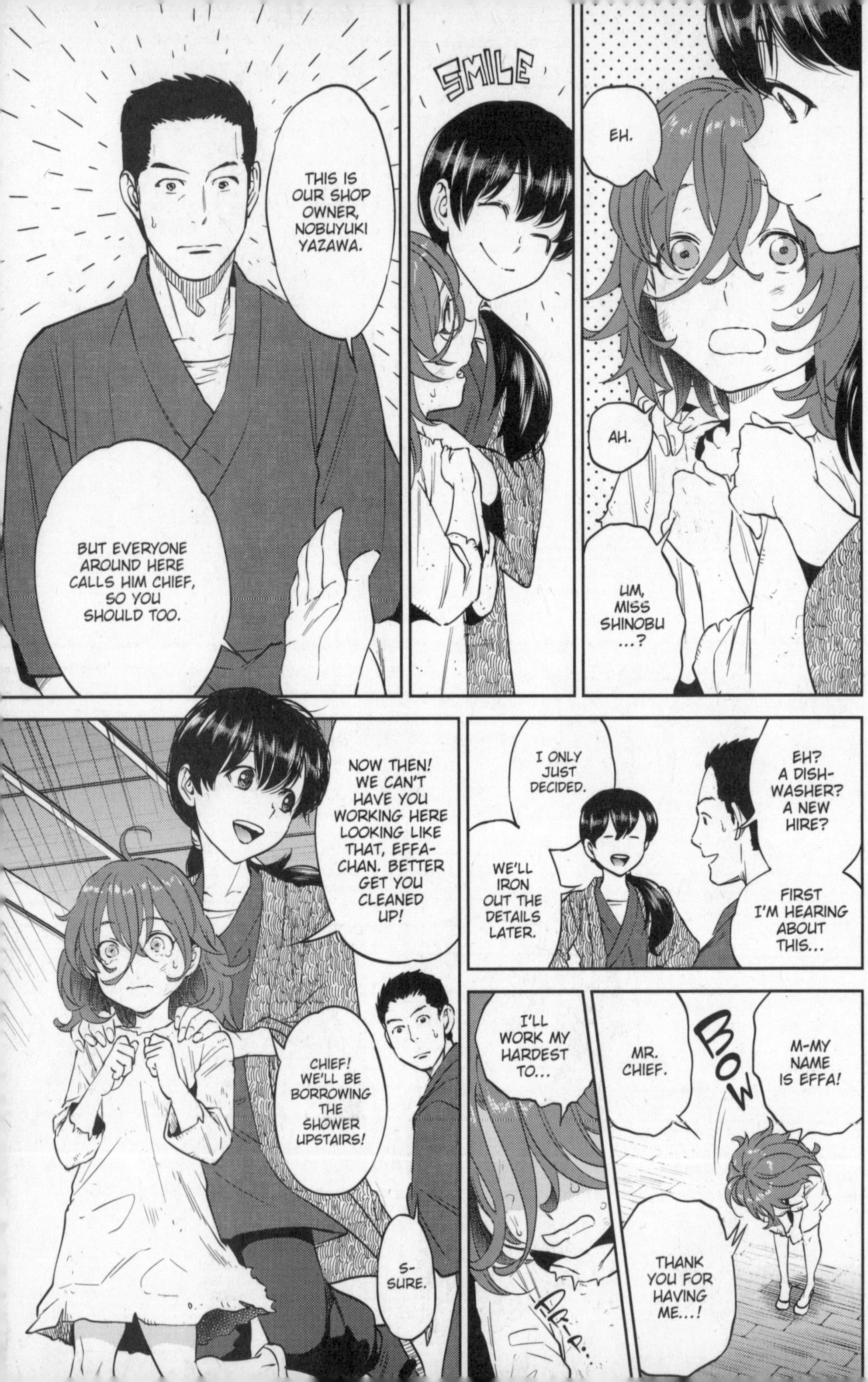
EH.
AH.
UM, MISS SHINOBU...?
SMILE
THIS IS OUR SHOP OWNER, NOBUYUKI YAZAWA.
BUT EVERYONE AROUND HERE CALLS HIM CHIEF, SO YOU SHOULD TOO.
EH? A DISH-WASHER? A NEW HIRE?
FIRST I'M HEARING ABOUT THIS...
I ONLY JUST DECIDED.
WE'LL IRON OUT THE DETAILS LATER.
M-MY NAME IS EFFA!
BOW
MR. CHIEF.
I'LL WORK MY HARDEST TO...
THANK YOU FOR HAVING ME...!
RRIP...
NOW THEN! WE CAN'T HAVE YOU WORKING HERE LOOKING LIKE THAT, EFFA-CHAN. BETTER GET YOU CLEANED UP!
CHIEF! WE'LL BE BORROWING THE SHOWER UPSTAIRS!
S-SURE.

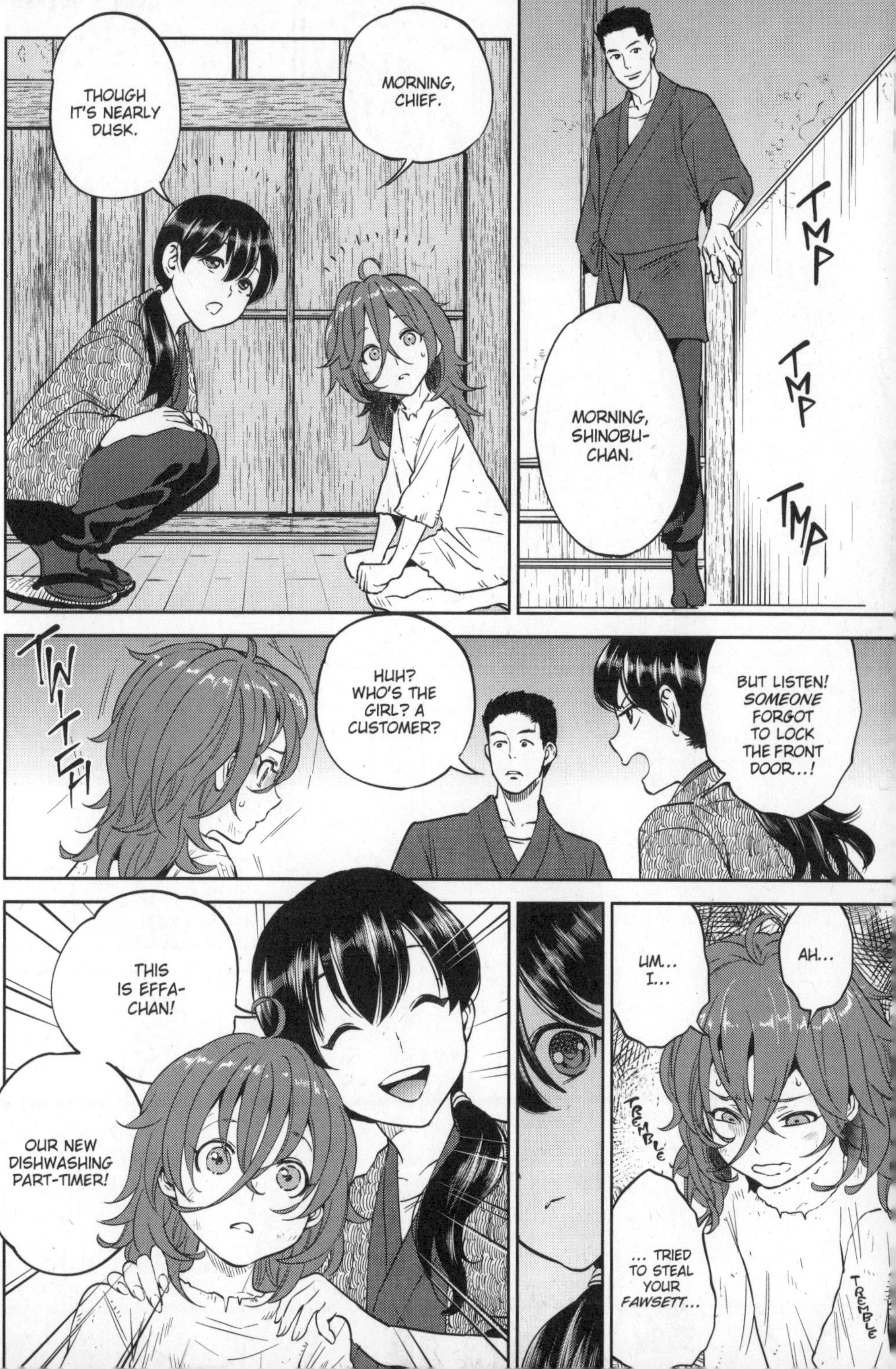
TMP
TMP
TMP
MORNING, SHINOBU-CHAN.
MORNING, CHIEF.
THOUGH IT'S NEARLY DUSK.
BUT LISTEN! SOMEONE FORGOT TO LOCK THE FRONT DOOR...!
HUH? WHO'S THE GIRL? A CUSTOMER?
TWITCH
AH...
UM... I...
TREMBLE
... TRIED TO STEAL YOUR FAWSETT...
TREMBLE
THIS IS EFFA-CHAN!
OUR NEW DISHWASHING PART-TIMER!

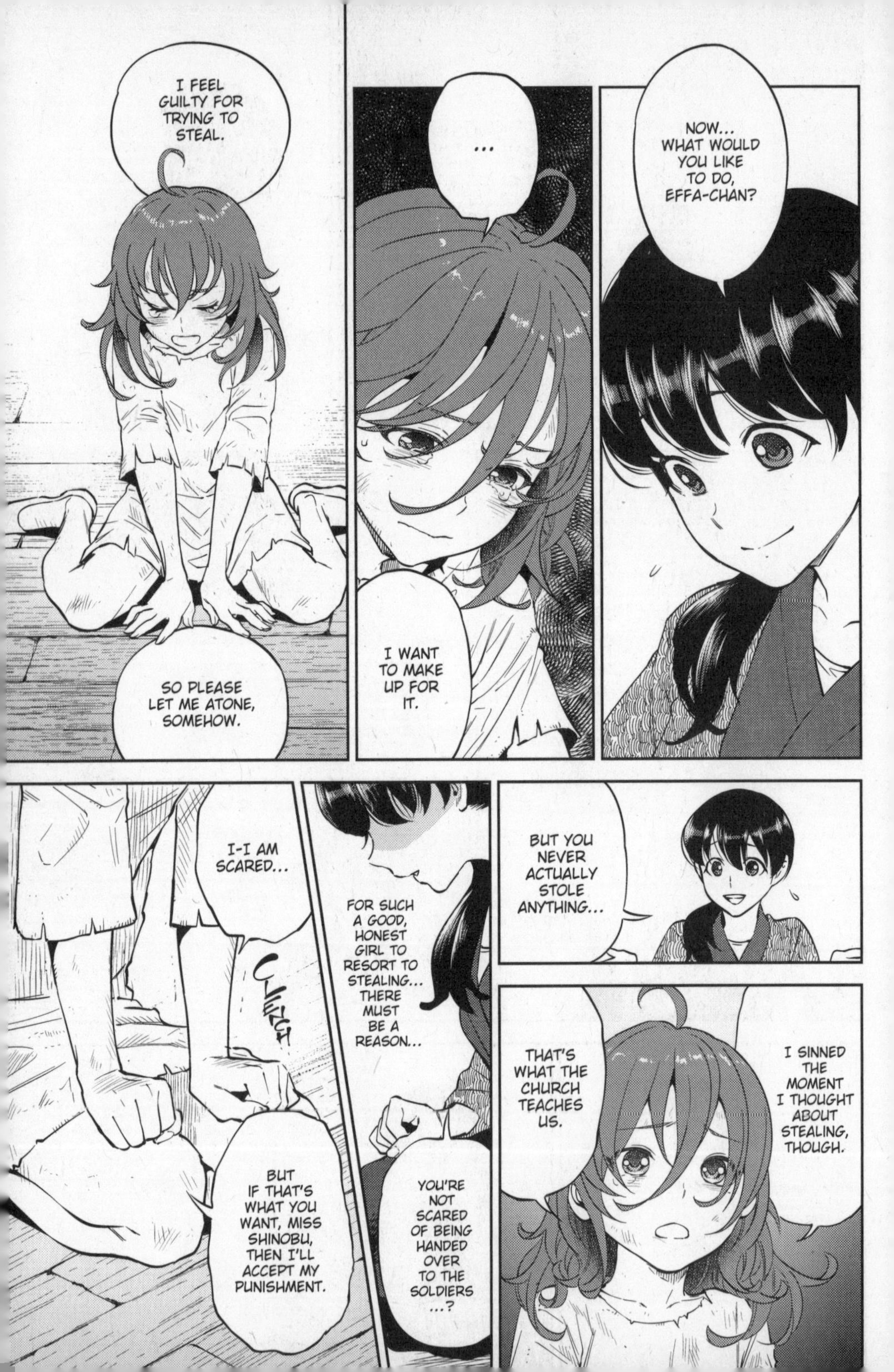
NOW... WHAT WOULD YOU LIKE TO DO, EFFA-CHAN?
...
I WANT TO MAKE UP FOR IT.
I FEEL GUILTY FOR TRYING TO STEAL.
SO PLEASE LET ME ATONE, SOMEHOW.
BUT YOU NEVER ACTUALLY STOLE ANYTHING...
I SINNED THE MOMENT I THOUGHT ABOUT STEALING, THOUGH.
THAT'S WHAT THE CHURCH TEACHES US.
FOR SUCH A GOOD, HONEST GIRL TO RESORT TO STEALING... THERE MUST BE A REASON...
YOU'RE NOT SCARED OF BEING HANDED OVER TO THE SOLDIERS ...?
I-I AM SCARED...
CLENCH
BUT IF THAT'S WHAT YOU WANT, MISS SHINOBU, THEN I'LL ACCEPT MY PUNISHMENT.

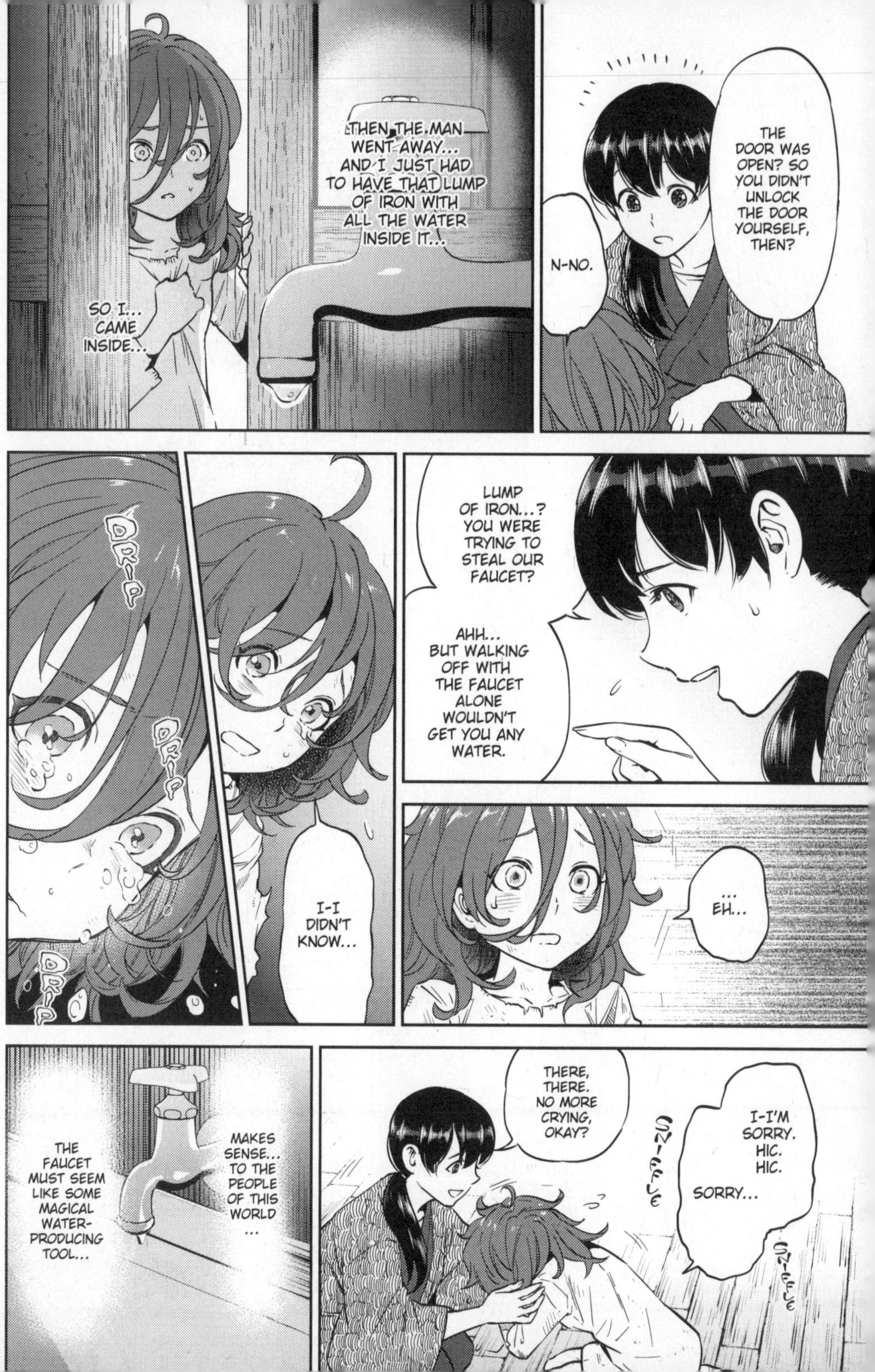
THE DOOR WAS OPEN? SO YOU DIDN'T UNLOCK THE DOOR YOURSELF, THEN?
N-NO.
THEN THE MAN WENT AWAY... AND I JUST HAD TO HAVE THAT LUMP OF IRON WITH ALL THE WATER INSIDE IT...
SO I... CAME INSIDE...
LUMP OF IRON...? YOU WERE TRYING TO STEAL OUR FAUCET?
AHH... BUT WALKING OFF WITH THE FAUCET ALONE WOULDN'T GET YOU ANY WATER.
... EH...
I-I DIDN'T KNOW...
DRIP
DRIP
DRIP
I-I'M SORRY. HIC. HIC.
SORRY...
THERE, THERE. NO MORE CRYING, OKAY?
SNIFFLE
SNIFFLE
MAKES SENSE... TO THE PEOPLE OF THIS WORLD...
THE FAUCET MUST SEEM LIKE SOME MAGICAL WATER-PRODUCING TOOL...

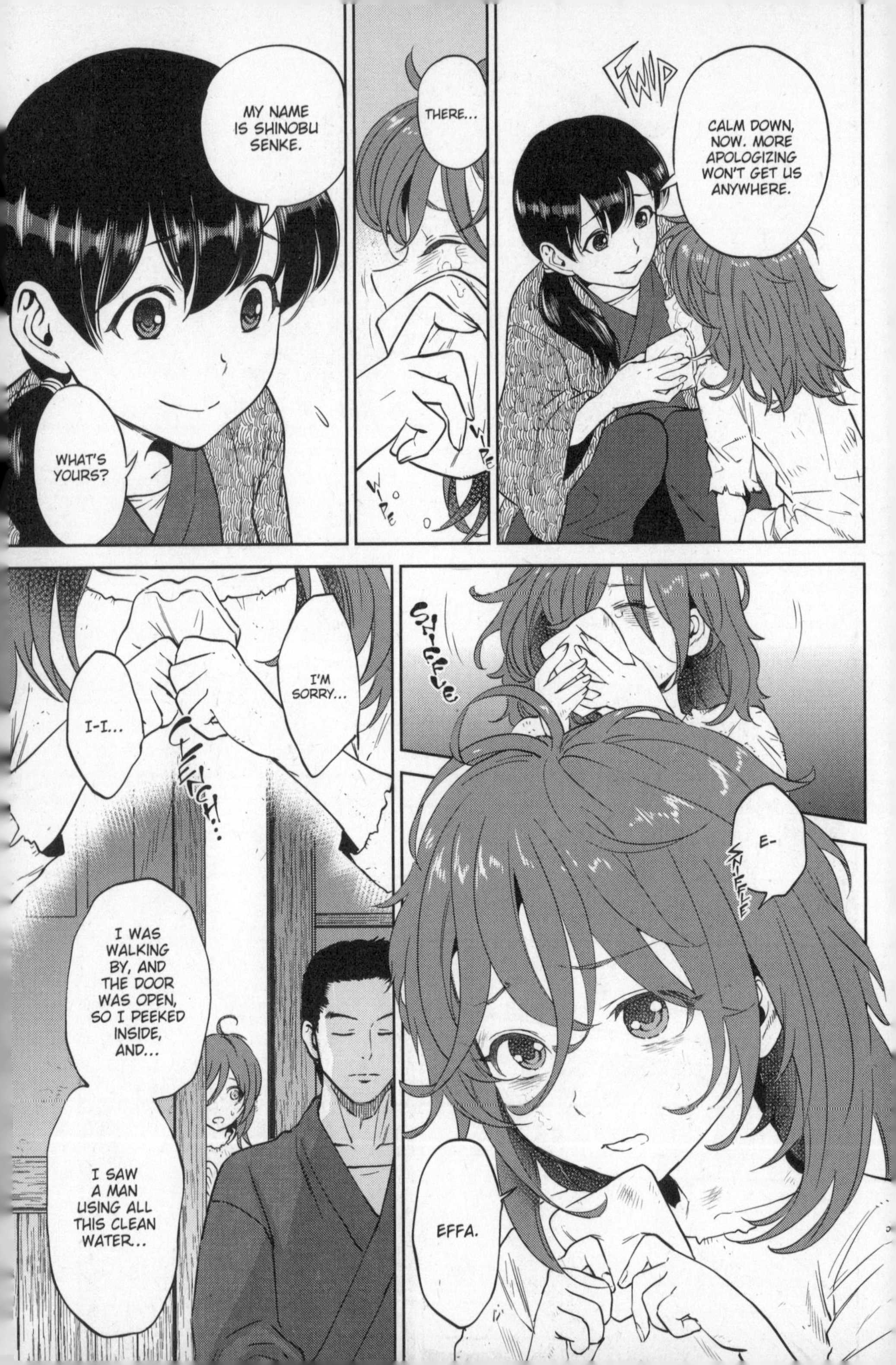
FWIP
CALM DOWN, NOW. MORE APOLOGIZING WON'T GET US ANYWHERE.
THERE...
WIPE
WIPE
MY NAME IS SHINOBU SENKE.
WHAT'S YOURS?
SNIFFLE
E-
SNIFFLE
EFFA.
I'M SORRY...
I-I...
CLENCH...
I WAS WALKING BY, AND THE DOOR WAS OPEN, SO I PEEKED INSIDE, AND...
I SAW A MAN USING ALL THIS CLEAN WATER...

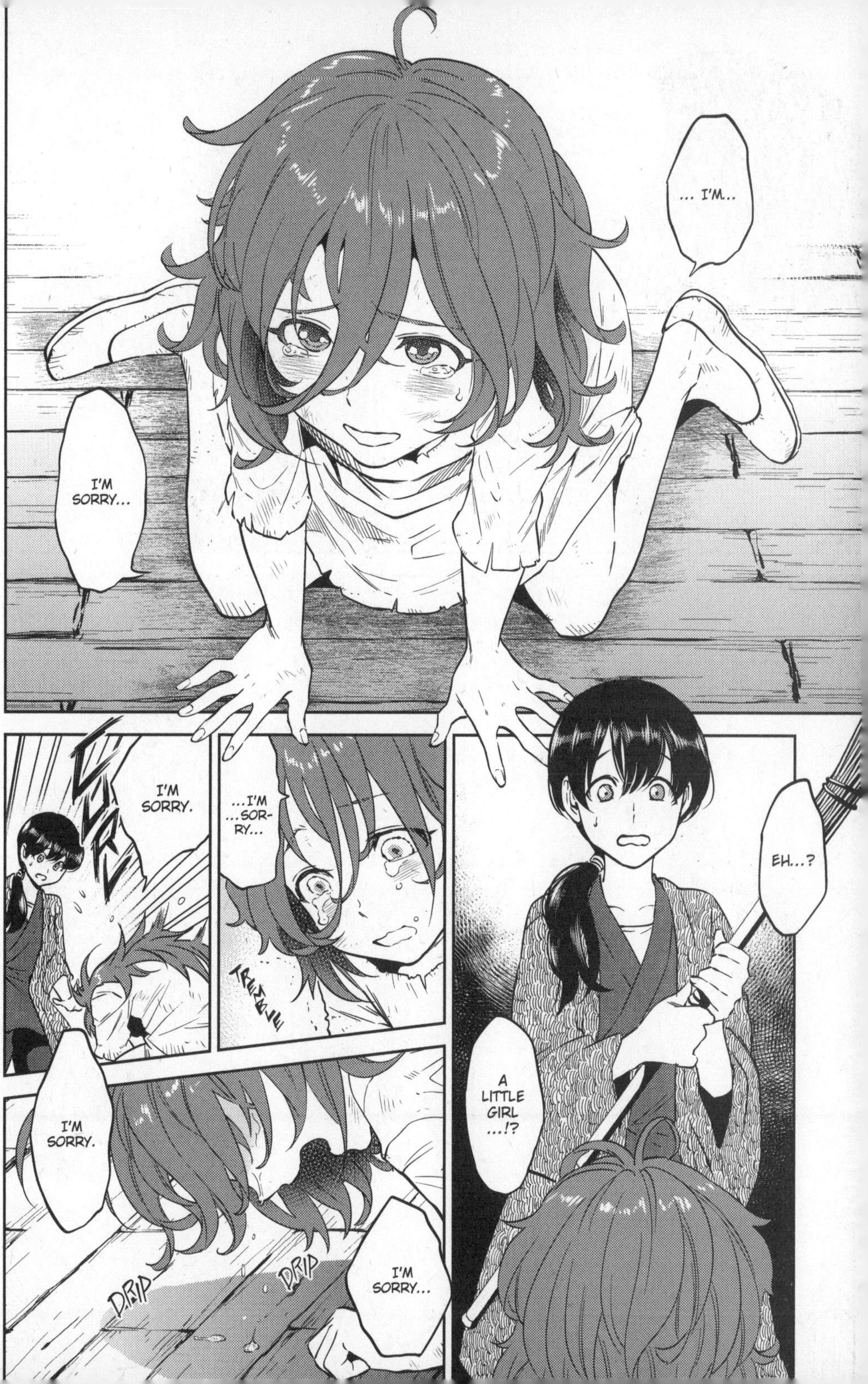
... I'M...
I'M SORRY...
EH...?
A LITTLE GIRL ...!?
...I'M ...SOR-RY...
TREMBLE
I'M SORRY.
I'M SORRY...
DRIP
I'M SORRY.
DRIP

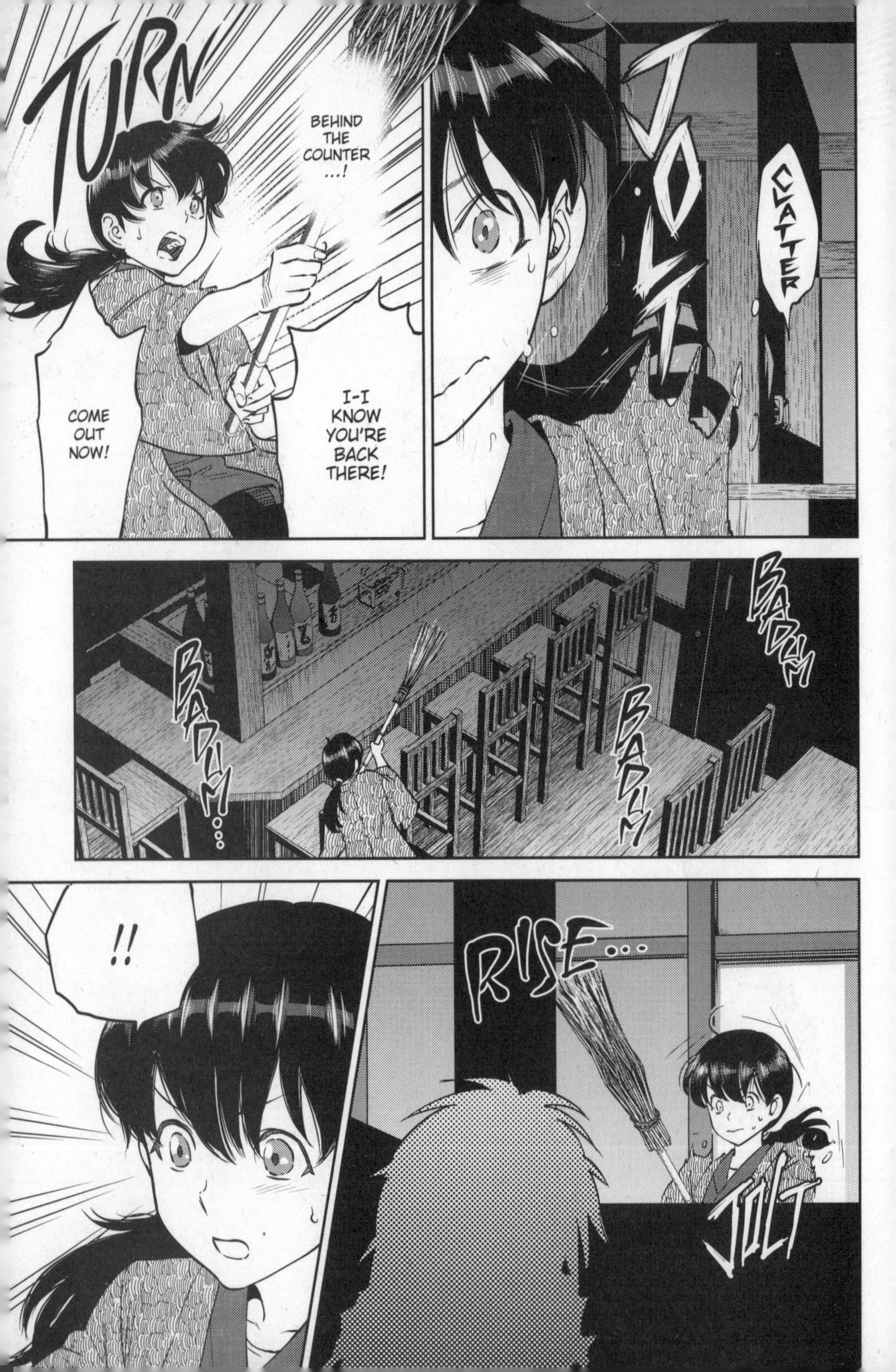
CLATTER
JOLT
TURN
BEHIND THE COUNTER ...!
I-I KNOW YOU'RE BACK THERE!
COME OUT NOW!
BADUM
BADUM
BADUM...
RISE...
JOLT
!!

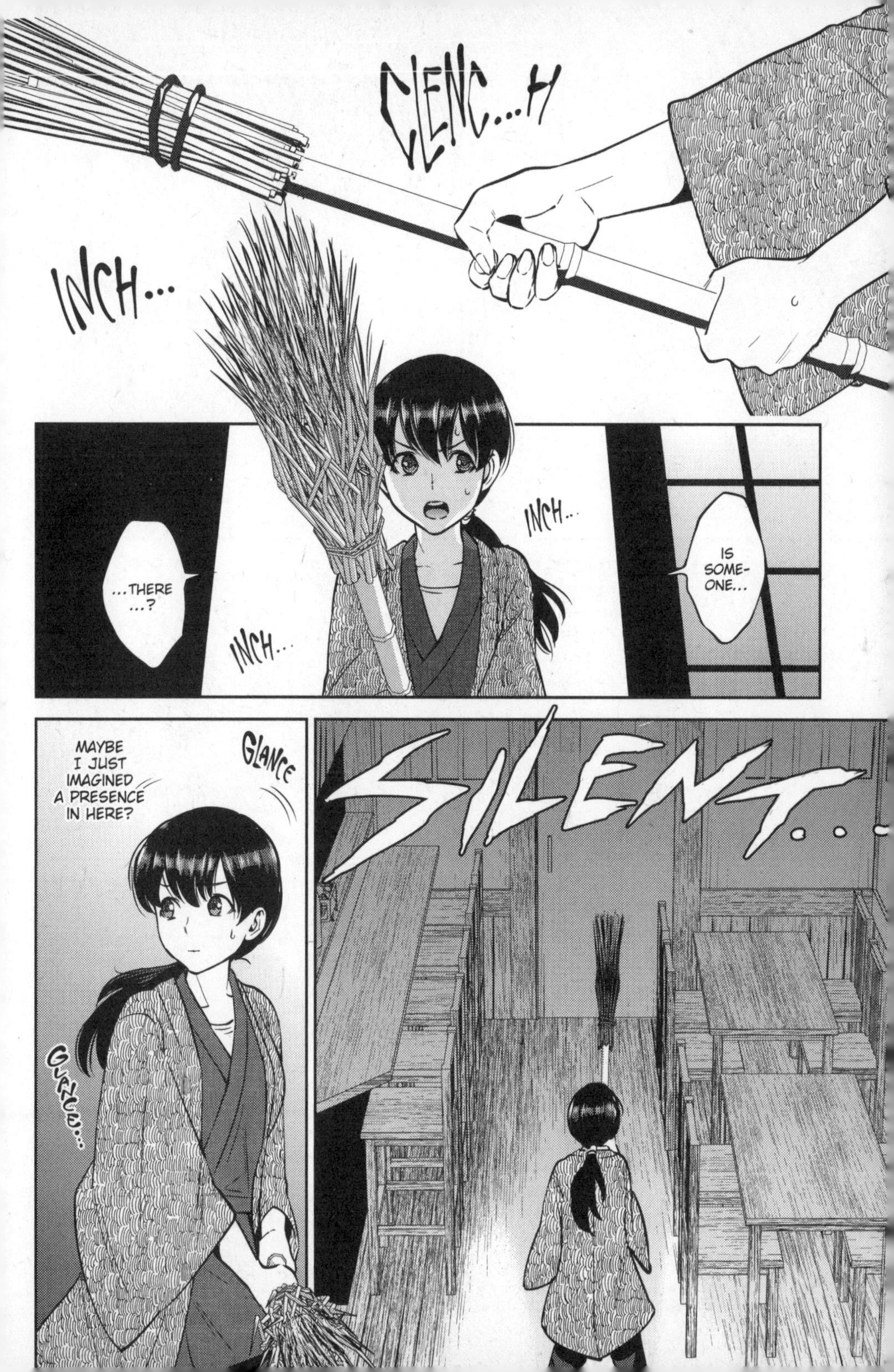
CLENC...H
INCH...
IS SOME-ONE...
INCH...
...THERE ...?
INCH...
SILENT...
GLANCE
MAYBE I JUST IMAGINED A PRESENCE IN HERE?
GLANCE...

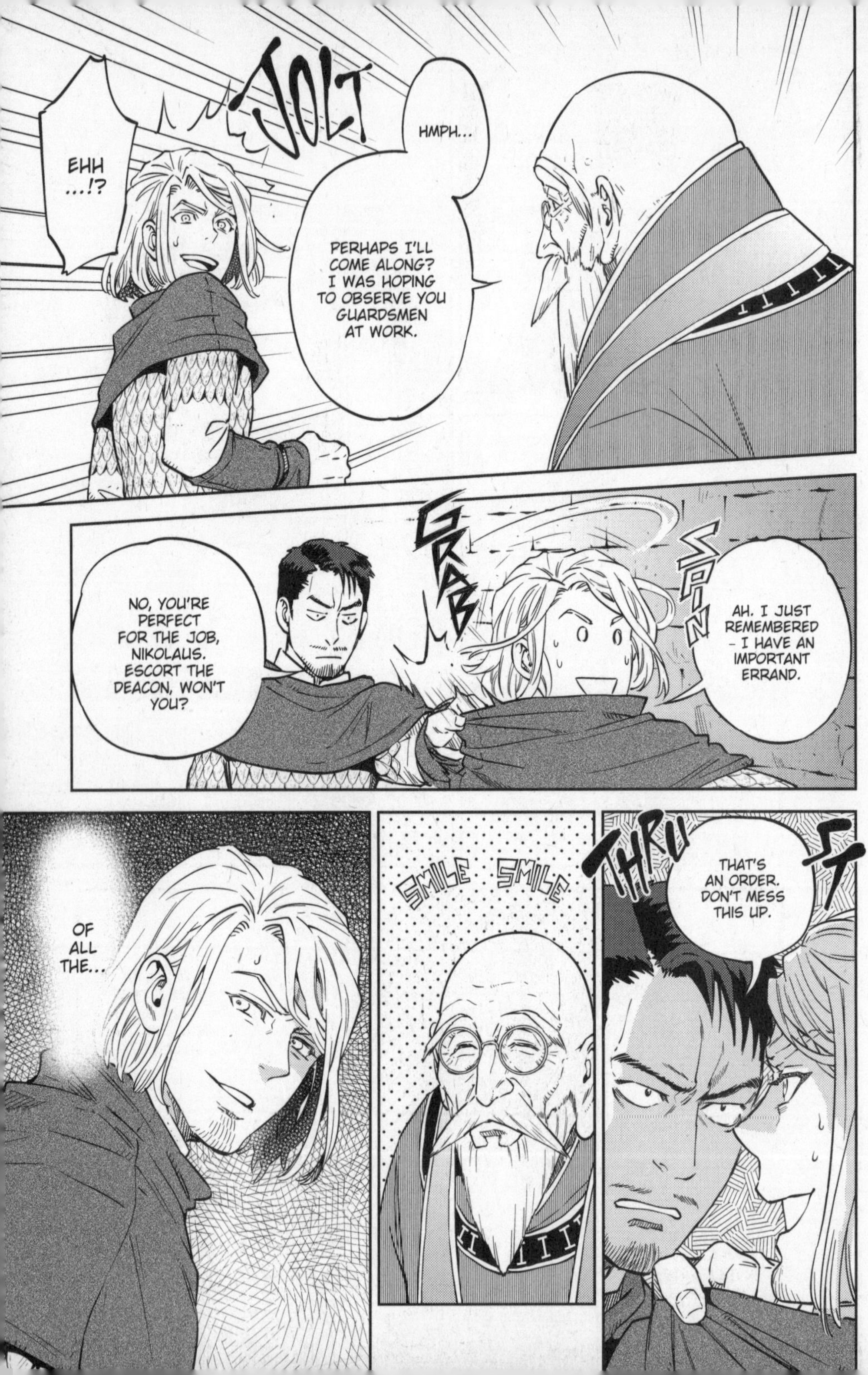
HMPH...
PERHAPS I'LL COME ALONG? I WAS HOPING TO OBSERVE YOU GUARDSMEN AT WORK.
JOLT
EHH ...!?
SPIN
AH. I JUST REMEMBERED - I HAVE AN IMPORTANT ERRAND.
GRAB
NO, YOU'RE PERFECT FOR THE JOB, NIKOLAUS. ESCORT THE DEACON, WON'T YOU?
THRUST
THAT'S AN ORDER. DON'T MESS THIS UP.
SMILE SMILE
OF ALL THE...

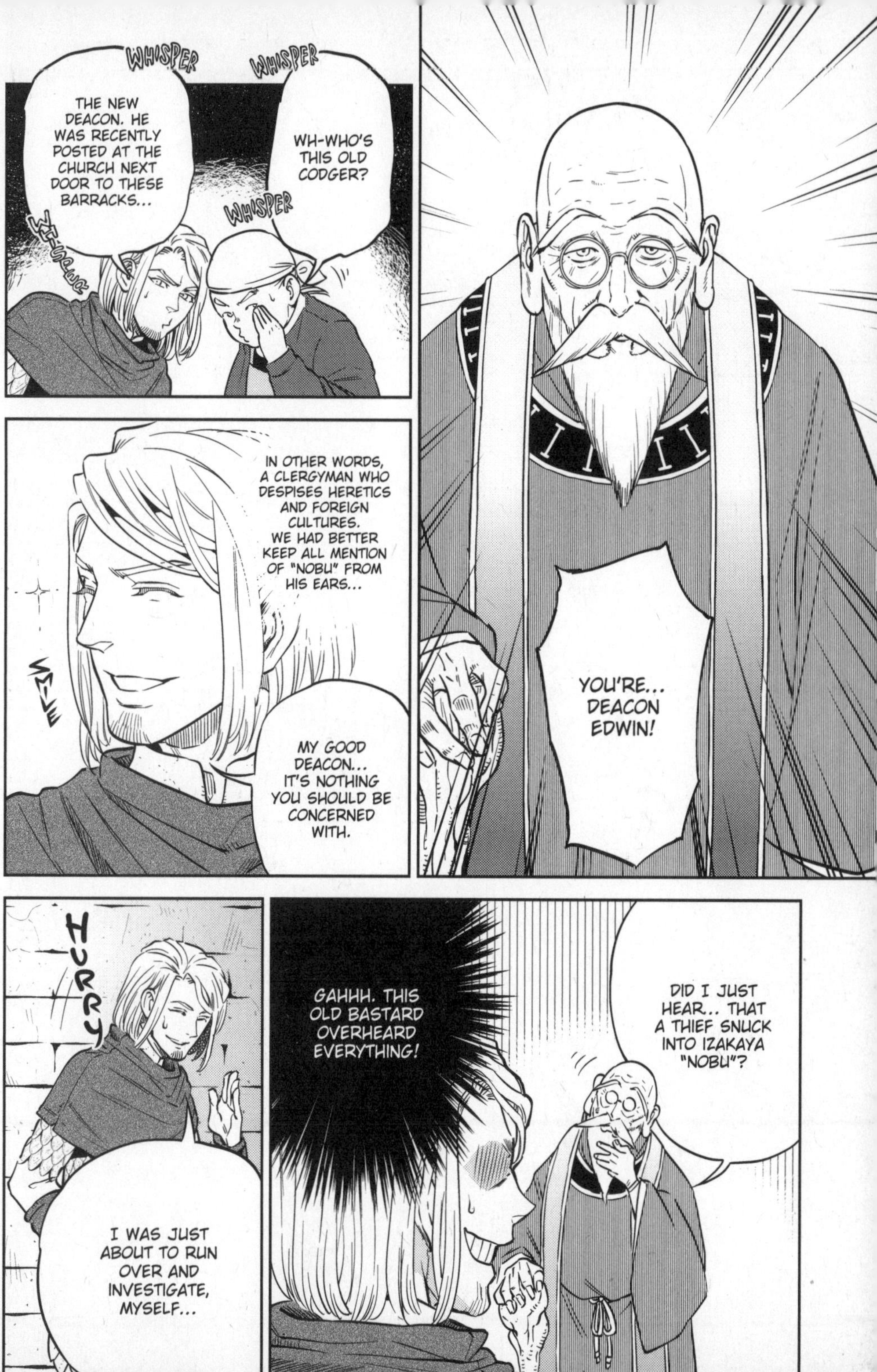
YOU'RE... DEACON EDWIN!
WHISPER
WHISPER
WH-WHO'S THIS OLD CODGER?
WHISPER
THE NEW DEACON. HE WAS RECENTLY POSTED AT THE CHURCH NEXT DOOR TO THESE BARRACKS...
IN OTHER WORDS, A CLERGYMAN WHO DESPISES HERETICS AND FOREIGN CULTURES. WE HAD BETTER KEEP ALL MENTION OF "NOBU" FROM HIS EARS...
SMILE
MY GOOD DEACON... IT'S NOTHING YOU SHOULD BE CONCERNED WITH.
DID I JUST HEAR... THAT A THIEF SNUCK INTO IZAKAYA "NOBU"?
GAHHH. THIS OLD BASTARD OVERHEARD EVERYTHING!
HURRY
I WAS JUST ABOUT TO RUN OVER AND INVESTIGATE, MYSELF...

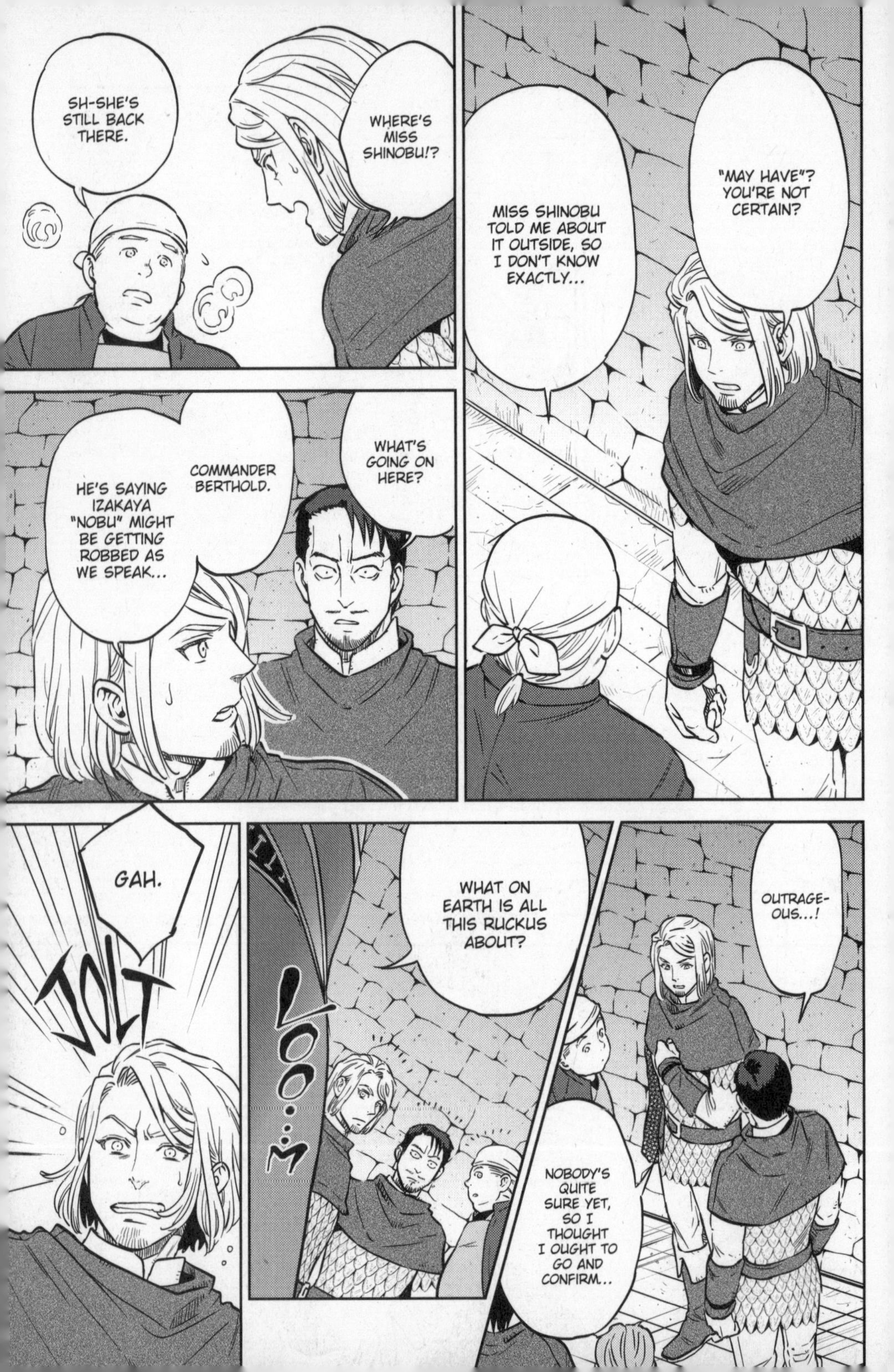
"MAY HAVE"? YOU'RE NOT CERTAIN?
MISS SHINOBU TOLD ME ABOUT IT OUTSIDE, SO I DON'T KNOW EXACTLY...
WHERE'S MISS SHINOBU!?
SH-SHE'S STILL BACK THERE.
WHAT'S GOING ON HERE?
COMMANDER BERTHOLD.
HE'S SAYING IZAKAYA "NOBU" MIGHT BE GETTING ROBBED AS WE SPEAK...
OUTRAGE-OUS...!
NOBODY'S QUITE SURE YET, SO I THOUGHT I OUGHT TO GO AND CONFIRM..
WHAT ON EARTH IS ALL THIS RUCKUS ABOUT?
VOO...M
GAH.
JOLT

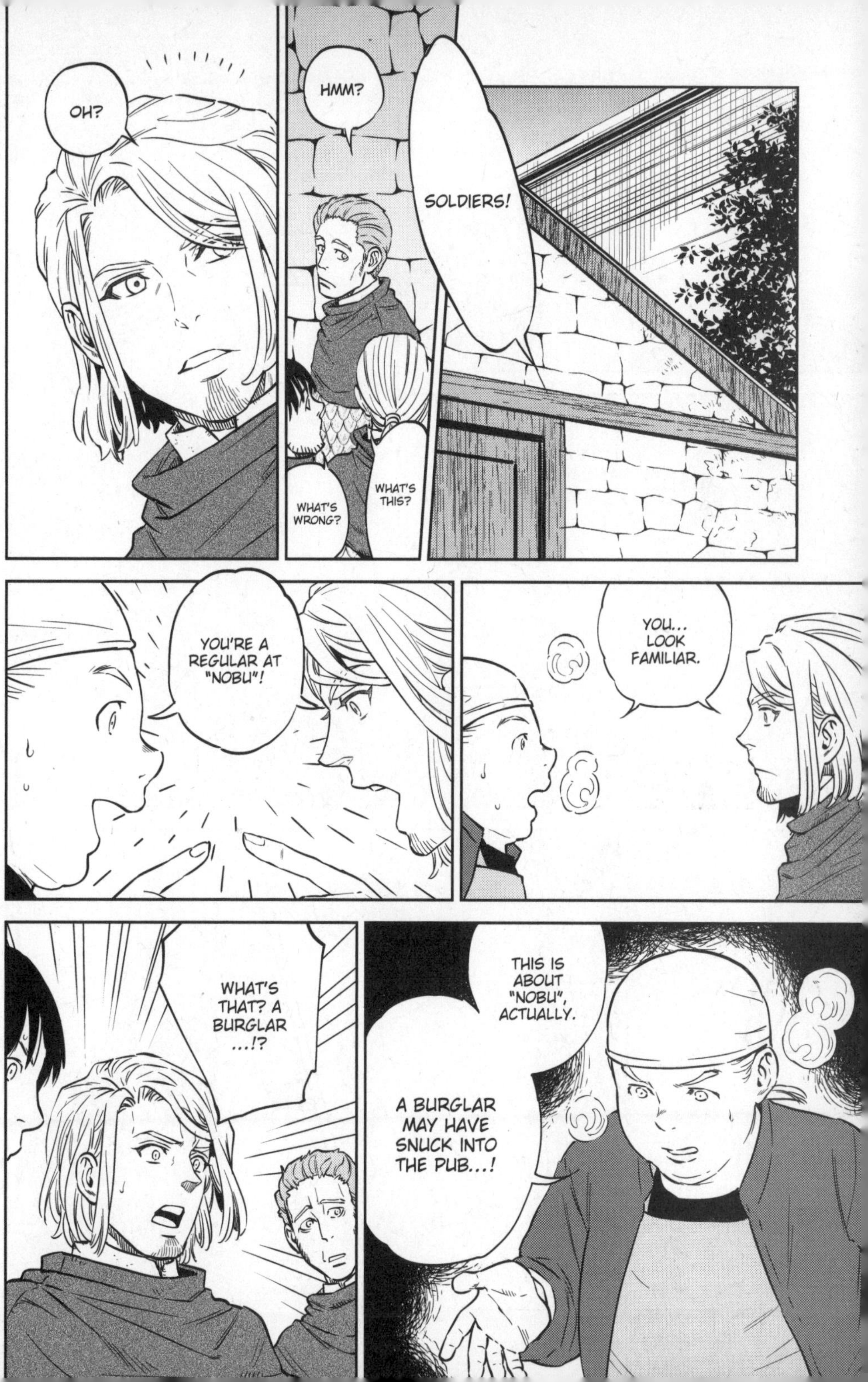
SOLDIERS!
HMM?
WHAT'S THIS?
WHAT'S WRONG?
OH?
YOU... LOOK FAMILIAR.
YOU'RE A REGULAR AT "NOBU"!
THIS IS ABOUT "NOBU", ACTUALLY.
A BURGLAR MAY HAVE SNUCK INTO THE PUB...!
WHAT'S THAT? A BURGLAR ...!?

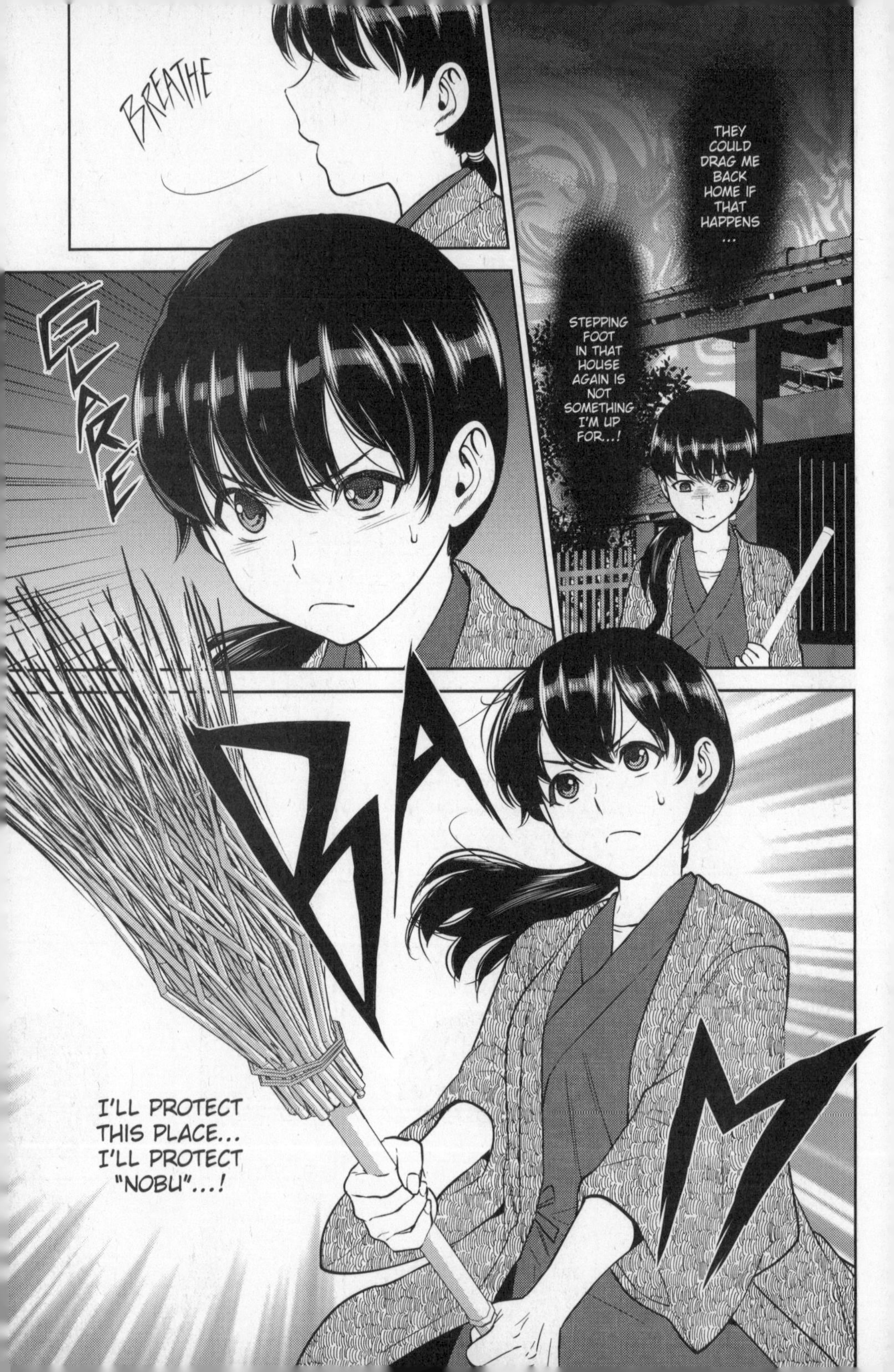
THEY COULD DRAG ME BACK HOME IF THAT HAPPENS...
STEPPING FOOT IN THAT HOUSE AGAIN IS NOT SOMETHING I'M UP FOR...!
BREATHE
GLARE
BAM
I'LL PROTECT THIS PLACE... I'LL PROTECT "NOBU"...!

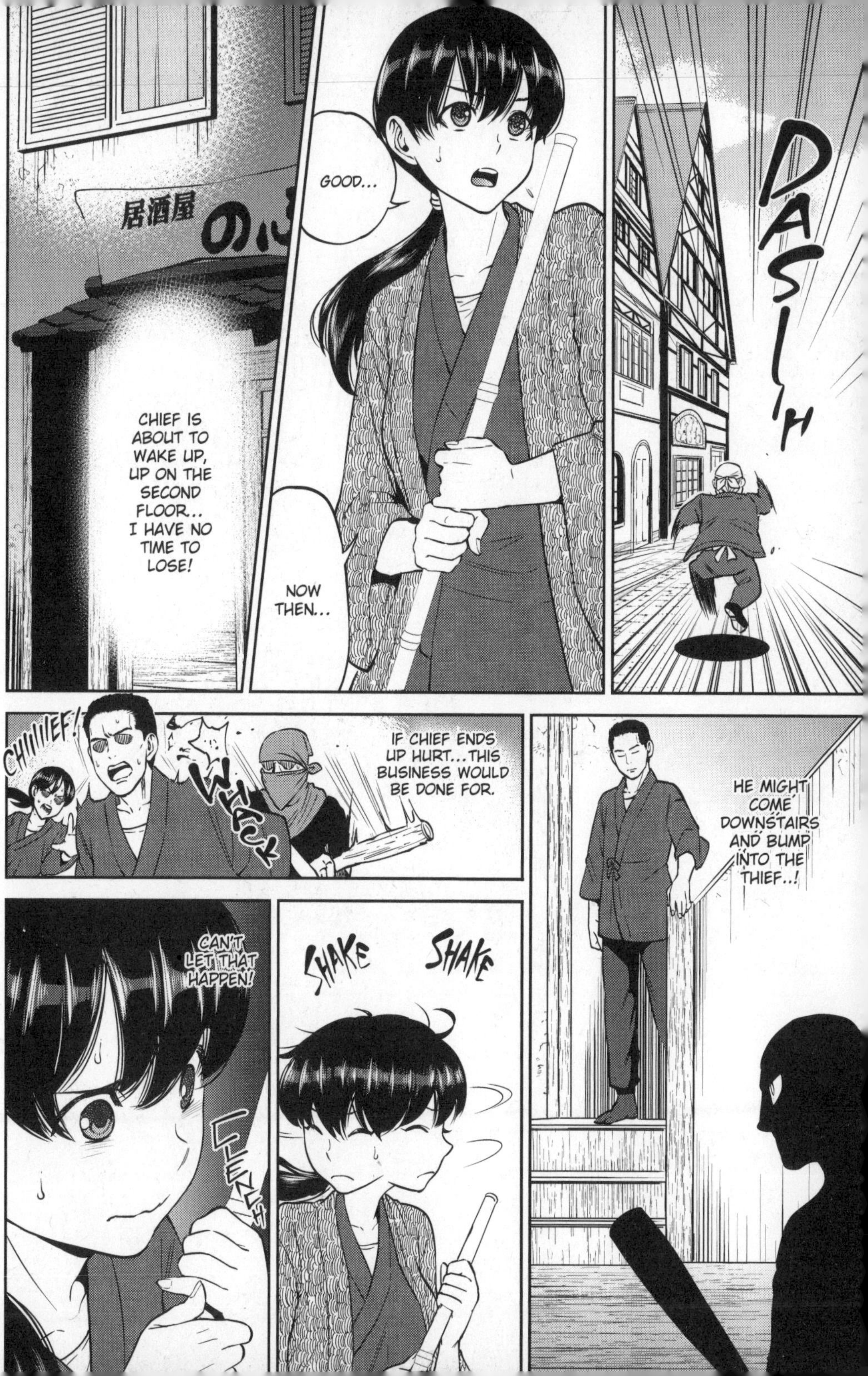
DASH
GOOD...
NOW THEN...
CHIEF IS ABOUT TO WAKE UP, UP ON THE SECOND FLOOR... I HAVE NO TIME TO LOSE!
居酒屋
HE MIGHT COME DOWNSTAIRS AND BUMP INTO THE THIEF..!
IF CHIEF ENDS UP HURT...THIS BUSINESS WOULD BE DONE FOR.
WHACK
CHIIIIEF!
SHAKE
SHAKE
CAN'T LET THAT HAPPEN!
CLENCH

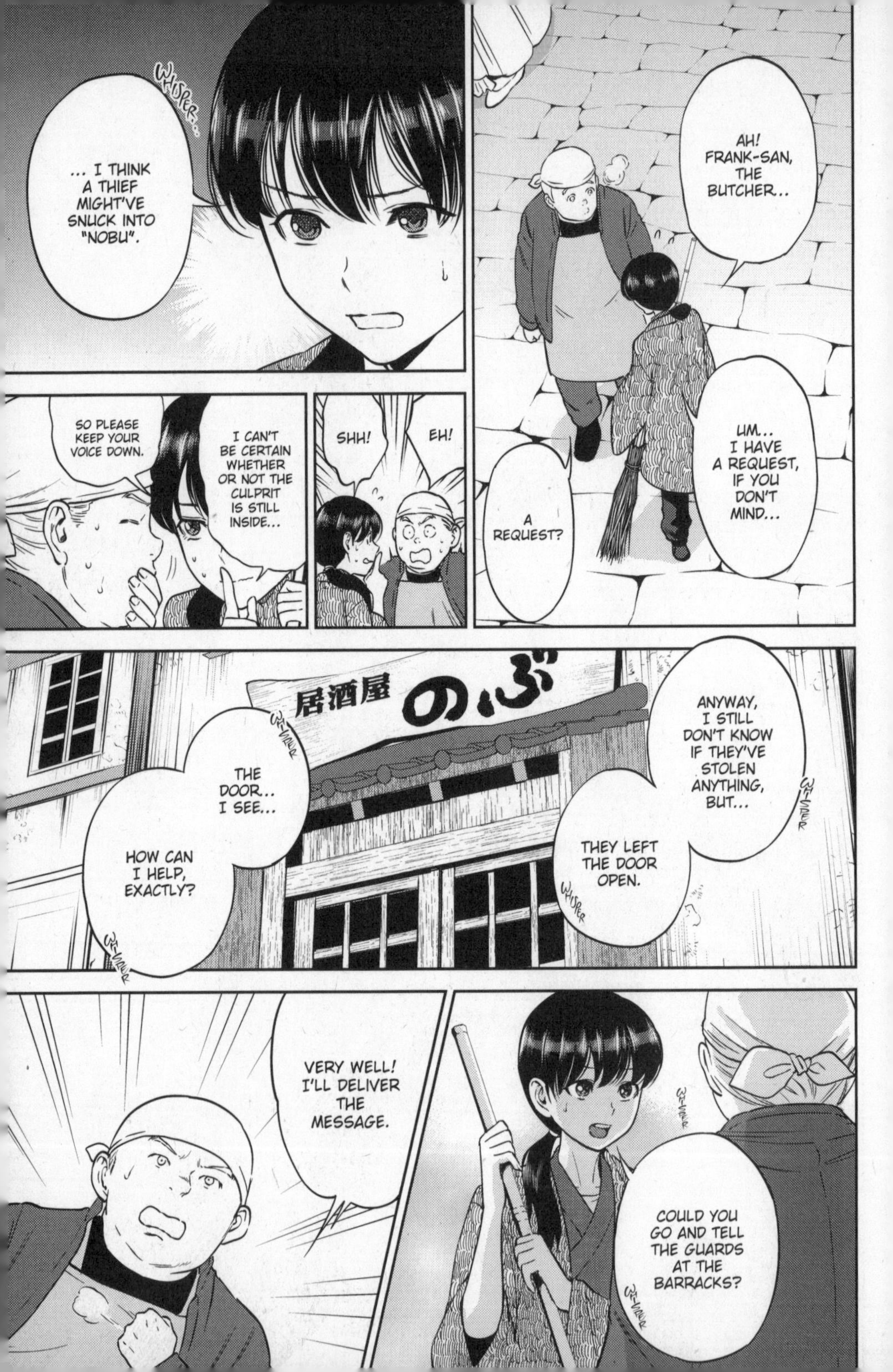
AH! FRANK-SAN, THE BUTCHER...
UM... I HAVE A REQUEST, IF YOU DON'T MIND...
A REQUEST?
WHISPER...
... I THINK A THIEF MIGHT'VE SNUCK INTO "NOBU".
EH!
SHH!
I CAN'T BE CERTAIN WHETHER OR NOT THE CULPRIT IS STILL INSIDE...
SO PLEASE KEEP YOUR VOICE DOWN.
居酒屋 のぶ
ANYWAY, I STILL DON'T KNOW IF THEY'VE STOLEN ANYTHING, BUT...
WHISPER
THEY LEFT THE DOOR OPEN.
WHISPER
THE DOOR... I SEE...
WHISPER
HOW CAN I HELP, EXACTLY?
WHISPER
WHISPER
COULD YOU GO AND TELL THE GUARDS AT THE BARRACKS?
WHISPER
VERY WELL! I'LL DELIVER THE MESSAGE.

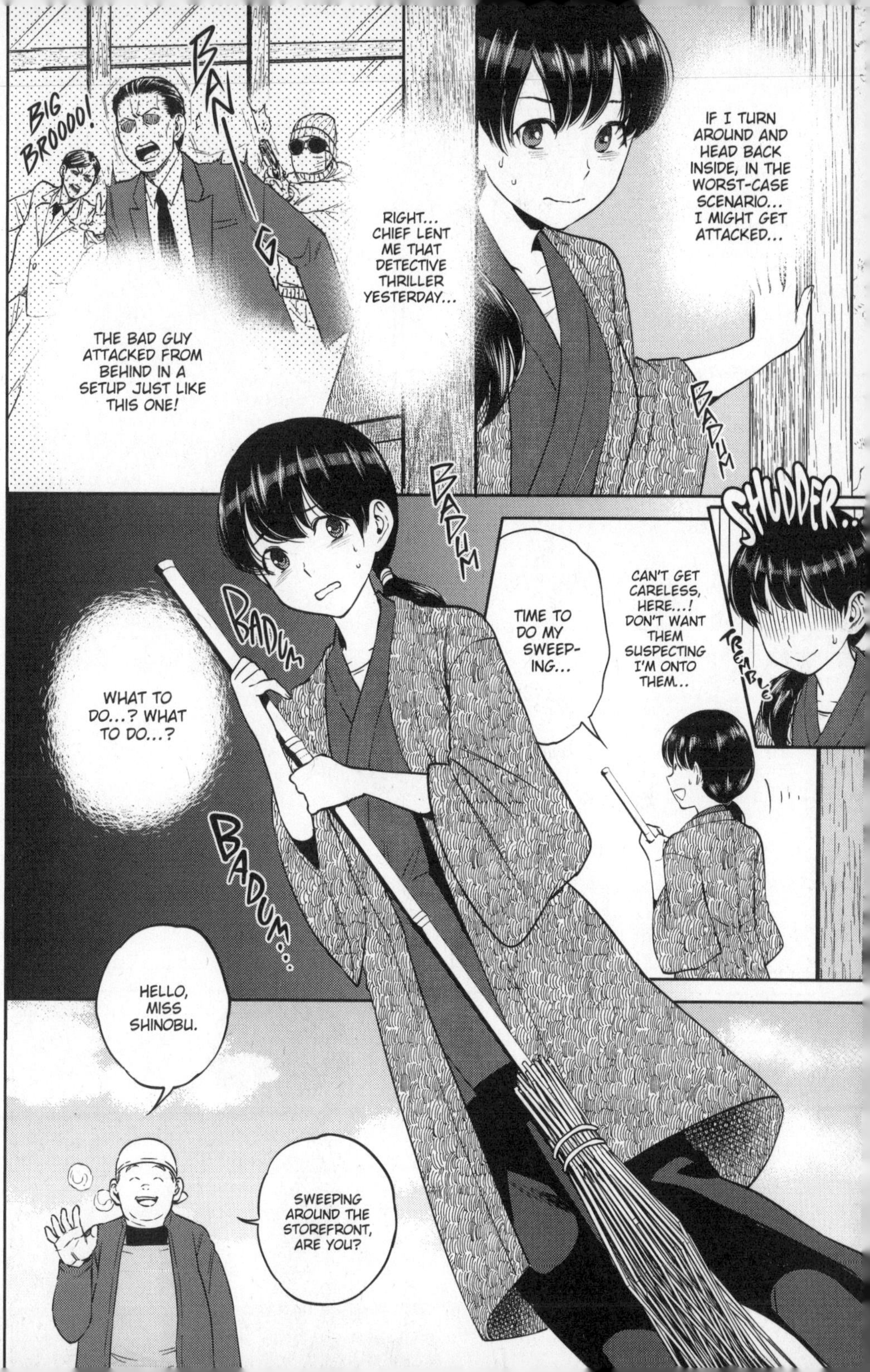
IF I TURN AROUND AND HEAD BACK INSIDE, IN THE WORST-CASE SCENARIO... I MIGHT GET ATTACKED...
BADUM
RIGHT... CHIEF LENT ME THAT DETECTIVE THRILLER YESTERDAY...
BANG
BIG BROOOOO!
THE BAD GUY ATTACKED FROM BEHIND IN A SETUP JUST LIKE THIS ONE!
SHUDDER...
TREMBLE
CAN'T GET CARELESS, HERE...! DON'T WANT THEM SUSPECTING I'M ONTO THEM...
TIME TO DO MY SWEEP-ING...
BADUM
BADUM
WHAT TO DO...? WHAT TO DO...?
BADUM...
HELLO, MISS SHINOBU.
SWEEPING AROUND THE STOREFRONT, ARE YOU?

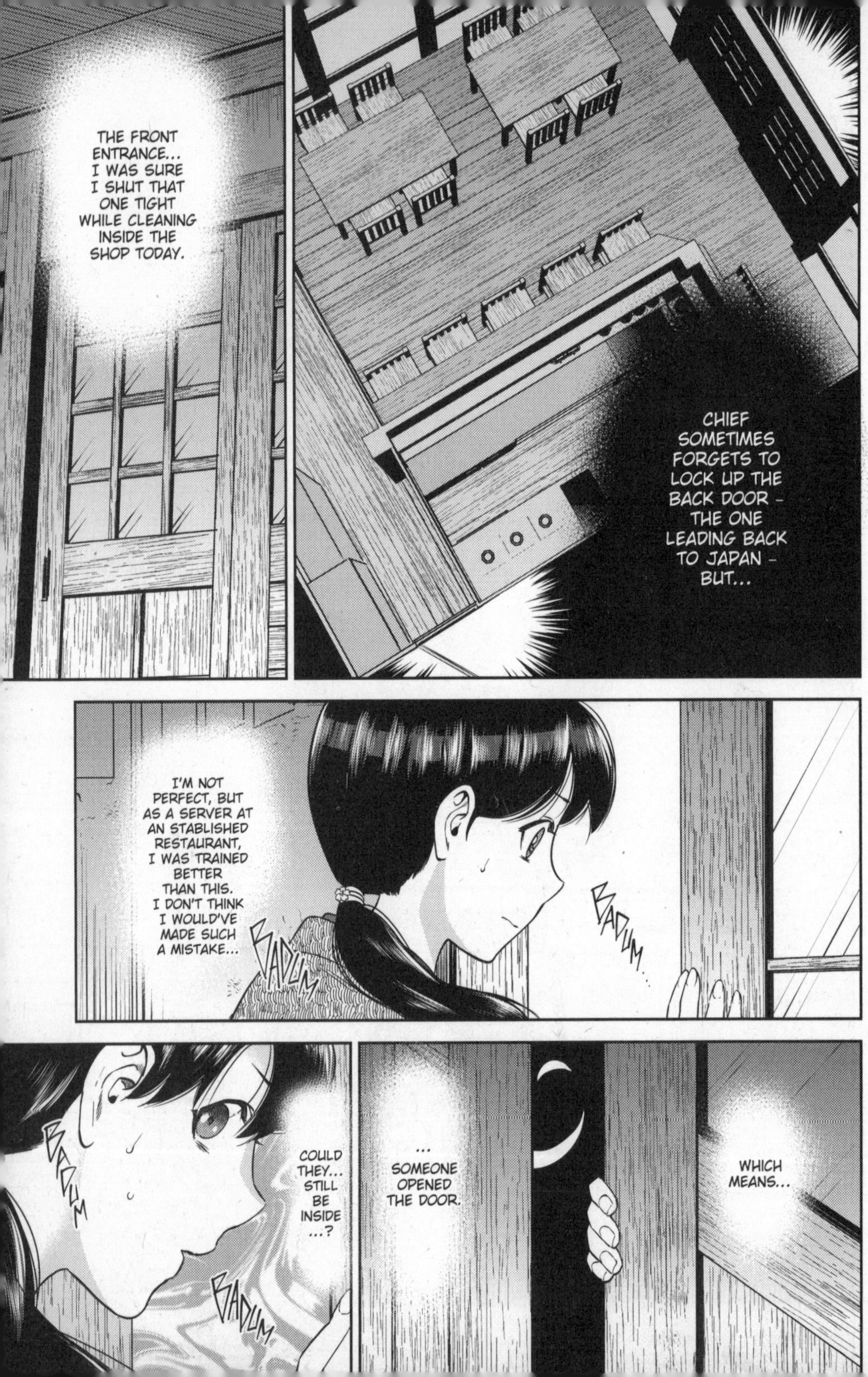
CHIEF SOMETIMES FORGETS TO LOCK UP THE BACK DOOR - THE ONE LEADING BACK TO JAPAN - BUT...
THE FRONT ENTRANCE... I WAS SURE I SHUT THAT ONE TIGHT WHILE CLEANING INSIDE THE SHOP TODAY.
BADUM...
I'M NOT PERFECT, BUT AS A SERVER AT AN STABLISHED RESTAURANT, I WAS TRAINED BETTER THAN THIS. I DON'T THINK I WOULD'VE MADE SUCH A MISTAKE...
BADUM
WHICH MEANS...
... SOMEONE OPENED THE DOOR.
COULD THEY... STILL BE INSIDE ...?
BADUM
BADUM

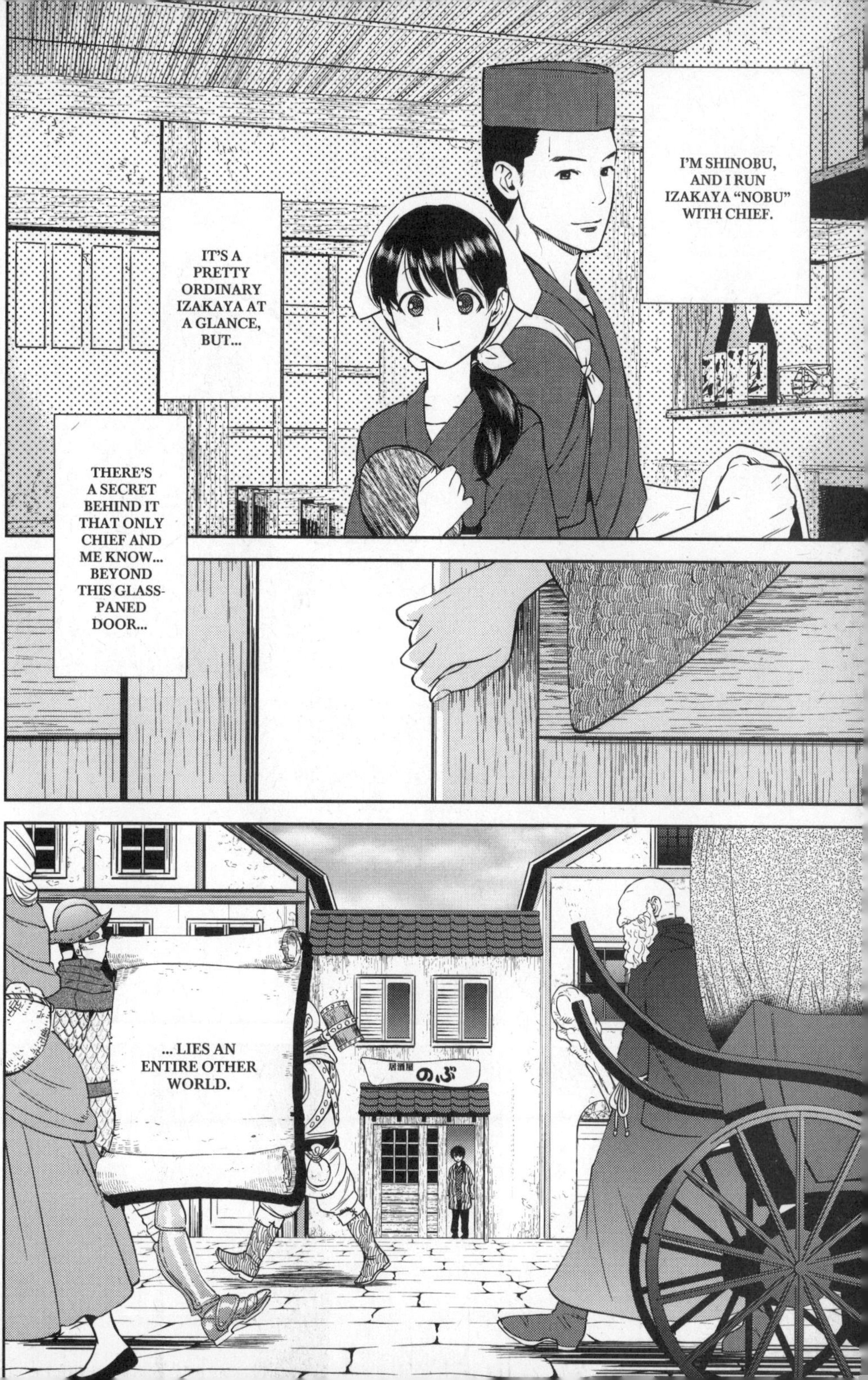
I'M SHINOBU, AND I RUN IZAKAYA "NOBU" WITH CHIEF.
IT'S A PRETTY ORDINARY IZAKAYA AT A GLANCE, BUT...
THERE'S A SECRET BEHIND IT THAT ONLY CHIEF AND ME KNOW... BEYOND THIS GLASS-PANED DOOR...
居酒屋 のぶ
... LIES AN ENTIRE OTHER WORLD.

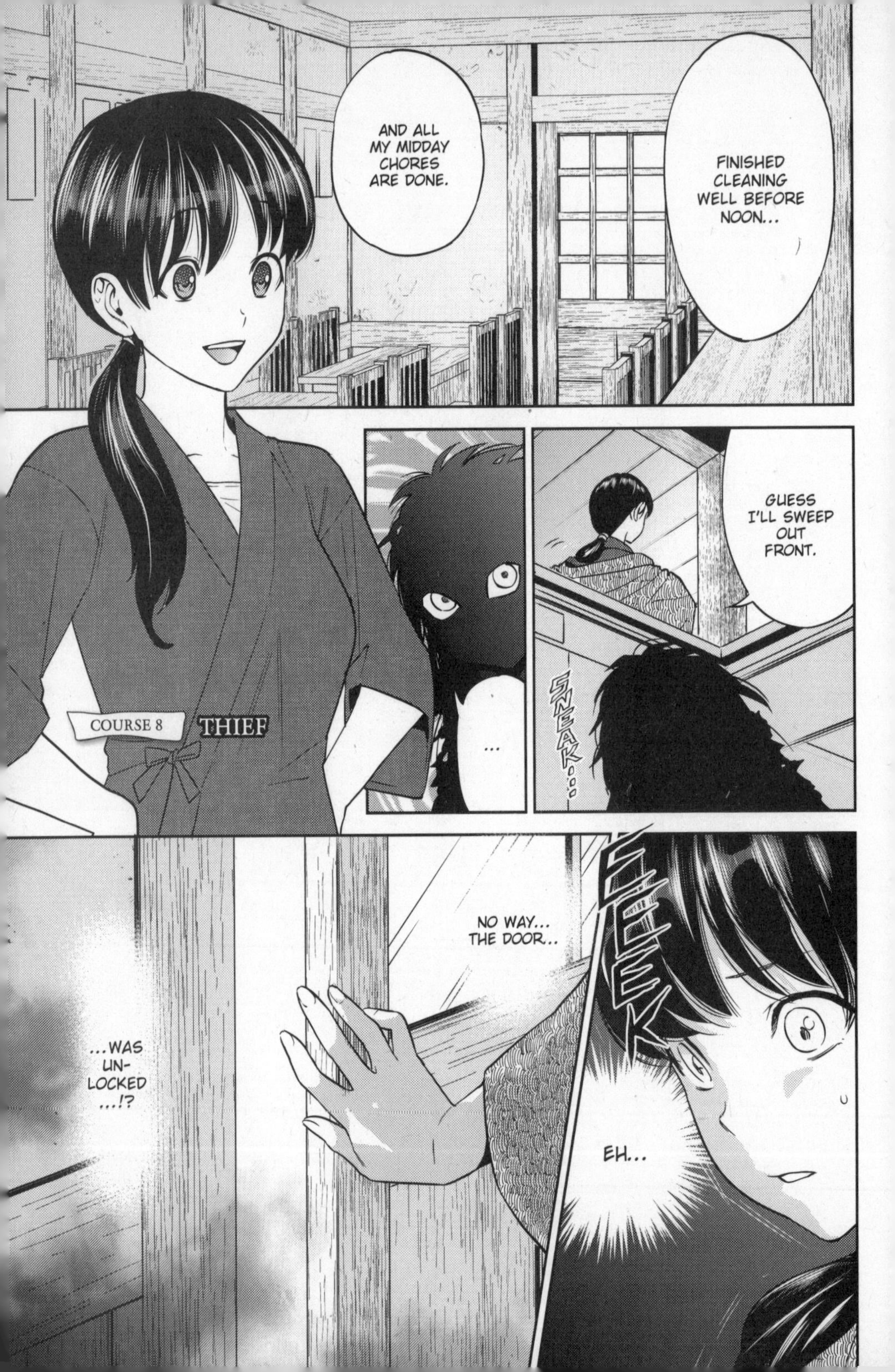
FINISHED CLEANING WELL BEFORE NOON...
AND ALL MY MIDDAY CHORES ARE DONE.
GUESS I'LL SWEEP OUT FRONT.
SNEAK...
...
COURSE 8
THIEF
NO WAY... THE DOOR...
...WAS UN-LOCKED ...!?
EH...

OTHERWORLDLY IZAKAYA

NOBU

Kisu Tempura

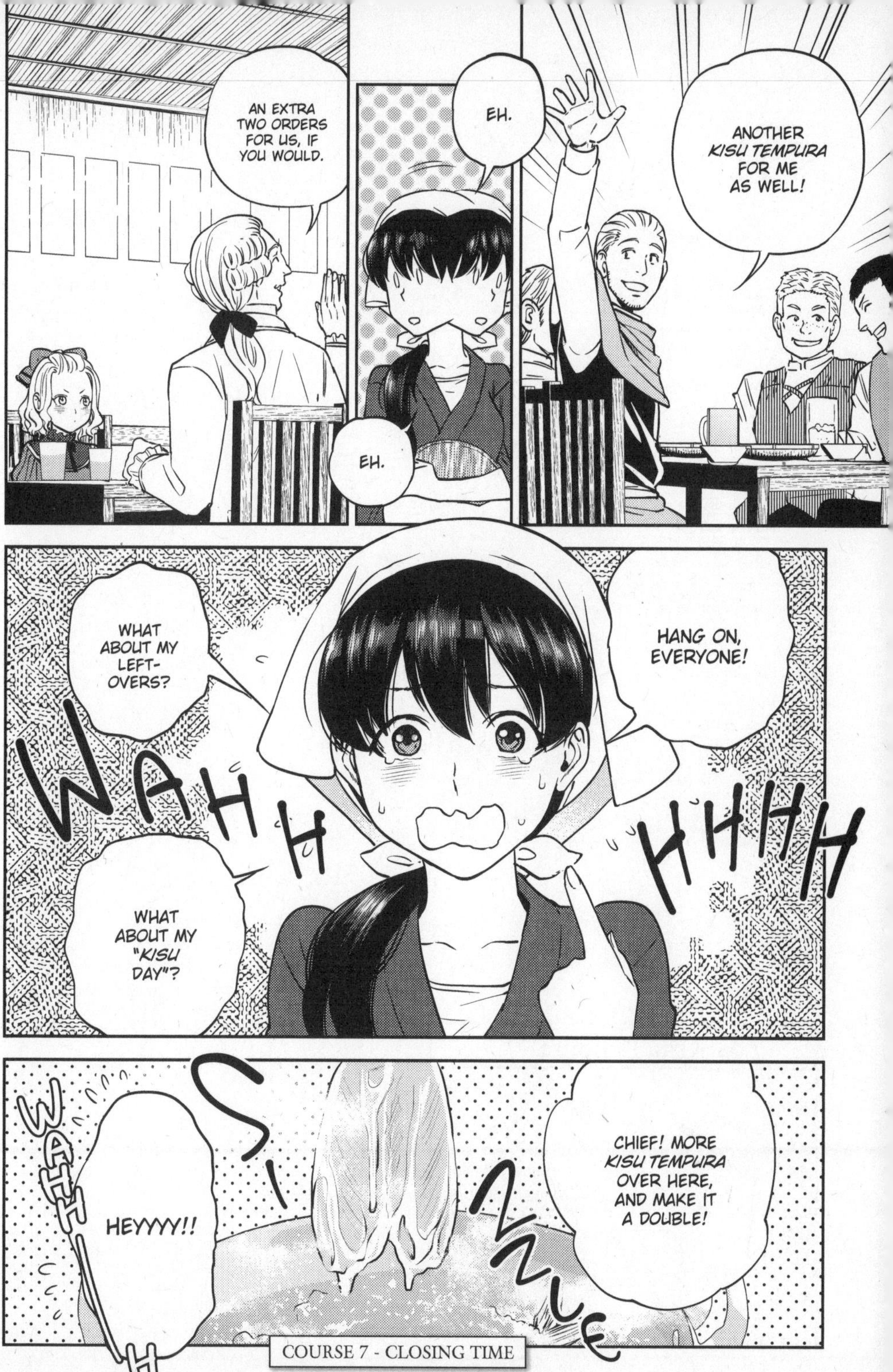
ANOTHER KISU TEMPURA FOR ME AS WELL!
EH.
EH.
AN EXTRA TWO ORDERS FOR US, IF YOU WOULD.
HANG ON, EVERYONE!
WHAT ABOUT MY LEFT-OVERS?
WAHHHHHHH
WHAT ABOUT MY "KISU DAY"?
CHIEF! MORE KISU TEMPURA OVER HERE, AND MAKE IT A DOUBLE!
SIZZLE
HEYYYY!!
WAHH—H

COURSE 7 - CLOSING TIME

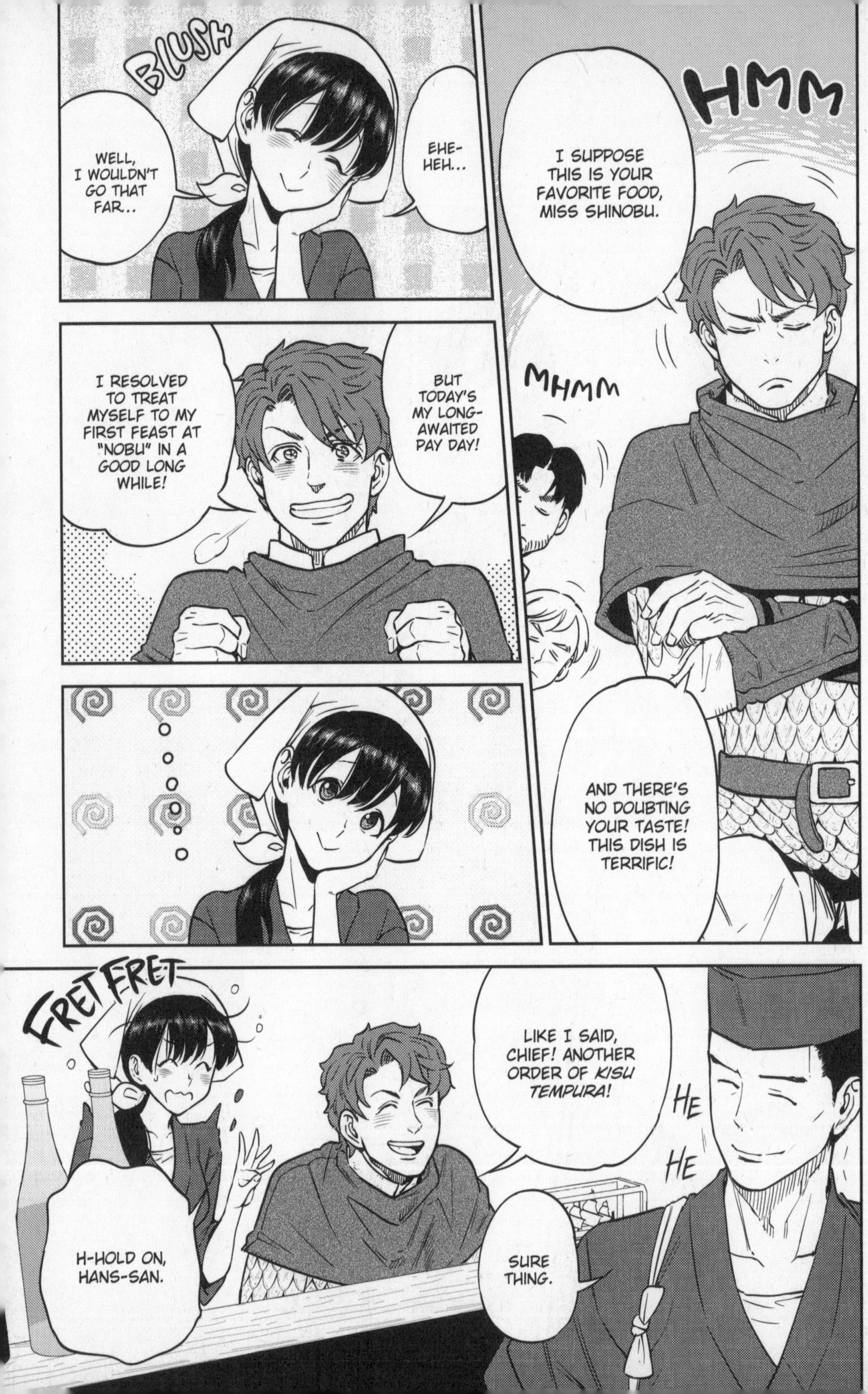
HMM
I SUPPOSE THIS IS YOUR FAVORITE FOOD, MISS SHINOBU.
MHMM
AND THERE'S NO DOUBTING YOUR TASTE! THIS DISH IS TERRIFIC!
BLUSH
EHE-HEH...
WELL, I WOULDN'T GO THAT FAR...
BUT TODAY'S MY LONG-AWAITED PAY DAY!
I RESOLVED TO TREAT MYSELF TO MY FIRST FEAST AT "NOBU" IN A GOOD LONG WHILE!
LIKE I SAID, CHIEF! ANOTHER ORDER OF *KISU TEMPURA*!
HE HE
SURE THING.
FRET FRET
H-HOLD ON, HANS-SAN.

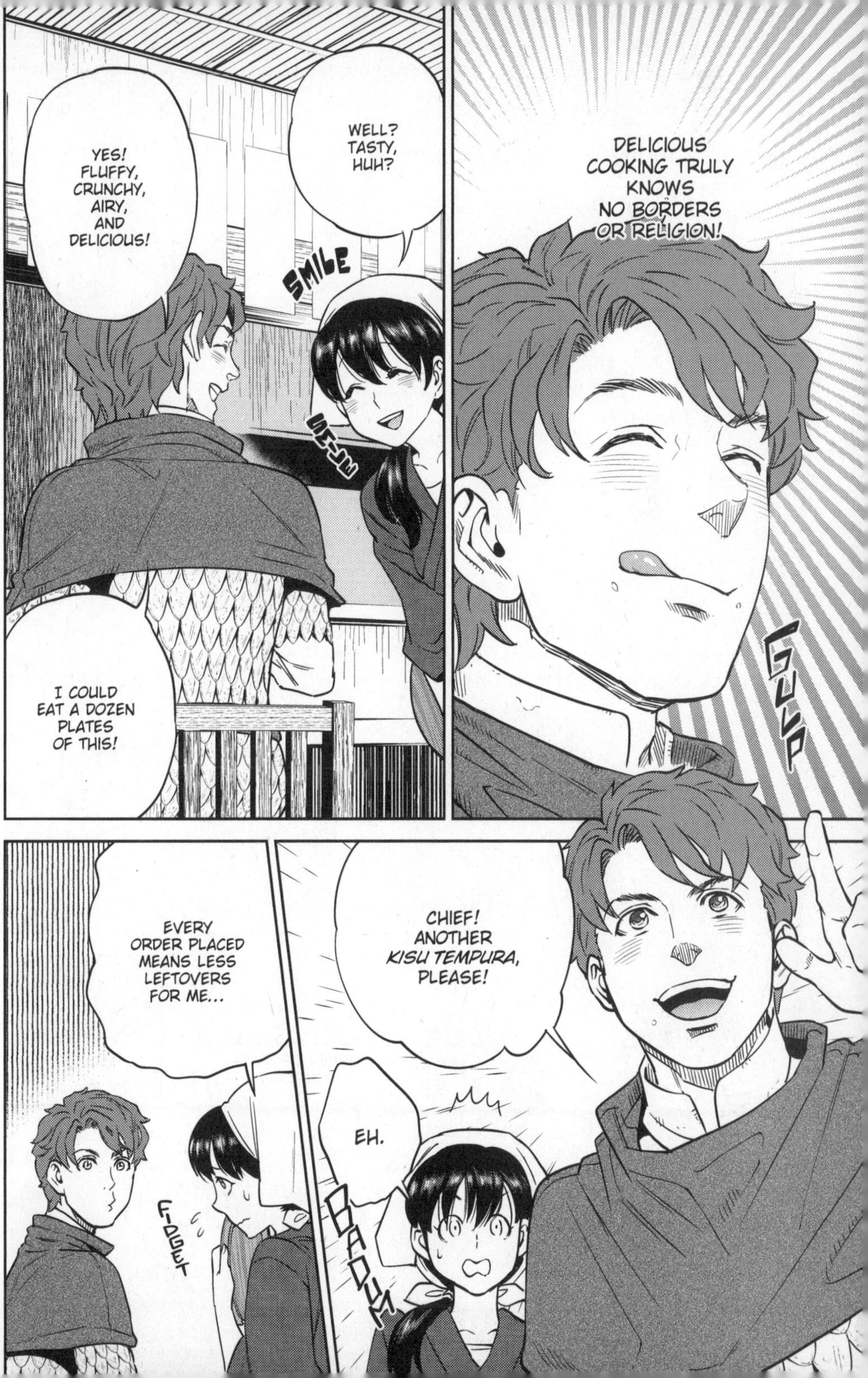
DELICIOUS COOKING TRULY KNOWS NO BORDERS OR RELIGION!
GULP
WELL? TASTY, HUH?
SMILE
YES! FLUFFY, CRUNCHY, AIRY, AND DELICIOUS!
I COULD EAT A DOZEN PLATES OF THIS!
CHIEF! ANOTHER *KISU TEMPURA*, PLEASE!
EH.
BADUM
EVERY ORDER PLACED MEANS LESS LEFTOVERS FOR ME...
FIDGET

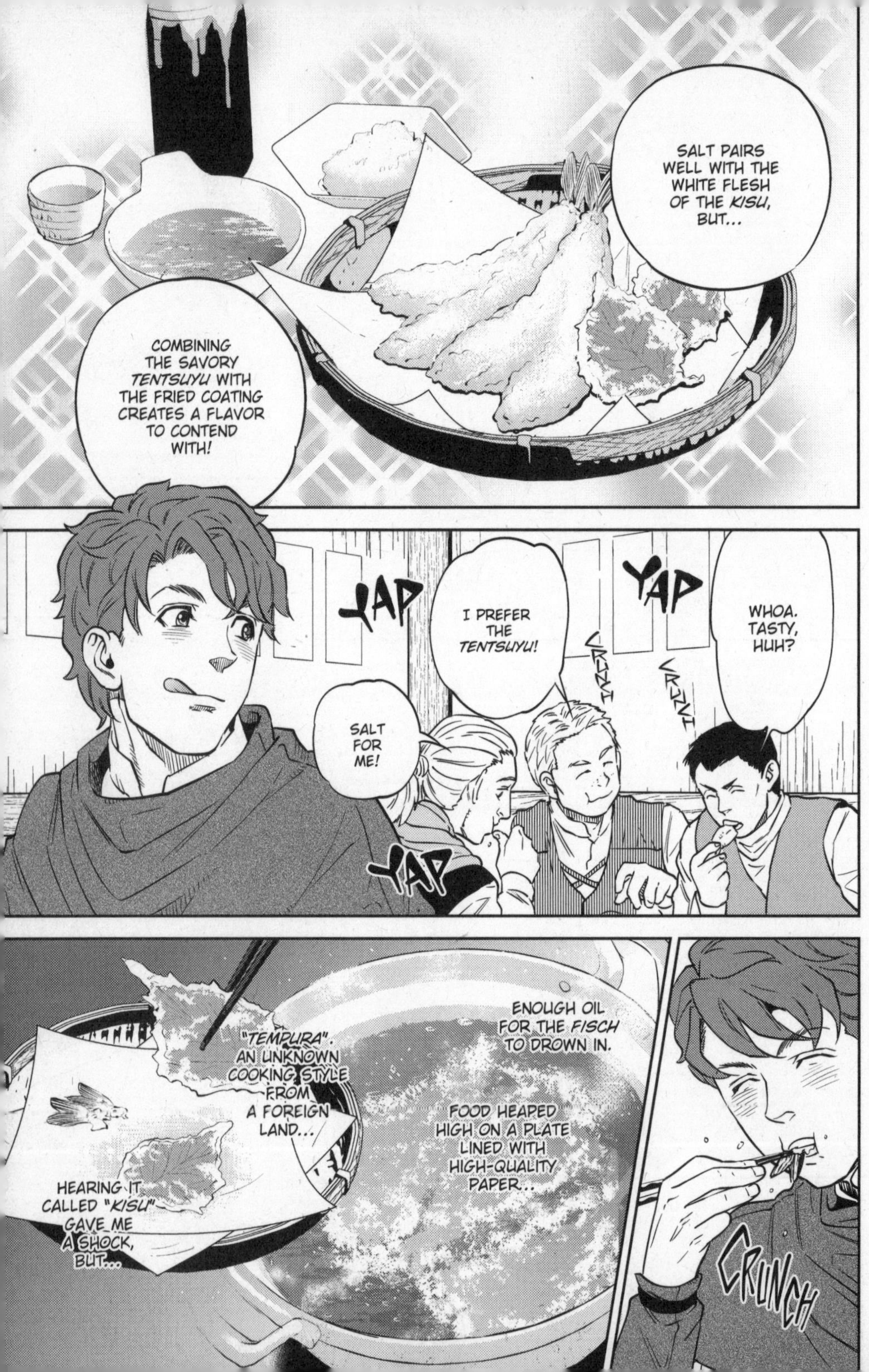
SALT PAIRS WELL WITH THE WHITE FLESH OF THE *KISU*, BUT...
COMBINING THE SAVORY *TENTSUYU* WITH THE FRIED COATING CREATES A FLAVOR TO CONTEND WITH!
WHOA. TASTY, HUH?
YAP
CRUNCH
I PREFER THE *TENTSUYU*!
CRUNCH
YAP
SALT FOR ME!
YAP
CRUNCH
ENOUGH OIL FOR THE *FISCH* TO DROWN IN.
"*TEMPURA*". AN UNKNOWN COOKING STYLE FROM A FOREIGN LAND...
FOOD HEAPED HIGH ON A PLATE LINED WITH HIGH-QUALITY PAPER...
HEARING IT CALLED "*KISU*" GAVE ME A SHOCK, BUT...

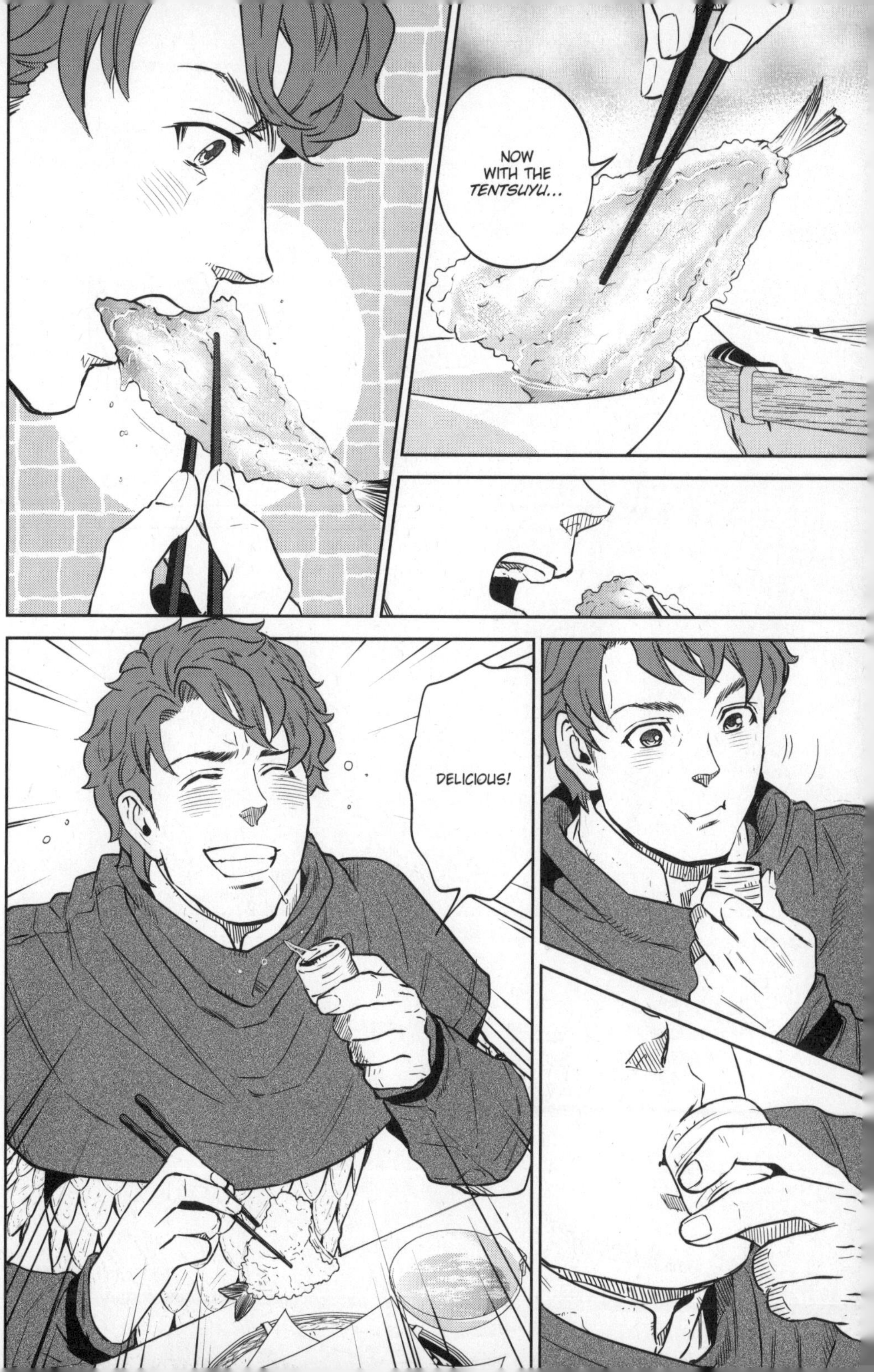
NOW WITH THE *TENTSUYU*...
DELICIOUS!

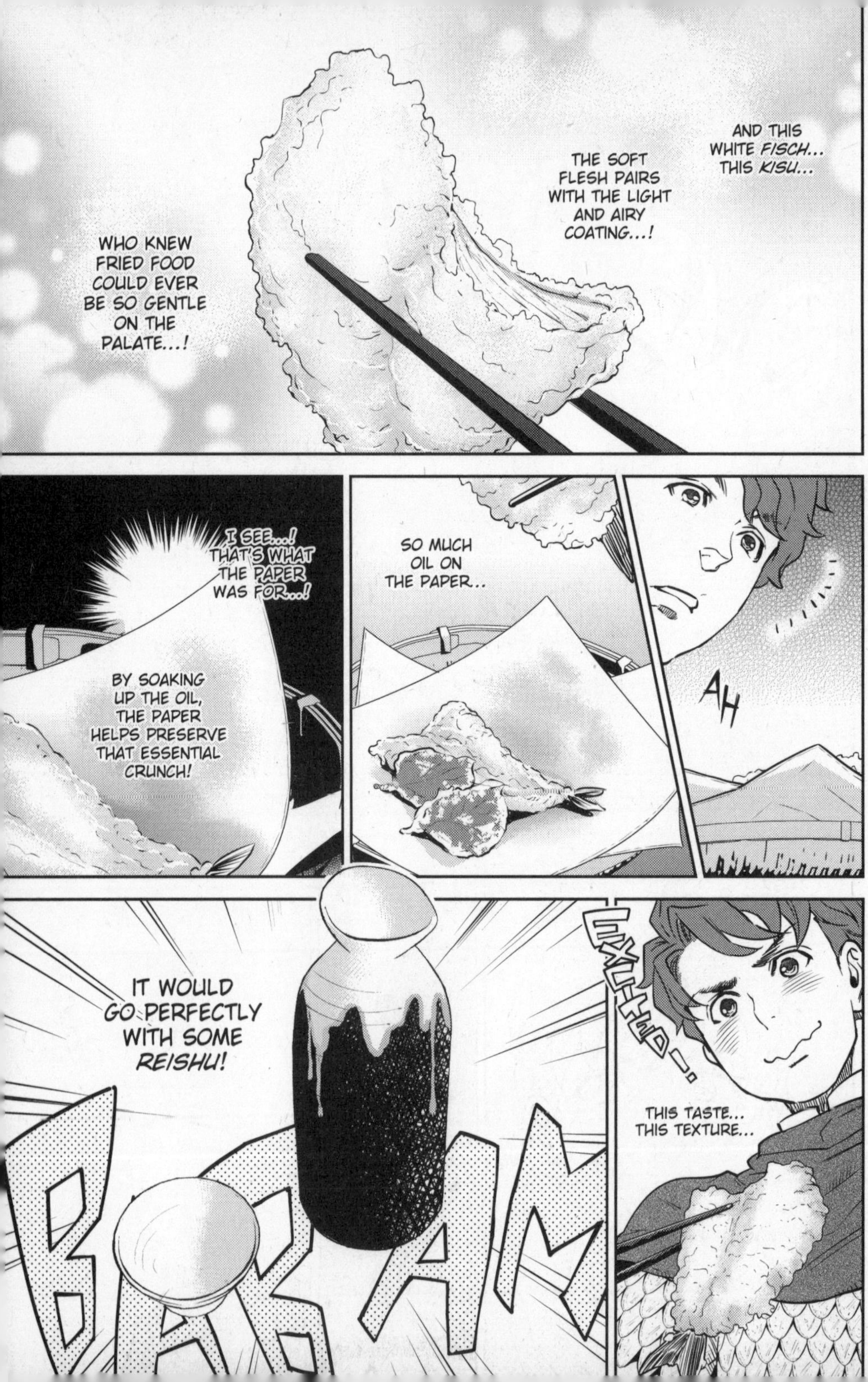
AND THIS WHITE *FISCH*... THIS *KISU*...
THE SOFT FLESH PAIRS WITH THE LIGHT AND AIRY COATING...!
WHO KNEW FRIED FOOD COULD EVER BE SO GENTLE ON THE PALATE...!
AH
SO MUCH OIL ON THE PAPER...
I SEE...! THAT'S WHAT THE PAPER WAS FOR...!
BY SOAKING UP THE OIL, THE PAPER HELPS PRESERVE THAT ESSENTIAL CRUNCH!
THIS TASTE... THIS TEXTURE...
IT WOULD GO PERFECTLY WITH SOME *REISHU*!
BABAM

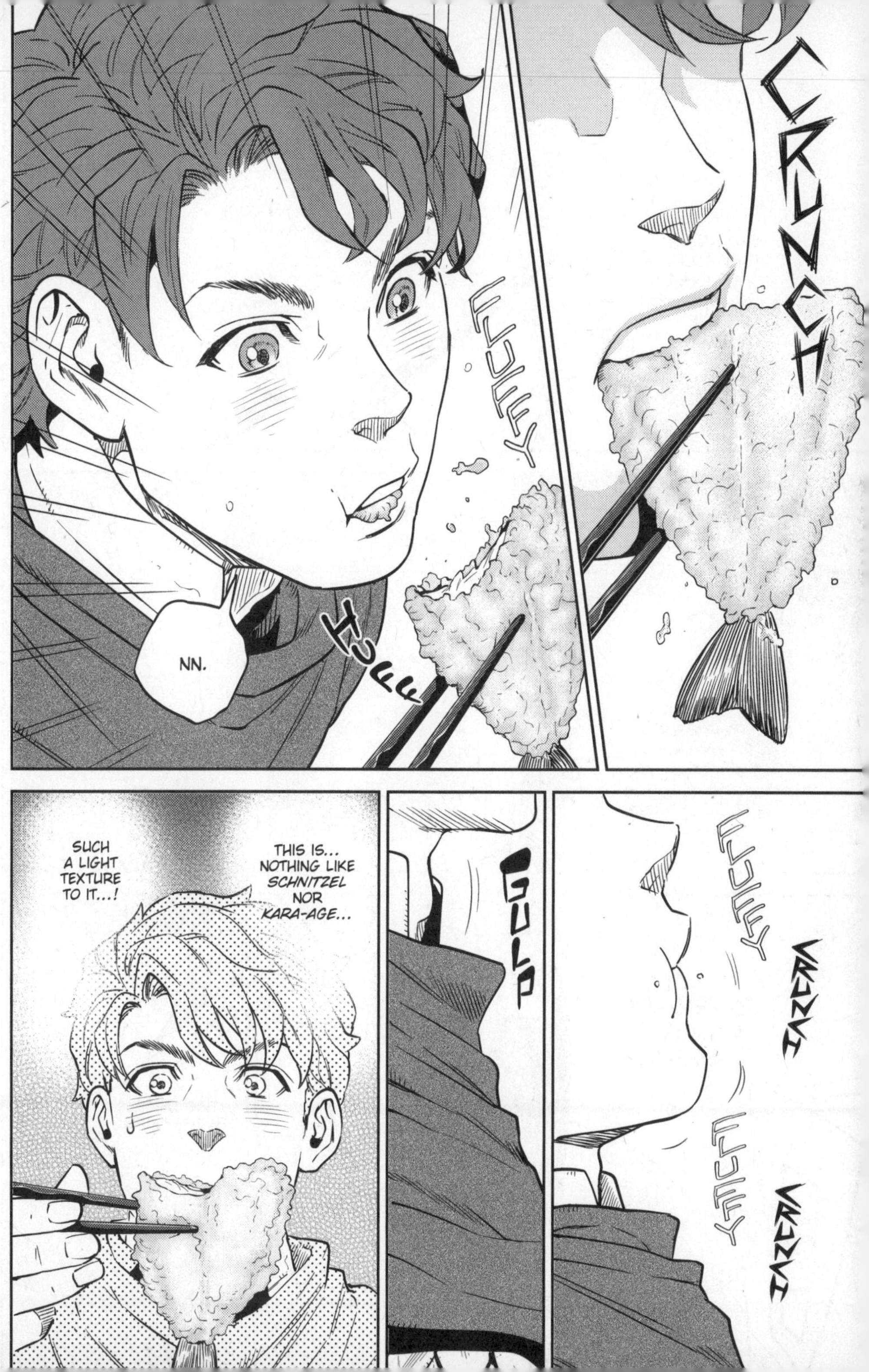
CRUNCH
FLUFFY
HUFF
NN.
FLUFFY
CRUNCH
FLUFFY
CRUNCH
GULP
THIS IS... NOTHING LIKE SCHNITZEL NOR KARA-AGE...
SUCH A LIGHT TEXTURE TO IT...!

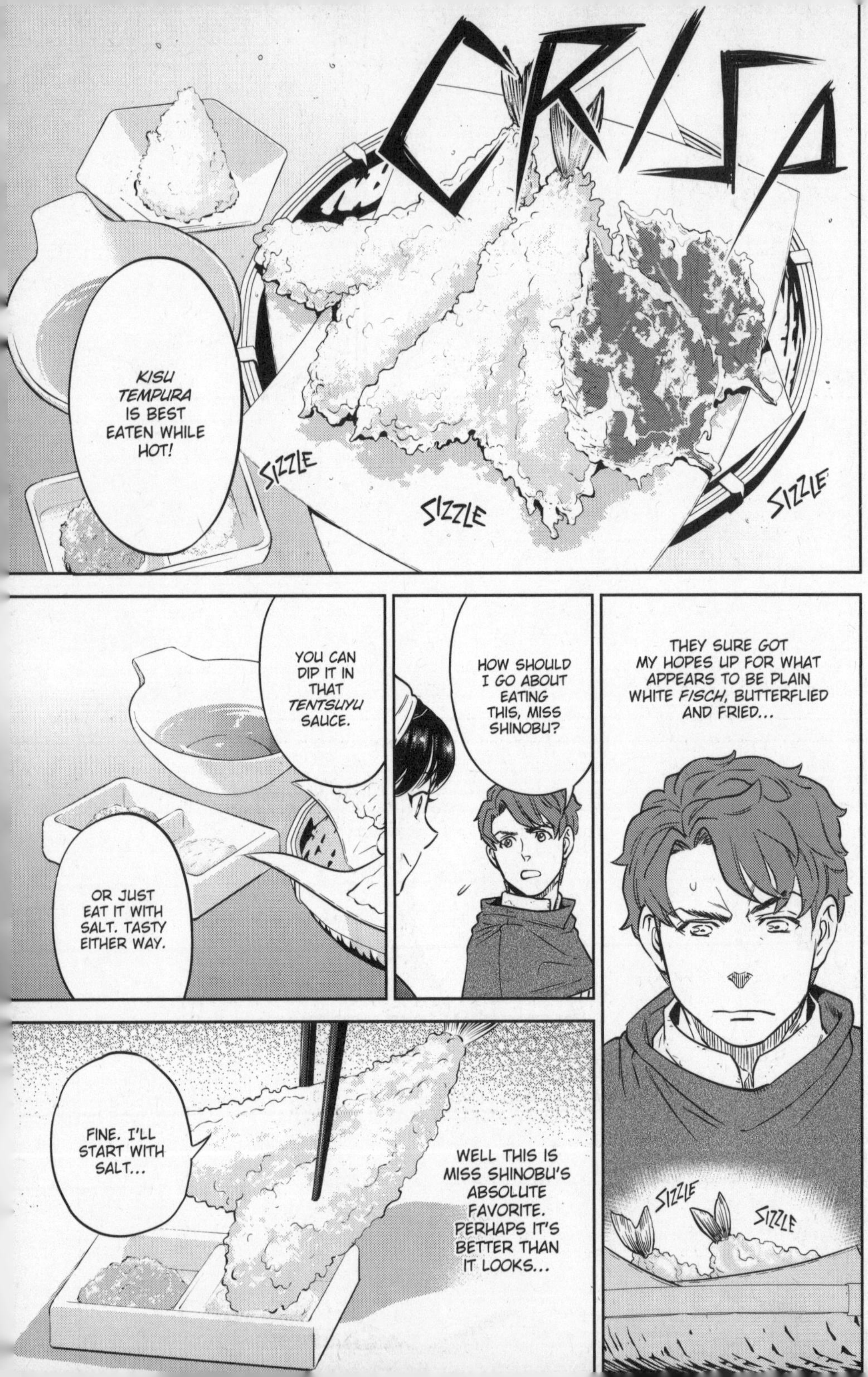
CRISP
KISU TEMPURA IS BEST EATEN WHILE HOT!
SIZZLE
SIZZLE
SIZZLE
THEY SURE GOT MY HOPES UP FOR WHAT APPEARS TO BE PLAIN WHITE *FISCH*, BUTTERFLIED AND FRIED...
WELL THIS IS MISS SHINOBU'S ABSOLUTE FAVORITE. PERHAPS IT'S BETTER THAN IT LOOKS...
SIZZLE
SIZZLE
HOW SHOULD I GO ABOUT EATING THIS, MISS SHINOBU?
YOU CAN DIP IT IN THAT *TENTSUYU* SAUCE.
OR JUST EAT IT WITH SALT. TASTY EITHER WAY.
FINE. I'LL START WITH SALT...

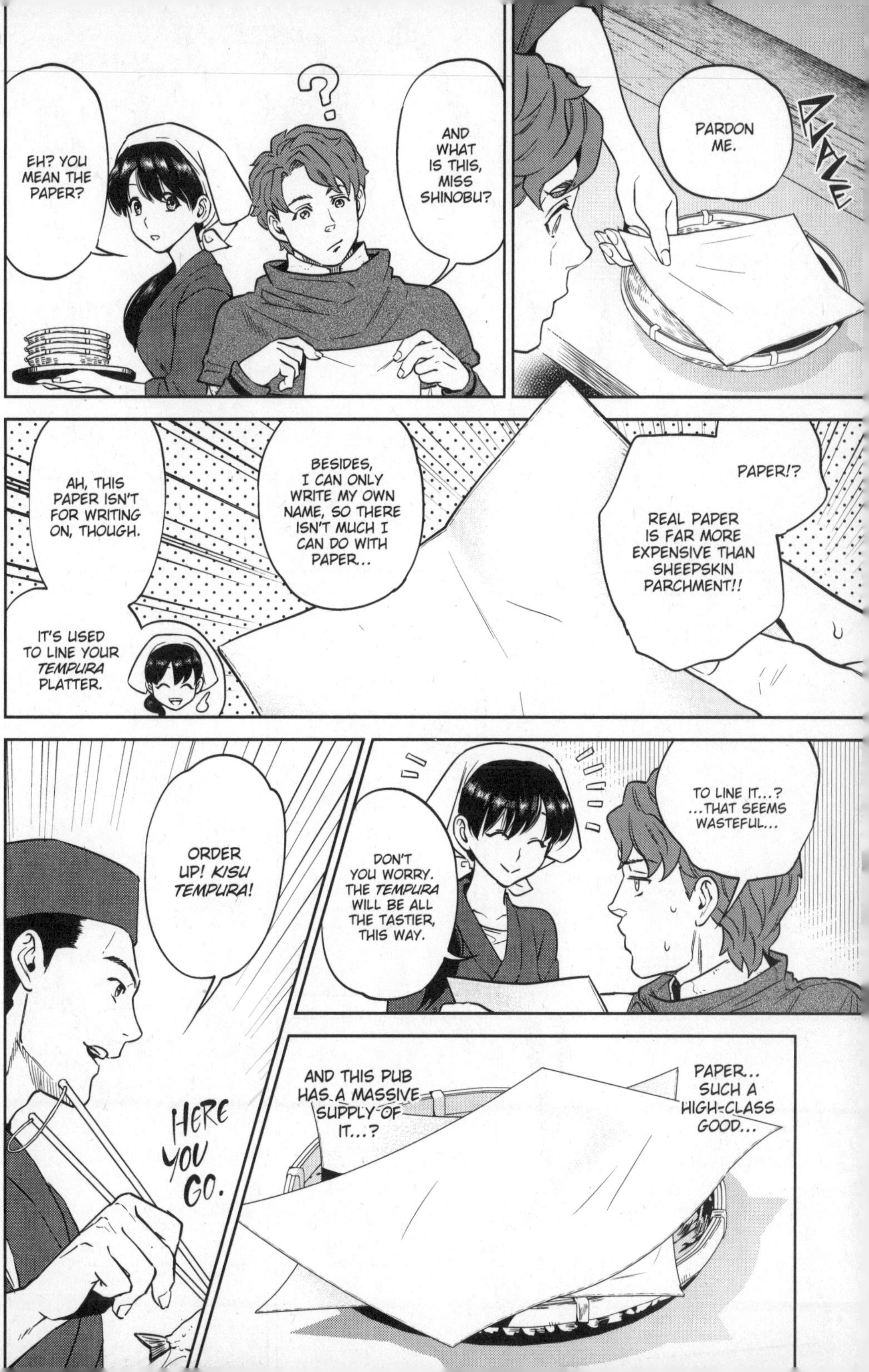
PARDON ME.
AND WHAT IS THIS, MISS SHINOBU?
EH? YOU MEAN THE PAPER?
PAPER!?
REAL PAPER IS FAR MORE EXPENSIVE THAN SHEEPSKIN PARCHMENT!!
BESIDES, I CAN ONLY WRITE MY OWN NAME, SO THERE ISN'T MUCH I CAN DO WITH PAPER...
AH, THIS PAPER ISN'T FOR WRITING ON, THOUGH.
IT'S USED TO LINE YOUR *TEMPURA* PLATTER.
TO LINE IT...? ...THAT SEEMS WASTEFUL...
DON'T YOU WORRY. THE *TEMPURA* WILL BE ALL THE TASTIER, THIS WAY.
PAPER... SUCH A HIGH-CLASS GOOD...
AND THIS PUB HAS A MASSIVE SUPPLY OF IT...?
ORDER UP! *KISU TEMPURA*!
HERE YOU GO.

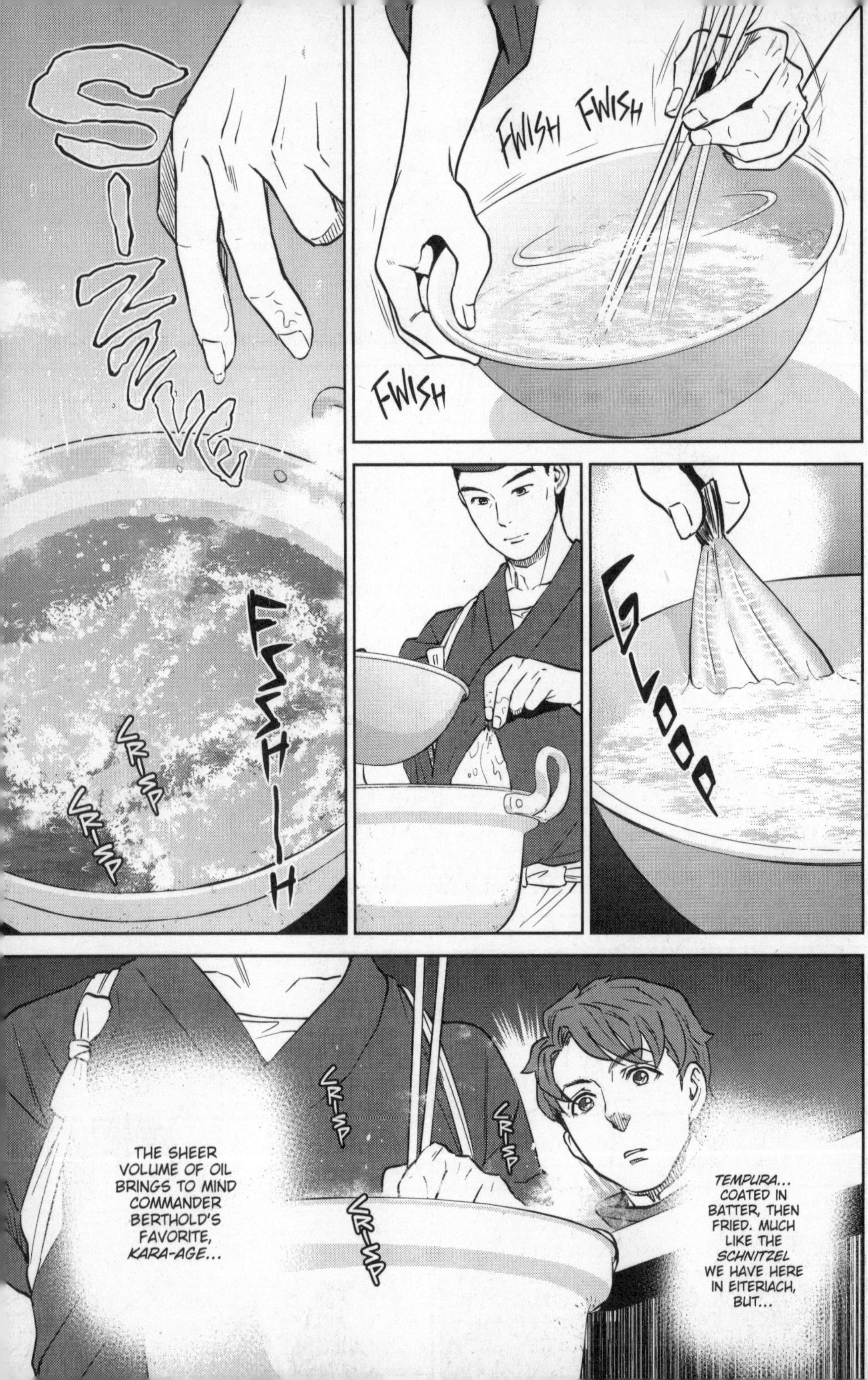
FWISH FWISH
FWISH
GLOOOP
S-I-NNGG
FSSH—H
CRISP
CRISP
TEMPURA... COATED IN BATTER, THEN FRIED. MUCH LIKE THE *SCHNITZEL* WE HAVE HERE IN EITERIACH, BUT...
CRISP
CRISP
CRISP
THE SHEER VOLUME OF OIL BRINGS TO MIND COMMANDER BERTHOLD'S FAVORITE, *KARA-AGE*...

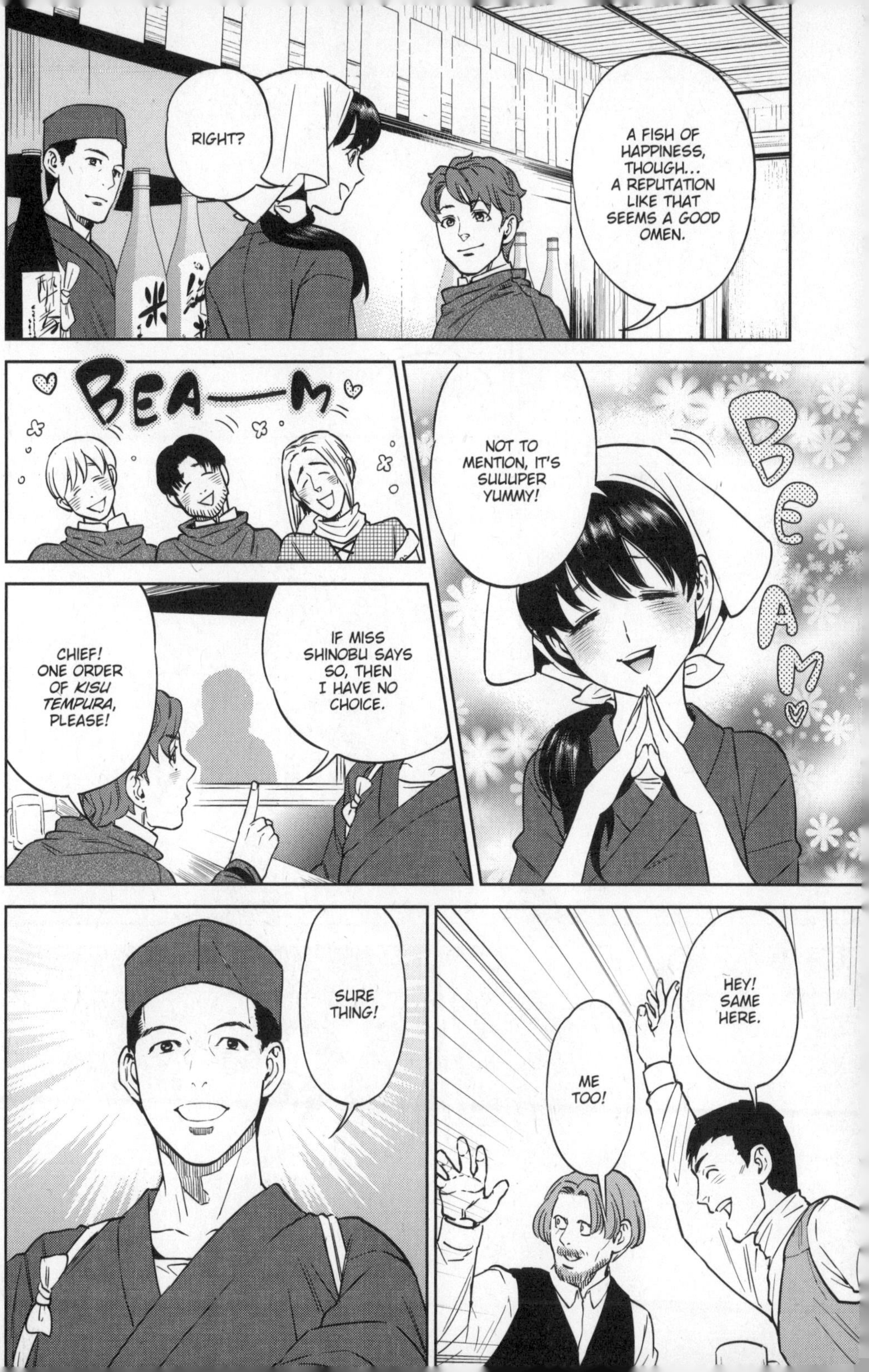
A FISH OF HAPPINESS, THOUGH... A REPUTATION LIKE THAT SEEMS A GOOD OMEN.
RIGHT?
BEAM♡
NOT TO MENTION, IT'S SUUUPER YUMMY!
BEA—M
IF MISS SHINOBU SAYS SO, THEN I HAVE NO CHOICE.
CHIEF! ONE ORDER OF *KISU TEMPURA*, PLEASE!
HEY! SAME HERE.
ME TOO!
SURE THING!

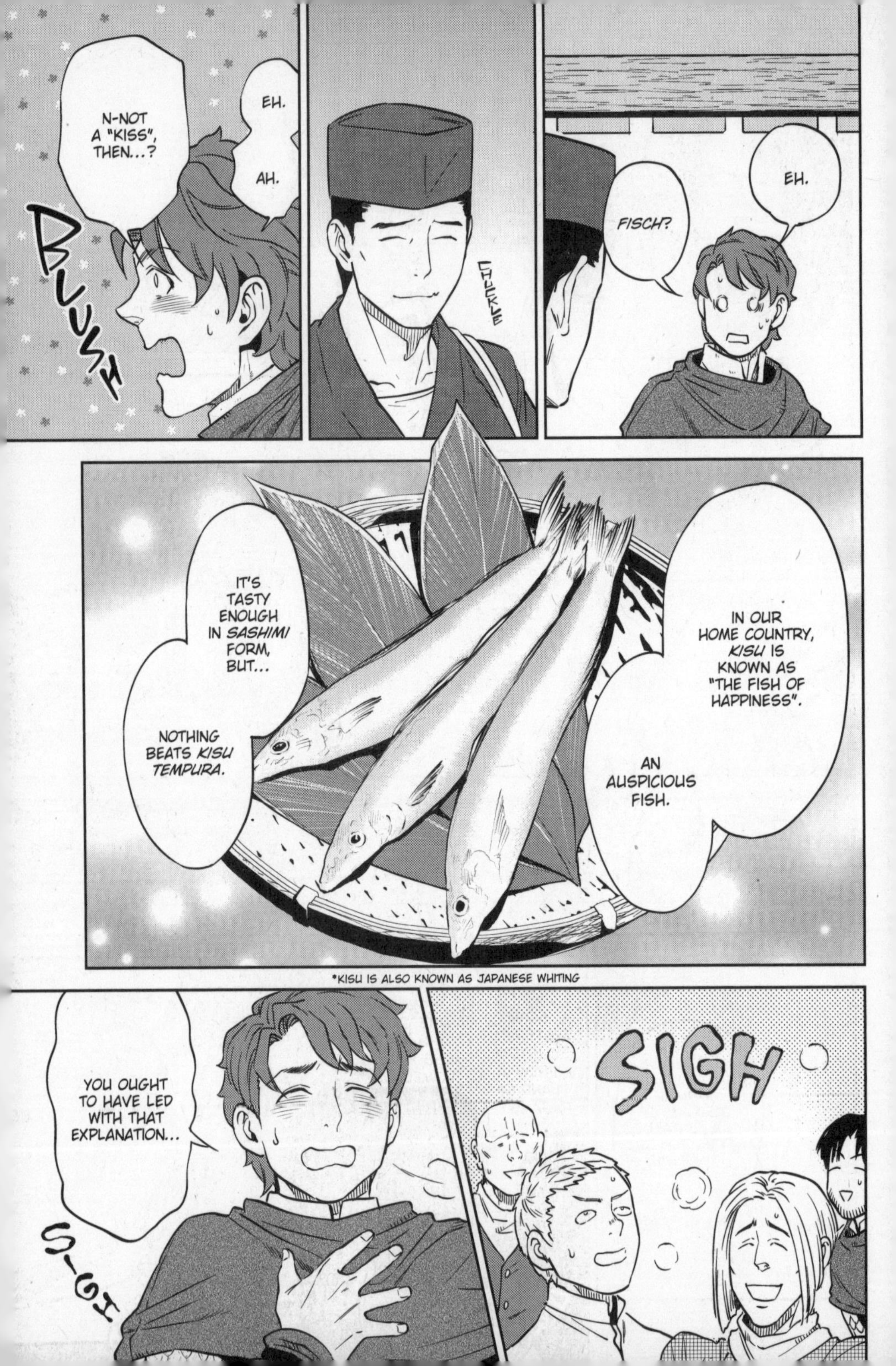
EH.
FISCH?
CHUCKLE
EH.
AH.
N-NOT A "KISS", THEN...?
BLUSH
IN OUR HOME COUNTRY, KISU IS KNOWN AS "THE FISH OF HAPPINESS".
AN AUSPICIOUS FISH.
IT'S TASTY ENOUGH IN SASHIMI FORM, BUT...
NOTHING BEATS KISU TEMPURA.
*KISU IS ALSO KNOWN AS JAPANESE WHITING
SIGH
YOU OUGHT TO HAVE LED WITH THAT EXPLANATION...
S-GI

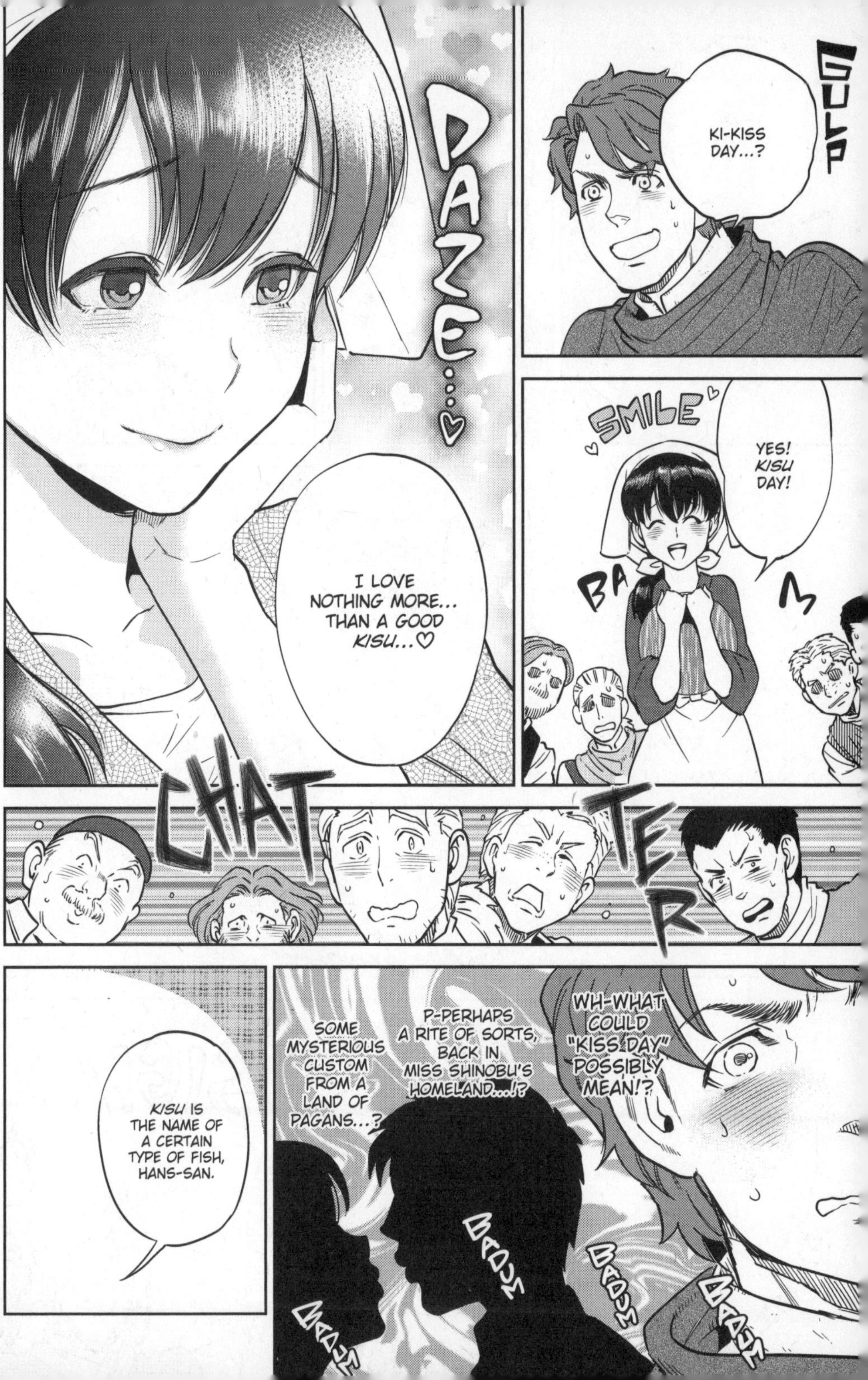
GULP
KI-KISS DAY...?
SMILE
YES! KISU DAY!
BAM
DAZE...♡
I LOVE NOTHING MORE... THAN A GOOD KISU...♡
CHATTER
WH-WHAT COULD "KISS DAY" POSSIBLY MEAN!?
P-PERHAPS A RITE OF SORTS, BACK IN MISS SHINOBU'S HOMELAND...!?
SOME MYSTERIOUS CUSTOM FROM A LAND OF PAGANS...?
BADUM
BADUM
BADUM
BADUM
KISU IS THE NAME OF A CERTAIN TYPE OF FISH, HANS-SAN.

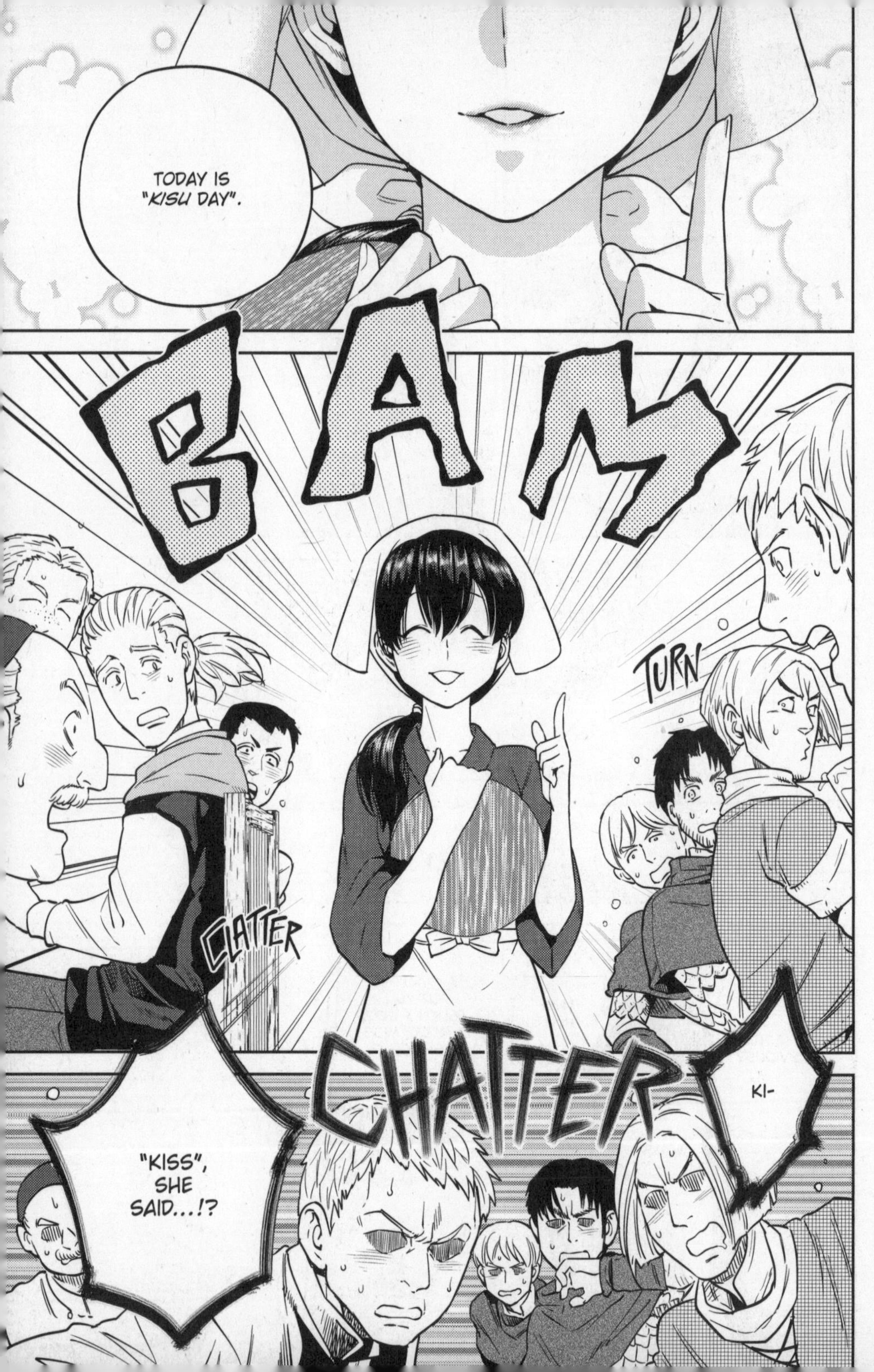
TODAY IS "KISU DAY".
BAM
TURN
CLATTER
KI-
CHATTER
"KISS", SHE SAID...!?

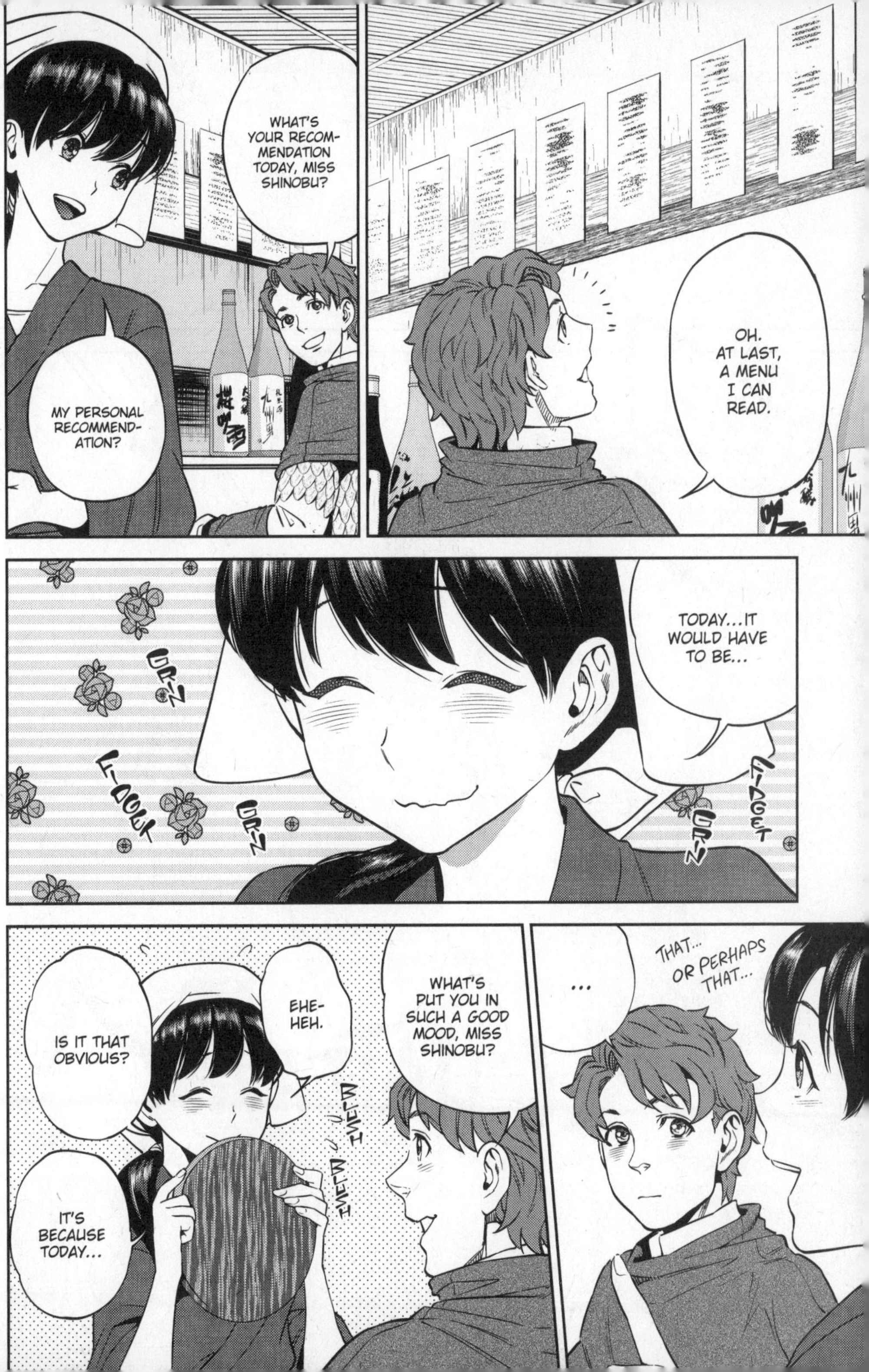
OH. AT LAST, A MENU I CAN READ.
WHAT'S YOUR RECOMMENDATION TODAY, MISS SHINOBU?
MY PERSONAL RECOMMENDATION?
TODAY...IT WOULD HAVE TO BE...
FIDGET
GRIN
GRIN
GRIN
FIDGET
GRIN
THAT... OR PERHAPS THAT...
...
WHAT'S PUT YOU IN SUCH A GOOD MOOD, MISS SHINOBU?
EHE-HEH.
IS IT THAT OBVIOUS?
IT'S BECAUSE TODAY...

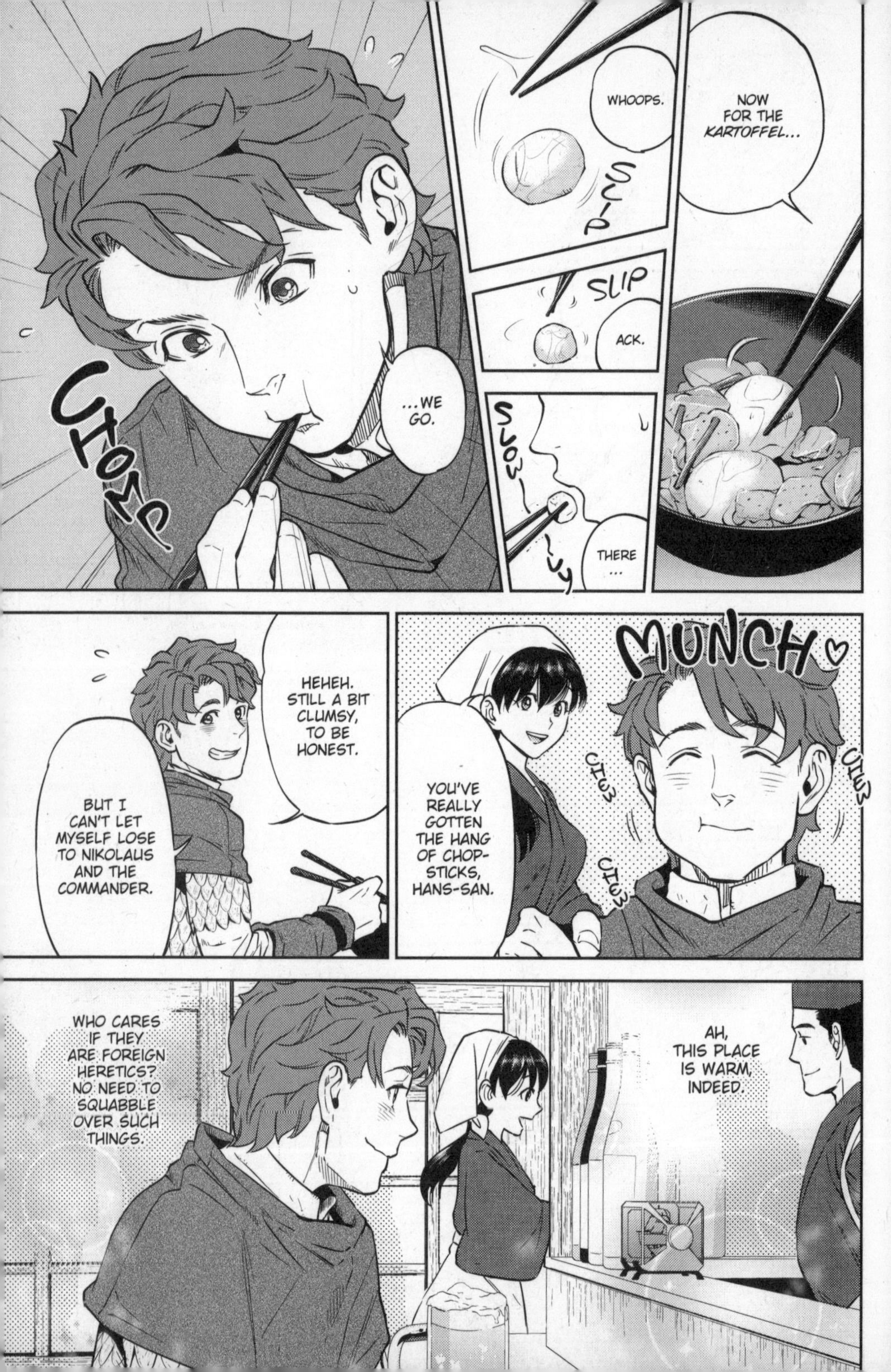
NOW FOR THE KARTOFFEL...
WHOOPS.
SLIP
SLIP
ACK.
SLOWLY
THERE...
...WE GO.
CHOMP
MUNCH
CHEW
CHEW
CHEW
YOU'VE REALLY GOTTEN THE HANG OF CHOP-STICKS, HANS-SAN.
HEHEH. STILL A BIT CLUMSY, TO BE HONEST.
BUT I CAN'T LET MYSELF LOSE TO NIKOLAUS AND THE COMMANDER.
AH, THIS PLACE IS WARM, INDEED.
WHO CARES IF THEY ARE FOREIGN HERETICS? NO NEED TO SQUABBLE OVER SUCH THINGS.

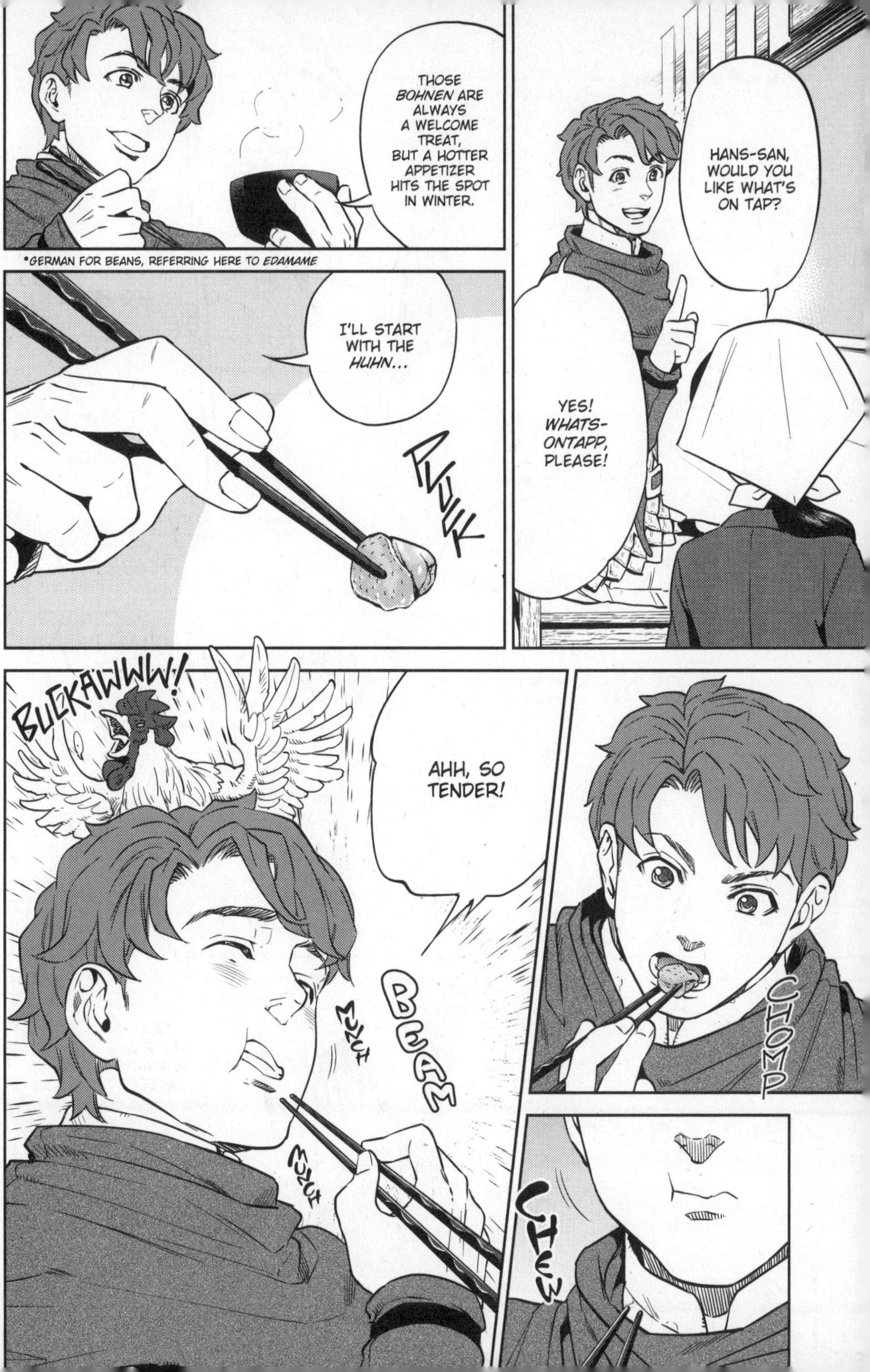
HANS-SAN, WOULD YOU LIKE WHAT'S ON TAP?
YES! WHATS-ONTAPP, PLEASE!
THOSE *BOHNEN* ARE ALWAYS A WELCOME TREAT, BUT A HOTTER APPETIZER HITS THE SPOT IN WINTER.
*GERMAN FOR BEANS, REFERRING HERE TO *EDAMAME*
I'LL START WITH THE *HUHN*...
PWUUK
CHOMP
CHEW
AHH, SO TENDER!
BUCKAWWW!
BEAM
MUNCH
MUNCH

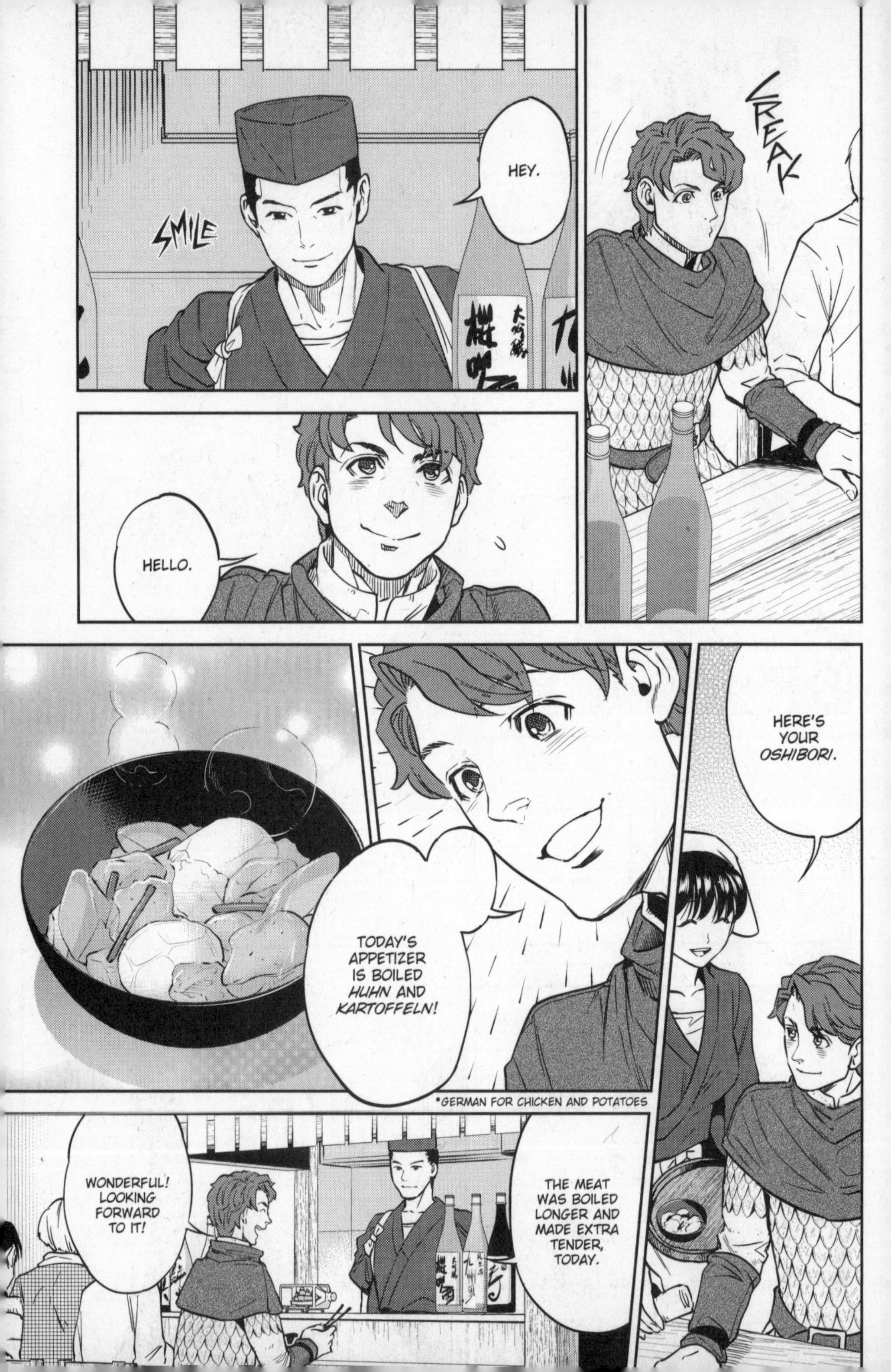
CREAK
HEY.
SMILE
HELLO.
HERE'S YOUR OSHIBORI.
TODAY'S APPETIZER IS BOILED *HUHN* AND *KARTOFFELN*!
*GERMAN FOR CHICKEN AND POTATOES
THE MEAT WAS BOILED LONGER AND MADE EXTRA TENDER, TODAY.
WONDERFUL! LOOKING FORWARD TO IT!

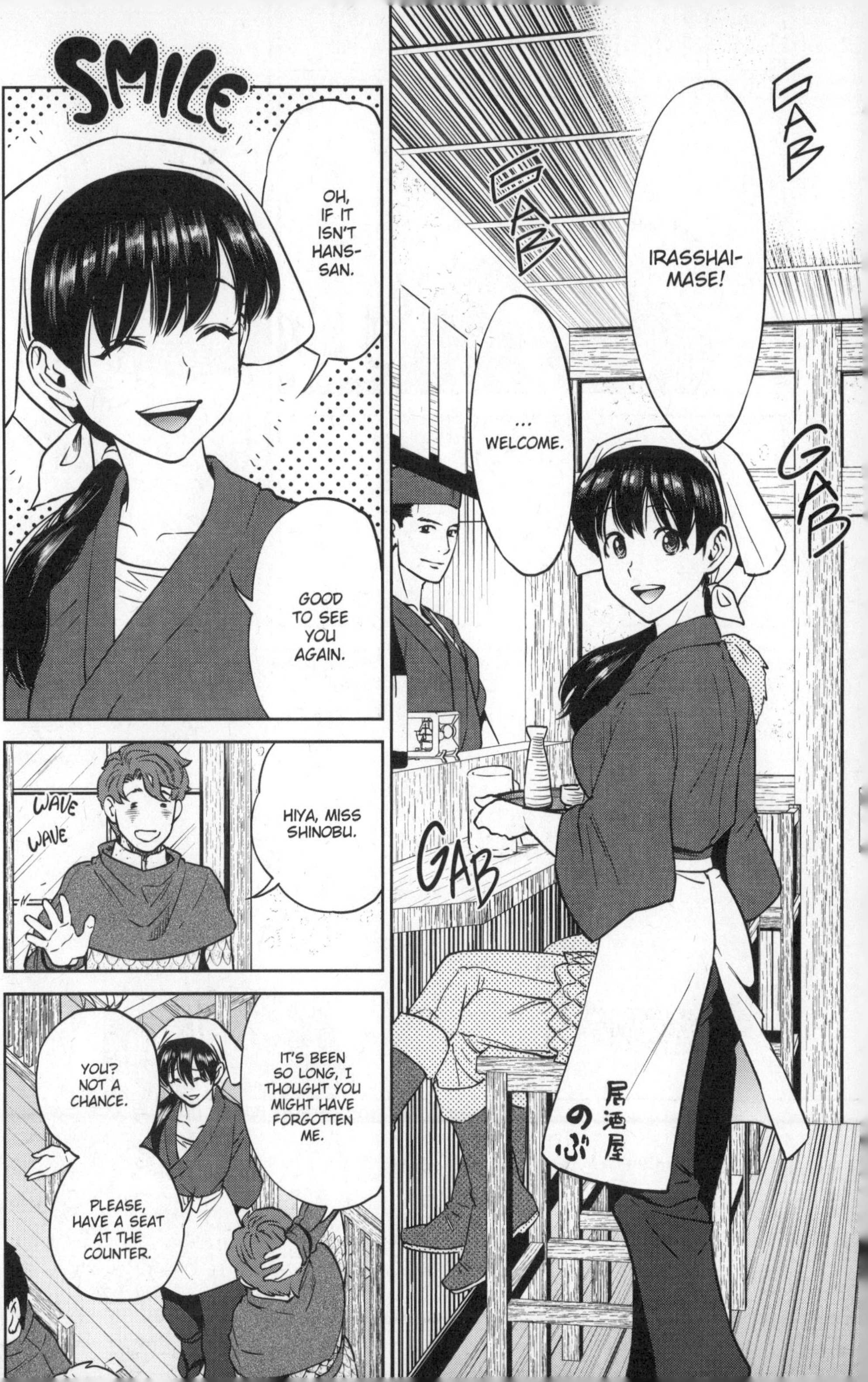
GAB
IRASSHAI-MASE!
GAB
... WELCOME.
GAB
GAB
居酒屋
のぶ
SMILE
OH, IF IT ISN'T HANS-SAN.
GOOD TO SEE YOU AGAIN.
HIYA, MISS SHINOBU.
WAVE
WAVE
IT'S BEEN SO LONG, I THOUGHT YOU MIGHT HAVE FORGOTTEN ME.
YOU? NOT A CHANCE.
PLEASE, HAVE A SEAT AT THE COUNTER.

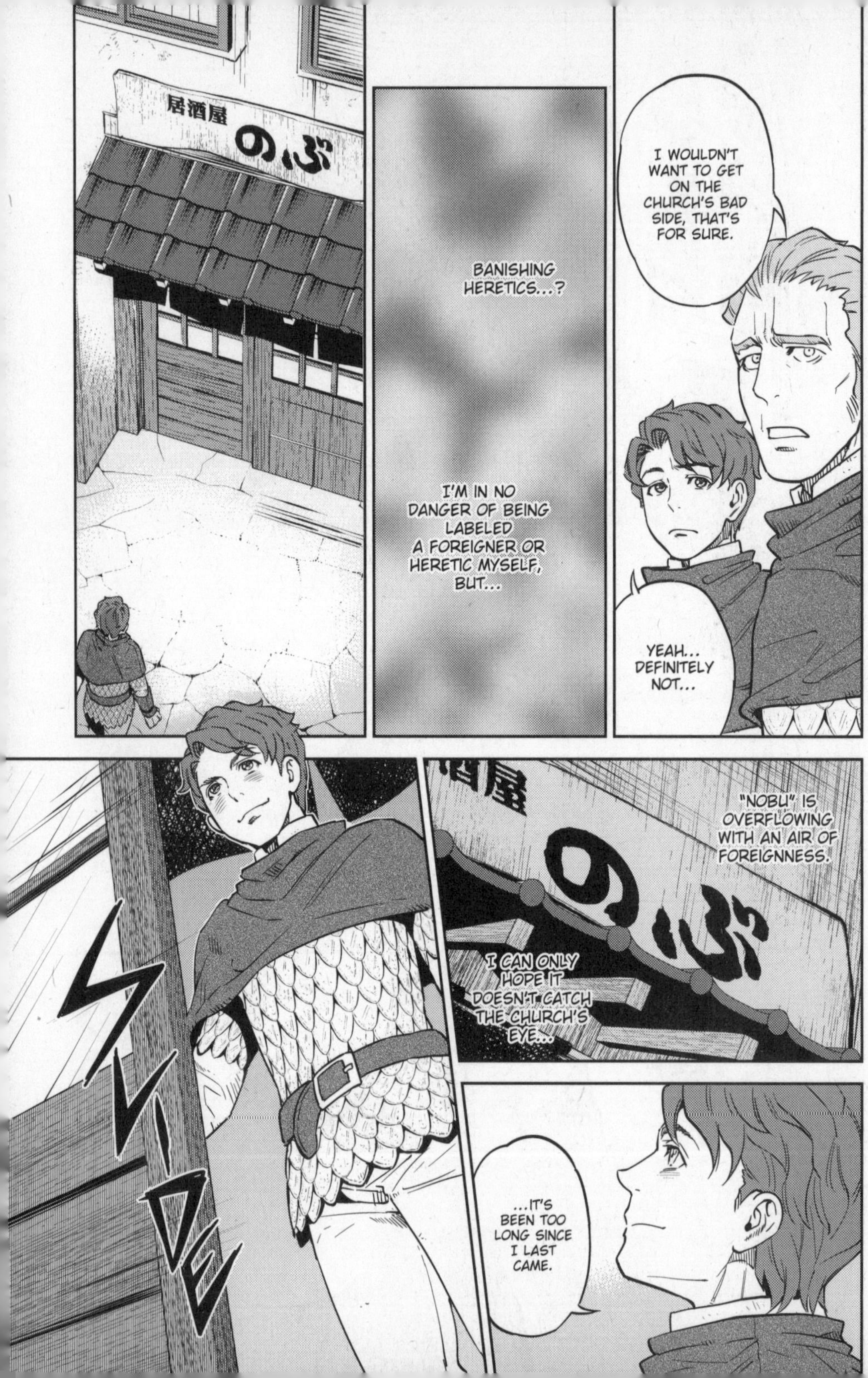
I WOULDN'T WANT TO GET ON THE CHURCH'S BAD SIDE, THAT'S FOR SURE.
YEAH... DEFINITELY NOT...
BANISHING HERETICS...?
I'M IN NO DANGER OF BEING LABELED A FOREIGNER OR HERETIC MYSELF, BUT...
居酒屋
のぶ
"NOBU" IS OVERFLOWING WITH AN AIR OF FOREIGNNESS.
I CAN ONLY HOPE IT DOESN'T CATCH THE CHURCH'S EYE...
...IT'S BEEN TOO LONG SINCE I LAST CAME.
SLIDE

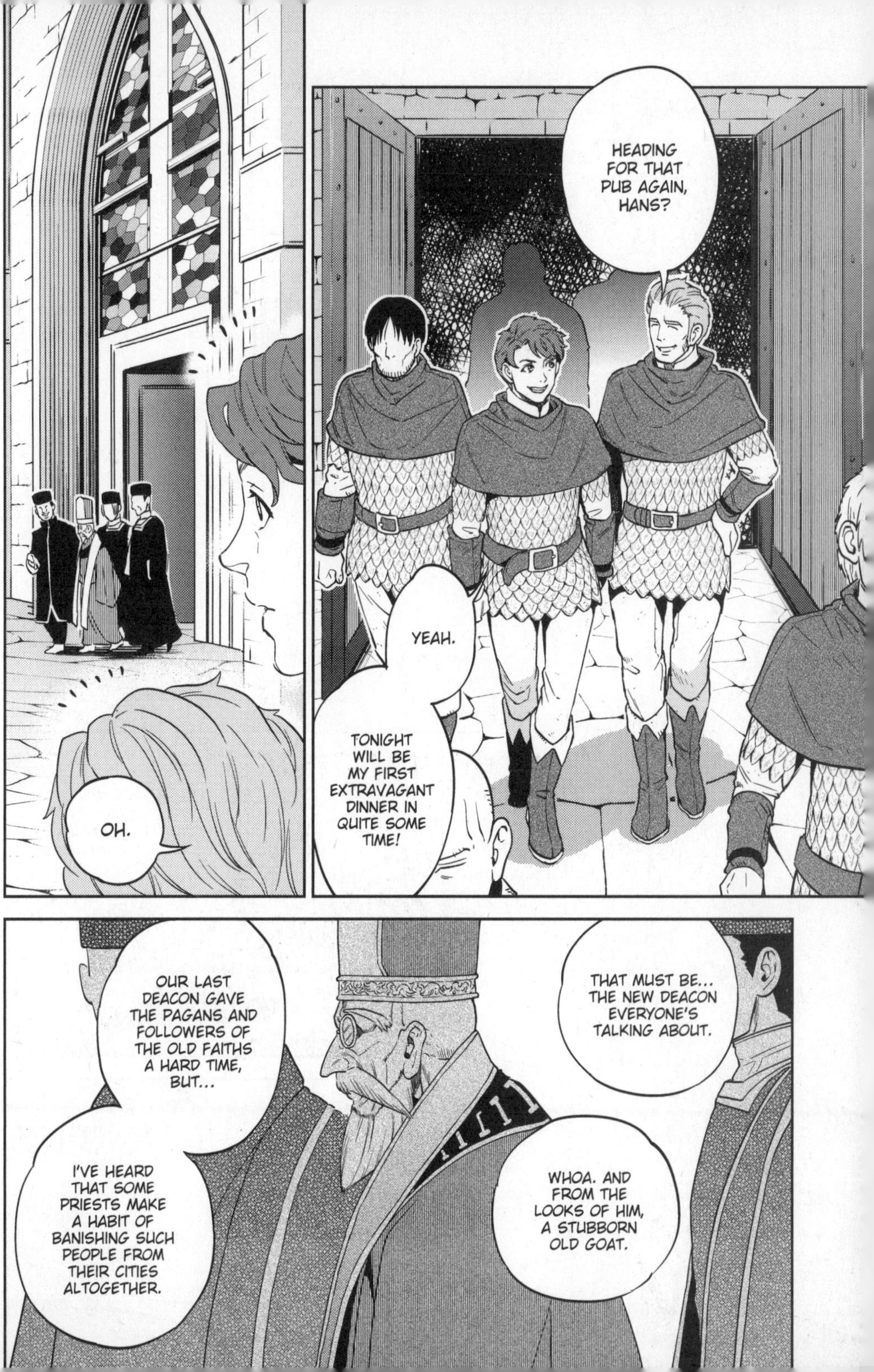
HEADING FOR THAT PUB AGAIN, HANS?
YEAH.
TONIGHT WILL BE MY FIRST EXTRAVAGANT DINNER IN QUITE SOME TIME!
OH.
THAT MUST BE... THE NEW DEACON EVERYONE'S TALKING ABOUT.
WHOA. AND FROM THE LOOKS OF HIM, A STUBBORN OLD GOAT.
OUR LAST DEACON GAVE THE PAGANS AND FOLLOWERS OF THE OLD FAITHS A HARD TIME, BUT...
I'VE HEARD THAT SOME PRIESTS MAKE A HABIT OF BANISHING SUCH PEOPLE FROM THEIR CITIES ALTOGETHER.

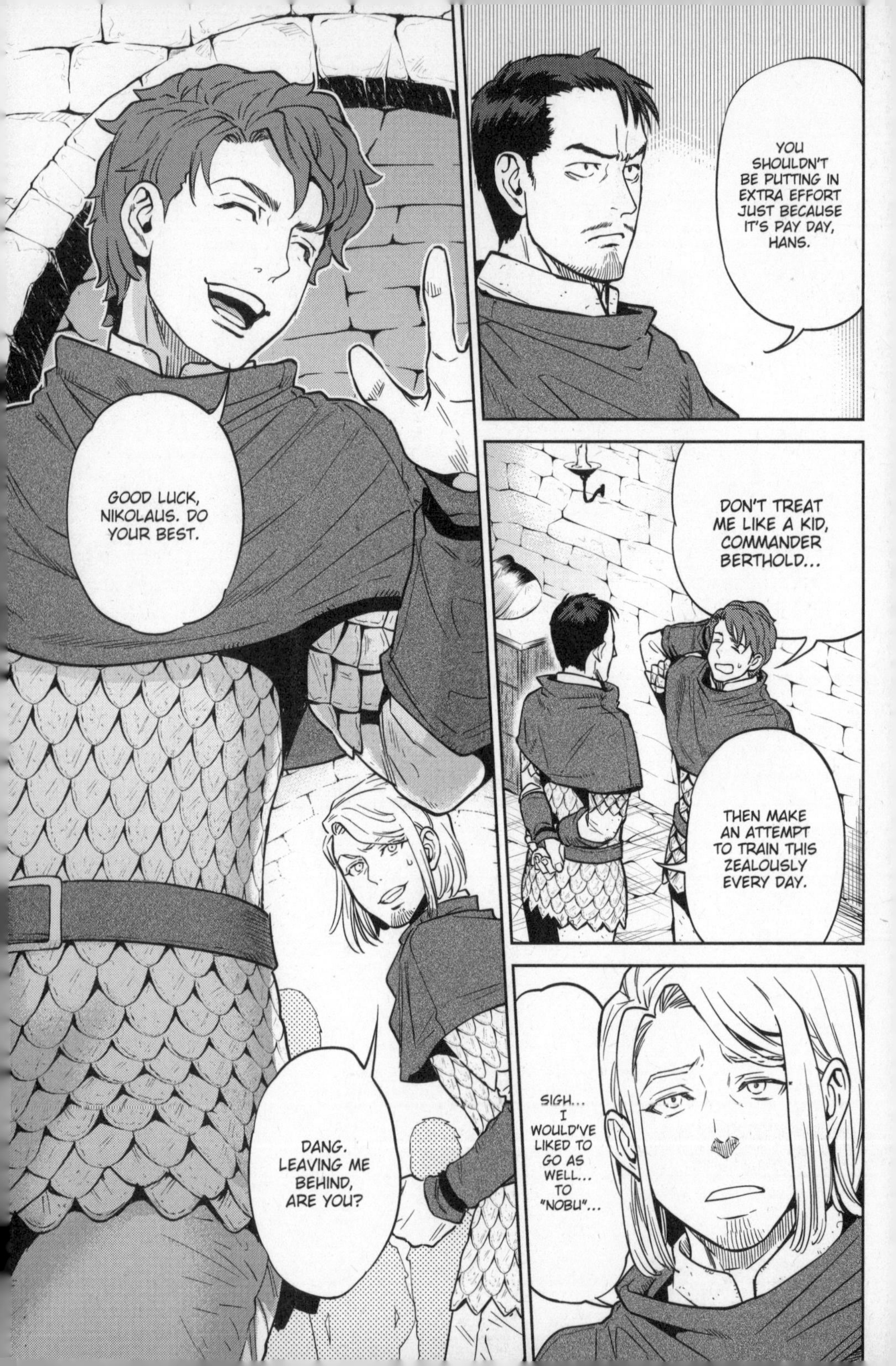
YOU SHOULDN'T BE PUTTING IN EXTRA EFFORT JUST BECAUSE IT'S PAY DAY, HANS.
DON'T TREAT ME LIKE A KID, COMMANDER BERTHOLD...
THEN MAKE AN ATTEMPT TO TRAIN THIS ZEALOUSLY EVERY DAY.
SIGH... I WOULD'VE LIKED TO GO AS WELL... TO "NOBU"...
GOOD LUCK, NIKOLAUS. DO YOUR BEST.
DANG. LEAVING ME BEHIND, ARE YOU?

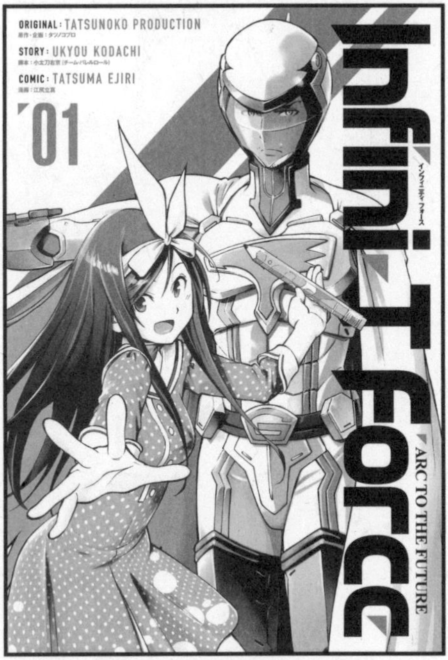
ORIGINAL: TATSUNOKO PRODUCTION
STORY: UKYOU KODACHI
COMIC: TATSUMA EJIRI
'01
Infini-T Force
ARC TO THE FUTURE

INFINI-T FORCE VOL.1
ISBN-13: 978-1772940503

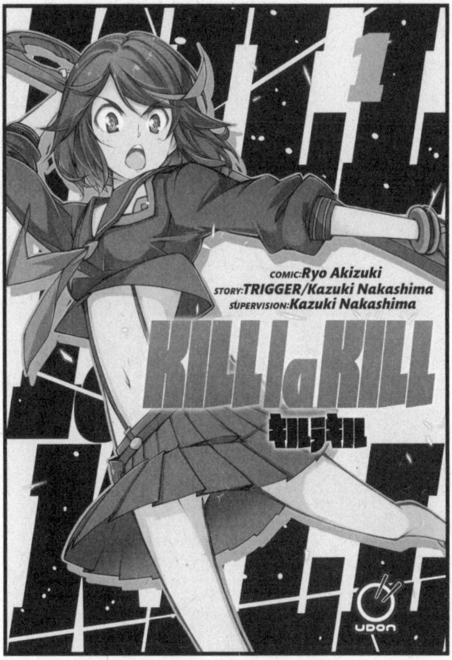
1
COMIC: Ryo Akizuki
STORY: TRIGGER/Kazuki Nakashima
SUPERVISION: Kazuki Nakashima
KILL la KILL
キルラキル
UDON

KILL LA KILL VOL.1
ISBN-13: 978-1927925492

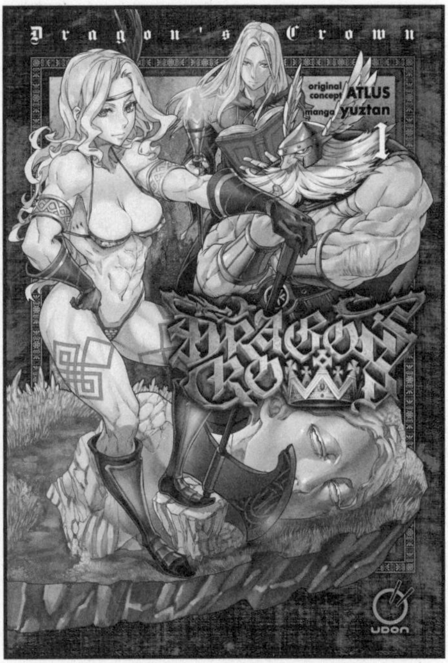
Dragon's Crown
original concept ATLUS
manga yuztan
1
DRAGON'S CROWN
UDON

DRAGON'S CROWN VOL.1
ISBN-13: 978-1772940480

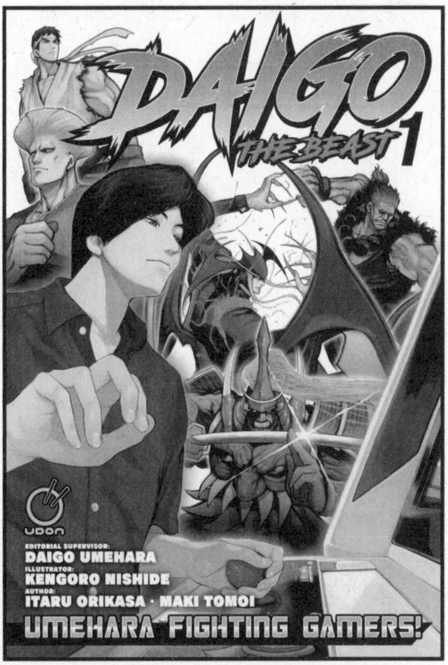
DAIGO
THE BEAST 1
UDON
EDITORIAL SUPERVISOR:
DAIGO UMEHARA
ILLUSTRATOR:
KENGORO NISHIDE
AUTHOR:
ITARU ORIKASA · MAKI TOMOI
UMEHARA FIGHTING GAMERS!

DAIGO THE BEAST VOL.1
ISBN-13: 978-1772940572

OTHERWORLDLY IZAKAYA

「NOBU」② 2

ENGLISH EDITION
Translation: CALEB D. COOK
Typesetting: MIYOKO HOSOYAMA
Sound Effects: JEANNIE LEE
Art Touch-ups: MERIKO ROBERT
Associate Editor: M. CHANDLER

UDON STAFF
Chief of Operations: ERIK KO
Director of Publishing: MATT MOYLAN
VP of Sales: JOHN SHABLESKI
Senior Producer: LONG VO
Marketing Manager: JENNY MYUNG
Japanese Liaisons: STEVEN CUMMINGS
ANNA KAWASHIMA

Original Story
NATSUYA SEMIKAWA

Manga
VIRGINIA NITOUHEI

Character Design
KURURI

ISEKAI IZAKAYA "NOBU" Volume 2

©Virginia-Nitouhei 2016
©Natsuya Semikawa,Kururi/TAKARAJIMASHA

First published in Japan in 2016 by KADOKAWA CORPORATION, Tokyo.
English translation rights arranged with KADOKAWA CORPORATION, Tokyo.
through TUTTLE–MORI GENCY, INC., Tokyo.

English language version published by UDON Entertainment Inc.
118 Tower Hill Road, C1, PO Box 20008
Richmond Hill, Ontario, L4K 0K0 CANADA

www.UDONentertainment.com

First Printing: November 2018
ISBN-13: 978-1-77294-068-8
ISBN-10: 1-77294-068-2

Printed in Canada